The
Grammar

3
Level

The Grammar Level 3

지은이 Kwon Ki Ha, Nexus Contents Development Team
펴낸이 임상진
펴낸곳 (주)넥서스

출판신고 1992년 4월 3일 제311-2002-2호 2-4
10880 경기도 파주시 지목로 5
Tel (02)330-5500 Fax (02)330-5555

ISBN 979-11-6165-100-2 54740
        979-11-5752-011-4 (SET)

가격은 뒤표지에 있습니다.
잘못 만들어진 책은 구입처에서 바꾸어 드립니다.

www.nexusEDU.kr

The Grammar

Kwon Ki Ha, Nexus Contents Development Team

3
Level

NEXUS Edu

Features

단순히 문법을 기계적으로 암기하는 시대는 지나가고 있습니다. 요즘은 문법의 개념설명을 전달하는 데 있어서 핵심적이고 문장 중심의 문법 포인트를 찾아 반복 학습하는 방법을 권하고 있으며, 그 효과도 뛰어납니다.

이 교재에서는 영어 독해 능력뿐만 아니라 Writing 능력도 동시에 향상시킬 수 있도록 어법에 초점을 맞추어 구성했으며, 불필요한 문법 부분을 과감히 삭제하여 여러분이 보다 핵심적인 부분만을 단시간에 학습하도록 구성하였습니다.

가정법 법칙을 암기하는 것보다 이해하는 방법을, 수동태를 만드는 방법보다 사용하는 방법을, 명사의 종류보다는 명사의 다양한 표현 방법을 강조하고 있습니다. 이 책을 학습하다보면 어법이 문법이 아닌 이유를 알게 될 것입니다.

암기, 법칙, 용법이라는 용어를 사용하기보다는, 이해와 복습만으로 어법을 가까운 친구로 만들 수 있도록 구성하였습니다. 어법 문제를 푸는 핵심을 집중 강조하고 있으며 독해에서는 길고 까다로운 구성의 문장을 집중적으로 분석할 수 있는 방법을 제시하고 있습니다.

이 교재에서는 문장 구성상 중요하고 자주 등장하는 표현들을 제목으로 정했습니다. 어법은 실제 20여 개의 제목만으로도 충분하지만, 어휘나 문제 적용을 위해 31개의 unit으로 만들어 여러분들이 보다 효율적으로 핵심적인 부분만 학습할 수 있도록 구성하였습니다.

본 교재를 통해 여러분이 쉽고 즐겁게 영어 공부를 할 수 있고, 그것을 통해 여러분의 영어 실력을 향상시키는 데 조금이나마 도움이 되었으면 합니다.

저자 권 기 하

Concise and Core
Grammar Points!

The Grammar Series

Concise and core grammar

자주 사용하지 않는 문법은 배제하고 핵심적인 부분만을 간결하고 정확하게 예문 중심으로 이해할 수 있도록 구성되어 있다.

A variety of question types

각 unit의 이해력을 점검할 수 있는 Exercise와 수능 유형의 문제로 구성된 Further study를 학습함으로 다양한 문제를 접할 수 있다.

Preparation for tests

내신 대비뿐만 아니라 수능시험에 대비하는 최적의 문법 참고서이다.

Extensive reading

다양하고 유익한 종류의 글을 통해 문장 분석 능력과 어법을 향상시킬 수 있다.

Writing-based learning

어법 문제의 핵심 요점을 집중 강조하고 있으며, 쓰기 위주로 문제 유형을 구성하여 다양한 영어시험에 대비할 수 있다.

Features

Grammar Point

문법 포인트 설명: 한글 주석과 영문 예문을 분리하여 문장의 예문 패턴을 집중적으로 비교 분석할 수 있도록 구성

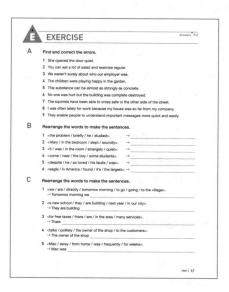

Exercise

배운 내용의 개념과 규칙 등을 확인하는 연습문제

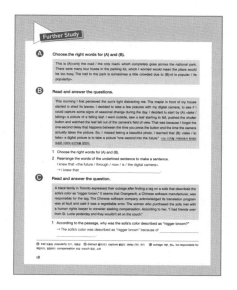

Further Study

짧은 읽기 지문을 통해 각 단원에서 배운 문법 포인트를 체크해 볼 수 있도록 문제 구성. 문법이 확장되어 지문 안에서 잘못된 문장을 수정할 수 있는 능력을 기를 수 있도록 구성

부록

각 단원에서 배운 기본 문법 포인트들을 표로 정리하여 기본적 문법 사항을 놓치지 않도록 구성. 본문에서 다루지 않은 기본 사항과 보충적인 문법 사항을 수록

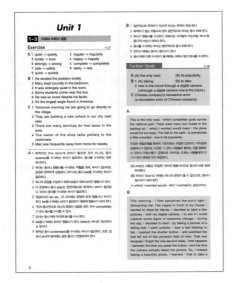

정답 및 해설

각 Unit의 연습문제를 풀이하고 정답을 수록하였으며 Further Study의 각 지문을 알기 쉽게 분석

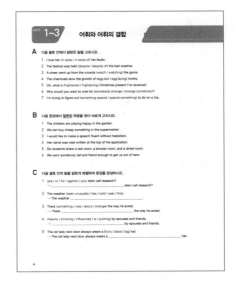

Workbook

기초 문법 확인 문제 외에도 내신 완벽 대비를 위한 객관식, 서술형 문제를 유닛별로 구성하여 자기주도학습을 할 수 있도록 구성

이 책을 공부하는 방법 – 하루에 한 Chapter, 31일 완성!

한 Unit에 어법을 설명하는 부분과 EXERCISE가 각각 2쪽씩 구성되었으며, 실전 문제를 다루는 FURTHER STUDY가 있습니다. 하루에 한 Unit을 기준으로 31일 만에 완성하도록 구성한 교재입니다. 하지만 매일 하루에 한 Unit을 완성하기 힘들다면, 하루에 작은 제목으로 나눈 2쪽을 완성하는 것도 하나의 방법입니다. 이러한 방법으로 일주일에 2~3unit을 완성한다면 부담 없이 어법을 완성할 수 있을 것입니다. 하지만 모든 언어가 그러하듯 반복 학습이 중요하므로 교재를 두 번 이상 볼 것을 권합니다.

이 책을 공부하는 방법 – 암기가 아니라 이해와 반복!

이제 어법을 암기하겠다는 생각을 버리고, 이해하겠다는 생각으로 교재를 접해야 합니다. 먼저, 읽으면서 이해가 어려운 부분을 표시하세요. 이러한 어려운 부분은 EXERCISE나 FURTHER STUDY에 다시 나오며, 해설지에 상세한 설명이 들어있으므로 궁금함을 해결할 수 있습니다. 그리고 두 번째 반복학습 단계에서 부담 없이 중요한 부분을 다시 학습할 수 있습니다.

이 책을 공부하는 방법 – 끊어읽기와 문장구조!

영어의 문법 문제는 단순히 암기만 하지 않고 문맥에서 필요한 형태가 무엇인지를 알면 해결되는 것이 요즘 추세입니다. 그렇다면 문장의 구조를 파악하는 것이 가장 우선적으로 해결해야 할 과제이며 핵심이 될 것입니다. 이러한 문제를 해결하는 방법이 바로 글을 읽을 때 의미 단위마다 끊어읽기를 하는 것입니다.

문장의 끊어읽기는 어법과 독해의 고민을 해결하는 출발점입니다. 우리말을 읽을 때 중요하거나 까다로운 부분에 밑줄을 치면 집중력이 생기고 문제의 실마리가 되는 경우와 같습니다. 단, 끊어읽기는 어법상 의미 단위를 알아야 하며, 글을 읽는 습관으로 자리 잡아야 합니다.

▲ Contents

Contents

The

Part I

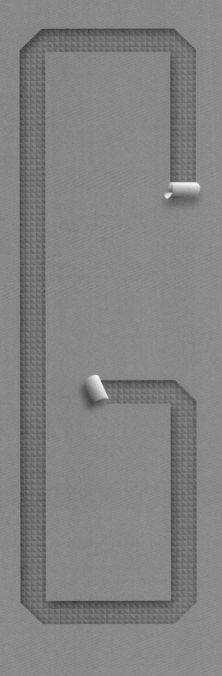

Questions

1 어휘와 어휘가 결합하는 데에도 어떤 원칙이 있는가?
2 명사와 명사, 형용사와 형용사는 그냥 연결되는가?
3 복잡하지 않게 어휘끼리 서로 연결하는 원칙은?

Answers

1 문장은 같은 품사나 다른 품사의 어휘들이 서로 연결된 것이다. 원칙은 부사가 동사와 부사를, 형용사는 다른 형용사나 명사를 수식한다는 것이다.

2 부사, 형용사 그리고 명사가 같은 품사끼리 나란히 나열되기도 한다. 이들이 연결되는 데에는 간단한 원칙이 있다.

3 부사나 형용사가 같은 품사끼리 연결되는 경우, 일반적으로 밖(외부)에서 안(내면, 성질)으로, 작은 단위에서 큰 단위로 이어진다.

1 명사/형용사/분사+**명사**, **명사**+분사/형용사/형용사구

1 명사+명사(noun+noun)

(1) 단수명사+명사(singular noun+noun)

> * book reviews 책 서평
> * bottle rockets 물병 로켓
> * computer parts 컴퓨터 부품
> * car accidents 자동차 사고
> * school buses 학교 버스
> * flower gardens 화단

(2) 동명사+명사(gerund+noun)

> * **chewing** gum(=gum for chewing) 씹는 껌
> * **drinking** water(=water for drinking) 마시는 물
> * a **living** room(=a room for living) 거실(주거용 공간)
> * a **parking** lot (=a lot for parking) 주차장

2 분사+명사(participle+noun)

(1) 현재분사+명사(present participle+noun)
The chemicals slow the growth of **egg-laying** moths.
Oh, what a **frightening** Christmas present I've received!

(2) 과거분사+명사(past participle+noun)
I told the **surprised** patient that most adults have fatty livers.
The **used** car export of Korea has rapid growth.

3 명사+형용사(noun+adjective)

(1) the money / *(which is)* **available** to pay back the loan
the man / *(who is)* **sincere** in his professions
an engineer / *(who is)* **reluctant** to learn new skills

(2) 명사+형용사구 (noun+adjective phrase)
the distance / **from** the Earth to the Sun
the crowds / **against** some of the Australian players
the country / **under** pressure from the terrorists

4 명사+분사(noun+participle)

A cheer went up from the crowds / **watching** the game.
There is never a fee to the candidate / **applying** for the position.
He should return the money / **taken** away by force.
The equipment / **provided** to his employees is properly used.

1

(1) 명사+명사 형태에서 앞의 명사는 형용사 역할을 하므로 반드시 단수형태가 온다.

> 예외: 복수형(단수 취급) 명사+명사
> *arms race 무기 경쟁
> *customs office 세관
> *news letter 뉴스 기사
> *physics class 물리학 수업

(2) 동명사(-ing)는 명사+명사 형태로 사용되며, 목적이나 용도를 나타낸다.

2 현재분사(-ing)는 명사를 수식할 수 있으며, 이 경우 명사는 능동적 역할을 한다.

(1)
> * a dancing lady
> * falling leaves
> * an evil-smelling pond

(2) 과거분사는 명사를 수식하는 형용사 역할을 하며, 이 경우 명사가 수동적인 역할을 한다.

> * the provided food
> * a broken arrow
> * a newly built ship

3

(1) 뒤의 형용사가 앞의 명사를 수식하는 경우, 사이에 <u>관계대명사+be동사</u>가 생략되어 있다.

(2) 전치사+명사는 앞의 명사를 수식하는 형용사구 역할을 하기도 한다.

4
분사가 다른 수식어와 함께 있는 경우, 뒤에서 앞의 명사를 수식한다.
* 분사의 주어는 앞의 명사이며, 그 명사가 능동적인 주어이면 -ing, 수동적 주어이면 -ed를 쓴다.
– which was taken
– which was provided

2 ▶ 형용사+**형용사**, 부사+**형용사/부사**

1 형용사의 위치(position)와 순서(order)

(1) 형용사의 위치(position of adjective)

I crossed the **mountain** /(which was) **white** with snow overnight.
We should not use the raw **materials** / **harmful** to environment.
I'm trying to figure out **something special** to do on a trip.
Why do you want to vote for **somebody strange**?

(2) 형용사의 순서(order of adjective)

The artist was dressed in a **dirty old navy blue** suit.
He is driving a **huge blue American** truck with huge wheels.
That is the Mont Blanc, **the highest white** mountain in Europe.
She has **the most beautiful red** fingernails I've ever seen.

(3) 나열되는 형용사(parallel adjectives)

Protein makes your skin **moist, white, soft and smooth**.
Its blossoms are **large, white and pretty hard** to miss.
Her hair was **long, but dirty and poorly combed**.
Whether this idea is **valuable or worthless** doesn't concern us.

1

(1) 형용사는 형용사+명사의 순서로 쓰이지만, 반드시 그런 것은 아니다.
- 명사+형용사(뒤에서 앞으로 수식): 명사 뒤에 관계대명사+be동사가 생략된 것이다.
- 명사+형용사: -thing와 -body로 끝나는 명사는 형용사가 뒤에 위치한다.

(2) 형용사가 여러 개 등장하면 일반적으로 크기-모양-성질(age, color, 출신)-재료의 순서로 나열한다.
- 밖(외형)에서 안(성질)으로
- 비교급(comparative), 최상급(superlative) 형용사 우대!

(3) 형용사가 3개 이상이면 comma(쉼표)로 연결하며, 마지막에만 접속사(conjunction)를 붙인다.

---

2 부사의 위치(position of adverb)

(1) 동사+부사(verb+adverb)

What breeds of dogs can live / **happily** in a small apartment?
She is sensitive and gets ill / **easily** from mishandled food.
This bridge type is **very** expensive but is **really** beautiful.

(2) 동사+목적어+부사

I like him / **simply** because he is kind.
He spoke English / **fluently** without stopping to think of grammar.
He gave me a lift / **after** the party. I felt comfortable in the car.

(3) 부사의 순서: 방-장-시간의 순서(manner-place-time)

They certainly spoke / **loudly** at **the time** of the tea party.
I heard him playing the piano / **very softly** in **the background**.
I heard that you did **well** / **in the test last night**. Well done!

2

(1) 부사는 일반적으로 동사나 목적어의 뒤에 위치한다.
- 동사+부사
- 동사+보어+부사
- 부사+형용사

(2) 부사는 뒤에서 앞의 동사를 수식하지만, 목적어나 보어가 있는 경우는 그 뒤에 위치한다.

(3) 부사가 여러 개 등장하면 방법-장소-시간의 순서로 나열한다.

왕래 발착 동사 뒤에는 보통 장소-방법-시간의 순서로 나열한다.

3 ▸ 전치사+명사(Preposition+Noun)

1 전치사의 의미

(1) 전치사는 반드시 명사 앞에!(preposition+noun/pronoun/gerund)

I fell asleep / **during** the film.

I could do nothing / **without** him.

She kept worrying / **about** drowning in the ocean.

(2) 전치사는 하나의 덩어리를 만든다!

You've heard the report / **about** babies born in this hospital.

She is wearing a dress / **of** silk and wool.

She went out / **without** paying her bill for the operation.

I asked / **about** what he did to celebrate his achievement.

(3) 전치사+that절

> * in that S+V : 「~라는 점에 있어서」
> * except that S+V : 「~라는 점을 제외하고」

Men differ from animals **in that** they can think and speak.

I know nothing about him **except that** he lives next door.

2 여러 단어가 하나의 전치사 역할

* because of	~ 때문에(=owing to, thanks to)	
* in spite of	~ 에도 불구하고(=despite)	
* in front of	~ 앞에서	
* next to	~ 옆에서(=by)	+ 명사
* instead of	~ 대신에	
* according to	~ 에 따르면	
* up to	~ 까지	

I love her **in spite of** her faults. – I love her **in spite** her faults. (×)

I love her **despite** her faults. – I love her **despite of** her faults. (×)

Is my seat **next to** that lady's? – Is my seat **next** that lady's? (×)

3 전치사의 다양한 위치와 의미

What are you crying **for**?

Are you **for** or **against**?

What are friends **for**?

I must be **off** now.

What is the weather **like**?

What are you **up to**?

Today, it's **on** me.

Let him **in** after lunch.

1

(1) 전치사 뒤에는 반드시 명사(대명사, 동명사, 명사절 등)가 온다.
- 전치사+명사
- 전치사+대명사
- 전치사+동명사

- 형용사구
- 형용사구
- 부사구
- 부사구

(3) 전치사는 일반적으로 명사와 결합하지만, that절과 결합하여 쓰이는 예외가 있다.

2

2개 이상의 여러 단어가 하나의 전치사 역할을 하는 경우이다.
전치사 뒤에는 반드시 명사(구)가 오므로, 전치사 뒤에 문장이 올 수 없다.

3

- 왜 우니? (what ~for=why 왜)
- 날씨가 어때? (be like: ~와 같다)
- 찬성이니 반대니?
- 오늘 뭐 할거니?
- 친구 좋은 게 뭐니?
- 오늘은 내가 한턱 낸다.
- 이제 그만 가봐야겠어요.
- 그를 점심 이후에 들여보내.

EXERCISE

Answers P.2

A Find and correct the errors.

1 She opened the door quiet.

2 You can eat a lot of salad and exercise regular.

3 We weren't surely about who our employer was.

4 The children were playing happy in the garden.

5 This substance can be almost as strongly as concrete.

6 No one was hurt but the building was complete destroyed.

7 The squirrels have been able to cross safe to the other side of the street.

8 I was often lately for work because my house was so far from my company.

9 They enable people to understand important messages more quick and easily.

B Rearrange the words to make the sentences.

1 <the problem / briefly / he / studied>.   → _____

2 <Mary / in the bedroom / slept / soundly>.   → _____

3 <it / was / in the room / strangely / quiet>. → _____

4 <come / near / the boy / some students>.   → _____

5 <despite / he / so loved / his faults / was>. → _____

6 <eagle / in America / found / it's / the largest>. → _____

C Rearrange the words to make the sentences.

1 <we / are / directly / tomorrow morning / to go / going / to the village>.
   → Tomorrow morning we _____

2 <a new school / they / are building / next year / in our city>.
   → They are building _____

3 <for free taxes / there / are / in the area / many services>.
   → There _____

4 <talks / politely / the owner of the shop / to the customers>.
   → The owner of the shop _____

5 <Mac / away / from home / was / frequently / for weeks>.
   → Mac was _____

A Choose the right words for (A) and (B).

This is (A)<only the road / the only road> which completely goes across the national park. There were many tour buses in the parking lot, which I worried would mean the place would be too busy. The trail to the park is sometimes a little crowded due to (B)<it is popular / its popularity>.

B Read and answer the questions.

This morning I first perceived the sun's light distracting me. The maple in front of my house started to shed its leaves. I decided to take a few pictures with my digital camera, to see if I could capture some signs of seasonal change during the day. I decided to start by (A) <take / taking> a picture of a falling leaf. I went outside, saw a leaf starting to fall, pushed the shutter button and watched the leaf fall out of the camera's field of view. That was because I forgot the one-second delay that happens between the time you press the button and the time the camera actually takes the picture. So, I missed taking a beautiful photo. I learned that (B) <take / to take> a digital picture is to take a picture "one second into the future." 나는 디지털 카메라에서 현재의 모습은 미래의 순간임을 알았다.

1 Choose the right words for (A) and (B).

2 Rearrange the words of the underlined sentence to make a sentence.

   I knew that <the future / through / now / is / the digital camera>.

   → I knew that _____.

C Read and answer the question.

A black family in Toronto expressed their outrage after finding a tag on a sofa that described the sofa's color as "nigger brown." It seems that Orangesoft, a Chinese software manufacturer, was responsible for the tag. The Chinese software company acknowledged its translation program was at fault and said it was a regrettable error. The woman who purchased the sofa met with a human rights lawyer to consider seeking compensation. According to her, "I had friends over from St. Lucia yesterday and they wouldn't sit on the couch."

1 According to the passage, why was the sofa's color described as "nigger brown?"

   → The sofa's color was described as "nigger brown" because of _____

   _____.

A trail 오솔길 popularity 인기, 대중성 **B** distract 흩뜨리다 capture 붙잡다 delay 지연, 연기 **C** outrage 격분, 분노 be responsible for 책임지다, 담당하다 compensation 보상 couch 침상, 소파

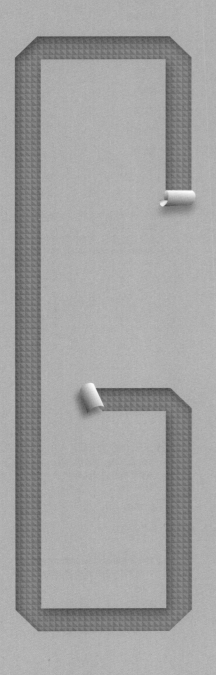

Unit 2

문장의 구성 1

1 단순 문장(Simple Sentence)–주어의 형태
2 단순 문장(Simple Sentence)–동사의 형태

Questions

1 모든 문장은 반드시 주어 + 동사로 구성되는가?
2 주어와 동사, 동사와 목적어의 관계는 무엇인가?
3 목적어의 위치는 어디이며, 목적어의 형태는 어떤가?

Answers

1 영어의 모든 문장은 주어 + 동사로 구성된다.
2 가장 많이 등장하는 문장은 주어 + 동사 + 목적어이다. 자동사는 목적어가 없으며, 타동사는 목적어를 반드시 필요로 하므로, 이 경우 타동사가 쓰인다.
3 목적어는 반드시 명사의 형태(명사, 대명사, 동명사, 명사구, 명사절)가 오는 지 확인해야 한다.

---

① 주어 S(Subject)–명사나 대명사의 형태가 온다.
② 동사 V(Verb)–목적어를 필요로 하는 동사와 필요하지 않는 동사가 있다.
③ 목적어 O(Object)–명사나 대명사의 형태와 명사 역할을 하는 구나 절이 온다.
④ 보어 C(Complement)–신분을 나타낼 때 명사와 대명사, 상태를 나타낼 때 형용사가 온다.
⑤ 구(Phrase)와 절(Clause)–구나 절은 명사, 형용사, 부사의 역할을 한다.

1 단순 문장(Simple Sentence)–주어의 형태

1 구와 절

(1) 구(phrase)

Everybody in our neighborhood knows **Mary's new friends**.
To stay in this country / is to destroy our valuable lives.
The street **leading to the school** / is very wide.
The thief ran away / **at the sight of the policeman**.

(2) 절(clause)

What you know / is not as important as who you are.
I can't understand / **what you want**.
The problem is / **that we can't speak English**.
Tell me the reason / **why you are so angry**.
He was talking on the telephone / **when the doorbell rang**.

1
(1) 구: 주어+동사의 문장형태가 아닌, 2개 이상의 어휘가 명사, 형용사, 부사 역할을 한다.
– 명사역할(목적어)
– 명사역할(주어, 보어)
– 형용사역할
– 부사역할

(2) 하나의 문장으로서, 명사(주어, 목적어, 보어), 형용사, 부사의 역할을 한다.
– 주어절
– 목적어절
– 보어절
– 형용사절
– 부사절

2 문장의 구성(sentence word order)

You should listen / carefully. (주어+동사+부사)
I waited / at the corner till 11:30.
He kept silent / at all times. (주어+동사+보어+부사)
He became a teacher / in New York City.
He got good marks / in all subjects. (주어+동사+목적어+부사)
I ate my meal / by the front windows.
My grandfather bought me a book. (주어+동사+목적어+목적어)
He bought his son a Macintosh computer.
They wanted me to change my mind. (주어+동사+목적어+보어)
He made me very comfortable.

2
하나의 완전한 문장은 주어(subject)와 동사(verb)가 있어야 한다.
문장의 주어+동사 뒤에는 목적어(object), 보어(complement), 그리고 부사 등이 올 수 있다.

3 주어(subject)의 종류

(1) 주어로 쓰이는 구(phrase)

The price of oil nowadays / is still heavily discounted.
To lose a loved one suddenly / is painful to everyone.
Taking a walk in the woods / is one of my favorite pastime.

(2) 주어로 쓰이는 절(clause)

The fact that you work here / makes you different.
Whether he succeed or not / depends on the choice.
How you do it during meetings / can affect your promotion.

3
(1) 주어 위치에는 명사뿐만이 아니라 명사 역할을 하는 구(phrase)가 올 수 있다.
– 명사구
– to부정사
– 동명사

(2) 하나의 절(that절, what절, 의문사절 등)이 문장의 주어로 올 수 있다.
– 동격절
– 접속사절
– 의문사절

EXERCISE

Answers P.3

A   Identify the subjects in the following sentences.

1 What you told me is going to come true again.

2 Working in this company will be a good experience.

3 Speaking another language opens new doors for us.

4 The only way to study in this country is to join the party.

5 A lot of people in my class attend the class in the evening.

6 One of the people whom I admire most is my class teacher.

7 Everybody in the neighborhood participated in a Christmas festival.

8 The test they took yesterday consisted of long scenario questions.

B   Identify the adverbial phrase or clause in the following sentences.

1 Mary left her surfboard at the beach.

2 Thousands of languages exist in the world.

3 Hong Kong has seen a rapid increase in its population.

4 There are a lot of police cars near my house at night.

5 Earthquakes also occur in the area near the Nansei Islands.

6 Mike didn't show up at Jill's party because he had a headache.

7 Coal and oil were formed from plant remains millions of years ago.

C   Identify S(subject), V(verb), O(object), and C(complement).

1 Einstein took a job in a Swiss patent office.

2 I thanked my friend for lending me some money.

3 Only a few people are satisfied with their jobs.

4 I took a course called The Study of Islam in Singapore.

5 Hindus call their religious tradition the eternal teaching.

6 A group of scientists brought help and hope to poor farmers.

7 The dream that I had last night was fantastic.

8 The sellers would allow us to stay through closing as their guests.

9 The helicopter tour enabled us to see all the places we couldn't drive to.

*patent: 특허

2 ▶ 단순 문장(Simple Sentence)–동사의 형태

1 목적어가 필요 없는 동사–자동사

(1) 자동사(주어+동사–subject+verb)

The sun **is shining** / all day long.

I **waited** / in the city for two months.

There **remains** no agreement / on where to store the waste.

(2) 자동사(주어+동사+보어–subject+verb+complement)

* keep, stay, remain+형	~ 한 상태로 남아있다
* become, turn, grow, get, fall+형	~ 한 상태가 되다
* appear, seem / prove+형	~ 인 것 같다, ~임이 판명되다

They **remained** quiet / about the new proposals.

These books **seem** (to be) popular / with the kids.

2 목적어를 필요로 하는 동사–타동사

(1) 자동사와 타동사의 겸용이다!(ergative verb)

By second grade, he **learns** in the school's resource room.

Jeff was **learning** German and had almost mastered Latin.

My stomach seemed to **hurt** a little bit after drinking soda.

Don't try to **hurt** somebody financially using foul plays.

(2) 타동사로만 쓰인다!

① situate, locate, defeat, lay, raise, arouse, lack, feed, marry 등		
② leave=start from	reach=arrive in	discuss=talk about
enter=go into	resemble=look like	answer=reply to

How old was prince Charles when he **married** princess Diana?

Will you turn down the radio while I **answer** the phone?

3 혼동하기 쉬운 자 · 타동사

* lie-lay-lain	* lay-laid-laid
* sit-sat-sat	* seat-seated-seated
* rise-rose-risen	* raise-raised-raised
* arise-arose-arisen	* arouse-aroused-aroused

I love it when a cat **lies** in front of a fire on its back!

We **laid** the baby down, washed, fed and wrapped in cloths.

1

(1) 목적어 없이 주어+동사만으로 하나의 문장을 만들며, 목적어가 필요 없다.
자동사는 수동태(be+과거분사)를 만들 수 없으며, 부사나 보어와 결합할 수 있다.

(2) 주어의 상태나 성질을 설명하는 동사들은 뒤에 주격보어가 와야 문장이 완성된다.

– appear, seem, prove 뒤의 to be는 종종 생략된다.

2

(1) 대부분 동사는 목적어의 유무와 의미에 따라 자동사와 타동사를 겸한다.

– 자동사

– 타동사

– 자동사

– 타동사

① 반드시 목적어를 필요로 하는 타동사가 있다.
② 자동사+전치사는 타동사의 역할과 같다.
〈타동사=자동사+전치사〉

= was married to

= reply to

3

자. 눕다, 놓여 있다	타. 눕히다
자. 앉다	타. 앉히다
자. 일어나다	타. 올리다
자. 발생하다	타. 깨우다

E EXERCISE

A Choose the right words.

1 To tell you the truth, I <waited / waited for> your letter so long.

2 The student frequently appears <angry / angrily> and exhausted.

3 Was Cinderella happy when she <married / married with> the prince?

4 The city council <discussed / discussed about> the matter and decided to take action.

5 The name of the town has remained <familiar / familiarly> after more than a century.

6 When he <entered / entered into > the room, the door was locked from the outside.

B Complete each sentence using the words in the box.

call	stop	turn	drive	hurt	change

1 The doctor _____calls_____ at the end of the week.

They used to _____call_____ the town Charlotte after his only daughter.

2 Failing in realizing his dream, he _____(e)d to Hong Kong.

I normally _____ the handle in a clockwise direction.

3 I've never deliberately _____ any animals.

My fingers started to _____ a lot and my wrists got very sore.

4 You look just the same. You haven't _____(e)d at all.

You don't have to _____ your password regularly.

C Rearrange the words to complete the sentences.

1 He <answer / kept / and / did not / silent / anything>.

〈그는 침묵을 지키고 어떤 대답도 하지 않았다.〉

→ He _____

2 The house <to / seemed / for the couple / be / large enough>.

〈그 집은 그 부부에게 충분한 크기인 것 같다.〉

→ The house _____

3 The apartments <strong / despite / remained / a few earthquakes>.

〈아파트들은 몇 번의 지진에도 불구하고 튼튼한 상태로 남아있었다.〉

→ The apartments _____

4 I feel <me / your product / to / looks / familiar>. Where could I have seen it?

〈너의 제품은 눈에 익은 것 같다. 내가 어디서 보았을까?〉

→ I feel _____ Where could I have seen it?

A Choose the right words for (A), (B) and (C).

Where do you place a baby turtle if you can't discover either of its parents? Usually young turtles are left to live for themselves as soon as they hatch. The answer to how you (A) <raise / rise> one is simple: (B) <leave / start> it alone. Turtles are protected by international agreements, and cannot legally be taken from the wild. If you (C) <find / found> them on the road, bring them into the bush or near watering holes.

B Read and answer the questions. 기출 응용

Mom was an extraordinarily clean person. After feeding my brother and me breakfast, she would scrub, mop, and (A) <dust / to dust> everything. As we grew older, Mom made sure we did our part by keeping our rooms (B) <neat /neatly>. Outside, she would tend a small flower garden, which was the envy of the neighborhood. With Mom, everything she touched (C) <turned / turning> to gold. She didn't believe in doing anything halfway. She often told us that we always had to do our best in whatever we did.

1 Choose the correct words for (A), (B) and (C).
2 According to the passage, mom wants children to be <industrious / economical>.

C Read and answer the questions.

In the middle of the night the sound of a wailing young child who has a fever (A) <pierce / pierces> the air. ① A feverish child will feel very hot or burning but may him or herself feel cold. ② The first step parents need to take with a feverish child is to get that fever down. ③ The reality of dealing with a feverish child can send some parents into a panic. ④ Taking your kid's temperature really (B) <make / makes> one's life crazy, especially at 3:00 in the morning. ⑤ Sometimes, parents can't understand that the fever itself isn't dangerous, but it could be a sign that there is an illness that could cause the child some uneasiness.

1 Choose the correct words for the blanks.
2 Where would the following sentence best fit?

Doctors sympathize with such parents, but note that one can't ignore a fever.

A legally 법적으로 bush 수풀, 숲 **B** scrub 문지르다 mop 청소하다 neat 정돈된 **C** wail 울부짖다 pierce 관통하다 panic 공포

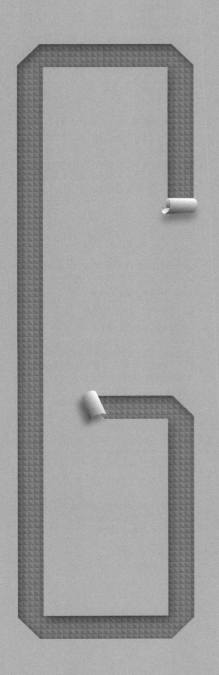

Unit 3

문장의 구성 2

Questions

1 동사에 따라 목적어가 달라질 수 있을까?

2 주격보어를 필요로 하는 동사는 무엇인가?

3 목적격 보어로 동사원형, to부정사, 분사가 오는 기준은?

Answers

1 목적어로 to부정사와 동명사를 취하는 경우만 구분하면 된다. 별도로 암기하는 것보다 평상시에 동사에 to부정사나 -ing를 붙여 함께 사용하는 습관을 들인다.

2 상태를 설명하는 동사(remain, keep, seem, appear)와 감각동사(look, sound, smell, taste, feel)의 경우가 그렇다.

3 동사 중에서 a) 사역/지각동사, b) 목적격 보어로 to부정사가 오는 동사, c) 목적어와 목적격 보어의 관계를 유념해야 한다.

1 ▶ 단순 문장(Simple Sentence) – 목적어의 종류

1 목적어(Object)의 형태

(1) 목적어로 쓰이는 구(phrases)

He killed **a walnut tree** last year. Now he misses **it** a lot.
We are enjoying **hearing all** about your adventures.
I want **to know** about a lecturer job in Australia.
I wonder **how to send videos** from this camera to an e-mail.

(2) 목적어로 쓰이는 절(clauses)

This training program gave me **what I really needed**.
I believe **that animal intelligence can be measured**.
He wonders **what I like most and least about Japan**.

2 목적어(Object)의 종류

(1) S+V+O (subject+verb+object)

We can kill **multiple birds** / with one stone.
The news surprised **many market observers**.
The children threw **snowballs** / made of ice and dust.

(2) S+V+Indirect Object(간·목) + Direct Object(직·목)

> 1. bring, give, lend, pay, sell, send, show, tell, write 등
> 2. buy, cook, do, find, get, make, order 등
> 3. ask

He **gave** me a book.   → He gave a book / **to** me.

I **told** him a ghost story.   → I told a ghost story / **to** him.

Please **order** me a meal.   → Please order a meal / **for** me.

Will you **do** me a favor?   → Will you do a favor / **for** me?

Mary **asked** me your name   → Mary asked your name / **of** me.

May I **ask** you a question?   → May I ask a question / **of** you?

(3) S+V+Indirect Object(간·목) + Direct Object(직·목)

I used to **envy** him his well-shaped figure.

= I used to envy his well-shaped figure.

The war **cost** me my father and my property.

= I lost my father and my property because of the war.

The car **cost** me two thousand pounds.

= I paid two thousand pounds to buy the car.

1

(1) 명사만이 목적어로 오지만, 명사 역할의 구(phrase)가 목적어로 올 수도 있다.

– 명사/대명사

– 동명사

– to부정사

– 의문사 + to부정사

(2) 목적어 위치에는 명사 역할을 하는 하나의 문장이 올 수도 있다.
– what절

– that절

– what절

2

(1) 타동사는 반드시 목적어를 필요로 한다. 주어+동사+목적어 뒤에 수식어나 부사가 올 수 있다.

(2) 목적어가 2개(S+V+I.O+D.O)인 경우는 '~에게 ...를'로 해석한다.

~ 에게…를 (동사)해주다

~ 에게…를 (동사)해주다

~ 에게…를 묻다

목적어가 2개인 경우 직접목적어와 간접목적어의 위치를 바꾸고 전치사를 써 3형식 문장으로 사용하기도 한다.

> * do+간접목적어+직접목적어
> do me good
> do me harm
> do me damage
> do me justice
> do me a favor

(3) 목적어가 2개인 경우, 해석에 주의해야 하는 동사들이 있다.
– 부러워하다. 시기하다

– 앗아가다

– ~에게 비용을 들게 하다

E EXERCISE

A Underline the object in the following sentences.

1 She insists that what Amy needs is discipline.

2 I don't know who broke the window yesterday.

3 I gave what I had and what I could give to the winners.

4 I used to envy a main character in the dramas or movies.

5 I wonder how to properly and correctly convey this emotion.

6 Most of the people asked if Christmas was Santa's or Jesus' birthday.

7 He collected butterflies and various oddments from around the world.

8 I am enjoying cooking and sharing delicious food with my family.

B Rearrange the words to make the sentences.

1 a long letter / her friend / wrote / she → _____

2 her / some flowers / on her birthday / he / gave → _____

3 us / what to do / told / nobody → _____

4 sent / a letter / to / we / the people we met → _____

5 cook / dinner / me / let / for you → _____

6 me / has bought / my father / a good gift / for → _____

7 will / I / try to / find / those books / you → _____

C Complete the sentences using the given words.

1 Will _____ a favor? (do)
   〈부탁 하나 할까요?〉

2 Please _____ to the station. (tell)
   〈내게 역으로 가는 길을 좀 말해주세요.〉

3 He _____ take a cab. (lend)
   〈그는 내가 택시를 타도록 얼마의 돈을 빌려주었다.〉

4 Dave _____ I wanted to listen to. (bring)
   〈Dave는 내가 듣고 싶었던 노래 테이프를 가져다 주었다.〉

5 They _____ but my answer wasn't there. (ask)
   〈그들은 내게 답을 물었으나 나는 답을 하지 않았다.〉

2 단순 문장(Simple Sentence)–보어의 형태

1 보어(Complement)로 사용되는 구와 절(phrase and clause)

He is **energetic** and **thorough** in his teaching duties.
My intention is **to try** to open that debate.
One of my hobbies is **making** dollhouses and **decorating** them.
The trouble is **that he only thinks of himself**.
This is **what I need for the new yard**.

> **1**
> 주어나 목적어를 설명해주는 보어는 명사나 형용사의 형태가 와야 한다.
> – 명사구(to부정사)
> – 명사구(동명사)
> – 명사절(that 절)
> – 명사절(관계대명사절)

2 주격보어(subjective complement)

(1) 주어+동사+형용사 (subject+verb+adjective)

turn red	turn sour	go blind	go mad
come true	come loose	grow tall	grow old
run dry	run short	fall short	fall asleep

She **remained** silent during the debate.
The fog **grew thicker** later in the morning.

> **2**
> (1) 동사 뒤에는 주어의 상태나 성질을 설명하는 형용사가 보어로 온다.
> 자동사 뒤에 형용사가 오면 '~하게 되다'가 되는 표현들이 있다.

(2) 주어+동사+보어 (subject+verb+complement)

look	sound	smell	taste	feel

She **looked** white and pale in the desert.
Her music **sounds** good and should not be heard alone.
The food **smells** delicious, oniony, heavy, and hearty

> (2) 느낌과 감각을 나타내는 동사 뒤에는 상태를 나타내는 형용사가 보어로 온다.
>
> > * 효과적인 기억 방법
> > S+look good.
> > sound good.
> > smell good.
> > taste good.
> > feel good.

3 목적격보어(objective complement)

The people elected him / **president** twice.
My mother often leaves the door / **open**.
We want you / **to finish** the job quickly before exam day.
I noticed her / **eating** her lunch alone in the cafeteria.
I heard my name / **called** out on the radio this morning.
I helped her / **carry** her baggage to the church.

> **3**
> – 명사
> – 형용사
> – to부정사
> – 지각동사+O+현재분사
> – 지각동사+O+과거분사
> – 사역동사+O+동사원형
> 목적어를 설명하는 목적격보어는 문장의 동사에 따라 다양한 형태가 온다.

4 S+V+O+to부정사(to-infinitive)

expect, want, allow, tell, ask, encourage, persuade, cause, enable, advise, teach, order, warn, forbid 등	+목적어+to부정사 (목적격보어)

He didn't allow me **to smoke** in the building.
The cold weather caused us **to bond** with each other.

> **4**
> 동사가 지각/사역동사인 경우 목적격보어로 to부정사가 올 수 없다.
> 대부분 동사의 경우, 목적격보어로 동사가 오려면 to부정사 형태를 취한다.

EXERCISE

A Choose the right words.

1 You look <happy / happily> today.

2 Keep <silent / silently> while we are singing.

3 In summer the roses smell so <sweet / sweetly>.

4 That music sounds too <loudly / loud> in this night.

5 I feel very <comfortable / comfortably> with the housekeeper.

6 He asked me how <beautiful / beautifully> the butterfly looked.

B Underline the complement in the following sentences.

1 I advised Mary to think well before starting.

2 She found the book a little too hard to read.

3 This is what happened when you took a week off.

4 When the hall lights went out, the crowd went mad.

5 I watched him take his first steps and say his first words.

6 He called him Uncle Cave Man because he lived in a cave.

7 The location has changed, but the tradition remains the same.

8 The problem is that he just doesn't understand ethnic minorities.   *minority: 소수민족

C Write the right words to complete the sentences.

1 What caused _____*him to be changed*_____ so much?
〈그는 무슨 이유로 그렇게 많이 변했나요?〉

2 Darry's chair feels _____ against my back.
〈Darry의 의자는 부드러웠지만 등이 닿는 데는 딱딱했다.〉

3 National income fell _____ by 11 percent of maximum.
〈국가의 수입은 최대 11퍼센트 정도까지 부족하게 되었다.〉

4 I think this job will enable _____ an expert in this field.
〈내 생각에 이 일은 내가 이 분야에서 전문가가 되도록 해줄 것이다.〉

5 My parents always encourage _____ in my daily life.
〈우리 부모님께서는 항상 내게 매일매일 열심히 일하라고 격려하신다.〉

6 A screw never comes _____ from the handle under normal use.
〈정상적으로 사용했을 때 손잡이에서 나사가 헐거워지지 않는다.〉

A Choose the right words for (A) and (B).

> Jane heard her father's loud and angry voice. Growing very (A) <pale / palely>, she ran out into the hall. To her surprise, her father was already halfway upstairs, and his face turned red with rage. In the hall below she saw her stepmother looking troubled and getting (B) <angry / angrily>.

B Read the passage and answer the question.

> I lost touch with you for a while and the cell phone number I had for you no longer works. I have been thinking about you off and on, but I haven't dared to even dream of writing a letter. I can offer you no more than my childish best wishes for your birthday. Nonetheless, I hope these lines bring (A) <joy you / you joy>. I wish that I could show you how real my feelings for you are. I wish that I could (B) <give / keep> you this card personally instead of mailing it to you. Would you let me give you these wishes in the future? Happy Birthday.

1 Choose the right words for (A) and (B).

 C Read the passage and answer the questions.

> It was a long car ride to the hospital. His dad told me how my friend, Dick, had had a mental disorder for many years. He assured me that whatever happened was out of our control; we had to let Fate do its job. I walked in as Dick yelled at the staffs who tried to comfort him. The reaction to medication he was taking made him think they were poisoning his food. Sometimes he drifted in and out of consciousness. Still, he made friends at the hospital. To my surprise, he was everybody's favorite patient. The nurses said he was "crazy but funny." Some nurses could often rely on him to make them laugh when they were too stressed. They also said he had a family who cared for him through everything, and 그것이 그를 살아있게 해준 것이다.

1 Rearrange the words to have the same meaning as the underlined part.
   <alive / kept / him / what>
   → that is _____

2 According to the passage, what made the mental patient get better in the hospital?
   → <Harmony / Staff> made the patient adapt himself to life and get better.

Ⓐ rage 격노, 분노 stepmother 새엄마   Ⓑ no more than 단지(=only) nonetheless 그럼에도 불구하고 childish 유치한
Ⓒ mental disorder 정신질환 fate 운명 yell 고함치다

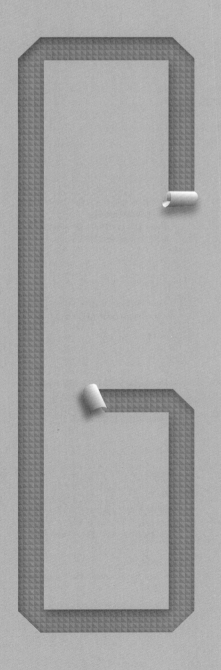

Unit 4

문장의 연결

1. 복합 문장(Compound Sentence)−접속사
2. 병렬 구조(Parallelism)

Questions

1. 영어는 정말 반복을 싫어하는가?
2. 같은 표현이 반복되지 않아야 한다면 그 원칙은?
3. 접속사의 의미와 역할은 정확히 무엇일까?

Answers

1. 영어는 표현의 반복을 싫어하며, 표현을 연결하는 접속사의 앞과 뒤는 같은 형태의 표현이 온다.
2. 접속사와 어법단위(to부정사, 동명사 등)를 기준하여 반복되는 표현은 생략한다.
3. 영어의 반복되는 표현을 연결하거나 문장을 연결하는 접속사는 and, but, or, so, for 등이 있다. 이들은 단독으로 사용되기도 하지만, 'either A or B' 처럼 특정한 형태를 취하기도 하므로 그 형태를 잘 익혀두어야 한다.

복합 문장(Compound Sentence) – 접속사

1 복합 문장 만들기

| addition 부가 | She washed my car **and** then polished it. |
| | She studied in Chicago **and** worked in Pittsburgh. |

| contrast 대조 | She sold her car, **but** she couldn't help regretting it. |
| | Julie gave me some food, **yet** it was not enough. |

| choice 선택 | Put on your coat, **or** you'll catch a cold. |
| | You can park your car by the road **or** on the road. |

| result 결과 | He couldn't find his pen, **so** he wrote in pencil. |
| | My mom is always tired, **so** I help her with her chores. |

| reason 이유 | Mary rarely stays in hotels, **for** she can't afford it. |
| | I couldn't explain it, **for** I knew nothing about it. |

1
2개 이상의 문장이나 표현이 연결되어 있는 경우를 복합 문장이라 한다.
연결된 각각의 문장과 표현들 사이에는 접속사(conjunction)를 사용한다.

2 접속사 – and, but(=yet), nor(=and ~not)

He phoned **and** left a message yesterday.
Immigration began long before **and** continues now.

We got ready to get on the train, **but** the train didn't stop.
She hates math, **but** she gets good grades in it.

She hasn't been to Japan, **nor** has she been to China.
They won't go to the beach tomorrow, **nor** the day after.

2
일반적으로 반복되는 표현은 접속사 뒤에서 다시 반복하지 않는다.
접속사 앞에 comma가 올 수 있으며, 종종 이러한 comma는 생략되기도 한다.

– nor 뒤에서는 V+S로 도치된다.(~and she hasn't been to China.)

3 접속사 – so, for

We didn't want to watch the film, **so** we went straight back.
We got into an argument, **so** we stopped talking again.
We were bored yesterday, **for** there was nothing to do.
I must leave early, **for** I have a long way to go.

3
접속사 so와 for의 뒤에는 같은 내용이 반복되더라도 완전한 문장이 와야 한다.
접속사 for는 반드시 뒷문장의 처음에 오며, 뒤이어 완전한 문장이 따른다.

4 복합 문장을 만드는 접속사

Jim **not only** built his own house **but** designed it himself as well.
He was **both** training them in theater **and** acting with skills.
I can **either** leave now **or** stay for another hour.
I **neither** know what happened **nor** care to.

4
either A or B, neither A nor B,
not only A but also B, both A and B
등 에서 B에는 A의 내용이 반복되지 않는다.

– care to 뒤에 know what happened가 생략

E EXERCISE

Answers P.6

A Choose the right words.

1 She opened the door <and / so> the frog was sitting there.

2 The country lane was very narrow, winding, <and / but> muddy.

3 The king could not sleep, <so / but> he gave an order to bring a book.

4 I looked for a place to dance <or / for> listen to the music that I loved.

5 Jason finally left New York for Korea, <for / yet> he wanted to see his son.

6 Mary was very confused, <nor / yet> she didn't know why all of this happened.

7 When Charles heard this, he ran away, <for / so> he was afraid of being beaten.

B Complete each sentence using the words in the box.

nor	for	but	or	and	so

1 The world isn't square, _____ is it triangular.

2 I will take either math _____ English class in the spring semester.

3 The cat is either taken in _____ put outside by the parents.

4 Bottled water is neither cleaner _____ greener than tap water.

5 Jennifer is incredibly busy, _____ she has much work and four children.

6 He not only built his own house, _____ made every piece of furniture in it.

C Rewrite the sentences using the given conjunctions.

1 I took the books back to the store. I complained about them. (and)

→ _____*I took the books back to the store and complained about them.*_____

2 Your father phoned this afternoon. He didn't leave a message. (but)

→ _____

3 I didn't want to get home late. I ran straight back. (so)

→ _____

4 Mari was not in class all day long. She was not at home. (nor)

→ _____

5 I'm not a leader now. I do not want to be a leader. (nor)

→ _____

2 병렬 구조(Parallel Structure)

1 접속사에 의한 연결(connecting with conjunction)

Joe is intelligent and creation. (×)
Joe is **intelligent** and **creative**. (○)

My hobby is collecting stamps and to listen to pop music. (×)
My hobby is **collecting** stamps and **listening** to pop music. (○)

Tom finished the job slowly but perfect. (×)
Tom finished the job **slowly** but **perfectly**. (○)

Bob not only met Tom but also to have dinner with him. (×)
Bob not only **met** Tom but also **had** dinner with him. (○)

Both diligence and sincere are required in this job. (×)
Both **diligence** and **sincerity** are required in this job. (○)

You must either clean the room or to wash the dishes. (×)
You must either **clean** the room or **wash** the dishes. (○)

A language is learned by making and correct mistakes. (×)
A language is learned by **making** and **correcting** mistakes. (○)

1 두 개 이상의 단어가 and, or, but 등 등위 접속사로 연결될 때는, 연결되는 단어들이 동일한 문법 요소(명사+and+명사, 동사+and+동사, 형용사+but+형용사 등)로 결합된다.

2 복합 문장(compound sentence)을 만드는 접속사

(1) 동일한 형태의 A, B

* either A or B	A, B 둘 중의 하나
* neither A nor B	A, B 둘 다 아닌
* not only A but also B	A뿐만 아니라 B도
= B as well as A	

A recipe for pound cake calls for **either** water **or** milk.
They don't take life seriously, **either** dancing **or** playing sports.
The growth will **neither** stop **nor** slow down due to the oil price.
It's a place to **not only** write **but** share music and movies.

2

(1) 복합 문장에서 or, nor, but, also 등의 뒤에는 같은 내용이 반복되지 않으며, 앞과 뒤에는 서로 문법적으로 동일한 어구가 와야 한다.

(2) 동사는 B에 일치

Not only my father **but also** my brothers <u>are</u> drummers.
My father **as well as** my brothers <u>is</u> a drummer.
Neither my brothers **nor** my father <u>is</u> a drummer.
Either my father **or** my brothers <u>are</u> drummers.

(2) A와 B를 동반하는 표현이 주어로 올 때는 B에 동사가 일치된다.
– 주어: my brothers

– 주어: my father

– 주어: my father

– 주어: my brothers

E EXERCISE

A Find and correct the errors.

1 We finished the work slowly and accurate.

2 You must either clean the room or to wash the dishes.

3 Overpopulation causes poverty and hinder development.

4 Bob not only met Tom but also to have dinner with him.

5 My home offers me a feeling of secure, warmth, and love.

6 Use this site to find out if famous people are dead or live.

7 Today, our world produces enough food and nourishing every human.

8 The top 32 teams reached the finals and competing to win the trophy.

B Add 'is' or 'are' to each sentence.

1 Both the students and the teacher _____ planning to go there.

2 Not only the students but also the teacher _____ planning to go there.

3 Either the teacher or the students _____ planning to go there.

4 Neither the students nor the teacher _____ planning to go there.

5 The students as well as the teacher _____ planning to go there.

C Rewrite the sentences using the given words.

1 He does not have a bag. He does not have books. (neither A nor B)
→ _____ *He has neither a bag nor books.* _____

2 We can fly to New York, or we can take a train. (either A or B)
→ _____

3 Coal is an irreplaceable natural resource. (both A and B)
→ _____

4 The mosquito spreads a disease. The fly spreads a disease. (not only A but also B)
→ _____

5 Spiderman isn't going to the party. Batman isn't going to the party. (neither A nor B)
→ _____

6 Medical education can be fun. Medical education can be educational. (B as well as A)
→ _____

Choose the right word. 기출 응용

In order to make their dream come true, Mike and Amy decided not to waste money. By living temporarily with Mike's parents and (A) <cut / cutting> their leisure expenses, they hoped to save enough money to buy a modest house in two years.

 Read and answer the questions in English.

There lived a simple man who was the person responsible for sweeping floors and for keeping windows clean. He really did a good job, (A) <for / or> he was highly self-reliant and attentive to details. He had only a little money but he had good credit. (B) <So / But> a new rabbi came and insisted that everyone who lived and worked within its walls had to be educated enough to read and write. (C) <Still / So>, he was illiterate and said to the rabbi, "I do my job well and long to continue to do it." The rabbi frowned and said, "I am sorry to ask you to leave. It's my belief that everyone in this place should be literate. 가서 읽고 쓰는 것을 배우시오. 그리고 돌아오시오"

1 Choose the right words for (A), (B) and (C).

2 Translate the Korean into English.

→ Go _____.

C **Read and answer the question.**

Our bodies already knows how to cure themselves and be healthy. Occasionally we choose not to listen to our bodies because we don't want to hear that we shouldn't be eating chocolate, drinking coffee or whatever else our body is sending signals about. It is easier to sit on the couch in front of the TV and eat ice cream than to go out for a walk in nature. Both will make us feel good temporarily, but <will increase / and / our energy / for the rest of the day / eating / healthy foods / walking>.

1 Rearrange the words to complete the sentence.

→ but _____

Ⓐ **come true** 실현되다 **temporarily** 일시적으로 **modest** 겸손한, 알맞은 Ⓑ **attentive** 주의 깊은 **responsible** 책임있는, 담당하는 **detail** 상세, 세부 **rabbi** 유대 교회의 목사 **illiterate** 문맹의 Ⓒ **couch** 침상, 소파 **signal** 신호

Unit 5

문장의 일치

Questions

1 동사의 형태는 무엇을 기준으로 변하는가?
2 무조건 단수취급을 하는 경우는?

Answers

1 동사의 형태는 시제와 수(단수, 복수)에 따라 정해진다.
2 영어는 수와 양을 나타내는 표현이 다르며, each와 every처럼 단수 취급하는 경우도 있다. 우선, 주어가 무엇인지를 파악하는 습관을 길러야 한다.

1 ▶ 주어와 동사의 일치(Subject-Verb Agreement)

1 주어의 단수/복수 구분(singular number / plural number)

The best way to learn a second language **is** to hear it spoken.
People struggling to learn a second language **need** patience.
The desire to help others **is** always a double-edged sword.
Most children who have run away from home **commit** a crime.

> 1
> 주어에 수식어가 붙어 있는 경우, 수식을 받는 명사가 주어이다.
>
> − double-edged: 양날의

2 주어가 분수, 수량 표현(fractional number, quantity)

Half of the students **don't** listen to the speaker.
One third of the apples in the basket **are** rotten and dirty.
A few animals in the zoo **are** roaming here and there.
Few apples **are** showing internal damage from moth.

> 2
> 분수표현 뒤에 복수명사가 오면 복수동사, 단수명사가 오면 단수동사가 따른다.
>
> − 주어인 A few, Few 뒤에는 복수동사가, A little, Little 뒤에는 단수동사가 온다.

3 There+동사+주어(There+Verb+Subject)

There was a big automobile accident in our community.
There remains another major reason why they go there.
There need to be seven spaces between the letters.
There have been a number of earthquakes in recent history.

> 3
> 'There 동사+주어' 순서의 문장에서 동사의 수는 동사 뒤의 주어와 일치한다.

4 a number of / the number of

* a number of	많은 (= many)	〈 + 복수동사〉
* the number of	～의 수	〈 + 단수동사〉

A number of opportunities **are** available for promoting services.
The number of opportunities **is** only limited by our own efforts.

A number of buildings **are** situated inside the zoo.
The number of buildings **is** increasing along the shorelines.

> 4
> The는 수식을 받을 때 붙이므로, 'The number of+명사'는 뒤에서 앞으로 해석 (～의 수)!

5 의문문의 주어(subject of question sentence)

Why are **Susan and Alex** late for the meeting?
Who broke the windows of some cars in the parking lot?
What percentage of the people in the world is illiterate?
Why was **one of the students** excluded from the exam?

> 5
> 의문문에서 주어를 먼저 찾는 것이 중요하며, 의문사가 주어인 의문대명사에 주의해야 한다.

EXERCISE

A Choose the right words.

1 A number of problems resulting from the use of the text <is / are> discussed.

2 The number of passengers on domestic ship <was / were> great.

3 Two thirds of the food we eat <is / are> produced here in the UK.

4 Over two-thirds of students <has / have> written down a password.

5 Last year half of the site's visitors <was / were> at least 25 years old.

6 Half of the water used at home <is / are> used for waste disposal through the toilet.

7 Recently there <has / have> been changes in the laws in the USA.

8 There <has / have> been much debate about the ill effects of television viewing.

B Correct the errors in subject-verb agreement.

1 There were a terrible earthquake in Japan last year.

2 A study concludes that few people thinks the race is cruel.

3 About half of the students in the class receives scholarships.

4 About two thirds of the Chinese people lives in flood zones.

5 Beside the houses there stand a rock that resembles a peacock.

6 Who decide that the workday is from 9 to 5, instead of 11 to 4?

7 A sort of drumbeat have been sounding for a couple of days.

8 The variety of language spoken in Europe have a direct impact on the policy.

C Fill in blanks using the given words.

1 About two-thirds of the world's gold output _____ from South Africa. (come)

2 A research shows that more men than women _____ buying perfume. (be)

3 The number of adults in Asian population _____ been increasing. (have)

4 Sixty-five percent of the people in the United States _____ in cities. (live)

5 I wonder what _____ going to happen on the way to the party. (be)

6 How many students _____ going to attend the meeting? (be)

7 There _____ some food safety tips you need to keep in mind. (be)

8 There _____ to be so much trouble right now in the Middle East. (seem)

2 ▶ 주어+단수동사

1 주어가 Every, Each

Every man, woman, and child deserves peace.

Everyone of my friends remembers the great school days.

Each student and teacher is equipped with a lap top in a class.

Each picture in the book appears at least twice.

One of the hardest parts of my job is to help the poor.

One of the world's most eminent scientists returns to our lab.

1
주어가 Every, Each, One of ~ 등이 오면 동사는 항상 단수동사와 결합한다.
every는 단수취급을 하지만, every two days(2년마다)에서는 복수표현을 사용한다.

– lab=laboratory

2 주어가 시간(time), 거리(distance), 가격(price), 무게(weight)

Seven and seven is fourteen.

Three hours is the maximum length of time allowed for the race.

Five miles is a long distance for a child to walk.

Thirty dollars is all I can afford to pay.

Ten kilograms is the maximum weight limit allowed for a package.

2
주어가 숫자를 동반하는 시간, 거리, 가격, 무게 등인 경우 단수동사와 결합한다.
이 경우 복수개념이 아니라 '~라는 무게, ~라는 가격' 등의 의미를 지니기 때문이다.

3 -s로 끝나는 단수명사

arms	means	forces
mathematics	politics	physics
ethics	statistics	athletics
economics	linguistics	measles
mumps	diabetes	

3

– 무기, 수단, 군대

– 수학, 정치학, 물리학

– 윤리학, 통계학, 체육

– 경제학, 언어학, 홍역[míːzəlz]

– 이하선염, 당뇨병[dàiəbíːtis]

원칙적으로 학문명, 질병명 등에 붙이는 -s는 복수가 아니라 단수로 취급한다
일반적으로 명사 뒤의 -s가 의미를 바꾸는 방법으로 쓰인 경우(arms, means, customs 등) 단수 취급한다.

Statistics is the study of how to summarize and analyze data.

Politics in Europe **is** a bit different than it is in the United States.

The news about world hunger **has** not been all bad.

Measles remains a leading cause of children's death here.

4 주어가 동명사 / to부정사(gerund/to-infinitive)

Getting to know students **is** a huge advantage.

Helping others is as easy as clicking on a link.

Losing ten pounds makes you feel more attractive to others.

To learn a second language **is** very important to the social future.

To help others **is** all right, but it shouldn't be a burden on you.

To attempt to make it is like looking for a needle in a haystack.

4
주어가 동명사이거나 to부정사인 경우 단수동사와 결합한다.

– haystack: 건초더미

E EXERCISE

A **Choose the right words.**

1 Every lady and gentleman <has / have> a part in the game.

2 Every bird I have mentioned <make / makes> very long journeys.

3 Mathematics <has / have> been helpful in practical ways for centuries.

4 Washing the dishes <are / is> hard work when you can barely get out of bed.

5 One of the students in each group <dance / dances> dressed in banana fibers.

6 Studying a foreign language <make / makes> us more aware of other cultures.

7 Ten years <are / is> enough to start a family, grow kids, and get them into school.

B **Write the correct form of the given verbs in a simple present tense.**

1 Each of the students _____ three favorite films. (choose)

2 Every member of this club _____ the same T-shirt. (wear)

3 Economics _____ how you manage your possessions. (mean)

4 Keeping a pet _____ a positive effect on your health. (have)

5 Thirty dollars _____ an unreasonable price for the comb. (be)

6 The number of animals _____ to be similar to last year. (appear)

7 Almost all the information provided on the Web site _____ accurate. (be)

C **Rearrange the words to complete the sentences.**

1 is / ten dollars / all / have left / I
→ Ten dollars _____

2 has brought / child / each / some / food
→ Each _____

3 worse / the news / was / I / had expected / than
→ The news _____

4 its / has / image / own / every / flower
→ Every _____

5 of / them / each / the answer / has
→ Each _____

6 is / as fun / making / ice cream and pies / as / dressing a doll
→ Making _____

A Choose the right words for (A), (B) and (C).

People get passionate and heated when talking about politics. Politics (A) <are / is> a zero-sum game. In politics, one party wins and the other loses. If possible, you should not get involved in (B) <it / them>, because in an environment politics (C) <are / is> a matter of life and death.

B Read and answer the questions in English.

Every year 20,000 Polish young people disappear, which is large enough to fill a medium-sized town. The 'caregivers' children meet after running away from home (A) <are / is> taking advantage of their difficulties and most of them have gone unpunished. Most children who (B) <has / have> run away from home either commit crimes or become crime victims. An increasing number of Polish teenage girls (C) <decide / decides> to run off abroad. Polish law doesn't provide sufficient solutions to this. Neither the parents of the missing teenagers nor the police who chase them (D) <has / have> the power to take their passports to block them from leaving the country. This is a large loophole in Polish legislation.

1 Choose the right words.

2 According to the passage, how could Polish law try to block the young runaways?
   → Polish law could try to block the young runaways by _____.

C Read and answer the question.

<of / Russian women / the number / has / more than / doubled / who / smoke> since the breakup of the Soviet Union. In 1992, just seven percent of women smoked, compared to almost 15 percent by 2003. Over the same period, the number of men who smoke has risen from 56 percent to 62 percent. The Russian government needs to recognize the fact that smoking kills one in every two smokers, and unless it takes urgent action, millions more Russians will die from cigarettes. The findings emphasized that the greatest increase in smoking rates has occurred among the least educated, distinctly so among women. In a sign that the Russian government will take immediate action on the tobacco epidemic, it adopted a law on joining the World Health Organization's Framework Convention on Tobacco Control (FCTC).

1 Rearrange the words to complete the sentence.
   → The number of _____.

A politics 정치학 get involved in ~에 관련되다   **B** loophole 총구멍, 헛점 legislation 법률   **C** breakdown 붕괴 urgent 긴급한 epidemic 유행병, 전염병

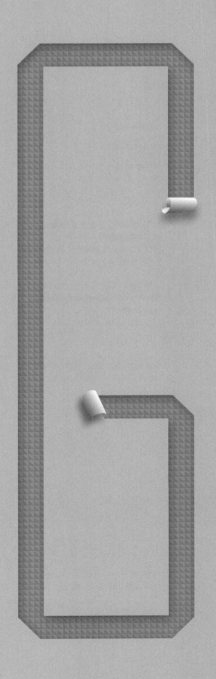

Unit 6

부정문과 도치문장

----

1 부정의 문장
2 도치의 문장

Questions

1 부정어는 본래 위치는 어디일까?
2 부정어는 위치를 바꿀 수 있는가?
3 부정어 No와 Not의 차이는 무엇이지?

Answers

1 부정표현(not)의 위치는 can't(=can not)를 연상하면 알 수 있듯이, 조동사와 be동사의 뒤이며, 일반동사 앞이다. 유사한 부정부사들(never, seldom 등)도 바로 이 위치에 온다.

2 부정어가 주어(No, None, Few 등)로 오는 경우를 제외하고도, 부정부사를 문장의 앞에 둘 수 있다. 이것은 부정을 강조하기 위함이며, 이 경우 뒤에는 V+S로 도치된다.

3 No는 홀로 쓰이지 않고 반드시 명사와 함께 붙어 사용된다. not은 부정부사로서, 조동사와 be동사의 다음, 그리고 일반동사의 앞에 등장하는 특성이 있다.

1 ▶ 부정의 문장(Negative Sentence)

1 부정을 만드는 'not'과 'no'

aren't (=are not)	mustn't (=must not)	haven't (=have not)
wasn't (=was not)	shouldn't (=should not)	hadn't (=had not)
weren't (=were not)	won't (=will not)	hasn't (=has not)
can't (=can not)	couldn't (=could not)	wouldn't (=would not)
ain't (=am not, isn't, aren't를 나타내는 비공식 표현)		

There are **no** mountains here. You **won't** see **any** mountains.
No automobiles are permitted in the park on Sundays.
When I became ill, I had **no** choice but to cancel my trip.

We haven**'t** got **any** information from the government's side.
He didn**'t** want **any** headstone on his grave.
She doesn**'t** support **any** particular candidate or party.

> **1**
> 동사를 부정하는 not은 원칙적으로 조동사 뒤, 일반동사(본동사)의 앞에 온다.
> * no는 단수명사나 복수명사의 앞에서 형용사처럼 쓰이며, not ~any로 바꿀 수 있다.
>
> = no information
> = no headstone
> = no particular ~

2 부분부정(partial negation)

"**Everybody doesn't** need a college education," Jim said.
Scholars discovered that **not all** types of fat are harmful.

Laughter is **not always** the best form of medicine.
Online banking may **never completely** replace a walk-in bank.

> **2**
> '전체'를 의미하는 대명사(all, both, every)가 부정어와 결합하는 경우
> * '완전'을 의미하는 부사가 부정어와 결합하는 경우—'완전히 ~하는 것은 아니다'
>
> '완전' 의미의 부사
> always, altogether, fully, exactly, completely 등

3 부정표현들

(1) 부정어가 주어

* none	(= no+명사)	아무도 ~않다
* neither	(= not+either)	(둘 중) 아무도 ~않다(단수 취급)
* nothing	(= not ~anything)	아무것도 ~않다
* nobody	(= not ~anybody)	아무도 ~않다
* nowhere	(부사, 명사)	아무데도 ~없다

Neither horse showed signs of illness.
None of them had to stand in line for hours to buy bread.
Nothing except your fears stands in your way.

> **3**
> (1) nobody와 no one은 사람에게 사용하며, none은 사람과 사물에 사용한다.

(2) 부정표현을 중복하지 않는다!
They would **never** discuss **anything** about the accident.
No one can find the cave **anywhere** in the mountain.
We would **hardly** find **anybody** else who is alive.

> (2) 부정어가 있는 문장에서는 nothing, no one, nobody 등 대신에 any ~를 사용한다.
> - never ~nothing (×)
> - no ~nowhere (×)
> - hardly ~nobody (×)

E EXERCISE

A Choose the right words.

1 I looked everywhere for Jane but I couldn't find her <anywhere / nowhere>.

2 There wasn't <any / none> left in the vending machine.

3 It looks very nice, but I have <ever / never> used such a bad raincoat!

4 I kept asking them questions, but <anyone / no one / someone> replied.

5 I asked Tim for advice but he could do <anything / nothing / something>.

6 If you haven't <ever / never / not> met her before, don't judge her by this book.

7 A policeman knocked at the door, but there was <anybody / nobody> in the house.

B Complete the sentences using 'nobody', 'nothing', 'anybody', or 'anything'.

1 That house is empty. _____Nobody_____ lives there.

2 He didn't tell _____ but Bailey obviously knew.

3 I could not find _____ who was in a similar situation.

4 I mentioned it years ago, but _____ agreed with me.

5 Harry was gone away. _____ knows where he is now.

6 She walked softly, looked sweetly, and said _____ all the time.

7 I was waiting for e-mail, but I didn't receive _____ in the mail.

C Rewrite the sentences using 'no', 'nobody', 'nothing', or 'nowhere'.

1 I haven't any free time today.
→ I _____ *have no free time today.* _____

2 There is not any student that knows the answer.
→ There is _____

3 I didn't send any message to anyone. I'm not a spammer.
→ I sent _____

4 We don't want anything to happen to your twins.
→ We want _____

5 There is not anywhere to hide from the solar rays.
→ There's _____

6 His wife complains that she doesn't have any food left to feed the family.
→ His wife complains that she has _____

2 ▶ 도치의 문장 (Inversion Sentence)

1 장소, 방향의 부사＋동사＋주어

In the doorway stood her father all day long.
Above the fireplace was a portrait of the Duke.
Here comes the bus which we are waiting for.

문학적이고 형식적인 글에서 장소나 방향의 부사가 문두에 오면 보통 V+S로 도치된다.

be동사의 경우는 반드시 도치가 되며, 주어가 대명사인 경우에는 도치가 발생하지 않으므로 문장 해석에 주의한다.

2 부정부사(negative adverb)

(1) 부정부사의 위치(position of negative adverb)

never	rarely	seldom	hardly	scarcely	barely	little

We could **barely** see the road in the fog.
We are **seldom** aware of why we do it.
She **never** confessed having such a problem.

(1) 부정부사의 위치는 not과 마찬가지로 be동사와 조동사의 뒤, 일반동사의 앞이다.

(2) 부정부사＋V＋S (negative+verb+subject)

I'll **never** do that again. → **Never** will I do that again.
He was **rarely** beaten. → **Rarely** was he beaten.
He **hardly** ever sings. → **Hardly** ever does he sing.

(2) 부정어가 문장 앞에 가면 뒤에는 동사(조동사, be동사, do)+주어의 순서로 도치된다.

– 일반동사의 경우 'do'동사가 도치된다.

(3) 부정부사구＋V＋S (negative adverbial+V+S)

Not until September / did he reach the Hungarian capital.
Not only / did she let me sleep in her house, but she fed me.
First of all, **in no way** / was I upset by your comments.

(3) not only, not until, 부정사구 등이 문두에 오면 뒤에는 V+S로 도치된다.

> * 자주 쓰이는 부정부사구
> in no way, on no account,
> under no circumstances,
> at no time, by no means,
> anything but 등

3 Only ~＋V＋S(verb+subject)

Only once / did I go to the concert when I was in England.
Only when he restores liberty / can we praise him.

Only by train / can you reach this beautiful view.
Only in Kenya / can you be killed by hippos and lions.

Only+부사(Only after, Only then, Only when 등)가 문두에 오면 도치된다.
* Only+전치사(Only by ~, Only in ~, Only with ~ 등)가 문두에 오는 경우에도 V+S로 도치된다.

4 So＋V＋S / Neither V＋S– ' ～도 마찬가지야.'

A: He majored politics.　　B: **So did** my father.
A: I was a singer.　　　　B: **So was** I.

A: Fleming isn't a liar.　　B: **Neither is** Mary.
A: He didn't want money.　B: **Neither did** I.

긍정문에서 So＋V＋S, 부정문에서는 Neither V＋S로 표현한다.
= I was a singer, too.

= Mary isn't a liar, either.

EXERCISE

A Match the beginning of each sentence with the most appropriate ending.

1 *Under no circumstances*   *a. can they use nuclear weapons.*

2 Not only   b. did I hear from my grandparents.

3 Above the fireplace   c. will it be cold enough to snow in Korea.

4 Not a single word   d. was I startled, but I was disappointed.   *startle: 놀라게하다

5 Only in Kenya   e. was a picture of a lady who looked familiar.

6 Hardly   f. did I complain yesterday about the weather.

7 Not until January   g. can you see so clever lions.

B Choose the right answer of the question.

1 A: He will join the study group.   B: a. So will I.

2 A: He is expecting to have a Thanksgiving day.   B: b. So am I.

3 A: I want to be a singer.   B: a. So did I.

4 A: I tried to jump over the pole.   B: b. So do I.

5 A: Mary doesn't know the truth.   B: a. Neither do I.

6 A: Mary hasn't known the truth.   B: b. Neither have I.

7 A: Our family won't visit the country.   B: a. Neither has my family.

8 A: Our family hasn't visited the country.   B: b. Neither will my family.

C Change each sentence so that it begins with a negative word.

1 We rarely go to the movies.

→ Rarely _____ *do we go to the movies.* _____

2 I hardly ever checked the weather.

→ Hardly _____

3 The mail scarcely ever arrives before noon.

→ Scarcely _____

4 I have never known Rosa to be dishonest.

→ Never _____

5 Babies in the room seldom slept through the night.

→ Seldom _____

Choose the right word. 기출 응용

I was five years old when my father introduced me to motor sports. Dad thought it was a normal family outing to go to a car racing event. (A) Little <did he / he did> know that he was fueling his son with a passion that would last for a lifetime.

 Read and answer the questions.

Fans were often used not only in Japan, but also in Europe as well. But, only in Japan <open and close / without / does / the taxi door / your touching it>. You may think (A) <anything / nothing> is familiar here in Japan; everything is new experience! It's a surprise that in Japan cell phones can be used for banking and ticket gate passes. You find exclusive luxury cellphone stores that require a membership before making a purchase only in Japan. Only in Japan (B) <can you / you can> find a mixture of many beans in food, such as bean cakes and bean rice. These are the reasons so many foreigners enjoy living in Japan.

1 Choose the right words for (A) and (B).

2 Rearrange the words to complete the sentence.
→ Only in Japan _____ .

ⓒ Read and answer the question.

Humor therapy is the art of using humor and laughter for the relief of physical and emotional difficulties. (A) It is said that "a cheerful heart is a good medicine, but a downcast spirit dries up the bones." (B) The only side effects of humor therapy is that it can cause sadness, mental hurt, and alienation in persons who are not receptive to it. (C) Some people may consider humor for the sick or injured as inappropriate or harmful. (D) Therefore, it is important to know when humor will be therapeutic and when it will be appropriate. (E) We should use it cautiously in cases where the sensitivity of the person is either uncertain or unknown.

1 Where would the following sentence best fit?

However, not everyone will appreciate humor therapy.

ⓐ passion 열정 last 지속하다 ⓑ exclusive 고급의, 독립적인 luxury 사치, 호화 bean 콩 ⓒ therapy 치료 mental illness 정신병 downcast 아래로 향한, 풀이 죽은 alienation 소외 sensitivity 민감성

Part II

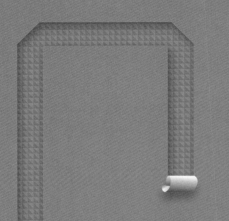

Questions

1 명사절을 이끄는 접속사에는 어떤 것이 있는가?
2 전치사 뒤에는 접속사 that S+V가 올 수 없는가?

Answers

1 that, if(목적어), whether는 주어, 목적어, 보어 역할을 하는 접속사이다.
2 전치사 뒤에는 명사가 오며, 원칙적으로 접속사(that, if, whether) 절은 전치사와 결합할 수 없다.

명사절 (S+V+Noun Clauses)

1 if와 whether의 명사절

I don't know **if** Eric is at home today.
I wonder **if** Alice will go to Chicago.
We are not certain **if** the bus stops here.

Whether he will come or not is a mystery to me.
I wonder **whether** the world is being run by smart people.
The problem is **whether** Koreans buy at home or from abroad.

> **1**
> if S+V는 목적어로 쓰일 때에만 '~인지 아닌지'의 의미를 지닌다.
> whether S+V는 명사절(주어, 목적어, 보어)과 부사절에서 모두 '~인지 아닌지'로 사용된다.
> if S+V와 whether S+V 절의 경우, 뒤에 'or not'이 올 수도 있다.

2 접속사(conjunction) that으로 시작하는 명사절

(1) that이 이끄는 명사절(noun clause)
　　It is essential **that** we take care of ourselves. 〈주어절〉
　　That the job market is changing is obvious.

　　I know **that** the Earth is not flat. 〈목적절〉
　　I recall **that** he won the prize a few years ago.

　　The important thing is **that** there has been progress. 〈보어절〉
　　The problem is **that** nobody wants to be our leader.

(2) that이 이끄는 목적절(object clause)
　　We insisted **that** all the workers **should** take two days off.
　　I proposed **that** our boat **go** to the beach right now.
　　I recommended **that** he not **be** punished for his crimes.
　　She demanded **that** she **be** allowed to continue her studies.

(3) 동격절(appositive clause)
　　The claim that brighter lighting reduces crime is unfounded.
　　The news that he won the prize came during Thanksgiving.
　　He expressed **the opinion that** Jane showed signs of illness.
　　The minister shared **the news that** he had Alzheimer's.

> **2**
> (1) 접속사 that은 문장의 주어, 목적어, 보어절을 이끌며, 목적절에서는 생략할 수 있다
> 접속사 that의 뒤에는 하나의 완전한 문장이 온다.
>
> (2) 주절에 주장동사나 당연표현(necessary, important, vital) 등이 오면 that절에 '당연'의미의 'should'가 오며, 생략시 동사원형을 둔다.
>
> > * 주장동사: insist, demand, order, propose, recommend 등
>
> (3) 동격절인 The fact(news, opinion, claim, report 등)+that S+V는 '~라는'으로 해석한다.
> 일반적으로 The 명사(The fact, The news...)는 생략하기도 한다.

3 여러 가지 명사절

You should consider **what** effects it may have on your child.
I wonder **how come** he left so suddenly and got scared.
I remember **what** he said to me yesterday.

> **3**
> 의문문이나 관계사절이 문장의 명사절로 올 수 있다.
> – 의문사절
>
> – 의문사절(how come=why)
>
> – 관계사절

E EXERCISE

A Put in the conjunction 'that' where appropriate.

1 I am proud I made the best choice for my life.

2 I was convinced I was right and he was wrong.

3 We proposed the reports be filed within 40 days.

4 We are certain all these injuries are from boat rides.

5 He insisted the accident had happened on the sidewalk.

6 It is critical you understand clearly what she is saying.

7 The fact he is moving so well means he will walk again.

8 The belief arthritis pain is related to the weather is wrong.   *arthritis: 관절염

B Complete each sentence using the given words.

1 We insisted that we _____ more creative. (be)

2 I recommended that she not _____ _____ at all. (punish)

3 He demanded that we _____ _____ for the repair. (pay)

4 It is vital that we _____ _____ able to defend ourselves. (be)

5 It is important that we _____ not _____ the same mistakes. (make)

6 The students requested that the test _____ _____ on Monday. (give)

7 The governor proposed that funds _____ _____ in four primary areas. (use)

C Rewrite the sentences using 'if' or 'whether'.

1 Can people communicate with dolphins?

→ I wonder _____ *if people can communicate with dolphins.* _____

2 Will Mr. Ted use the prize money to buy another house?

→ Do you know if _____

3 Did Peter get bonuses for doing a good job?

→ I wonder whether _____

4 Is Chicago located north or south of the equator?

→ I can't remember if _____

5 Do insects have blood and ears?

→ Can you tell me whether _____

6 Does he have letters of recommendation?

→ I don't know if _____

2 ▶ that S+V

1 동사＋전치사＝동사＋that절

We **insisted on** putting candles on the X-mas tree.
=We **insisted that** we should put candles on the X-mas tree.

I never **heard of** his doing a dishonest thing.
=I never **heard that** he did a dishonest thing.

1
전치사 뒤에는 that절이 올 수 없으므로, 전치사 없이 <u>동사+that절</u>이 된다.

2 형용사＋that절

(1) be＋형용사＋전치사＝be＋형용사＋that절

* be afraid **of** = be afraid **that S+V**	~를 두려워하다
* be aware **of** = be aware **that S+V**	~를 인식하다
* be sorry **for** = be sorry **that S+V**	~를 유감스러워하다
* be certain **of** = be certain **that S+V**	~를 확신하다
* be confident **of** = be confident **that S+V**	~를 확신하다
* be sure **of** = be sure **that S+V**	~를 확신하다
* be convinced **of** = be convinced **that S+V**	~를 확신하다

Dick **was aware of** the difference between the two functions.
=Dick **was aware that** the two functions are different.

(1) 전치사 뒤에는 반드시 명사의 형태(명사, 대명사, 동명사)가 와야 한다.
목적어로 명사절이 오면 전치사가 함께 사용될 수 없으므로 전치사를 삭제해야 한다.

(2) be＋감정형용사 뒤의 that절

* be furious **that**	* be fortunate **that**	
* be proud **that**	* be glad **that**	
* be pleased **that**	* be worried **that**	＋주어＋동사
* be horrified **that**	* be surprised **that**	
* be shocked **that**	* be delighted **that**	

I am glad **that** you're feeling better today.
I am sorry **that** I missed class yesterday.
I was disappointed **that** the peace conference failed.

(2) be＋형용사(과거분사) 뒤의 <u>that+S+V</u>는 목적절을 이끌며, that은 완전한 문장을 이끈다.

3 형용사＋to부정사 / that S+V

* be sorry **to** = be sorry **that S+V**	* be afraid **to** = be afraid **that S+V**
* be happy **to** = be happy **that S+V**	* be likely **to** = be likely **that S+V**
* be anxious **to** = be anxious **that S+V**	

Kathy is sorry **to leave** her mother behind.
I am sorry **that** he missed his chance to be a hero.

3
감정이나 행동, 상황을 나타내는 형용사가 to부정사나 that절과 결합할 수 있다.
두 문장의 주어가 같으면 to부정사와, 다르면 that절과 결합을 한다.

E EXERCISE

A Complete the sentences using preposition 'of' or 'that'.

1 Jimmy was aware _____*that*_____ these two accidents were different.

2 Now I feel jealous _____ the experiences she has had.

3 I was suspicious _____ the government and what they were really doing.

4 He was proud _____ me because I worked hard to be more independent.

5 I was furious _____ I paid fifteen dollars plus another twenty for snacks.

6 They were unaware _____ using the name of 'Princess Isabella' was taboo.

7 I was ashamed _____ the available clinical data was only a cloud of smoke.

B Rewrite each pair of sentences using 'that-clauses'.

1 We might be late. I was sure. → *I was sure that we might be late.*

2 Garry sent us the flowers. I was pleased. → _____

3 Mary was asked to resign. I was worried. → _____

4 They enjoyed the party. I was delighted. → _____

5 He is in a pessimistic mood. I am sorry. → _____

6 We are anxious. The uniform cost you much. → _____

7 I'd get infected with disease. He is afraid. → _____

8 Jimmy hurt the bird. I was frightened. → _____

C Complete the sentences using the given words.

1 I was disappointed that ____*we weren't in the first class seats.*____ (first class seat)
〈나는 우리가 1등석에 앉지 못해 실망했다.〉

2 Michael was anxious that _____ (missing)
〈Michael은 여권 분실한 것을 걱정스러워했다.〉

3 He was happy that _____ (come)
〈그는 그들이 파티에 온다는 사실에 행복해 했다.〉

4 They were afraid that _____ (talk, the police)
〈그들은 내가 경찰에게 말한 것을 걱정스러워 했다.〉

5 They were confident of _____ (achieve, a growth of)
〈그들은 4%의 성장을 성취할 것으로 확신했다.〉

A Choose the right words for (A) and (B). 기출 응용

One day a truck hit a pedestrian on the street. The driver argued (A) <that / when> the careless pedestrian was to blame for the accident. It was difficult to determine exactly where the accident had taken place. Many witnesses insisted (B) <that / if> the accident had taken place on the crosswalk. So, the driver was held responsible for the accident.

B Read and answer the question.

During the season, I usually dance around when there is a big game. My heart rate runs high and I usually lose about 5 pounds from not eating when Denver loses a game. My husband thinks (A) that I'm a lunatic, but he appreciates the enthusiasm. Anyway, last May, we found out (B) that I was pregnant and I was worried about the fact (C) that I might miss some football. After the preseason began, I told myself (D) that I should be calmer and more reserved. But something was different last night. I was a little surprised that I myself shouted and threw the clocks. As the 3rd quarter rolled into the 4th quarter (E) that I was pumping my fists and bouncing up and down in my seat. Why couldn't I calm down and just let the game go?

1 Choose one of (A) ~ (E) which should not have the conjunction 'that'.

C Read and answer the questions.

There is a new proposal by the administration to provide $500 million to study the global warming problem. Are you concerned about climate change — global warming? <u>I'm aware that global warming exists.</u> I understand that scientific evidence supports the claim that we've had about a one degree centigrade rise in average temperatures over the last century. I'm also aware of the recent discoveries that seem to have nailed down the conclusion that much of it is man-made. I can't say <a long-term concern / that / is / or not / whether>.

1 Rearrange the words to complete the sentence.
   → I can't say _____ .

2 Rewrite the underlined sentence into a simple one using 'of'.
   → I'm aware _____ .

A pedestrian 보행자 argue 주장하다 witness 목격자 **B** lunatic 광적인, 미치광이 appreciate 인정하다, 감사하다 enthusiasm 열정, 열광 pregnant 임신한 reserved 말없는, 내성적인 fist 주먹 **C** administration 행정부 centigrade 섭씨 nail down 못박다, 확정하다 conclusion 결론 long-term 장기간

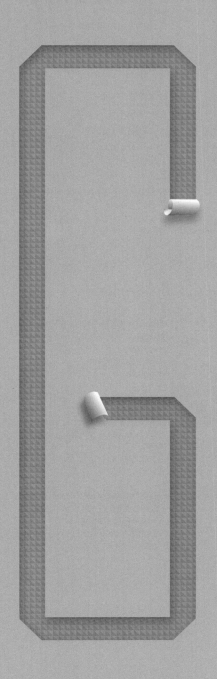

Questions

1 관계대명사 앞에서 끊어 읽으면 독해에 도움이 될까?

2 관계대명사의 어법과 독해를 해결하는 비법은 없을까?

3 왜 어법 시험에는 관계대명사가 꼭 등장할까?

Answers

1 관계대명사는 두 문장을 하나의 문장으로 연결한 것이므로 끊어서 두 문장으로 해석하면 쉬워진다.

2 관계대명사는 선행사를 대신하는 대명사 역할을 한다. 그래서, 관계사절에서 필요한 것이 주어인지, 목적어인지, 소유격인지, 부사인지를 판단하면 어법 문제를 쉽게 해결한다.

3 우리말에 없는 표현이기 때문이다. 관계대명사만 확실하게 이해해도 영어의 부담이 확 줄어들 것이다.

형용사절－관계대명사(Relative Pronoun) Ⅰ

1 관계대명사의 종류와 격 – who, which, that

선행사(antecedent)	주격(subjective case)	목적격(objective case)	소유격(possessive case)
사람	who	whom	whose
사물	which	which	of which, whose
사물, 사람	that	that	

This is the man / **who** loved me.
This is the man / **whom(=who)** I loved.
This is the man / **whose** son I loved.

There lived a woman / **who** had no children of her own.
This is the gentleman / **whom(=who)** we have admired.
I know a guy / **whose** feet are too big for his bed.

1

관계대명사절은 앞의 선행사나 내용을 보충
설명하는 형용사절의 역할을 한다.
관계대명사는 선행사를 대신하는 대명사로
서, 관계사절의 주어, 목적어, 소유격으로
쓰인다.
목적격 관계대명사 whom 대신 who를 사
용하기도 한다.

– 그 **남자가** 나를 사랑했다

– 그 **남자를** 내가 사랑했다

– 그 **남자의** 아들을 내가 사랑했다

– 그 여자는 ~

– 그 신사를

– 그 녀석의

2 관계대명사를 생략할 수 있다.

Have you got a laptop computer **(that)** I can use?
A woman **(whom)** my sister knows has just bought the house.

Tennis is the sport **(which)** I am fond of.
I must thank the people **(whom)** I got a present from.

2

관계대명사가 동사나 전치사의 목적어 일 때
생략할 수 있다.

3 명사＋현재분사／과거분사

Most people **living** in the city / have their own cars.
Most of the people **strolling** in the park / were teenagers.
He is gesturing towards the boxes / **lying** on the table.

He was the new minister / **appointed** by the president.
She was wearing a dress / **bought** in Paris.
A story **written** by a young girl / won the competition.

3

뒤에서 앞의 명사를 수식하는 분사는 관계대
명사＋동사로 바꿀 수 있다.
– who live
– who were strolling
– which lie

– who was appointed
– which was bought
– which was written
* 현재분사는 능동을, 과거분사는 수동을 나
타낸다.

4 관계대명사 that

The people **that**(=who) live next to me / are Italians.
Here is my servant / **that**(=whom) I have chosen.
We are enjoying the music / **that**(=which) plays on TV.

Hair is something **that** we can all live without.
I wish to thank Joe for all **that** he is able to offer.
Matrix is one of the best movies **that** I have ever seen.

4

that은 관계대명사 who와 which를 대신할
수 있으며, 제한적인 선행사(all, ~thing, 최
상급 등)가 올 때 주로 쓰인다.
현대 영어에서 반드시 that만을 사용해야 하
는 원칙은 사라지고 있다.

E EXERCISE

A   Choose the right words.

1   Hammers are tools <which / whom> are used to hit nails into wood.

2   A kangaroo is an animal <who / whose> babies are raised in a pouch.

3   Photographers are people <who / whom> are skilled at taking pictures.

4   A nurse is someone <whose / whom> most of us have met in hospitals.

5   An adjective is a word <that / of which> acts to modify a noun in a sentence.

6   A prisoner is a person <who / whose> is arrested and spends his time in a prison.

7   A giraffe is an animal <which / whose> neck is long enough to reach the tree top.

8   A miser is someone <who / whom> wouldn't spare a dime for anybody else in need.

B   Match the beginning of each sentence with the most appropriate ending.

1   *A widow is someone*   *a. whose husband has died.*

2   A pilot is a person   b. which cannot fly.

3   An alarm clock is a clock   c. who you don't know well.

4   A vegetarian is someone   d. which wakes you up.

5   A penguin is a kind of bird   e. who is trained to fly an aircraft.

6   A florist is someone   f. who doesn't eat meat.

7   A stranger is someone   g. who sells flowers.

C   Rewrite the underlined parts using the relative pronouns.

1   Do you know the woman <u>coming</u> toward us?

→ Do you know the woman ____*who is coming*____ toward us?

2   I came from a city <u>located</u> in the southern part of the country.

→ I came from a city _____ in the southern part of the country.

3   The children <u>attending</u> that school receive a good education.

→ The children _____ that school receive a good education.

4   They live in a house <u>built</u> in 1890.

→ They live in a house _____ in 1890.

5   Betty published the book <u>written</u> for children.

→ Betty published the book _____ for children.

2 ▶ 형용사절-관계대명사(Relative Pronoun) II

1 전치사+관계대명사(preposition+relative pronoun)

We need to understand the world / **which** we live **in**.
=We need to understand the world / **in which** we live.
=We need to understand the world / we live **in**.

He neglected the sports / **which** he had once been fond **of**.
=He neglected the sports / **of which** he had once been fond.
=He neglected the sports / he had once been fond **of**.

2 관계대명사 앞에 comma(,)를 둘 수 있다.

(1) 선행사, + 관계대명사(antecedent, + relative pronoun)

* who~: 그런데 그 사람이	* whom~: 그런데 그를	* whose~: 그런데 그 사람의
* which~: 그런데 그것이(을)	* of which~: 그런데 그것의	

She had three sons, **who** went abroad to study.
Our secretary, **who** can type fast, plans to quit work soon.
She was engaged to a sailor, **whom** she had met at Dartmouth.

They use lots of slang, **of which** the meanings we don't know.
I am teaching at the Oak center, **which** is just over the road.
Time magazine, **which** is available in Korea, is published weekly.

(2) 관계대명사 「, which」는 앞의 문장을 받기도 한다.
She was a little tense, **which** was understandable.
He said he was ill, **which** proved to be false.
He wanted to come, **which** was impossible.

3 선행사(antecedent)의 일부나 그룹을 나타내는 경우

most of whom	none of whom	some of whom
most of which	none of which	some of which

Our class has 20 students, **most of whom** are from Asia.
He talked about famous singers, **some of whom** he contacted with.
They are all friends, **many of whom** have lived in Japan for years.

I have tried many products, **most of which** I haven't liked.
Tens of azaleas, **some of which** are 3 meters high, adorn the yard.
The city has ten schools, **two of which** are junior colleges.

1
전치사의 목적어인 관계대명사는 생략하거나 전치사+관계대명사의 형태를 만들 수 있다.

― 관계대명사 생략

― 관계대명사 생략

2
사람이나 사물의 추가적 정보를 언급할 때 사용하며, 접속사+대명사로 해석한다.
관계대명사는 앞의 선행사를 한정하지 않고 별도의 주어나 목적어로 사용된다.
that은 이러한 형태로 사용할 수 없다.

― who는 three sons의 대명사

(2) 관계대명사 which는 문맥상 구(phrase)나 문장을 받기도 한다.
― which는 앞 전체 문장

― which는 앞의 to come을 받는다.

3
앞에 언급된 선행사의 일부나 그룹을 언급할 때 사용하는 형태이다.

EXERCISE

A Complete the sentences so that they mean the same as the first sentence.

1 That's the chair. I sat on it.

a. That's the chair _____ I sat on.

b. That's the chair _____ _____ I sat.

c. That's the chair I sat _____ .

2 They're the shops. I got these gifts from them.

a. They're the shops _____ I got these gifts from.

b. They're the shops _____ _____ I got these gifts.

c. They're the shops I got these gifts _____ .

B Match the beginning of each sentence with the most appropriate ending.

1 I had to travel first class,   a. which caused problems with electricity.

2 It snowed heavily all night,   b. which meant all the guests sat around the table.

3 The car uses very little petrol,   c. which meant that many trees were needed.

4 Saturday is a day off for all workers,   d. which certainly made his mom very happy.

5 Our dinner was 'family style',   e. which means it is quite cheap to run.

6 All ships were built of wood,   f. which means that roads are less crowded.

7 The ski season was beginning,   g. which meant reservations were necessary.

8 John did very well at school,   h. which cost double with no real advantage.

C Complete each sentence using relative pronoun.

1 우리는 약간의 돈을 마련했는데, 일부는 빌린 것이다.

→ We raised some money, ___*some of which*___ we borrowed.

2 단 3명만이 차를 보러 왔는데, 어느 한 명도 차를 사려지 않았다.

→ Only three people came to look at the car, _____ wanted to buy it.

3 그 가수는 팬들을 실망시켰는데, 팬들 중 일부는 홍콩에서 왔다.

→ The singer disappointed fans, _____ had traveled from Hong Kong.

4 그 부족은 세 종류의 언어를 사용했는데, 어느 하나도 오늘날 알려지지 않는다.

→ The tribe used 3 kinds of languages, _____ are known today.

5 그가 약 30권의 책을 추천했는데, 나는 그 대부분 책을 아직 읽지 않았다.

→ He recommended about 30 books, _____ I have not yet read.

A Choose the right words for (A) and (B).

> The Kangaroo is an animal (A) <which / whom> lives only in Australia. Australia is a fairly large country (B) <that / whom> is about the same size as the Continental USA. But most of its population lives only around the coastal areas, because two thirds of the country is desert.

B Read and answer the questions.

> Jealousy is something < breaks up / and distracts / which / your relationship / you>. You see jealousy is a feeling (A) <which / whom> can cause the breakup of a relationship even before you know it. I mean jealousy is something which is hard to control. Jealousy can make you do horrible things (B) <which / of which> you normally wouldn't even think about doing. Therefore, it is very important to know how to control jealousy in a relationship.

1 Choose the right words for (A) and (B).

2 Rearrange the words to complete the sentence.
   → Jealousy is something _____ .

C Read and answer the questions.

> The advertising campaign "Malaysia, Truly Asia" is commonly heard across the world. It is sponsored by the Malaysian Government. It is designed to attract foreign visitors to this country of 22 million people which boasts of a diverse ethnic and religious composition. 51 percent of the population is Malay, nearly all of whom are Muslim. Chinese make up 26 percent of the population, most of whom are Buddhists, while a small number are Christian. Indians constitute 7 percent of the population, most of which are Hindu. Various ethnic groups and migrant workers, most of whom are Indonesians, make up the remaining 16 percent of the population. In spite of the Muslim majority, Malaysia has these various ethnic groups, <mutually / respect / most of whom / its multi-religious society>.

1 Rearrange the words to complete the sentence.
   → Malaysia has these various ethnic groups, _____ .

2 Complete the following sentence to present the main idea of the passage.
   → _____ became the basis for Malaysia's multi-religious society.

Ⓐ coastal 해안의 Ⓑ jealousy 질투 breakup 붕괴, 분리 Ⓒ ethnic 인종의, 민족의 diverse 다양한 composition 구성, 성분 migrant 이주자 majority 다수

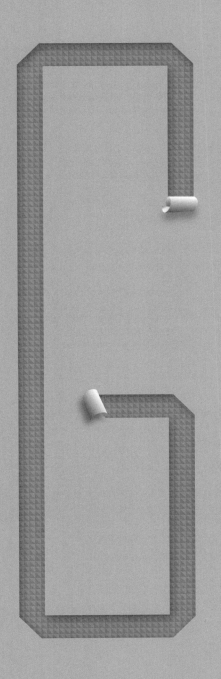

Unit 9

형용사절 문장 2

Questions

1 관계대명사와 관계부사는 무엇이 다른 거야?

2 관계대명사 what을 간단하게 기억하고 싶다.

3 접속사 that과 관계대명사 that을 어떻게 구분하지?

Answers

1 선행사가 관계사절에서 대명사 역할을 하면 관계대명사를, 부사 역할을 하면 관계부사를 사용한다.

2 관계대명사 what(=the thing which)은 선행사가 없으며 뒤에는 불완전한 문장이 온다.

3 접속사(that)는 단순히 절을 이끄는 안내자 역할이므로 뒤에 완전한 문장이, 관계대명사 뒤에는 불완전한 문장이 따른다.

형용사절 – 관계부사(Relative Adverb)

1 관계부사 when, where, why, how로 시작하는 문장

There was a time / **when** movies cost a dime.
August is the month / **when** the weather is usually the hottest.

A cafe is a small restaurant / **where** people can get a light meal.
That is the drawer / **where** I keep my jewelry.

There are several reasons / **why** we can't do that.
Can you give me any reason / **why** I should help you?

My uncle writes about / **how** he lives without credit cards.
I want to know the way / **that** he made the drawings.

> 1
> 시간, 장소, 이유, 방법을 나타내는 관계부사는 관계사절에서 부사로 사용된다.
> 선행사나 관계부사가 생략되기도 하지만, where는 예외적으로 생략하지 않는다.
>
> – how는 'the way how'의 형태로는 사용되지 않는다. the way that(=the way in which), the way, 또는 how로 사용된다.

2 관계부사 앞에 comma(,)를 둘 수 있다.(nonrestrictive clause)

The war happened in 1957, **when** I was still a baby.
He remembered his childhood, **when** he lived without cars.

We got back to Dublin, **where** we had dinner.
We had pizza in the cafe, **where** cockroaches roamed free.

> 2
> 쉼표 뒤의 when은 '그런데 그때', where는 '그리고 그곳에서'로 해석할 수 있다.

3 관계부사는 전치사+관계대명사 또는 that으로 대체가능하다.

I visited the old building / **where** he lived.
= I visited the old building / **in which** he lived.
= I visited the old building / he lived **in**.
= I visited the old building / **which** he lived **in**.
= I visited the old building / **that** he lived **in**.

I never forget the day / **when** I met you.
= I never forget the day / **on which** I met you.
= I never forget the day / **that** I met you.
= I never forget **the day** / I met you.

We found **how** Rachel escaped from the prison.
= We found **the way** Rachel escaped from the prison.
= We found the way **in which** Rachel escaped from the prison.
= We found the way **that** Rachel escaped from the prison.

> 3
> 관계부사는 관계사절에서 부사로 쓰이므로 전치사+관계대명사의 의미와 동일하다.
> 관계부사절은 관계부사 뒤에 완전한 하나의 문장이 따른다.
> 전치사+관계사 that은 불가능하다.
>
> – 관계부사
> – 전치사+관계대명사
> – that이 관계부사로 사용
> – 관계부사 생략
>
> – how 대신 in which 사용
> – how 대신 that을 사용

E EXERCISE

A Choose the right words.

1 That is the way <how / in which> we have been working.

2 Please fence off the area <when / where> the rabbits are kept.   *fence off 울타리로 구획하다

3 We'd hate the reason <why / which> we can't go out on Friday night.

4 She has never been to the shop <where / which> the crime occurred.

5 They aim to change the way <how / that> music is sold to the public.

6 He went back to the town <when / where> he spent his teenage years.

7 A cafe is the place <where / which> you can stay for brunch, lunch, and dinner.

B Complete the sentences using the 'relative pronouns' or 'relative adverbs'.

1 Our mini-van takes us to the restaurant ____where____ we will have lunch.
   There is the large restaurant ___which(that)___ gives you a fine view of London.

2 A playground is a place _____ children can have fun outdoors.
   The gallery became the place _____ children often visited.

3 I live next to the church _____ was constructed in 1517.
   This is the church _____ we are getting married.

4 School is the place _____ I can feel comfortable.
   School is the place _____ our students spend most of their time in.

5 We remember the time _____ he took a snowboard and couldn't stop.
   We shared his memories of the time _____ he spent with his animals.

C Combine the sentences using either 'where' or 'when'.

1 There was a time. Philippine basketball used to rule Asia then.
   → There was a time _when Philippine basketball used to rule Asia._

2 There was a time. Dinosaurs dominated the earth then.
   → There was a time _____

3 The miser hid his money in the ceiling. It was safe from robbers there.
   → The miser hid his money in the ceiling _____

4 She has just left the restaurant. She works as a waitress there.
   → She has just left the restaurant _____

5 Summer is the time of year. We enjoy the warm weather then.
   → Summer is the time of year _____

2 관계사절의 다른 형태(Relative Clause)

1 관계대명사 what(=the thing which)

(1) what의 역할

He gave me **what** I needed to survive.
These sunglasses are just **what** we've always wanted.
Professors say leaders are known by **what they do**.
He is not known for **what he has**, but **what he is**.

(2) what+명사

According to their demand he gave them **what money** he had.
The soldiers ate **what food** they could find in the woodland.
He will give them **what information** he has collected.

1

(1) what(=the thing which)은 선행사를 포함한 관계대명사이므로 선행사를 두지 않는다.

— 그들의 행동
— 그의 재산/그의 인간됨

(2) what+명사는 '얼마 안되는 모든 것'을 나타내는 표현이다.
— all the little money (which)
— all the little food (which)
— all the little information (which)

2 that: 접속사와 관계대명사(conjunction and relative pronoun)

(1) 관계대명사

I called the lady **that(=whom)** I had purchased dolls from.
I bought a book **that(=which)** was written 300 years ago.
The boys gave me something **that** I had never thought about.
This is the man and the dog **that** you are looking for.

(2) 접속사의 구분

I told the lady **that** the vet didn't do any blood test. (접속사)
The hat belongs to the lady **that** drove my dog to the vet. (관계대명사)

2

(1) that은 관계대명사 who, whom, which 를 대신할 수 있다.
선행사가 all, -thing, 사람과 사물, 최상급 등의 특수한 경우에 that을 사용한다.

(2) 접속사 뒤에는 완전한 문장이 온다.
— 접속사 that + 완전한 문장
— 관계대명사 that + 불완전한 문장

3 복합관계사(compound relative)

I'm supposed to give it to **whoever** asks for free.
You can of course vote for **whomever** you want.
He seems in the end to find **whatever** he is looking for.

Whatever you're saying, the music has to feel the same way.
Whichever you choose, I hope you have a good time here.
Whoever wins the race, you will be guaranteed to profit.

Wherever you go in Australia, we promise unique experiences.
Whenever I feel blue, I take a deep breath repeatedly.

No police force, **however** large, can protect everyone.
However similar it may be, each egg is identical with itself.

3

— anyone who
— anyone whom
— anything that

— no matter what
— no matter which
— no matter who

ever는 관계대명사나 관계부사 뒤에 붙으며, that과 why 뒤에는 사용하지 않는다.

however+형용사/부사+S+V는 '아무리 ~ 해도'의 부사절을 나타낸다.

EXERCISE

A Choose the right words.

1 He will give you everything <that / what> you are seeking.

2 Never tell anyone <that / what> you have seen and heard tonight.

3 We will discuss specifically <who / what> information she obtained.

4 <Whoever / Whichever> you choose, you will be satisfied with the choice.

5 I was so stupid that I misunderstood <that / what> they wanted to say.

6 <Wherever / Whichever> you travel around the world, you'll see Koreans.

B Match the beginning of each sentence with the most appropriate ending.

1 As a mayor, I would like to meet
a. whenever you go out in the tropics.

2 You can find the polar bear
b. whoever wants to buy it.

3 Your messages will be sent automatically
c. whoever is in charge in the committee.

4 You will have to take water with you to drink
d. whichever is offered by the provider.

5 I will sell the ship at market prices to
e. wherever you want to send them.

6 You will have to take
f. wherever you live in the arctic.

7 My class teacher doesn't mind
g. whoever is elected a class president.

C Rearrange the words to complete each sentence.

1 I won't tell <anyone / you / what / me / asked>.
〈나는 네가 나에게 물어본 것을 누구에게도 말하지 않을 거야.〉
→ I won't tell _____

2 The delivered goods are not <I / what / ordered / have>.
〈배달된 상품은 내가 주문한 것이 아닙니다.〉
→ The delivered goods are not _____

3 Why didn't you tell the doctor <died / that / of / your mom / lung cancer>?
〈왜 너는 의사에게 어머니가 폐암으로 돌아가신 것을 말하지 않았니?〉
→ Why didn't you tell the doctor _____

4 Paul has scolded <have not saved / that / what / I / I earned>.
〈Paul은 내가 버는 돈을 저축하지 않았다고 꾸짖었다.〉
→ Paul has scolded _____

5 Levan declared <what / has gained / that he / aimed for / he>.
〈Levan은 그가 목표로 한 것을 얻었다고 선언했다.〉
→ Levan declared _____

A Choose the right words for (A) and (B).

> Everyone has three things in common with everybody else in this world. The three things are: Needs, Wants and Dreams. (A) <That / What> most people need to discover is that almost anything can be achieved in their lifetimes. There are only a few details (B) <that / what> stand between you and the accomplishment of your dreams.

B Read and answer the questions.

> One of the most exciting moments in life is (A) <how / when> a person is finally old enough to get a license. This is the time (B) <when / which> one can have independence and go wherever one desires whenever one wants. A person no longer has to depend on someone else to get around all the time. However, driving a vehicle is also one of the biggest responsibilities one will ever have and must not be taken lightly. This is (C) <which / why> everyone is required to take a written test before they are allowed to get a license. The time has come for you to take your driver's license test! Are you fully prepared? Make sure that you pass your road test the first time with lots of practice. Learn how you can be completely ready for the big test by visiting http://www.roadtesttips.com.

1 Choose the right words for (A), (B) and (C).

2 Choose the word which best represents the purpose of the passage.
  → This passage means to <advertise / search> an Internet site for road tests.

C Read and answer the question. 기출 응용

> Schubert spent his whole life in poverty. But he had one noble purpose in life. That was to write down the beautiful musical thoughts which seemed to flow from his brain in an endless rush of melody. As one of the most productive composers, Schubert wrote music as freely as one would write a friendly letter. 그는 그의 내부에 있는 것을 단지 작곡했다, and brought us a rich treasure of music.

1 Rearrange the words to have the same meaning as the underlined part.
  He just <produced / in / him / what / was>
  → He just _____ .

Ⓐ in common 공통된 achievable 완수할 수 있는 detail 세부, 상세 achievement 성취, 업적, 성적 Ⓑ independence 독립 vehicle 탈 것, 차량 Ⓒ noble 고상한 composer 작곡가 treasure 보물

Unit 10

의문문
- -

1 의문사 의문문

2 간접의문문

Questions

1 간접의문문이란 무엇인가?

2 의문대명사란 무엇을 말하는 것이지?

3 간접의문문에서 가장 중요한 내용만 알면 좋겠는데!

Answers

1 의문문은 「의문사+동사+주어~」의 순서이지만, 의문문이 문장의 일부로 문장 속에 들어올 때는 평서문의 순서인 「의문사+주어+동사~」로 변하게 되는 것을 간접의문문이라고 부른다. 의문사가 주어 역할하는 의문대명사나 생각 동사가 등장하는 경우 혼란을 준다.

2 의문사이면서 문장의 주어(~는,이,가)나 목적어(~를) 역할을 하는 의문사이다. 예: who(누구가), which(어느 것이) 등.

3 생각동사로 물을 때의 간접의문문과 문장의 주어인 의문대명사가 의문사로 올 때에는, 의문대명사가 의문사와 주어를 겸하므로 간접의문문에서 순서가 바뀔 필요가 없는 경우이다. 《의문사+do you think+주어+동사》로 기억한다.

1 의문사 의문문(Question-word Questions)

1 의문사+동사(be, 조동사)+주어

When did you start to see results from your program?
Where did you get so small sausage made of pork?
Why are you getting on my nerves?

> 1
> 의문사는 'when 언제, where 어디서, what 무엇을, how 어떻게, why 왜'로 해석된다.
> – get on one's nerve 신경을 건드리다

2 의문사가 주어, 목적어

What do you know about Thanksgiving?
Who took the cookie from the cookie jar?
Whom did you see at the award ceremony?

> 2
> 의문사가 문장의 주어(Subject)나 목적어(Object)로 사용되기도 한다.
> – 주어: 누구가
> – 목적어: 누구를

3 전치사+의문사(question word), 의문사+명사/형용사/부사

From whom did the U.S. get their independence?
For what reason do you devote yourself to the church?

Which day of the week were you born on?
How large is China's defence budget this year?

> 3
> 의문사는 전치사와 결합할 수 있으며, 의문사 뒤에 명사가 올 수도 있다.
> 의문사와 함께 쓰이는 전치사나 명사는 분리되지 않는다.

4 부정의문문(negative question)

Why don't you get back into bed?
What doesn't it matter to our foreign policy?
Who doesn't want to be a millionaire?

> 4
> 부정의문문을 사용하여 내용을 강조한다.
> – 권유
> – 중요하다
> – ~되고 싶다

5 주의할 표현

> What is ~ like?
> What ~for?(= why~?)
> Why not~?(= Why don't you~?)
> What if I should fail again? (= What shall I do~?)

> 5
> – ~은 어떻게 생겼느냐?
> – 왜 ~하니?
> – ~하지 그래(권유)
> – 또 실패하면 어떻게 하지?

6 의문문의 답변

A: Will it rain tomorrow?
B: I hope **not**. (=I hope it will **not** rain tomorrow.)
   I hope **so**. (=I hope it will rain tomorrow.)
   I am afraid **not**. (=I am afraid that it will **not** rain tomorrow.)
   I am afraid **so**. (=I am afraid that it will rain tomorrow.)

> 6
> – I'm afraid ~: 유감스럽지만

EXERCISE

A **Change the 'How+adjective questions' into 'What+noun questions'.**

1 How old is the church building?   What is _the age of the church building?_

2 How wide is the highway lane?   What is _____

3 How long is the bridge?   What length _____

4 How deep is the Atlantic ocean?   What is _____

5 How big is an oil tanker?   What size _____

6 How far is the moon from here?   What distance _____

7 How high is the sky from here?   What height _____

B **Match each sentence on the left with one on the right.**

1 *How long has his sister been dead?* ....   a. *She passed away three years ago.*

2 What time do you want to have a meeting?   b. It took me five hours.

3 What frightened you as a kid?   c. The math test keeps me from going.

4 How long did it take you to drive to Seoul?   d. How about eleven or eleven-thirty?

5 How often do earthquakes occur?   e. I couldn't reach anybody except Paul.

6 Whose car did you borrow yesterday?   f. It depends on the region or the continent.

7 Why can't you go fishing tomorrow?   g. Nightmares scared me most.

C **Complete each sentence using the given words.**

1 Mary는 영어를 얼마나 잘 하니? (speak)
    → How _well does Mary speak English?_

2 무슨 일로 오셨나요? (bring)
    → What _____

3 어느 신발이 나에게 가장 잘 어울리니? (suit)
    → Which _____

4 우리 'Men In Black II' 보러 가는 게 어때? (go see)
    → Why _____

5 그 사람이 어떻게 생겼니? (look)
    → What _____

6 무엇 때문에 너는 시장에 출마하기로 결정했니? (run for)
    → What _____

2 ▶ 간접의문문 (Indirect Questions)

1 의문사로 시작하는 명사절 – Indirect Questions(간접의문문)

when	where	why	how	
who	whom	whose	what	which

What he felt about it is not stated officially.

I don't know **what he's doing** right now with pictures.

All you have to know is **what you want to do** with your blog.

Tell me **when** you signed the contract.

Could you tell me **how** far it is to the bank?

I just wonder **whom** she'll vote for in the elections.

2 주의할 간접의문문

My father asked me **which** college I wanted to attend.

We wonder **whose** house he will visit with a new baby.

We don't know **what** kind of job he would take at this time.

I don't remember **who** ordered this pork-cutlet and Coke.

I wonder **who** has left the car in front of our house.

Nobody knows **which** is pure gold, and **which** is artificial.

I wonder **what** she will look **like** as an adult.

A bus driver must know **how long** it takes to go there.

I asked **with whom** she wants to work in the future.

3 의문사+do you think+주어+동사

> * 의문사 + do you think(생각동사)+주어+동사
> 〈생각동사 : suppose, guess, believe, imagine 등〉

What is he?＋Do you think?

→ **What** do you think he is?

How long does it take?＋Do you guess?

→ **How long** do you guess **it takes**?

Where do you think **he lives**?

Why do you suppose **Hitler committed suicide**?

How long do you imagine **you will be here**?

1

의문사는 반드시 '누가, 언제, 어디서, 무엇을, 어떻게, 왜'처럼 해석한다.

의문사절은 문장에서 주어, 보어, 목적어 역할을 하며, 이 경우 평서문의 순서(의문사+S+V)가 되어야 한다.

– 주어절

– 목적절

– 보어절

2

– 의문사+명사의 형태로 쓰여서 의문사는 형용사 역할을 한다.

– 의문사가 문장의 주어 역할을 하여, 간접의문문이 의문사+동사~의 순서가 된다.

– 의문사는 전치사나 형용사와 짝을 이루어 사용되기도 한다.

3

의문사로 시작하는 질문은 'Yes', 'No'의 답이 나올 수 없다.

상대방의 생각을 묻는 질문에 'Yes', 'No'의 답이 필요하지 않으므로 문장의 순서는 의문사+do you think+S+V의 순서가 되어야 한다.

 **EXERCISE**

A Underline the errors and correct them.

1 Do you think who would apply for this job?

2 Could you tell me what is the weather like today?

3 Please tell me when did you receive the letter.

4 Nobody knows whose side will the decider take.

5 Who made it is important, but where was it made isn't.

6 Do you suppose how long the baby has been left alone at home?

B Complete each sentence using the given words.

1 A: Oops! Where ___*did I put*___ my key? Don't you have it? (put)
   B: It's better to ask Micky where ___*it is*___ . I saw her using it. (be)

2 A: Mr. Park is a recent immigrant. How long _____ in this country? (be)
   B: I have no idea. Please ask him how long _____ here. (live)

3 A: I called you up several times last night. Where _____ last night? (go)
   B: I visited Jimmy with my parents. I wonder why _____ . (call)

4 A: Where should _____ a bus to go downtown? (ride)
   B: I am a stranger here. I lost myself. I don't know where _____ . (be)

C Change these question-word questions to a noun clause.

1 "How much does it cost?"   → He asks me ___*how much it costs.*___

2 "Which one does she want?"   → Let's ask her _____

3 "Who left this bag here?"   → Tell me _____

4 "Whose painting will win the prize?" → I haven't any idea _____

5 "What would he like for his birthday?" → Do you know _____

6 "Where do Bill and Teresa live?"   → Do you know _____

7 "What's the weather like?"   → I asked him _____

8 "Why did they leave the country?" → She wondered _____

Choose the right words.

Just imagine (A) <what the world would / what would the world> be like if there were a universally accepted language. Our world would definitely be a better place for all our future generations. There would be easier communication and a less hostile and friendlier relationship among people.

 Read and answer the questions.

What are riches and what do they have to do with you? The answer you give shows exactly (A) <what do you / what you> think of your life. Some of you will visualize riches as an unlimited supply of money; a large estate; a fancy yacht; a personal jet, etc. These are but objects that reflect (B) <who are you / who you are>, and they are the tools that you use to live your life. However, the real reason for wanting riches is to be happy. Your riches will reflect your level of achievement; your achievements will reflect your level of happiness. If you are not happy with your life, then go start achieving something, and soon you will see both happiness and riches.

1 Choose the right words for (A) and (B).
2 According to the passage, what is the real purpose of wanting riches?
   → The purpose of wanting riches is _____.

C **Read and answer the question.**

<expanding / you / are / is / wondering / why / your waistline>? Current research suggests that many factors work together to influence your weight. These include genetics, eating habits, hormones and psychological factors. However, your intimate friends can influence your weight even more than anything else. If your close friends become obese, it's likely you'll become obese, too. The effect has much more to do with social norms: whom we look to when considering appropriate social behavior. Having fat friends makes being fat seem to be more acceptable. Consciously or unconsciously, people look to friends when deciding how much to eat, how much to exercise and how much weight is 'too much'.

1 Rearrange the words to complete the sentence.
   → Are you _____?

Ⓐ **definitely** 분명히 **hostile** 적대적인   Ⓑ **estate** 재산, 사유지 **reflect** 반영하다, 반사하다 **achievement** 성취, 달성   Ⓒ **genetics** 유전학 **obese** 살찐, 뚱뚱한 **norm** 기준, 표준 **consciously** 의식적으로

Questions

1 접속사 뒤에 문장이 아니라 분사가 오는 경우는?

2 시간의 부사절에서는 왜 미래시제가 불가능할까?

3 시간의 부사절에서 가장 중요한 사항은 뭐지?

Answers

1 가능하면 간단하게 표현하려는 속성이다. 접속사 뒤에 분사만 온다면 그 사이에 「주어+동사~」의 문장을 생략하여 간단하게 분사로 줄여서 표현한 것이다.

2 시간의 순서를 따지는 경우와 시제가 구분되는 가정법에서 이런 변칙이 발생한다. 시간과 조건을 나타내는 부사절에서만 현재시제가 미래시제를 대신한다.

3 since(~이래로)가 있는 경우 완료시제가 따른다는 것과 시간의 부사절에서는 미래시제 대신 현재시제를 사용한다는 사실!

1 ▶ 시간의 문장 (Time Clauses) I

1 시간의 부사절에서는 미래 대신 현재를 사용

I'll do it **when** I finish writing this letter.
Owen will move to a new flat **after** their baby is born.
I'll be dead **by the time** they find a cure for the common cold.
We wonder **when** Tom **will** come to Korea.

1
시간을 나타내는 부사절에서 미래는 현재로,
미래완료는 현재완료 시제로 나타낸다.
* 시간을 나타내는 명사절 (주어, 목적어, 보
어)에서는 미래를 미래로 표현한다.
– 부사절

– 명사절 : 미래를 표현함

2 접속사 before, after

(1) 접속사+S+V

After she graduates, she will open her own shop.
After she graduated, she opened her own shop.
After we had finished reading the novel, he looked out.

He will leave Seoul **before** she comes here.
It was not long **before** he came to his senses.
Hill had not waited long **before** he turned the corner.

2
(1) 두 사건의 발생 시점이 서로 달라, 前이나
  後의 내용을 언급할 때 사용한다.
– 시간 부사절: 미래 대신 현재시제 사용

– 일의 전후관계 명확: 동일 시제 사용

– 일의 전후관계 구분: 대과거 사용
 (전 · 후관계가 분명할 때는 동일 시제를 사
 용하는 경향이 있다.)

(2) 접속사, 전치사, 부사로 변신

He arrived here seven hours **after the fire** had started.
Within a day **after the fire**, I revisited the scene of the fire.
The war ended in 1953. I have never visited Korea **after**.

(2) before, after, since 등은 접속사
  +S+V, 전치사+명사, 부사로 사용된다.
– 접속사

– 전치사

– 부사

3 접속사 while, when

I will look after the children **while** she goes to London.
I have read sixty pages, **while** he has read only thirty.
He was having dinner **when** the telephone rang.

3
두 사건이 동시에 발생한 것을 나타낼 때 사
용한다. while은 ' ~인 반면에'의 의미도 있
다.

4 접속사 since

* S + 현재완료~, since S+과거
* S + 과거완료~, since S+과거(or 과거완료)

I **have been** in politics **since** I was at university.
Ever since you arrived, you **have been** causing trouble.

I **had wanted** to come **ever since** I was a child.
He **had lived** a lonely life **ever since** he had been a boy.

4
– 과거에 시작 → 지금까지 계속

– 과거에 시작 → 그 후 얼마 기간만 계속

EXERCISE

A   Complete the sentences using given words.

1   After I _____finish_____ this report, I will call you back right away. (finish)

2   You will get a surprise the moment you _____ the door. (open)

3   John and I _____ chess since we started traveling together. (play)

4   His grandfather often asks when he _____ his college choice. (announce)

5   Perhaps it will rain when we _____ ready to do some work outside. (be)

6   Ever since you introduced me to Timmy, our household _____ much. (change)

7   By the time he _____ home, she will have cleaned the entire house. (get)

B   Match the beginning of each sentence with the most appropriate ending.

1   *The building had almost burnt down* ———— a. *by the time the fire brigade arrived.*

2   I've been focusing on modeling   b. until I get to my goal weight.

3   We will have to run to be at the gate   c. by the time medical help arrived.

4   I'm not going to get pregnant   d. since I moved to Hollywood.

5   He began to walk into the water   e. immediately after I receive my degree.

6   Robert was already dead   f. an hour before our flight leaves.

7   I'll apply to graduate school   g. as soon as he reached the shore.

*fire brigade: 소방대

C   Complete each sentence using the given words.

1   George and I have been close friends since _____he moved here in 1987._____ (move)

2   We haven't been to New York ever since _____ (kids)

3   He hasn't been able to hold a job since _____ (illness)

4   We have lived next door to each other since _____ (young)

5   I've been looking forward to seeing you since _____ (newspaper)

6   The young ones have been alone all day since _____ (go off to work)

7   I have visited him in hospital ever since _____ (accident)

2 ▶ 시간의 문장 (Time Clauses) II

1 not ~ until…

I **didn't** know the truth **until** yesterday.
= **Not until** yesterday did I know the truth.
= It was **not until** yesterday that I knew the truth.

1

not ~ until…: '…하고 나서야 ~하다'로 해석한다.
– 부정어+V+S: 도치
– It ~that… 강조표현

2 as long as '~하는 동안, ~하는 한', so long as '~하는 한'

As long as he is silent, he doesn't seem offensive.
I'm letting Richard sleep **as long as** he needs to.
So long as he doesn't actually touch it, he's fine.
I will not believe it **so long as** he does not tell me.

2

긍정문의 as는 일반적으로 부정문과 조건문에서 so로 바뀐다.
* so long as는 부정문과 조건문에서 주로 '하는 한'으로 해석된다.

3 접속사 as

As he grew richer, he became more ambitious.
As she was tired, she went to bed early.
Mother watched children **as** they played with small animals.
As we sow, so shall we reap.

3

as는 문맥에 따라 다양한 의미를 가진다.
– ~함에 따라
– ~ 때문에
– ~ 할 때, ~하면서
– ~대로, ~처럼

4 once, whenever, every time

Will my child's passport expire **once** he or she reaches 16?
Once he finishes high school he'll move on to college.
Why does my dog cry **whenever** it plays with a new toy?
Derek is known to cheat **every time** he plays chess.

4

once S+V의 경우는 '일단 ~하기만 하면'이란 뜻으로 조건의 의미를 나타낸다.

5 as soon as '~하자마자'

As soon as we get tickets, we will send them to you.
I wanted to hire you **as soon as** I saw your resume.
As soon as he started reading, students started laughing.

6 접속사+분사

He read the book **before going** to see the film.
We get stressed **when making** reservations via the Internet.

The car was stolen **while parked** on a London street.
Use a copy of the form **when asked** about a family history.

6

= before he went
= when we make
= while it was parked
= when you are asked
주절과 부사절의 주어가 동일하면, 부사절의 주어를 생략하고 동사를 분사로 만들어 표현하는 경향이 있다.

EXERCISE

A Choose the right words.

1 I will tell him the truth <while / when> he returns.

2 <Since / As soon as> he arrives, we will have some lunch.

3 <Once / while> I have finished with your photo, I will e-mail it to you.

4 I think Steven can remain as our manager <while / until> he retires.

5 Pray for each other while <talked / talking> together on the phone.

6 <By the time / Since> you leave high school, you can be an expert in the skill.

7 Ever <since / until> she stopped drinking caffeine, Jane has been more studious.

B Match the beginning of each sentence with the most appropriate ending.

1 He takes pictures of the landscape below   a. until they're adopted.

2 He didn't find he'd left his bag in the cafe   b. as long as she stays reasonably quiet.

3 We will work to cure your disease   c. every time he rides in a helicopter.

4 They will keep the dogs   d. while you are our patient.

5 I will let Hayley stay up until midnight   e. as long as she puts on weight.

6 She won't be too thin   f. until he arrived home.

C Rewrite the following sentences using the given words.

1 I plan to try it again. I have some free time. (once)
   → *I plan to try it again once I have some free time.*

2 I will take good care of your kids. You are away. (while)
   → _____

3 He always feels excited and does his best. He plays golf. (every time)
   → _____

4 I never thought about people holding babies. My son was born. (until)
   → _____

5 Don't jump out. You can be safe. You stay in the lifeboat. (only so long as)
   → _____

6 The city is pleasant for tourists. There is no crime. (so long as)
   → _____

7 It is not very difficult, so don't be afraid. You can ask about any problems. (as)
   → _____

Further Study

A Choose the right words for (A) and (B).

In spite of wandering deep in the forests for months, I only encountered bears a few times. Whenever (A) <ran / running> away from me, they beat a hasty retreat. Meeting up with both mothers and their cubs might have been a little dangerous, though. So we made a bit of noise (B) <as / like> we advanced, giving the mother bear and her cubs plenty of time to move away.

 ## B Read and answer the questions.

Purchasing of office paper has been on the decrease for more than a year, and lower demand reduced prices in the first half of 2006. A purchasing and price recovery this year remains very much in doubt. Economists believe sales volume (A) <remains / will remain> the same until the first quarter of 2007. Market prices peaked at the end of 2004 and (B) <have been falling / were falling> ever since. Most buyers believe it might be fruitless to try to recoup lost revenues because there hasn't been any improvement in demand. Some buyers believe <will stay / until / the fourth / quarter / prices / flat>.

1 Choose the right words for (A) and (B).

2 Rearrange the words to complete the sentence.
→ Some buyers believe _____ .

C Read and answer the question.

<u>내가 15세부터 10년간 담배를 피워왔고, 또 계속 피운다면</u> how long will I live? Though the health risks of smoking are not uniform across all smokers, smokers die 10 years younger on average than non-smokers. One in three smokers die early from smoking-related diseases. However, quitting the habit at age 50 can halve the smoking-related risks, while quitting at age about 30 can practically eliminate them altogether. Smoking makes it 3 to 4 times more likely that you will get heart disease, and twice as likely that you will have a stroke. Stroke victims will tell you just how much painful such illnesses are, if they can still talk. Half of all teenagers that smoke will die from smoking-related diseases. On average, they will lose 16 valuable years of life.

1 Rearrange the words to have the same meaning as the underlined part.
If I <and smoke / for 10 years / since / have been / smoking / 15 years old / continually>
→ If I _____ .

Ⓐ wander 방랑하다, 배회하다 retreat 후퇴, 퇴각 cub 새끼 Ⓑ quarter 4분의 1 contract 계약 recoup 보충하다, 되찾다 revenue 소득, 수입
Ⓒ quit 중단하다 halve ~을 2등분하다, 반으로 나누다 eliminate 제거하다

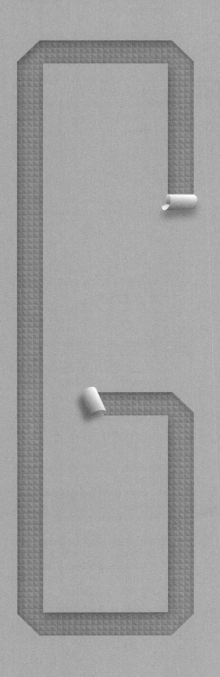

Questions

1 단순조건문과 가정법의 차이는 무엇인가?

2 가정법의 명칭이 왜 가정법 과거, 가정법 과거완료인가?

3 가정을 표현 할 때 반드시 접속사 If가 필요한가?

Answers

1 가정의 내용은 실현가능성이 없거나 돌이킬 수 없는 내용을 상상하는, 한마디로 꿈을 그리는 것이다. 이러한 가정의 문장에는 일정한 규칙이 따른다.

2 가정법의 명칭(가정법 과거, 가정법 과거완료)을 암기하는 것보다 '현재에 대한 가정'과 '과거에 대한 가정'으로 기억하는 것이 편리하다. 가정법 문장도 현재와 과거에 대한 가정만 주로 사용됨을 알아두자.

3 「~라면 …할 텐데.」를 단순히 「~할 텐데」로 줄여 말할 수 있듯이, 가정법의 주절만으로 표현할 수 있으며, 주절만으로도 가정법 문장인지 이해할 수 있어야 한다.

1 조건·가정의 문장(Conditional Clauses)

1 부사절을 이끄는 If

If oil is mixed with water, it floats.
If I wash the dishes, Sally dries them.
If someone is at the door, it must be Peter.
If I **tell** my manager about my illness, will he keep it secret?
If you **keep** telling a lie, people will come to believe it.

1
단순한 사실, 진리, 또는 예측을 나타낸다.
– 정해진 규칙
– 현재 사실

– 추측

– 조건의 부사절에서는 미래시제를 현재로 표현한다.

2 If절의 시제 〈미래 → 현재 → 과거〉

내용	If절의 시제	주절의 시제
미래 내용	If S+현재시제	S+will+동사원형
현재 내용 가정	If S+과거시제	S+would/could/might+동사원형
과거 내용 가정	If S+과거완료시제	S+would/could/might+현재완료

2
조건과 시간의 부사절에서는 미래 대신 반드시 현재시제를 사용해야 한다.
If절의 동사: 미래시제는 현재를, 현재의 가정은 과거시제, 과거의 가정은 과거완료시제를 사용한다.

3 가정의 문장

(1) 현재 사실의 가정 (untrue in the present)

> * If+S+과거동사 (were), S+would(could, might)+동사원형 ~.
> S가 (지금) 만약 ~한다면,   S는 ~할 텐데.

If I **had** enough money, I **would** buy the car now.
(= Did I have enough money, I would~.)
If I **were** you, I **would** take the money right now.
If it were not for the sun, all the living things would die.

3
(1) 현재 일어날 수 없는 사실을 가정하며, If절에 과거동사(be동사는 were)가 온다.

– If를 생략할 수 있으며, 이 경우 V+S의 순서로 도치된다.

= Without the sun, all the ~.

(2) 과거 사실의 가정

> * If+S+had p.p. ~, S+would(could, might)+have p.p. ~.
> S가 만약 ~했었다면,   S는 ~했을 텐데.

If I **had taken** his advice, I **could have succeeded.**
(= **Had I** taken his advice, I **could have succeeded.**)
I took a taxi to go home, **otherwise** I would have arrived too late.
If it had not been for the sun, all animals would have disappeared.

(2) 지나버린 과거 사실의 가정이며, If절의 동사로 반드시 과거완료(had+과거분사)가 온다.

– If를 생략할 수 있으며, 이 경우 V+S의 순서로 도치된다.
= If I hadn't taken taxi ~, I would have arrive ~.
= Without the sun, all animals ~.

(3) 현재와 과거 사실의 혼합 가정

If I **had** not **taken** a taxi then, I **would** not **be** here now.
If I **had worked** hard in my youth, I **would be** happier now.

(3) 혼합 가정법은 If절은 과거 내용(If+had+과거분사)이지만, 주절은 현재 내용(S+would/could/might+동사원형), 즉 실현되지 못한 과거의 일이 현재까지 영향을 미치는 경우 사용한다.

EXERCISE

A

Match the beginning of each sentence with the most appropriate ending.

1 *If anybody asks you what you are doing,*   a. *you can say you are with me.*

2 If you don't know what's going on,   b. you can take photos of the sunset.

3 If you stay here until night,   c. you can keep asking her about it.

4 If you are ready before eight,   d. I will ask my first question.

5 If you are ready for the interview,   e. we can catch the early train.

6 If there is much cloud,   f. allow extra time before drinking.

7 If water is very cold,   g. fog will not form over land.

B

Complete each sentence using the given words.

1 If she were a better dancer, _____*her feet would not hurt*_____ . (hurt)

2 If I were a rabbit, I _____ to a fairly high level quickly. (hop)

3 If I were ten years younger, I _____ to Poland with my family. (return)

4 If we had not been so greedy, it _____ . (never happen)

5 If my nose were shorter, I _____ quite pretty. (be)

6 If I had never studied English, my life _____ much simpler now. (be)

7 If I had been born in the time of Einstein, I _____ a genius. (consider)

8 If cars hadn't been invented, we _____ pollution now. (have)

C

Complete the sentences using the given words.

1 If I _____ their address, I would write a short letter to them. (have)

2 If it _____ a little warmer, it wouldn't be so cold outside. (be)

3 If we _____ less, there will be less air pollution. (drive)

4 If I _____ the car then, I would have saved some money. (buy)

5 If he _____ her back, she might not have been caught in the hurricane. (bring)

6 If I _____ on the radio then, she would have heard the news. (turn)

7 If they _____ earlier then, they would not be late now. (start)

2 ▶ 소망 · 가정의 문장 (Wish and Conditional Sentence)

1 If절이 없지만 가정의 내용

A wise man **does** not do such a thing. (현재 사실)
A wise man **did** not do such a thing. (과거 사실)
A wise man **would** not **do** such a thing. (현재의 가정)
A wise man **would** not **have done** such a thing. (과거의 가정)

> I appreciate your help. (네 도움에 감사한다.)
> I would appreciate your help. (네 도움이 있으면 고마울 텐데.)
> I would have appreciated your help. (네 도움이 있었다면 고마웠을 텐데.)

1
가정법에서 if절이 생략되는 경우, 주절의 가정법 표현(would, would have+과거분사)을 보고 가정의 의미를 이해한다.

– ~하지 않을 텐데
– ~하지 않았을 텐데

– 현재 사실
– 현재 내용 가정
– 과거 내용 가정

2 I wish ~ 와 as if(= as though)

I wish I knew the truth now.
I wish I had known the truth then.

He looks **as if** (= **as though**) he were angry.
He talks **as if** he knew all the secrets.
He looks **as if** he had seen a monster.
He looks **as if** he had been angry.

2
– 지금 ~라면 좋을 텐데
– 그때 ~했더라면 좋을 텐데

– 지금 마치 ~처럼
– 마치 ~했던 것처럼

> * 주의 : 불확실한 내용에서 as if는 가정법을 사용하지 않기도 한다.
> It looks as if it's going to rain.

3 It is time ~.'지금 ~할 때이다.'

It is time that I **went** to bed.
= **It is time** to go to bed.
= **It is time** that you **should** go to bed.

3
It is time 주어+과거동사.
= It is time to부정사

> 〈가정법 문장〉
> '이제 ~해야 할 때이다'는 '지금 ~를 해야 하는데 사실은 하지 않고 있다'는 것을 나타내므로 가정법 문장이다.

4 If를 대신하는 표현들

(1) **without** '~가 없다면, ~가 없었다면'
   Without your help, I **could** not **finish** it.
   (= **If it were not for** your help, I **could** not **finish** it.)

   Without your help, I **could** not **have finished** it.
   (= **If it had not been for** your help, I **could** not **have finished** it.)

(2) You cannot get anything **unless** you pay for it.
   What do you do **once** you achieve your big goals?
   We started early. **Otherwise**, we could not have been in time.

4

= Were it not for ~

= Had it not been for ~

unless ~ ~하지 않으면(= if ~ not)
once ~ 일단 ~하기만 하면
otherwise (부사) 그렇지 않으면

EXERCISE

A Choose the right words.

1 Now it is time that we <leave / left> the past.

2 Now he talks as if he <knew / know> something about it.

3 I wish I <knew / had known> this information 10 years ago.

4 If it had not been for the dog, he would not <be / have been> found.

5 Without the world war, she wouldn't <meet / have met> her husband.

6 It is estimated that without the moon, tides would not <exist / have existed>.

7 If it had not been for the police, they might not <be / have been> alive now.

B Match these parts to make conditional sentences.

1 Without your help,   a. otherwise he would not be so fast.

2 Had it not been for air and water,   b. that we finally did something about it.

3 It is about time   c. I could not have finished the work.

4 Had I not returned the money bag to the owner,   d. I could have become rich.

5 If it were not for e-mail,   e. none of us would have existed.

6 We don't reuse or recycle most of cans,   f. which would save us money.

7 He is a tennis player,   g. how would we send this information?

C Complete the conversations using 'could' or 'could have'.

1 A: I'm angry that he deceived me again. I _____*could kill*_____ him. (kill)
   B: You look extremely angry.

2 A: I had a very boring summer night at home yesterday.
   B: Why did you stay at home? You _____ to the beach. (go)

3 A: Where have you been this summer? John tried to reach you.
   B: I _____, but I didn't want to. (call him up)

4 A: I heard that you joined the Mickey Mouse club?
   B: No. I _____, but I decided not to. (apply)

5 A: Tickets are on sale now online. It's a pity you paid too much.
   B: I _____ over twenty dollars. (save)

6 A: Have you finished your work?
   B: I spent all night working on it. I _____ for over a week now. (sleep)

Further Study

A Choose the right words for (A) and (B).

If I (A) <am / were> prime minister, my top priority would be the national educational and economic systems. As prime minister, I (B) <will / would> also grant money for education and health issues. A good country must have competent teachers and medical staff. A prime minister should pay more attention to the pensioners and the handicapped people.

B Read and answer the questions.

Have you heard about cars not using gas but water? Many major car manufacturers are already building automobiles that use this technology, but the facts aren't well known around the world. If the technology (A) <is / were> fully revealed to the general public now, what would happen? We use fossil fuel, such as petroleum and natural gas, to generate energy for transportation. If everyone (B) <turn / turned> to water to run their cars, there (C) <will / would> be much chaos in the oil industry because of sudden demand decrease. The chaos would have a heavy impact on the economy and many people would not make a living.

1 Choose the right words for (A), (B) and (C).

2 According to the passage, what would happen if we used water for running cars?
   → If we used water for running cars, many people would lose _____.

C Read and answer the question. 기출 응용

Many people went outside around August 27 this year to observe the close encounter between Earth and Mars. On August 27, when Mars was closer to Earth than ever in human history, the one-way travel time of light was just 3 minutes and 6 seconds. Thus, if you had turned a light toward Mars that day, <u>그것은 화성까지 186초 만에 도달했을 텐데</u>. Mars was so bright that even the lights of the city didn't get in the way. If you missed this astronomical show, you're really out of luck. Mars will not be this close again until the year 2287.

1 Translate the Korean into English.
   → it _____.

Ⓐ prime minister 수상 priority 우선(권) pensioner 연금 수령자 Ⓑ petroleum 석유 chaos 혼란 make a living 꾸리다 Ⓒ time of light 광년 get in the way 방해하다 astronomical 천문학(상)의 out of luck 불행한

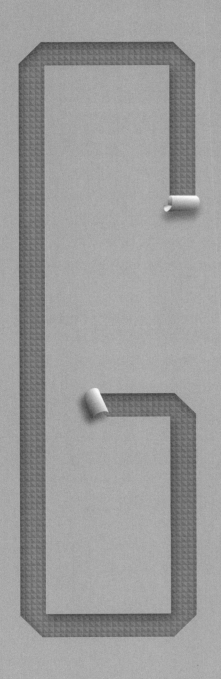

Unit 13

부사절 문장 – 원인 · 결과 · 목적

1 원인/이유의 문장
2 결과/목적의 문장

Questions

1 because와 because of의 차이점은 뭐지?
2 주의해야 할 까다로운 표현을 정리하고 싶은데?

Answers

1 접속사는 뒤에 문장이, 전치사는 뒤에 명사(구)가 와야 한다. because는 접속사이며, because of는 전치사이다.
2 result in과 result from의 표현과 That is why S+V~.와 That is because S+V~.의 적절한 사용 연습을 해야 한다.

1 원인/이유의 문장 (Cause/Reason Clauses)

1 접속사 as, because, since, for

He was absent from school, **for** he was very ill.
Tim is respected, **for** he hasn't betrayed his conscience.
I gestured for him to take it **since** he was there first.
I broke up with my boyfriend **because** he went overseas to study.
As it rained, we stayed at home.

* for 주어+동사: '왜냐하면' – 결과를 미리 말하고 원인을 밝히는 방법이다.
 – 왜냐하면
 – ~때문에
 – ~때문에
 – ~때문에

2 because / because of

Because it was hot, we went swimming.
= **Because of** the hot weather, we went swimming.

Because the car is expensive, we can't afford to buy it.
= **Because of** the high price, we can't afford to buy the car.

because는 접속사로서 뒤에는 완전한 문장(S+V ~)이 따른다.
because of는 전치사로 끝나게 되므로 뒤이어 명사나 명사구가 와야 한다.

3 ~때문에: due to, because of, on account of, owing to, thanks to

Because of the cold weather, we stayed home.
Due to the cold weather, we stayed home.
We stayed home **because of** the cold weather.
We stayed home **due to** the cold weather.

전치사로 끝나는 표현의 뒤에는 명사 형태인 목적격이 온다.
* 이유를 나타내는 전치사 표현은 주절(main clause)의 앞이나 뒤에 모두 올 수 있다.

4 야기하다: cause, lead to, result in

The fire **caused** the most severe damage in the third floor.
An air traffic controller's error **led to** a small plane crash.
The storms have **resulted in** the collapse of the building.
The collapse of the building has **resulted from** the storms.

'주어+원인동사+목적어'의 형태를 취하는 문장이다.

5 원인과 결과(cause and effect)

* <u>That is why</u> S+V~.	그것 때문에 ~.
* <u>That is because</u> S+V~.	그것은 ~ 때문이다.

Liberty means responsibility. **That is why** most people dread it.
Sam can't speak Russian. **That is why** he doesn't read the letter.
I am very breathless and **this is because** I've got lung cancer.
My throat is really sore. **This is because** I smoked heavily.

 – That's why + 결과의 내용
 – That's because + 원인의 내용

 **EXERCISE**

A Choose the right words to make the same meaning as the sentences below.

> * It snowed heavily. We could hardly see people.

1 <Because / Because of> the heavy snow, we could hardly see people.

2 It snowed heavily, <because / therefore> we could hardly see people.

3 We could hardly see people <because / therefore> it snowed heavily.

4 It snowed heavily, <since / so that> we could hardly see people.

5 We could hardly see people <because / because of> the heavy snow.

B Complete each sentence using the following words.

> [1~4] why   because   due to   [5~6] result in   result from

1 As predicted, _____ the global warming the sea level will rise.

2 People enjoyed listening to his stories. That is _____ he was invited.

3 He isn't selfish. That is _____ he has so many friends.

4 You may notice my eyes are red. This is _____ I wore contact lenses.

5 Most people feel that the Civil War _____ the slavery issue.

6 Fire from the ground _____ more damage to the plane in the sky.

C Rewrite the sentences using the given words.

1 He speaks English little. I talked to him through an interpreter. (so)
→ He _____ *speaks English little, so I talked to him through an interpreter.* _____

2 He got a stomach ulcer. Stress and spicy food caused his stomach ulcer. (result from)
→ His stomach ulcer _____

3 Enemies try to take back their areas. We need to defend our territory. (so)
→ Enemies try _____

4 The lid would not stay closed. My suitcase had become damaged. (because)
→ The lid _____

5 We animals are killed and butchered. We dislike and fear humans. (why)
→ We animals _____

2 ▶ 결과/목적의 문장 (Result and Purpose Clauses)

1 so, so that

I was bored, **so** I decided to write something to you.
I got a tight schedule, **so that** I decided to skip the meeting.

2 so ~ that, such ~ that

I dressed **so** quickly **that** I put my boots on the wrong feet.
They were **so** surprised **that** they couldn't utter a word.
He was **so** honest a boy **that** we all believed in him.

They got **such** a fright **that** they ran away again.
I was in **such** a panic **that** I didn't know it was him.
He often says **such** a stupid thing **that** I don't bother to listen.

3 as a result, therefore

He has been ill for months, and **as a result** he has lost his job.
We have a growing population, and we **therefore** need more food.

4 원인과 결과(cause and effect)

```
* S + result in + 결과        ~ 란 결과가 나오다.
* S + result from + 원인       ~ 때문이다.
```

Heavy smoking may **result in** lung cancer.
= Lung cancer may **result from** heavy smoking.

The earthquake **resulted in** a number of landslides.
The earthquake **resulted from** the motion of the earth's crust.

5 목적의 문장

I gave up my job **so that** I could take care of my mother.
Advice should be given **in order that** they can win the game.
Let's take the course **in order to** get a better job.

Everybody works hard **lest** he **should** fail again.
= Everybody works hard **in order that he may not** fail again.
= Everybody works hard **so as not to** fail again.

1
접속사로서 어떤 행동이나 상황의 결과(그래서)를 나타내는 표현이다.

2
어떤 동작의 결과를 나타내는 표현이며, that은 종종 생략되기도 한다.

> * so의 뒤에는 형용사나 부사만이 오며, 만약 명사가 온다면 어순은 <u>so + 형용사 + a(n) 명사</u>
> * such는 뒤에 명사가 오며, 만약 형용사가 온다면 어순은 <u>such + a(n) 형용사 + 명사</u>

3
결과를 나타내며, 문장의 앞이나 문장의 주어 다음에 쓰이기도 한다.

4

– landslide: 산사태

– crust: 껍질, 표면

5
<u>so that S+V = in order that S+V</u>
~하기 위하여
so as to = in order to

<u>lest+S should ~</u> ~하지 않기 위하여
= so that S may not
　(= in order that S may not)
= so as not to (= in order not to)

EXERCISE

A Complete each sentence with 'so' and 'such a'.

1 He was ___*such a*___ fool that no one could talk to him.
   He was ___*so*___ silly that no one could talk to him.

2 He was _____ tired that he didn't want to do anything.
   He had _____ tiring day that he didn't want to do anything.

3 I had _____ serious injury that I ended up in the hospital for days.
   I was injured _____ badly that I ended up in the hospital for days.

4 My throat is _____ sore that it is hard for me to swallow.
   I had _____ sore throat that it is hard for me to swallow.

B Complete the sentences so that they mean the same as the first sentence.

1 The railways are now in such a mess that it is hard to find a solution.
   = The railways are now so ___*messy*___ that it is hard to find a solution.

2 He spoke in such a soft voice that people barely heard him at first.
   = His voice was so _____ that people barely heard him at first.

3 Cathy is such a good pianist that I think she should write her own songs.
   = Cathy plays the piano so _____ that I think she should write her own songs.

4 It is such a pity that my brother can't watch this movie.
   = It is so _____ that my brother can't watch this movie.

5 Mary lives such a long way off that very little is known about her.
   = Mary lives so _____ that very little is known about her.

C Complete the sentences using the given words.

1 그 언덕은 너무 경사가 져서 자전거에서 내려 걸어가야 했다. (get off, walk)
   → The hill was so steep that ___*I had to get off my bike and walk.*___

2 Kerry는 심한 거짓말쟁이여서 누구도 그가 말하는 것을 믿지 않았다. (believe)
   → Kerry was _____ a dreadful liar that _____

3 겨울에는 너무 추워서 시냇물이 모두 얼어버렸다. (stream, freeze)
   → The winter was _____ bitterly cold that _____

4 Dick은 너무 젊어 보여서 누구나 그를 대학생으로 착각했다. (take ~ for⋯)
   → Dick looked _____ young that _____

5 차고 앞을 막지 않도록 주차해주세요. 감사합니다. (block)
   → Please park _____ the garage doors. Thank you.

A Choose the right words for (A) and (B).

> Chinese tend to 'hide the broken arm in the sleeve' a lot. They think appearance matters (A) <so / such> much that it's better to hide painful truth. However, last month when some products were found corrupt and unsafe in China, the Chinese government responded immediately to the problems that resulted (B) <from / in> many deaths around the globe.

B Read and answer the questions.

> Patients can have sugar pills(placebos) from doctors and gain improvements in their health; this is (A) <because / why> the mental comfort doctors give patients is often just as effective as medication. On average, around one third of people taking placebos for complaints including pain and headache will experience relief from symptoms. Even simply participating in a medical study can have a positive effect on a person's health. That's (B) <because / why> researchers make both participants and staff unaware of whether any particular patient receives placebos or real medication. About 90 percent of people taking placebos in studies see their symptoms improve.

1 Choose the right words for (A) and (B).

2 According to the passage, why do placebos sometimes work out?
  → Sometimes placebos work out because they give _____.

C Read and answer the question.

> Breast milk is more easily digested, as it doesn't cause gas in babies. Moreover, even though dairy milk is higher in iron it isn't easily absorbed, resulting in the baby receiving fewer vitamins than it should. As a result of human milk being easily digested, a baby feeds on it more frequently; it takes about half an hour to digest, whereas the dairy alternative takes around four hours. This explains why a bottle-fed child tends to sleep longer, which is not an advantage.

1 According to the passage, why do babies fed on dairy milk tend to sleep longer?
  → Babies fed on dairy milk tend to sleep longer because _____.

A sleeve 소매 matter 중요하다 corrupt 타락한, 부패한 respond to ~에 반응을 보이다 **B** pill 알약 medication 약물 치료 placebo 가짜 약 participant 참가자 symptom 증상 **C** absorb 흡수하다 digest 소화하다 alternative 대안 bottle-fed 우유로 자란

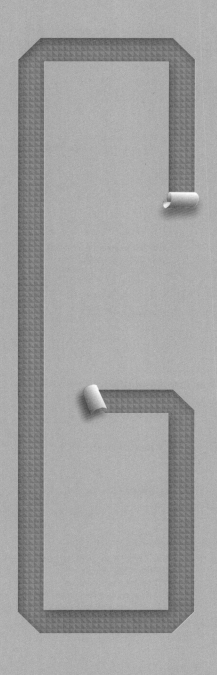

Unit 14

부사절 문장 – 대조

Questions

1 '양보'의 의미는 무엇인가?

2 다양한 연결사들을 보다 잘 기억하는 방법은 없을까?

3 연결사를 묻는 문제가 시험에 나올까?

Answers

1 '비록 ~이긴 하지만'으로 해석되는 경우를 양보(concession)라고 부른다.
결국 대조적인 두 문장을 연결할 때 사용하는 표현이다.

2 조금씩 의미가 다르기 때문에 문장 안에서 그 활용을 이해해야 하지만, 유사
한 의미끼리 함께 기억하는 것이 편리하다.

3 어법이나 문장 완성 유형에서 자주 묻는 시험유형이다. 영어에서는 연결어를
많이 사용하므로, 많은 연결사를 익혀두면 독해 문제를 풀 때 유리하다.

1 대조의 문장 – 양보절(Concessive clauses)

1 양보절

(1) though(= although)

Though he's lived for years in Paris, he writes in German.
Though he lives on a low income, he still aids the poor.
Although he hated me, he agreed to help me just the same.

(2) even though, even if

Even though Tom can't speak Chinese, I think he has to meet Mr. Wang. (= I know that Tom can't speak Chinese.)
Even if Tom can't speak Chinese, I think he has to meet Mr. Wang. (= I don't know if Tom speaks Chinese.)

(3) though+형용사(분사)

Although (we are) **poor**, we have our pride in our cultures.
Though (he was) **dying** of cancer, he painted every day.
Though (she was) **angry**, Lurie didn't say a word.

2 despite, in spite of(= with all, for all)

Despite the difference in their ages, they were close friends.
Despite working hard, too many families have low-income.

Mortgage applications rose **in spite of** rising interest rates.
He insisted on playing, **in spite of** the fact that he had a cold.

3 however+형/부사 = no matter how+형/부사

You can complete learning it, **however hard**, in your lifetime.
I am never defeated, **however fast** the enemy may attack.

However hard it may be, try not to yell at your partner.
Her life is celebrated **however short** or **long** it may be.

However much money is spent, more is always demanded.
However much food you consume, you will still be hungry.

4 형/부+as+S+V

Nervous as he was, he felt his heart rate became slower.
Fast as he may flee himself, his shadow never leave his side.

1

(1) 두 가지 내용을 대조할 때 사용하는 표현으로서 '비록 ~이긴 하지만'으로 해석한다.
주절에 still(여전히), nevertheless(그럼에도 불구하고), just the same(마찬가지로) 등과 함께 쓰이기도 한다.

(2) even though는 despite the fact that(~라는 사실에도 불구하고)를 나타낸다.
even if는 whether or not(~이든 아니든 간에)의 의미를 나타낸다.

(3) 부사절의 주어가 주절의 주어와 동일하면 접속사+형용사/현재분사/과거분사로 바꾸어 표현할 수 있다.

2

despite와 in spite of는 전치사로서 뒤에 명사나 동명사 형태가 온다.

– mortgage: 주택 담보 대출

3

however+형용사/부사는 '아무리 ~해도'로 해석하며, 'no matter how ~'와 같다.

– However + 부사

– However + 형용사

– However + 형용사 + 명사

4

형용사나 부사가 as S+V절 앞에 오면 일반적으로 양보절을 나타낸다.
= Though he was nervous, ~.
= Though he may flee himself fast, ~.

EXERCISE

A Choose the right words to complete the sentences.

> a. a rainy season
> c. rising interest rates
> e. his recent illness
>
> b. all the precautions
> d. an excellent resume and recommendations
> f. the relatively positive news

1 The local economy has remained strong despite ___*the high cost of living*___

2 A child runs into the street in spite of _____

3 This year we had so little rain in spite of _____

4 He didn't get the job despite _____

5 The demand for home purchase loans was up in spite of _____

6 The company's stock is down 12 percent despite _____

7 He continued to work on various projects despite _____

B Complete the sentences with your opinion using given words.

1 Although we were desperately hungry, ____*we had no time for lunch.*____ (lunch)

2 Even though I'm only 18, _____ (a rental car)

3 Although he can be a creative man, _____ (lack)

4 Though he didn't stop working all day, _____ (tired)

5 Even though his English was very good, _____ (fluently)

6 Although we set off early in the morning, _____ (arrive)

7 Although you cannot see them, _____ (spiders)

C Make necessary changes to complete the sentences.

1 It is expensive. He is determined to buy it.
→ However expensive ____*it is, he is determined to buy it.*____

2 He works hard. He still has to take work home with him.
→ However hard _____

3 You complain much. The UK has an excellent schooling system.
→ However much _____

4 You feel sorry. There are some things you can't just take back.
→ No matter how sorry _____

5 The night may be dark. Somehow the sun rises once again.
→ No matter how dark _____

2 ▶ 대조의 문장 – 연결사(Connective)

1 접속사 however, still, yet

I won't oppose your design; I can't, **however**, approve of it.
A man can betray me. **However**, a machine won't betray me.

We knew he wouldn't win. **Yet** he kept on trying all summer.
She is so tired, **yet** she can't sleep.

I tried again, "What's showing?" **Still** no reply.
He is very poor **still** I love him very much.

1
however(그러나)는 쉼표를 써서 문장의 중간이나 문장 앞에서 독립적으로 사용된다.
Still은 문장 앞에서 'Nevertheless 그럼에도 불구하고', Yet은 문장 앞에서 'But 그러나'를 의미한다.

2 접속사 while, whereas

A few people have plenty of food, **while** the others go hungry.
They had to stand outside the store, **while** we got to sit inside.

In the UK the hottest month is July, **whereas** in Korea August is.
A self-confident person may look straight ahead, **whereas** a nervous person may bend slightly.

2
while은 '~동안에'와 '반면에'의 두 의미를 가지며, whereas는 '반면에'의 의미로 사용된다.

3 on the other hand, on the contrary, in contrast

He is a bad cook, but **on the other hand**, he bakes a good cake.
Geneva is pretty. **On the contrary** Akron is desolate with no tree.

Sleepwalkers may walk down stairs, remaining fast asleep.
Sleeptalkers, **in contrast**, stay still, but they talk too much.

3
on one hand – 한편으로는
on the other hand – 다른 한편으로는, 반면에

* on the contrary, in contrast –그와는 반대로, 대조적으로

4 nevertheless, instead, instead of

Life is always difficult. **Nevertheless** we should survive.
I had no power to win the game. **Nevertheless**, I did my best.

I did not tell him, **instead** I kept it private like a secret.
He decided to leave his country **instead of** staying and fighting.

4
nevertheless : 그럼에도 불구하고
instead : 그 대신에
instead of + 명사 : ~대신에

5 like / unlike

Like most singers he first began performing in church.
My dog acts **like** something is biting him on his back.
Unlike those in poorer countries, people here seldom go hungry.
Unlike death and taxes, pensions are no longer guaranteed.

5
like는 문장을 이끄는 접속사나 명사 앞에 쓰이는 전치사로서 '~처럼'의 의미이다.
unlike는 전치사로서 '~와 달리'의 의미이다.

E EXERCISE

A Choose the right words.

1 Can I use diesel fuel <instead / instead of> regular gas?

2 Why is she acting <like / unlike> she doesn't know me anymore?

3 You had better do regular exercise <instead / instead of> going on a diet.

4 Let's say goodbye <like / instead of> we said hello in a friendly kind of way.

5 We rely on our knowledge <like / unlike> our ancestors who relied on labor.

6 The American revolution was mostly bloodless <as / unlike> the French revolution.

7 The soldier didn't die immediately, but <instead / instead of> he survived two days.

8 It offers an entirely different landscape <like / unlike> the islands we have visited.

B Match each sentence on the left with one on the right.

1 *Snakes help protect farm crops.*   *a. Nevertheless, they are in danger of disappearing.*

2 I didn't feel like meeting his eyes.   b. whereas I prefer slim types.

3 My friend respects guys with muscle   c. Nevertheless, some smokers never quit smoking.

4 Smokers have the highest death rate.   d. Instead, I looked at his shoes.

5 Skinny ones are regarded as ugly,   e. like I believe in you.

6 I'm glad that you believe in me   f. However, he wishes to return back to the U.S.

7 The man is leaving the U.S.   g. while large women are thought to be beautiful.

C Complete the sentences with your opinions.

1 Some people lie in the sun in the summer, while others ___are in the shade___ .

2 The ants spent their days gathering food. However, grasshoppers _____.

3 Some people feel tired in the afternoon, while others _____.

4 We women talk too much, nevertheless we only _____.

5 It never rained at all this year, nevertheless we _____.

6 A lion left the rabbit sleeping soundly. Instead, he wanted _____.

7 Some try to darken their skin, while in other places light skin _____.

Further Study

A **Choose the right word.**

Mercury is much less like the Moon than scientists previously thought. (A) <Like / Unlike> the Moon, Mercury has huge cliffs, which range from hundreds of kilometers across the planet's surface. Mercury also has a surprisingly powerful gravity.

B **Read and answer the questions.**

Our soccer team gained third place at the tournament as we beat China 4:2. The Brazilian team celebrated a victory at the world competition after they defeated Japan 3:2 in overtime. I think our team could have achieved better results, but the Russian team was not very lucky in the semifinals match against Japan, where they suffered defeat in overtime. (A) <Nevertheless / Otherwise> we were excited to win the bronze and I think it was a great achievement for us. I'm very happy we won the bronze medal and I don't want to think about what would have happened if we had played better (B) <since / whereas> the bronze medal was a good result. To my mind, players should fight for victory in a game and at the same time should not forget about supporters.

1 Choose the right words for (A) and (B).

2 According to the passage, which team won the bronze in the world competition?
→ _____ won the bronze in the world competition.

C **Read and answer the question.**

Is it fair to want to live close to my work? My fiancée and I have a plan to move to New York City and the place I want to work at is located in the center of the city. I've suggested living right in the center of the city to walk to work, but she would like to live out in the suburbs. Whenever we talk about it, we get into an argument. Though her reasons are not that clear, I think it's because of noisy neighbors, along with a 'looking to the future' attitude that we might need a house for kids. She doesn't work currently, so it doesn't really matter to her where we live, whereas I must wake up an hour earlier every day if we live in the suburbs.

1 What is the possible reason why he doesn't want to live in the suburbs?
→ He doesn't want to live in the suburbs because _____ .

A Mercury 수성 cliff 낭떠러지 gravity 중력　**B** tournament 승자 진출전 celebrate 경축하다 defeat 패배시키다, 이기다 bronze 청동
C fiancée 약혼녀 suburbs 교외 currently 현재

96

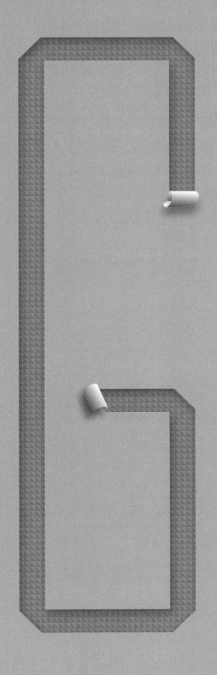

Unit 15

부사절 문장 – 비교

Questions

1 비교 문장은 어법이 중요한가, 작문이 중요한가?

2 비교 문장을 자연스럽게 해석하는 방법은?

3 비교 문장을 효과적으로 읽는 방법은?

Answers

1 물론 모두 중요하다. 특히, 쓰기(writing) 연습을 해 두면 어법과 독해가 저절로 해결된다.

2 원급(as ~ as…)이나 비교급은 자주 사용되는 표현이 있는데, 이것들 위주로 기억해두면 된다.

3 원급에서는 뒤의 as 앞에서, 비교급에서는 than 앞에서 끊어 읽어야 한다. 조각조각 끊어 읽기와 조각조각 연결하는 연습을 해보자!

원급의 비교(Positive degree)

1 비교의 대상

(1) A+닮다/다르다+B

A는 B를 닮았다	A는 B와 다르다(비교되다)
A [resemble / be like / look like / be similar to] B	A [differ from / be different from / be compared to / be comparable to] B

The climate of Korea is similar to **that** of Italy.
Tom's **appearance** is like his father's.

(2) 원급과 비교급에서 (positive and comparative degree)
The speed of a bus is not so fast as **that** of a train.
The speed of a plane is comparable to **that** of a missile.

He is older than **I** by three years.
The conclusion of the committee is very different from **the parents'**.

2 as와 like

(1) I was not **as** afraid **as** before joining in any activities.
Please tell me how you grew **such** a big pumpkin **as** this?
The roof was painted **the same** color **as** the living room.

(2) It **was like** a dream.　　　He still **feels like** a child.
He **looked like** an actor.　　The house **seemed like** a mansion.

3 원급 비교 (positive degree)

He writes **as slow / as** a dead snail, only a word per day.
Mars never appears to be **as large / as** the full Moon.

4 배수 표현 (multiples)

Angola is about **three times as** large **as** California.
= Angola is about **three times larger than** California.
= Angola is about **three times the size of** California.

Turtles lay eggs **many times as** many **as** crocodiles.
= Turtles lay eggs **many times more than** crocodiles.
= Turtles lay eggs **many times the number** of crocodiles.

1
'닮았다, 다르다' 등의 비교를 하는 두 대상은 격(주격 / 목적격 / 소유격)과 구문의 형태가 동일해야 한다.

– 한국의 기후와 이탈리아의 기후 비교

– Tom의 외모와 아버지의 외모를 비교

(2) 원급과 비교급의 비교 대상은 격(주격 / 목적격 / 소유격)과 형태가 동일하다.

– 주어인 he와 비교하는 대상은 주격이 된다.

2
(1) as ~ as: as는 '~만큼'
　　such as: as는 '~처럼, ~같은'
　　the same ~ as: as는 '~처럼, ~같은'

(2) 전치사 like는 '~처럼, ~같은'의 의미를 가지며, be, feel, look, seem과 함께 쓰인다.

3
as ~ as의 사이에는 형용사와 부사만이 쓰이며, 문맥에 맞는 품사가 와야 한다.
– Mars: 화성

4
배수는 2배(twice), 3배(three times), 4배(four times) 등으로 표현한다.

형용사는 ~ times the 명사(size, weight, number, amount 등)로 바꿀 수 있다.

EXERCISE

A **Choose the right words.**

1 Walking barefoot is not as <hard / hardly> as it looks.

2 Things went about as <smooth / smoothly> as you'd expect.

3 The poverty didn't look as <severe / severely> as it used to.

4 Cancer risks for dogs are similar to <humans / those for humans>.

5 Ten minutes seems <as / like> a longer time than ten hours.

6 Human auditory neurons are as sensitive as <that / those> of other mammals.

7 Yahoo Mail currently has about three times <as / than> many users as G-mail.

8 Flying between London and Paris causes ten times more CO_2 <as / than> the train.

B **Complete the sentences using the words in the box.**

as much as	as many as	as little as	as few as

1 Brands aren't worth _____as much as_____ we thought.

2 We only remember _____ 5% of our dreams.

3 Some tea in China cost six times _____ gold.

4 They are buying the school buses for _____ $1, 205.

5 Take away all but one red ball, or leave _____ possible.

6 If you aspire to live happily and healthily, eat _____ possible.

7 The Antarctic ice sheet is losing _____ 36 cubic miles of ice a year.

8 According to the latest Forbes rich list, India has _____ 36 billionaires.

C **Complete the sentences using the words in the box.**

hard	cheap	cold	popular	strong	fluent	low	valuable

1 I'm getting old. I can't work _____as hard as_____ I used to.

2 Are online friends _____ friends in real life?

3 It's freezing. It must be nearly _____ last winter.

4 Plastic is _____ steel but lighter and transparent.

5 Diamonds in industry are _____ they are with brides-to-be.

6 Prices have gone up. Things are not _____ they used to be.

7 He felt his Korean language was not quite _____ it had been.

2 ▶ 비교 문장 (Comparison Clauses)

1 비교 표현

(1) 비교급과 최상급 표현 (comparative and superlative)

I really need to be **more careful** than usual when driving.

They are **the most beautiful** gardens in the world.

Mitt will return when we need him **most**. 〈부사〉

I was **happiest** when I was on my own somewhere. 〈보어〉

(2) '아' 다르고 '어' 다르다

late 늦은, 늦게	later 더 늦은	→	latest 가장 늦은, 최신의
	latter 후자의	→	last 마지막의, 최후의
old 늙은	older 더 늙은	→	oldest 가장 나이 많은
	elder 윗사람의	→	eldest 가장 윗사람의
far 먼, 멀리	farther 더 먼	→	farthest 가장 먼
	further 더 이상의	→	furthest (정도가) 가장 심한

Tom was 10 hours **later** than I.   I like the **latter** part of the story.

He is **older** than I.   His **eldest** son is a doctor.

He walked **farther** than I.   I have nothing **further** to say.

2 비교급 표현의 강조

(1) 비교급의 강조

We have **far more serious** issues affecting the environment.

I think that doing is **rather more complicated** than saying.

It was **by far the worst** hospital I had ever seen in this city.

(2) The 비교급 ~, the 비교급 ~.

The more (he has), **the more** (he wants to have).

I found **the heavier** an object is, **the easier** it is to balance it.

The less a baby sleeps, **the more likely** it is to become fat.

3 less, least

They are helping others **less fortunate than** themselves.

I get my hair cut **less frequently than** once a year.

The UN has released **the Least Developed** Countries Report.

Immigration could have negative impact on **the least-skilled** workers.

1

형용사나 부사가 1음절이면 -er, -est를 붙이며, 2음절 이상은 대부분 more, most를 앞에 붙인다.

최상급에 the를 붙여야하지만, 부사나 보어로 쓰일 때에는 생략되기도 한다.

> * 주의할 비교급의 형태
> (1) hot-hotter-hottest:
>   1음절의 단모음+단자음으로 끝나면 자음 추가(예: big, fat, hot, sad, thin, wet 등)
> (2) alike-more alike-the most alike: a-로 시작하는 형용사는 보어로만 사용되는 형용사로서, 비교급은 반드시 more ~, most ~로 표현한다. (예: alike, afraid, ashamed 등)

(2) 비교 표현은 경우에 따라 달라진다. (현재 far의 비교 표현은 구분하지 않는 경향이 있다.)

2

(1) 비교 표현을 강조하기 위해 much, even, far, a bit, rather, by far(최상급) 등을 사용한다.

(2) The+비교급 S+V ~, the+비교급 S+V…: ~하면 할수록 점점 더 …하다.

> * 줄여서 사용하는 표현들
> The more, the better.
> The sooner, the better.
> (The) more haste, (the) less speed.

3

* less는 '덜 ~한', least는 '가장 적은'의 의미로서, 형용사, 부사, 명사와 함께 쓰인다.

* more, most와 반대 의미를 지닌 비교 표현이다.

EXERCISE

A

Write the comparative and superlative form of each word.

1 unhappy _____*unhappier*_____ _____*unhappiest*_____

2 black _____ _____

3 valuable _____ _____

4 disappointed _____ _____

5 pretty _____ _____

6 confident _____ _____

7 hot _____ _____

8 alike _____ _____

9 likely _____ _____

B

Match the beginning of each sentence with the most appropriate ending.

1 *The later the general election,* _____   a. *the better it will be for the government.*

2 The higher the temperature,   b. the better the view becomes.

3 The more courses a meal has,   c. the more expensive it becomes.

4 Once again, the more shops you stop by,   d. the more quickly you'll get well.

5 The higher we climb,   e. the greater the demand for ice cream.

6 Naturally, the more they issued,   f. the better price you will get.

7 The more you take care of your health,   g. the more worthless it became.

C

Write the comparative or superlative form of given words.

1 I feel much _____*more relaxed*_____ now because the exams are over. (relaxed)

2 Mothers are _____ than other women to work part time. (likely)

3 The bad news is that it is the _____ day of the year today. (hot)

4 The twins looked even _____ than usual. (alike)

5 How on earth are snakes _____ than harmless dogs? (dangerous)

6 Oil pollution may be the _____ cause of death among sea birds. (common)

7 India announces its new Nano, at $2,500 the _____ car in the world. (cheap)

8 How can I get the _____ news without surfing the web for it? (late)

Further Study

A Choose the right words for (A) and (B).

Scientists found that the heavier an object is the easier it is to balance it. Once everything is set in motion it resists change and movement. Also, once a weight has balance on a point, the object has a stable state. The (A) <greatest / greater> the weight, the more stable, therefore the lighter the (B) <better / worse>.

B Read and answer the questions.

While women have made notable gains in education since the 1980s, improvements in pay equity haven't been achieved. As early as one year out of college, women working full-time already earn (A) <less / more> than their male counterparts even when they work in the same field. Ten years after graduation, women fall further behind, earning only 68 percent as much (B) <as / than> men. Accounting for occupation, parenthood, position, and other factors associated with pay, <u>college-educated women still earn less than their male peers</u>. The research indicates that one-quarter of the pay gap remains unexplained and is likely due to sex discrimination.

1 Choose the right words for (A) and (B).

2 Rewrite the underlined sentence using 'as.'

→ College-educated women still don't _____ their male peers.

C Read and answer the question.

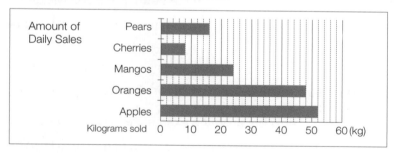

1 Choose all that doesn't agree to the graph.

① The weight of apples sold is the largest.
② The weight of oranges sold is three times greater than that of cherries sold.
③ The weight of mangos sold is three times greater than that of cherries sold.
④ The weight of pears and mangos combined is the same as that of oranges.
⑤ The weight of cherries and oranges put together is larger than that of apples.

A object 물체 stable 안정된 **B** equity 평등 counterpart 한 쪽, 상대방 peer 동료 discrimination 차별

Part III

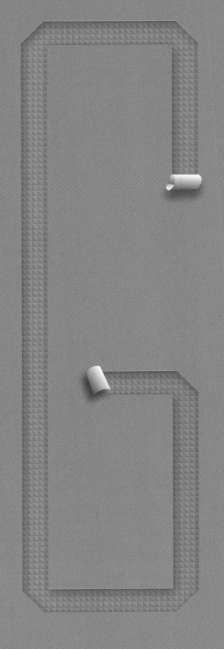

Unit 16

문장의 시제

1 동사의 단순시제
2 동사의 완료시제

Questions

1 단순시제와 완료시제를 꼭 구분해서 사용해야 하는가?
2 완료시제의 다양한 해석을 용법으로 외워야 하는가?
3 과거와 대과거를 정확히 구분하여 표현해야 하는가?

Answers

1 과거와 현재완료의 어감은 '아' 다르고 '어' 다르듯이 분명히 다르다. 그래서 내용상 완료시제가 필요한 경우는 완료형을 사용해야 한다. 완료형 문장이 어떤 경우에 사용되는지 알아야 한다.

2 아니다. 문법이 아니라 어법에는 법칙이란 것이 없다. 따라서, 완료시제의 다양한 해석 방법의 예를 익히고 문맥을 통해 의미 파악을 해야 한다.

3 시간적인 순서가 분명한 경우 반드시 대과거를 사용하지 않아도 된다. 대과거는 과거시제 이전에 발생한 일을 나타내는 방법일 뿐이다.

1 동사의 단순시제(Simple Tense)

1 시제의 구분(simple tense, perfect tense, continuous tense)

	과거	현재	미래
	과거완료 (pastperfect)	현재완료 (presentperfect)	미래완료 (futureperfect)

〈미래〉 Tom will study later.	〈미래 진행〉 Tom will be studying then.
〈현재〉 Tom studies now.	〈현재 진행〉 Tom is studying now.
〈과거〉 Tom studied then.	〈과거 진행〉 Tom was studying then.

2 미래시제(future)

Wherever you go, you **will find** the local people friendly.

Until you **start** the engine, nothing will happen.

If you **earn** much money, then you will pay income tax on it.

cf) I don't know **if** he **will** come here tomorrow.

I wonder **when** he **will** be able to solve it by himself.

3 현재시제(present)

When the moon **is** between the earth and the sun, it is dark.

I heard Venus **is** slightly smaller than the Earth.

Actually the game **begins** at three on Tuesday.

4 과거시제(past)

ago	yesterday	last year	just now	until	then
when a child	once	at that time			

Brian **went** to the new house **yesterday**.

When a child I often **played** with the son in the timber-yards.

5 단순과거와 현재완료의 차이

He **was** in prison for ten years.　　　(He is not in prison now.)

He **has been** in prison for ten years.　　(He is in prison now.)

His sister **suffered** from asthma all her life.

His sister **has suffered** from asthma all her life.

I **changed** the plan to visit China.

I **have changed** the plan to visit China.

2

시간과 조건을 나타내는 부사절에서는 미래 시제 대신 현재를 사용해야 한다.

– 시간의 부사절

– 조건의 부사절

– 명사절에서는 미래를 미래로 표현한다.

3

일반적인 사실, 변하지 않는 진리, 정해진 원칙, 확실한 미래의 일에는 현재를 사용한다.

* 주어가 3인칭 단수 현재이면 동사에 -s를 붙이는 기본적인 원칙에 주의한다.

4

과거시제는 단순히 과거에 발생한 일이며, 그 이후 상태는 그렇지 않거나 모르는 상태 이다.

* 명백한 과거를 나타내는 부사가 있는 경우 는 반드시 과거시제를 사용한다.

5

과거시제는 현재 그렇지 않거나 내용을 모르는 경우에, 현재 완료는 과거부터 지금까지 일이 진행되거나 영향을 미치는 경우에 쓴다.

– She is now dead.

– She is still alive.

– I didn't go.

– I'm not going.

EXERCISE

Answers P.24

A Choose the right words.

1 Morden won't be leaving until he <tells / will tell> the truth.

2 <Did you take / Have you taken> your medicines yesterday?

3 I <didn't get / haven't gotten> much attention when I was a child.

4 I wonder when you first <decided / have decided> to be a musician.

5 He <has returned / returned> from his trip the day before yesterday.

6 I <got / have gotten> a cold almost a month ago, but it wasn't serious.

7 As soon as he <receives / will receive> the order, he will start the operation.

B Choose the correct ending to each sentence.

1 *I finished the script* — *a. at the end of the last month.*
  I've finished the script — *b. and I am free to do what I want.*

2 I never tasted a durian in Thailand;   a. I hope I have the chance to.
  I have never tasted a durian in Thailand;   b. I wish I'd had the chance to.

3 I've lost my passport,   a. so I couldn't get on the plane.
  I lost my passport,   b. so I can't get on the plane.

4 Rosa suffered from diabetes all her life.   a. She is now dead.
  Rosa has suffered from diabetes all her life.   b. She's still alive.

C Write answers using the given words.

1 A: How long ago did you serve as a civil servant?
  B: _____ *I served as a civil servant three years ago.* _____ (three years ago)

2 A: When did you last visit Russia?
  B: _____ (when I was 14)

3 A: When did he go to the Italian restaurant?
  B: _____ (last night)

4 A: What time did the market close on Friday?
  B: _____ (at 7)

5 A: When did you read a Central Asian Writer's book?
  B: _____ (last year)

2 ▶ 동사의 완료시제 (Perfect Tense)

1 완료형의 다양한 해석

I **have** just **brought** three dogs to serve as guide dogs.
I **have** just **washed** some socks and I am now having tea.

She **has taught** at the university **for 10 years**.
How long **have** you **lived** in this house?

I **have found** the letter you were looking for. Here it is.
My ceiling **has fallen** and the kitchen is flooded.

Nothing like this **has ever happened** to us.
I**'ve seen** an ice storm personally in New Jersey.

2 주의해야 할 현재완료(present perfect tense)

(1) 완료 시제와 결합하는 since
My father **has played** the guitar since childhood.
There **have happened** many fires since this summer.

(2) have been to + 장소 / have gone to + 장소
My mother **has been to** Spain only once in her life.
I'm sorry but she **has** already **gone to** school.

3 시제에도 순서가 있다!−대과거(past perfect tense)

I **told** the guide that I **had lost** the air ticket the day before.
I **lost** the watch which my darling **had bought** for me.

I **knew** yesterday that John **had died** last year.
The little boy whom we **had given up** for lost **returned** safe.

4 "have+pp"는 지난 과거의 일!

He seems **to have been** a singer in his teens.
The Romans seem **to have had** a game like today's soccer.

The players are proud of **having won** the gold medal.
I told him about **having seen** the LA Dodgers win the game.

Having failed in the attempt twice, Tom didn't try again.
Having evolved over centuries, languages contain many cultures.

1
현재완료 시제는 과거에 발생한 일이 현재까지 영향을 미친다.
– ∼를 다 완료했다.

– 계속 ∼해왔다, 지금도 ∼한다.

– ∼한 결과 …하다.

– ∼한 적이 있다.
* just, already, yet, so far, up to now, ever 등은 주로 완료시제에 쓰인다.

2
since(∼이래로)가 있는 경우, 내용상 '∼해왔다'는 완료형 시제와 결합한다.

have been to + 장소: '∼에 갔다 왔다'
have gone to + 장소: '∼로 가버리고 여기 없다'

3
현재보다 앞선 시제는 과거와 현재완료, 과거와 현재완료보다 더 앞선 시제는 과거완료로 나타낸다.

말하는 시점이 과거나 현재완료일 때, 더 앞의 일은 대과거인 과거완료(had+p.p.)를 쓴다.

4
to부정사, 분사, 동명사에서는 주절의 시제보다 더 앞서 발생한 일에 완료형을 사용한다.
* 해석은 (주절의 시제보다) '옛날에, 그에 앞서, 그 전에'로 한다.

EXERCISE

A   **Choose the right words.**

1   I have <been / gone> to Hawaii eight times as a tourist.

2   He <has served / served> as our president since June 2003.

3   The night <ended / has ended> and it's time to rise and start.

4   Everybody has <been / gone> to the beach. They will soon be back.

5   Gas prices <went / have gone> up by 50%. Now prices are too high.

6   A hawk, which <have been / had been> very ill for a long time, tried to fly.

7   We <are / have been> waiting for the sun to show its face for forty minutes.

8   Yesterday I visited Hollywood. I <never / had never> visited the place before.

B   **Match the beginning of each sentence with the most appropriate ending.**

1   After she had tried on some jackets   a. he went back to where the rabbit had been.

2   When he retired as a chairman   b. she decided on the first one.

3   When the cook came back   c. she had worked for the company for two years.

4   After a lion missed the deer   d. he had already lost his memory.

5   Ever since Anne became a secretary   e. I have been dissatisfied with her work.

6   When I was walking along the beach   f. I said the cat had just tasted her food.

7   When Jane was promoted to the head   g. I noticed the tide had brought the starfish to shore.

C   **Complete each blank using given words.**

1   Oprah Winfrey is an amazing person. By the time she a) _____ (be) twelve, she b) _____ (already decide) on a career. Not long afterward, she got her first radio job. Although she c) _____ (have) any experience, she became a news reporter. When she got her own TV talk show, she d) _____ (already act) in a major Hollywood movie.

2   When she a) _____ (offer) a promotion to become a head of the department, Janet b) _____ (work) for an advertising company for two years. A few months later, Janet c) _____ (tell) her employers about her pregnancy. At first, they congratulated her on her pregnancy. Later that month, the personnel director told her that, due to her inability, they had to let her go. She d) _____ (ask) him why they e) _____ (promote) her for her excellence and now decided to let her go.

Further Study

A Choose the right words for (A) and (B). 기출 응용

Former U.S. President Jimmy Carter, who promotes Habitat for Humanity, (A) <has toured / toured> various countries since 1994. In the summer of 2001, he (B) <has visited / visited> Asan, Korea, to participate in a house-building project. It was part of Habitat for Humanity International's campaign to build houses for homeless people.

Read and answer the questions in English.

Recently, in my apartment complex there has been a birth of 8 puppies to my neighbor's dog. The dog is a little more protective than usual and she seems to protect her property a little more. My female Doberman(Dobi) who (A) <has lived / lives> at the complex longer has only known the female who just had puppies. Now since the puppies were born and kept in the house, my Dobi (B) <is / has been> acting very strange and frantic. She looks somewhat slower and sadder than usual. Does anyone have an explanation for this? She seems almost envious or jealous in a way.

1 Choose the right words for (A) and (B).

2 According to the passage, why has Dobi been acting strange?
   → Dobi has been acting strange, as _____ .

C Read and answer the questions in English.

<u>어떤 부부가 25년간 결혼생활을 했다</u> and was going to celebrate the husband's 60th birthday. A fairy showed up and said that because they had been such a sweet couple, she would give them one wish each. The wife said, "We've been so poor all these years, and I've never gotten to see the world. I wish we could travel all around the world." The fairy waved her wand and POOF! — she had the travel tickets in her hands. Next, it was the husband's turn. He hesitated about what to say and then said, "I'd like to be married to a woman 30 years younger than me." The fairy got upset and waved her wand and POOF!—he became 90 years old.

1 According to the passage, when did the man get married?
   → The husband <was married / has been married> at 35.

2 Translate the Korean into English.
   → A couple _____ .

A former 이전의 habitat 주거지 participate 참가하다   **B** apartment complex 아파트 단지 puppy 강아지 property 재산 jealous 질투하는
C fairy 요정 wand (요술)지팡이 turn 차례

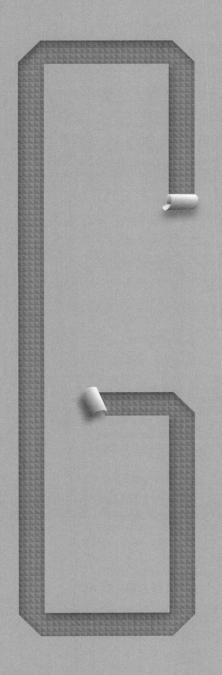

Questions

1 다양한 조동사의 의미를 외워야 한단 말입니까?

2 should, would, must... 복잡해서 정리가 안돼요!

Answers

1 조동사는 본동사를 보조하는 역할을 할 뿐이다. 그러므로, 조동사에는 다양한 용법이 있는 것이 아니라 다양한 의미나 어감을 갖고 있을 뿐이다. 기본적인 역할만 안다면 문맥을 통해 의미를 판단하면 된다.

2 would는 will의 과거형태인데, 다양한 위치에 등장한다. '~하고 싶다, ~하 곤 한다, ~를 고집하다 등' 다양하게 쓰이는 것은 암기해라. 과거의 일을 판단 하는 조동사+have+과거분사 표현은 상당히 중요한 표현이다.

Unit 17

1 ▶ 조동사의 다양한 의미

1 조동사의 종류–순수한 조동사

종류	의 미
should	* You **should** go and see it. (∼해야 한다) * Tom **shouldn't** go to bed so late.(∼하면 안된다)
will (would)	* I **will** not be late for work again.(∼할 것이다) * I **would** like to see the film. (∼하고 싶다) * She **would** play the piano when she was young. (∼하곤 했다)
can (could)	* You **can** read and write it. (∼할 수 있다) * It **can't be** five o'clock. (∼일리 없다) * You **can** borrow that pen. (∼해도 된다)
may (might)	* **May** we go now? (∼해도 된다) * He **may** come tomorrow. (∼할지도 모른다)
must (have to)	* We **must** go to the bank today. (∼해야 한다) * I **must not** touch the bag. (∼하지 말아야 한다) * She **must be** hungry. (∼임에 틀림없다)

1
조동사 뒤에는 반드시 동사원형이 오며, 부정표현은 조동사 뒤에 **not**을 붙인다.
= ∼go see it.

– 허락

> * 의미의 강한 정도
> ↓should : 현재나 미래시제
> ↓have to : 일반적 당위성
> ↓must : 주관적인 감정
>   미래시제에는 사용하지 않음.

2 조동사의 대체 어구(phrasal counterpart)

can(could)	be able to
will, shall	be going to, be about to
must	have to(=have got to – 구어체 표현)
should(=ought to)	be supposed to
would	used to
may(might)	be allowed to, be permitted to

2
유사한 의미의 일반동사로 대체 가능하다.
– ∼할 수 있다
– ∼할 예정이다
– ∼해야 한다
– ∼하기로 되어있다
– ∼하곤 했다
– ∼해도 된다

3 조동사의 종류–특수한 조동사

종류	의 미
ought to ∼해야 한다	* You **ought to** stay in bed. * You **ought** not to cook potatoes so long.
had better ∼하는 게 낫다	* You **had better** check if the door is locked. * You **had better** not go home now.
have to(=have got to) ∼해야 한다	* They'll **have to** take the course again. * They **didn't have to** check in.
used to ∼하곤 했었다	* I **used to** play tennis.
need ∼할 필요 있다	* He **needs** money. (∼를 필요로 하다) * You don't **need** to(=need not) start early.
dare 감히 ∼하다	* He **dares** to call(=dare call) me names. * He doesn't **dare** to(=dare not) touch me.

3
조동사의 형태는 아니지만 하나의 조동사 역할을 하므로 뒤에는 동사원형이 온다.
– ought to=should
– 부정표현: to 앞에 not
– 충고

– not 위치

– ∼해야 한다
– ∼할 필요 없다

– 조동사와 일반동사 겸용

– 조동사와 일반동사 겸용

EXERCISE

A Choose the right words.

1 You must come to school on time; you <must / need> not be late.

2 We <can't / needn't> see the chalkboard when we sit in the back row.

3 You <had better / ought to> not take pictures in the shade and the sun light.

4 We <didn't / had to> leave the meeting early. We couldn't stay until the end.

5 I have already finished all my homework, so I <didn't / don't> have to study today.

6 We can leave camp after midnight. We <can / needn't> stay until the next day.

7 The drivers <ought to / used to> stop before a crosswalk when a child is waiting.

B Choose the words which have the same meaning with the underlined parts.

a. ability	b. necessity	c. possibility	d. requesting
e. certainty	f. advising	g. asking for permission	

1 <u>May</u> I sit and stare at you for a while? _____g_____

2 <u>Can</u> you please help me find a camera? _____

3 Mary <u>must</u> be a good reader. She read 35 books in eighth grade. _____

4 When there is a lot of rainfall, the river <u>may</u> overflow its banks. _____

5 He likes musicals with plenty of dance. He <u>must</u> see *Mamma Mia*. _____

6 He has no map with him, but he <u>can</u> find himself miles out of town. _____

C Choose the right words to complete each sentence.

must	doesn't(don't) have to	must not

1 You ___must not___ drive when you are tired. It's dangerous.

2 He lives only a few blocks from his office. He _____ drive to work.

3 Liz finally got a car, so now she _____ walk to work.

4 Tommy, you _____ talk to your partner. Please keep silent.

5 You _____ read this book because it would be harmful to your morals.

6 When you see a toll-free number, you _____ pay for the phone call.

7 A dog is the only animal that _____ work for a living.

8 Take your time. You _____ hurry. Everything has a right time.

2 ▶ 까다로운 조동사

1 조동사 + 동사원형

현재의 일	□ may be ～일지 모른다
	□ must be ～임에 틀림없다
	□ cannot be ～일리 없다
	□ need not ～할 필요 없다
	□ should(=ought to) ～해야 한다

Children **may be** afraid of cats.

There **must be** thousands of stars in the sky.

A cook who eats only her own cooking **cannot be** a good cook.

You **need not** remove the bandage when you wash your hands.

Maybe one of us **ought to** tell her for her own sake.

> **1**
> 조동사+동사원형은 현재의 일에 대한 당연, 추측, 가능 등을 나타낸다.

2 조동사 + have + 과거분사(pp)

과거의 일 (조동사+have 과거분사)	□ may have+pp ～했었는지 모른다
	□ must have+pp ～했음에 틀림없다
	□ cannot have+pp ～했을 리 가없다
	□ need not have+pp ～할 필요가 없었는데
	□ should(=ought to) have+pp ～했어야만 했는데
	□ should not have+pp ～하지 말았어야 했는데

People **may have been** shocked by the earthquake.

The birds **must have seen** the light in the living room.

Those who failed **need not have been** disappointed so much.

I **should have done** it yesterday because it was my last chance.

Mary **should not have married** Tom then.

> **2**
> 조동사+have 과거분사는 과거에 발생한 일에 대한 당연, 추측, 가능 등을 나타낸다. 여기서 <u>have 과거분사</u>는 과거에 발생한 일임을 나타낸다.
>
> = ought to have pp

3 조동사 would, might, could

When I **was** young, I **could** run very fast.

He **said** that he **would** call back.

The phone is ringing. It **might** be Tim.

It's a nice day. We **could** go for a walk.

If I **had** much money, I **could** lend you money.

If he **knew** the fact, he **would** tell us what to do.

Don't eat that. It **could** be poisonous.

Don't touch that. It **might** be harmful to the children.

> **3**
> will, may, can의 과거형으로서 시제의 일치 형태에 나타난다.
>
> – would, might, could는 실제 사실이 아닌 내용을 가정하는 가정법 문장에도 쓰인다.(가정법 80페이지 참조)
>
> – 가정 : ～할 수 있을텐데
>
> – 가정 : ～할텐데

EXERCISE

A Choose the right words to complete the sentences.

must have been	can't have been	should have been	shouldn't have been

1 Jack ___*should have been*___ fired years ago. Nobody wants to listen to the guy.

2 You _____ waiting long. After all, I'm only five minutes late.

3 Vera _____ at the supermarket this morning. I didn't see her there.

4 The road is closed off now. There _____ an accident on South Street.

5 Henry _____ driving a car yesterday. He got into a car accident.

6 John _____ back here till 10, but he only arrived here after 11.

7 He knows a lot about flying planes. He _____ a pilot when he was young.

B Match each sentence on the left with one on the right.

1 You must have had a terrible night.   a. It should have been cleaned by now.

2 You should not have driven to your office.   b. How foolish I was!

3 The bathroom hasn't been cleaned.   c. It's a pity he stole a cellphone again.

4 You should have punished him then.   d. I heard a fire had broken out.

5 I should have driven under the speed limit. e. You'd better go to work by bus.

6 The beach had a beautiful sunset view.   i. He should not have married her.

7 James deeply regretted marrying her so soon. g. You should have seen it.

C Rewrite following sentences using 'should have' or 'shouldn't have'.

1 I wish you had taken that job in New York.

→ _____*You should have taken that job in New York.*_____

2 He walked out of the restaurant without paying his bill.

→ _____

3 Why did you waste such a golden chance for peace?

→ _____

4 I wish I had not worked so many part-time jobs.

→ _____

5 Why didn't you tell me Paris was such a nightmare?

→ _____

A Choose the right words. 기출 응용

The function of school is to produce knowledgeable people, but if schools only provide knowledge, they may destroy creativity. We often hear stories of ordinary people who, if education had focused on creativity, could have become great scientists. Those victims of education (A) <should receive / should have received> training to develop creative talents while in school. It really is a pity that they did not.

B Read and answer the questions in English.

Since blood types are inherited, you have the same blood type as your parents. However ① it is sometimes possible to prove that someone cannot possibly be the parent of a child. ② You might be unfortunate to discover that you (A) <cannot / must> have been adopted; ③ your adoptive parents (B) <ought / should> have told you about that already. ④ You can have blonde hair and Type-O blood, and your biological parents both have brown hair and Type-A blood on your birth certificate. ⑤ You can easily have different hair color and blood type from your biological parents, especially if you have a genetically recessive trait.

1 Choose the right words for (A) and (B).

2 Where would the following sentence best fit in ①~⑤?

However, this doesn't necessarily mean that you were adopted.

C Read and answer the question in English.

A 38-year-old Canadian businesswoman is seeking justice after she was thrown in jail by Saudi Arabia's religious police for sitting with a male colleague in a coffee shop in Jeddah. However this businesswoman didn't want to be arrested, she should not have broken the local law. If this businesswoman aimed to openly protest gender segregation by purposely getting arrested, I acknowledge her intention. Yet, if she was trying to actually conduct a business meeting, she should have known the local laws and followed them. If not, she shouldn't have been there or her husband should have been with her. When traveling abroad one must remember "When in Rome, <Romans / do / as / the / do>"

1 Rearrange the words to complete the sentence.
→ "When in Rome, _____."

A function 역할, 기능 creativity 독창성 pity 애석한 일, 동정 **B** inherit 상속하다, 물려받다 adopt 양자를 삼다, 채택하다 certificate 증명서 recessive 열성의 **C** religious 종교적인 racial segregation 인종 차별 arrest 체포하다

S+V+O+동사원형

1 사역동사
2 지각동사

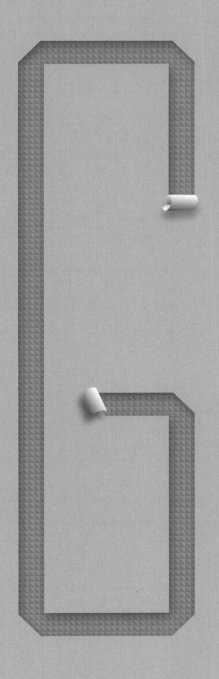

Questions

1 사역동사, 지각동사란 이름이 어렵다. 무슨 말이지?
2 사역동사와 지각동사를 없애면 정말 문제가 생길까?
3 어디에는 동사원형, 어디에는 to부정사… 정리가 필요한데!

Answers

1 사역(使役)동사는 '역할을 시키다', '역할을 맡기다'는 의미이다. 지각(知覺)동사는 '감각으로 알다'는 의미이다. 한마디로, 특별하게 '~하도록 시키다'와 '~하는 것을 보고 느끼다'는 동사가 영어에 자주 쓰이는 표현이므로 별도의 규칙을 가지고 있는 것이다.

2 매우 자주 사용하는 동사이므로 반드시 알아야 한다.

3 사역동사와 지각동사는 절대로 to부정사를 상대하지 않는다. 정해둔 의미 없이 아무렇게나 쓰이는 to부정사(不定詞)가 아니라, 문맥에 따라 동사원형, 현재분사, 과거분사가 목적보어로 올 뿐이다. 절대 목적어 뒤의 목적보어로 to부정사(不定詞)가 오지 않는다.

1 ▶ 사역동사(Causative Verb)

1 사역동사(causative verbs)−make, let, have, get

(1) 사역동사의 의미

I **made** him **wash** my car. (I **insisted** that he wash my car.)

I **let** him **wash** my car. (He **wanted** to wash my car.)

I **had** him **wash** my car. (I **asked** him to wash my car.)

* I **got** him **to wash** my car. (I **persuaded** him to wash my car.)

> 1
> 사역동사+object+동사원형에서 사역동사는 '어떤 일을 하도록 야기한다'는 의미이다.
> (1) make, let, have는 '시키다'의 의미를 지니지만 의미는 조금씩 다르다.
>
> − get동사는 내용상으로 사역동사의 의미를 가진다.
> (2) 목적어에게 어떤 일을 해달라고 요청하는 경우에 사용한다.

(2) have 동사

> * have + O(목적어) + 동사원형 : O가 능동적 동작
> * have + O(목적어) + 과거분사 : O가 수동적 동작

I had the plumber **repair** the leak.

Scofield had the waiter **bring** some tea.

I had the leak **repaired** and received the repair bills.

She had some tea **brought** in for herself.

He had his car **stolen** while he was shopping.

While travelling in Santiago, she had her bag **snatched**.

> − 도난당하다
> − 소매치기 당하다

(3) help 동사

My brother helped me **wash** my car yesterday.

My brother helped me **to wash** my car yesterday.

My brother helped **wash** my car yesterday.

My brother helped **to wash** my car yesterday.

> (3) help+목적어+동사원형(to부정사)의 형태로 사용된다.
>
> − to 생략

2 get 동사

> * get + 목적어 + to부정사 : 목적어를 설득하여 ～하도록 하다
> * get + 목적어 + 과거분사 : 목적어가 ～되어지도록 하다

The students got the teacher **to dismiss** class early.

Mary got her friends **to play** soccer after school.

I got my car **towed** for the first time in my life today.

I got my computer **checked** several times last month.

> 2
> 동사 get은 사역동사가 아니지만, '(설득하여) 시키다'는 의미를 지닌다.
>
> − 차를 견인당하다

3 사역동사의 수동태 (be+과거분사)+to부정사

I was made / **to inform** city council members of the news.

He is helped / **to master** daily activities like washing and shaving.

> 3
> 사역동사가 수동형태인 경우, 뒤에는 동사원형이 아니라 to부정사가 온다.
> * 「be+과거분사」에 이어 또 다른 동사가 연이어 올 수 없기 때문이다.

EXERCISE

A Choose the right words.

1 I'll have my assistant <book / to book> me a flight tomorrow.

2 In general, do you let others <make / makes> decisions for you?

3 What made you <started / start> reading the Harry Potter books?

4 He wished to have the meeting <postpone / postponed> to March 30.

5 I want to get the contract <to cancel / cancelled> but keep the service.

6 Understanding why parents get their children <eat / to eat> is important.

7 Have you ever let someone <take / taking> the blame for something you did?

B Complete each sentence using the given verbs in the correct form.

1 The doctor made the patient _____ in bed. (stay)

2 Peeling onions always makes me _____ . (cry)

3 Alice stopped at the service station to have the tank _____ . (fill)

4 Nick went to a doctor to have a wart on his nose _____ . (remove)   *wart: 사마귀

5 The teacher had the class _____ a 2000-word research paper. (write)

6 I got Rosa _____ me some money so I could go to a movie. (lend)

7 Casey got some kids in the neighborhood _____ out her garage. (clean)

8 I spilled some tomato sauce on my suit. I need to get my suit _____ . (clean)

C Rearrange the words to complete the sentences.

1 I got my friend <some pictures / to / take / my camera phone / using>.
 → I got my friend _____ *to take some pictures using my camera phone.* _____

2 Don't let your children <to be / grow up / cowboys>.
 → Don't let your children _____

3 Sometimes parents make <watching / their children / TV / stop>.
 → Sometimes parents make _____

4 They successfully helped the child <answer / to / the correct / reach>.
 → They successfully helped the child _____

5 I won't let my family <forget / my birthday / and close friends>.
 → I won't let my family _____

2 ▶ 지각동사(Verb of Perception)

1 지각동사+O(목적어)+do/doing/done

> * 지각동사 : see, watch, look at, hear, listen to, feel, smell, perceive, observe, notice 등

People noticed the robber **run** away from the house.
People noticed the robber **running** away from the house.
People noticed the robber **caught** by the police on the spot.

I felt someone **touch** me on the head.
Students observed the sun **rising** above the horizon.
We heard the Indian **beating** the drum from a distance.

I perceived the storm **approaching** apace from the South.
We noticed the little boy **sitting** on the wall of the cemetery.
The pupils listened to the teacher **reading** about the World War II.

2 동사+O(목적어)+현재분사/과거분사

I noticed smoke **rising** from the roof of a cabin.
I felt someone **looking** at me when I looked up there.
I heard you saw a man **stealing** a purse from a woman.

We noticed the horse **taken** up at the market.
I smiled as I saw the pictures **drawn** onto the walls.
My father never saw my works **exhibited** in the museum.

3 지각동사(be+과거분사)+to부정사/분사

The law was seen / **to be** on the students' side.
No one in the households was perceived / **to be** overweight.
He was overheard / **to say** that he hoped Mary would resign.
She was noticed / **to run** away from the house.

He was observed / **traveling** close to a shore in Hillsborough Bay.
She was seen / **watching** the farmer sow seed in the field.

He was seen / **seated** on a pile of earthen pots thrown away.
A robber man was seen / **beaten** to the ground by the police.

1
눈, 귀, 코, 입, 피부, 그리고 느낌으로 아는 것을 감각, 또는 지각(知覺)동사라고 한다.
S+지각동사+O+C의 문장에서 보어에는 동사원형이나 분사가 온다.
동사원형보다는 분사가 주로 사용되며, to부정사는 불가능하다.
– 동사원형 : 도망친다는 사실을 강조
– 현재분사 : 도망치는 동작 강조
– 과거분사 : 수동적 의미

2
현재분사는 의미상주어인 목적어가 직접 동작을 하는 능동적 의미를, 과거분사는 의미상주어인 목적어가 동작을 당하는 수동적인 의미를 나타낸다.

3
지각동사+목적어+동사원형은 수동태에서 동사원형이 to부정사로 바뀐다.
* S+V ~ 뒤에 또 다른 동사가 오려면 동사원형이 아니라 to부정사나 분사의 형태가 와야 한다.

seat–seated–seated 앉히다

beat–beat–beaten 때리다

E EXERCISE

A Choose the right words.

1 I screamed and felt my bag <pull / pulled> out of my hand.

2 In my entire life I have never seen her <to use / using> lipstick.

3 We noticed the robbers <standing / to stand> outside of the bank.

4 You can see the baby's heart <beaten / beating> on a television screen.

5 The inventor observes the tree <blooming / bloom> and fruiting everyday.

6 You can watch your money <drop / to drop> in value by watching the gold price.

7 Everybody heard the teacher <calling / called> out my name from the teachers' room.

B Complete each sentence using the words in the box.

sing	crawl	walk	whisper	happen	run	shout	call

1 I'd wake up and listen to the birds _____*singing*_____ in my backyard.

2 I heard somebody _____ that the war ended today.

3 Did anybody see the accident _____ yesterday?

4 I suddenly feel something _____ up my hand.

5 I saw Tim _____ on the streets of San Diego last night.

6 I thought I heard my name _____ behind the curtain.

7 Delano watched the two men _____ together in low voices.

C Rewrite these two sentences into one sentence.

1 I noticed her. She was eating her lunch alone in the cafeteria.

→ I noticed her _____*eating her lunch alone in the cafeteria.*_____

2 He was playing the guitar. I heard him.

→ I heard _____

3 Somebody grabbed her arm and pulled her.

→ Liz felt _____

4 He was dancing and singing beside the road. He was observed.

→ He was observed _____

5 The children lay down on the stage. They were noticed.

→ The children were noticed _____

A Choose the right words for (A) and (B).

When I fell ill, I was nearly dead within days. My close friend Joanne swooped in to support and (A) <got / helped> me locate doctors in San Francisco. She also let my friends (B) <know / to know> that they were needed. Joanne helped me gain the positive outlook I needed. She stressed the importance of surrounding myself with encouraging people.

B Read and answer the questions. 기출 응용

On most subway trains, the doors open automatically at each station. But when you are on the Metro, the subway in Paris, things are different. I watched a man on the Metro (A) <to try / try> to get off the train and (B) <fail / failed>. When the train came to his station, he got up and stood patiently in front of the door, waiting for it to open. It never opened. The train simply started up again and went on to the next station. In the Metro, you have to open the doors yourself by pushing a button, depressing a lever or sliding them.

1 Choose the correct words for (A) and (B).

2 According to the passage, who should operate the door to get off the Metro?
→ _____

C Read and answer the question.

When the Roboman arrived in the mail yesterday, I was really impressed. He had infrared vision, a color camera, and sonic sensors. Equipped with a sensor that can read microchips in identification cards, the robot recognized a woman approaching from behind, and turned to greet her by name. Now I have to get him to bounce a ball by himself. It is at this moment that my dreams of having him clean the house are gone. Sometimes it's very easy to think of a robot as a human being. But 그것이 너를 재미있게는 하겠지만, 집안일을 할 것으로는 기대하지 마라.

1 Translate the Korean into English.
→ it can make _____, but never expect _____.

A swoop 급강하하다, 단숨에 오다 positive 긍정적인 stress 강조하다   **B** Metro 지하철 depress 우울케하다, 내리누르다 slide 미끄러지게하다
C impress 감동시키다 infrared 적외선의 sonic sensor 소리 감지기 identification 신원확인

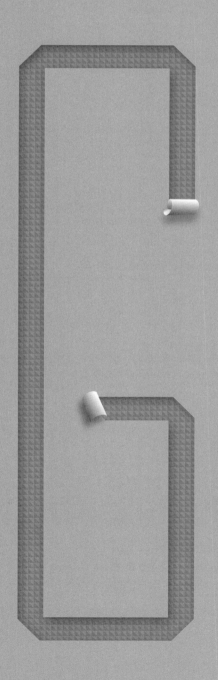

Questions

1 구동사는 우리가 사용하는 동사구, 2어동사와 무슨 관계가 있는가? 동사구는 하나의 동사로 대체할 수 있는가?

2 구동사를 만드는 원리가 궁금하다.

Answers

1 구동사는 동사가 전치사나 부사와 결합하여 별개의 동사를 만들어내는 표현이다. 익혀 외운다는 '숙어'라는 말처럼, 원래의 자동사나 타동사가 전치사 형태와 결합하여 조금 다른 의미의 표현을 만들어낸다. 우리는 이것을 동사구, 구동사, 또는 2어동사로 부르기도 한다.

2 구동사는 동사 원래의 의미와 달라지므로 하나의 동사처럼 익혀야 한다. 가장 중요한 것은 타동사+부사(원래는 전치사)의 목적어가 대명사일 경우 반드시 타동사+목적어+부사의 형태가 되어야 한다는 것이다.

구동사(Phrasal Verb)

1 전치사인가 부사인가?

> * **자동사** 뒤에는 보어, 부사, 전치사(in, on, off 등)가 올 수 있다.
> * **타동사** 뒤에는 목적어(명사형태)가 온다. 타동사와 결합하는 전치사를 부사로 부른다.

He **called** loudly / to the sailors and to the captain.
She **walked** up the street / to get a bite to eat.
Put the fruit pieces / carefully into a large bowl.
Never **put off** / what can be done today till tomorrow.

2 구동사(phrasal verb)란?

(1) 자동사+전치사(intransitive verb+preposition)
I will help you learn how to **cope with** the problem.
Soft drink sales greatly **depend on** weather and season.

(2) 타동사+부사(transitive verb+adverb)
Harold **turned off** the radio to focus on reading.
Can you **put off** the presentation until next Monday?

(3) 목적어가 없는 구동사
At the age of 6, the civil war **broke out** in Afghanistan.
When I **grow up**, I will have to take care of my parents.

3 구동사의 목적어

(1) 구동사의 목적어 위치

> * **구동사**의 목적어가 명사 : 타동사+목적어+부사 or 타동사+부사+목적어
> * **구동사**의 목적어가 대명사 : 타동사+목적어(대명사)+부사

We **threw away the ball** a few times in the second half.
We **threw the ball away** a few times in the second half.

I accidentally deleted a file. Any ideas on how to **get it back**?
I imagine a very touching song called *Don't call me up*.

(2) 구동사의 기억
I've tried to stop smoking, but I can't **give it up**.
Jim gave me a hat. When I **put it on**, I felt like a princess.
After I smoke a cigarette, I never **throw it away** in the street.

1
구동사는 동사가 전치사나 부사와 결합하여 만드는 동사의 덩어리이다.

– 자동사+부사
– 자동사+부사구
– 타동사+목적어
– 타동사+부사+목적어

2
(1) 자동사 뒤에 전치사가 와서 구동사를 만든다.

(2) 타동사 뒤에 부사가 와서 구동사를 만든다. 구동사에서 원래의 동사 의미는 변하게 된다.

(3) 구동사가 목적어 없이 사용되기도 한다.

3
(1) 구동사를 자동사와 타동사로 구분하는 것보다, 다양한 구동사 자체를 기억해야 한다.

(2) 구동사의 목적어로 대명사(it)를 함께 사용하면 효과적으로 기억할 수 있다.

 EXERCISE

A Complete each sentence using the words in the box.

> give   take   put   send   bring   get

1 We should not _____ on an impossible mission any more.
   Did Aladdin ask teenagers to _____ off their coats?

2 He is an alcoholic, and he should _____ it over.
   She wants the kids to _____ off the couch and get out the door.

3 She asked me to _____ out the campfire.
   Never _____ off until tomorrow what you can do today.

4 Our cultural traditions to _____ up children are very different.
   These results indicate that tourism may _____ about economic improvement.

B Complete each sentence using the words in the box.

> off   up   down   away   on

1 I gave _____ African studies because I found it depressing.
   She has put _____ with her noisy neighbors for years.

2 The rangers turned _____ all of the lights in the parking lot to make it dark.
   Saline City Council refused to cut _____ a walnut tree.

3 He has put _____ marriage to look after his family.
   Maybe other people should take _____ their shirts as well.

4 I won't miss him if he goes _____.
   Don't throw _____ that Christmas tree, instead recycle it!

C Complete the following sentences using the given words.

1 I got something to tell you. Will you please ____*call me back*____? (call back)

2 I'll be back to him after class, thus don't _____. (wake up)

3 Here is an application form. _____ and send it to us. (fill in)

4 I've got something in my left eye and I can't _____. (get out)

5 When you receive your parcel, please _____ for damage. (look over)

6 Once time is gone, we will never _____. (get back)

7 The maintenance light is still on. How can I _____? (switch off)

8 They're very similar. Indeed I can hardly _____. (tell apart)

2 ▶ 다양한 구동사

1 구동사(2어동사)

부사와 전치사	의미	examples(예)	
in, into, out	안, 밖	get in 들어가다 break in 침입하다 run into 우연히 만나다 break out 발발하다 figure out 이해하다 pick out 고르다 work out 운동하다	check in 숙박 수속하다 take in 받아들이다, 속이다 hand out 제출하다 speak out 솔직히 말하다 turn out 몰아내다, 생산하다 put out 끄다, 내놓다 make out 이해하다
on, off	켜진, 입은, 꺼진, 떨어져	put on 입다 go on 계속하다 live on ~을 먹고살다 count on 의지하다 get off 내리다, 출발하다 set off 시작하다 put off 연기하다 take off 벗다, 출발하다	keep on 계속하다 take on 떠맡다 depend on 의지하다 turn on 켜다 drop off 탈락시키다 give off (냄새를) 발산하다 turn off 끄다 pay off 빚을 청산하다
away, back	저멀리, 떨어져, 뒤로, 돌아와서	drive away 쫓아버리다 run away 도망치다 take away 앗아가다 keep back 숨기다 put back 되돌려 놓다	give away 주어버리다 keep away 멀리하다 put away 치우다 throw away 던져버리다 give back 돌려주다
up, down	위, 모두 아래	give up 포기하다 get up 일어나다 stay up 밤샘하다 set up 세우다 make up 구성하다 pick up 고르다	show up 나타나다 turn up 뒤집다, 나타나다 grow up 성장하다 bring up 기르다 call up 전화걸다 turn down 거절하다
for, over, by 등		look for 찾다 get through 겪다 drop by 잠깐 들르다 go over 검토하다 look after 돌보다	allow for 참작하다 get over 극복하다 laugh at 비웃다 come across 우연히 만나다 bring about 야기하다
3어동사		catch up with 따라 잡다 get through with 끝내다 look forward to 기대하다	make up for 보충하다 get on with 잘 지내다 put up with 참다

1

동사와 전치사가 결합하여 구동사를 만들 때,
동사 본래의 의미가 달라지게 된다.
전치사는 본래의 의미를 지니고 있으므로,
전치사나 부사를 중심으로 동사구를 기억한
다.

EXERCISE

A Complete the following sentences using the words in the box.

out	on	off	in	up	down	with

1 I can't figure _____out_____ what is going on here.

2 How late did you stay _____ on Christmas Eve?

3 I am really sad you did not get along _____ your friends.

4 Where did you grow _____ in Canada and where do you live now?

5 Do you know how water puts _____ the fire despite having oxygen?

6 Don't be afraid to turn _____ a job offer if it isn't right for your career goals.

B Complete the following sentences using the words in the box.

come	go	find	give	put	make	bring	grow	pick

1 How and when did you _____come_____ across these cards?

2 The streets _____ off the smell of cold ashes.

3 You must _____ on your own oxygen mask first in fire.

4 All you have to do is _____ up your mind to work at it.

5 I would like to _____ out the meaning behind their names.

6 I'll give you tips on how to _____ out apples at the grocery store.

7 I can't understand how volcanic eruption would _____ about earthquakes.

C Match these phrasal verbs with the explanations on the right.

1 When they <u>grow up</u>, they have to work for a living.

2 We have <u>gone through</u> many difficulties in that time.

3 Why don't you <u>call up</u> your mother?

4 My friend is going to <u>drop by</u> my house today.

5 Can you <u>live on</u> beer, water and vitamins?

6 I <u>came across</u> an interesting blog on immigration issues.

7 I can't <u>make out</u> what he means.

8 I will <u>pay</u> you <u>back</u> for this damage!

9 A trained nurse wants to <u>look after</u> the elderly.

a. get my revenge

b. find unexpectedly

c. take care of

d. visit

e. become adults

f. phone

g. understand

h. experience

i. support oneself

A Choose the right words for (A) and (B).

Even if (A) <putting / turning> a computer off once a day shortened its overall life by only a few days, it wouldn't pay to (B) <keep it on / keep on it> all the time. Probably the best compromise is to shut your computer down at the end of the day and turn it back on the next day.

B Read and answer the questions in English.

The ring on one's finger may get a little bit tighter during pregnancy. I'm just curious if I should take off my ring when my finger begins to swell. I wonder if I should (A) <keep it off / keep off it> until after the baby is born, and the swelling goes down. Frankly, I'd prefer to (B) <leave it on / leave on it> because I personally hate the thought of not wearing my wedding ring. I've been trying to ignore my finger which starts to swell like a sausage. However, I have contemplated buying an inexpensive, fake ring for the time being to wear instead of my wedding band. My friend (C) <took hers off / took off hers> when she was pregnant, and she wore a different, larger ring in its place.

1 Choose the right words for (A), (B) and (C).

2 What does the author think is the best way to avoid any problems with a ring finger?
   → You have to _____ .

C Read and answer the question in English. 기출 응용

Possibly the most effective way to focus on your goals <them / is / to / down / write>. Although this may sound like an obvious first step, it is a step that many people ignore. As a result, their goals often remain unfocused, and therefore unrealized. Go to a fairly quiet place where you are not likely to be disturbed. Make a list of every goal you have. Include goals about finances, relationships, and your career. Be as specific as possible.

1 Complete the sentence rearranging the words in the bracket.
   → Possibly the most effective way to focus on your goals _____ .

Ⓐ shorten 줄이다, 단축시키다 overall 종합의, 전체의 Ⓑ pregnancy 임신 swell 부풀다(swell–swelled–swollen) fake 가짜 Ⓒ fairly 상당히 finance 재정, 재무 specific 특유한, 특정한

현재분사와 과거분사

- -

1 현재분사와 과거분사
2 분사구문

Questions

1 왜 ing와 ed가 아니라 분사(分詞)라고 부를까?

2 현재분사와 과거분사를 확실하고 간단하게 기억하는 방법은?

3 왜 어법시험과 독해지문에는 분사가 자주 등장하지?

Answers

1 그냥 과거분사와 현재분사 2개가 있다는 의미로 사용하며, 영어로 '나누어진
것'이라는 participle로 표현할 뿐이다.

2 현재분사(-ing)는 '직접~하는'의 의미를, 과거분사(-ed)는 '~되어지는'의 수
동적인 의미로 해석하면 되는데!

3 우리말은 형용사가 발달되어 있으며, 영어는 동사가 매우 잘 발달되어 있다.
'노란, 누런, 샛노란, 누리끼리한, 노릿노릿한…'처럼 다양한 표현이 가능하
다. 영어에서 동사를 다양한 어감과 용도로 사용하는 방법이 바로 현재분사와
과거분사를 이용하는 것이다.

현재분사와 과거분사

1 형용사 역할의 분사 (-ing/-ed adjective)

(1) 분사 (-ing/-ed)+명사

They don't want to disturb **the sleeping child.**

Many of our residents complain about **the barking dog.**

Our company moved to **the well-heated building.**

The police arrested four men after they found **the stolen car.**

(2) 명사+분사(-ing/-ed)

The **student waiting** for me outdoors is my friend.

He was looking at **the guy wearing** the black hat.

People invited to the party should be close friends.

There are many **soldiers wounded** in the battlefield.

2 합성어 분사

People wish for **long-lasting** batteries for mobile phones.

Vitamin E helps promote **good-looking** skin.

I wanted to make some **half-boiled** eggs for my breakfast.

He pictured himself skiing on **snow-covered** slopes.

3 자동사+ing

the existing laws	the remaining players
the coming wars	the good-looking glasses
the occurring location	the falling price
the lying dog	the flying bat

The increase in smokers is due to **the falling price** of cigarettes.

How will **the coming wars** affect the world economy?

4 주어를 설명하는 주격보어, 목적어를 설명하는 목적격보어

(1) 주격 보어(subjective complement)-S+V+주격보어

People sat down under the tree / **reading** a novel.

The soldiers sat down / **wounded** on the back.

(2) 목적격 보어(objective complement)-S+V+목적어+목적보어

We found the child **lying** on the floor.

Please keep the door **closed** during the night.

1

(1) 분사는 명사의 앞뒤에서 명사를 수식하는 형용사의 역할을 한다.

– 능동 – 주어는 child

– 능동 – 주어는 dog

– 수동 – 주어는 building

– 수동 – 주어는 car

(2) 현재분사는 주어가 직접 동작을 하는 능동, 과거분사는 동작을 당하는 수동적 의미이다.
분사가 다른 수식어와 함께 있으면, 분사(-ing, -ed)는 뒤에서 앞의 명사를 수식한다.

– 수동 – 주어는 people

– 수동 – 주어는 soldiers

2

– 자. last 지속하다

– 자. look 보이다

– 타. boil 끓이다

– 타. cover 덮다

3

자동사는 수동형(be+과거분사)이 불가능하므로 현재분사(-ing) 형태로만 쓰인다.

– 현행법, 남은 선수들

– 다가오는 전쟁, 멋있는 안경

– 발생 현장, 하락하는 가격

– 누워있는 개, 날아가는 박쥐

4

(1) 주어를 설명해주는 보어 위치에 현재분사와 과거분사가 올 수 있다.

– 능동 – 주어는 people

– 수동 – 주어는 soldier

(2) 분사의 의미상 주어인 목적어가 능동적이면 현재분사, 수동적이면 과거분사

– 능동 – 주어는 child

– 수동 – 주어는 door

E EXERCISE

A Choose the right words.

1 Everyone in the call center heard him <yelled / yelling> at me.

2 Do you know what is the most <selling / sold> car in Germany?

3 The soldier caught the man <stealing / stole> a car in the garage.

4 A supermarket today sells a pack of four <boiled / boiling> eggs.

5 She is called Barbara and is married to a man <called / calling> Prince.

6 Didn't you notice him <chasing / chased> the dog up and down the mountain?

7 The film tells the story of a man <catching / caught> in the middle of the battles.

B Complete the sentences using the given words.

1 repair   a) I watched a tall man ___repairing___ the damage last night.
           b) I had a similar problem with a car ___repaired___ last month.

2 invite   a) We sent the letter _____ the members of the club.
           b) They announced the names of the guests _____ to the party.

3 provide   a) People _____ support often need to be supported themselves.
           b) The books _____ from the US are generally in English.

4 leave   a) They've all moved out _____ a mess behind.
           b) Cleaning up the waste _____ behind will cost nearly $1.5 billion.

5 lift   a) I saw a man _____ a heavy wooden box.
           b) We returned to find our luggage _____ out into the hallway.

6 write   a) The professor is interested in the student _____ a historical novel.
           b) The information is mostly from reports _____ in English.

C Rearrange the words to complete the sentences.

1 I noticed the horse <washing / while / eating / a box / my car>.
   → I noticed the horse _____

2 I love <covered / seeing / with snow / the surrounding Alps>.
   → I love _____

3 He wanted <before / the work / the start of summer / finished>.
   → He wanted _____

4 We discussed <brought up / the issue / the school fees / regarding>.   *school fee 수업료
   → We discussed _____

2 ▶ 분사구문(Participial Construction)

1 분사구문의 의미

Arriving at the park at 2 p.m., I took up a good position.
(=After I arrived at the park at 2 p.m., I~)
Not **knowing** how to use the tool, she looked around for help.
(=As she didn't know how to use the tool, she~)

Written in German, the letter was not easy to understand.
(=As it was written in Germany, the letter~)
Attacked on the head, he was not injured at all.
(=Though he was attacked on the head, he~)

1
분사구문은 하나의 독립된 절(접속사+S+V)
을 간결하게 줄인 형태이다.
* 현재분사는 능동을, 과거분사는 수동을 나
타내는 부사절을 만든다.
* 부정어는 분사 앞에 둔다.

> 자주 등장하는 분사구문
> * Judging from ~ ~로 판단하면
> * Considering ~ ~를 고려하면
> * Supposing ~ ~을 가정하면
> * Frankly speaking ~ 솔직히 말하면

2 다양한 분사구문

(1) 현재분사 구문

Saying good bye to my mother, I left the hometown.
Starting right now, you will arrive on time.
The typhoon hit the city, **causing** great damage.

(2) 과거분사 구문

Wounded by the hand, he was sent to the hospital.
Seen from the moon, the earth looks like a ball.
He went to bed, **pleased** with what she had done.

2
(1) 달리 표시가 없다면 주절의 주어가 분사
구문의 주어이다.
– 능동 – 주어는 I

– 능동 – 주어는 you

– 능동 – 주어는 typhoon

(2) 분사구문이 수동형태인 경우 being을
일반적으로 생략한다.
– 수동 – 주어는 he

– 수동 – 주어는 the earth

– 수동 – 주어는 He

3 접속사+분사(conjunction+participle)

When **entering** the room, he found his son was playing a videogame.
(=When he entered the room, he found~)
If **seen** and **attacked** by a dog, skunks would give off gas.
(=If **they were** seen and attacked by a dog, skunks~)

3
분사구문은 완전한 문장(접속사+S+V~)을
줄인 형태이며, 의미를 분명히 하기 위해 분
사 앞에 접속사를 제시할 수도 있다.

> * As expected
>   (=As it is expected)
> * More than doubled
>   (=More than it is doubled)
> * When accompanied with~
>   (=When you are accompanied with~)

4 with+목적어+분사

With night coming on, the wind roared in the pines above.
The boy ran to the school **with his dog following** close behind.
I saw a woman walking **with her arms folded** across her chest.
The picture shows a man seated **with his legs crossed**.

4
의미상주어인 목적어가 능동이면 현재분사,
수동이면 과거분사를 사용한다.

EXERCISE

A   Choose the right words.

1   If <asked / asking>, I will tell him the truth.

2   <Keeping / Kept> the bear in the dark, she usually feeds it once a day.

3   <Taken / Taking> the books, Mrs. Cohen didn't say a word to Danny.

4   After <obtained / obtaining> a visa, Saka wished to enter Indonesia again.

5   <Contained / Containing> cholesterol, animal fat is dangerous in large amounts.

6   <Attacked / Attacking> from the rear, they would move the aircraft back and forth.

7   <Expected / Expecting> to fly in space, Vela intends to manufacture jet-like vehicles.

B   Match the beginning of each sentence with the most appropriate ending.

1   Breaking windows of a building,   a. he was just looking around the shop.

2   Hit by the car from the rear,   b. the policeman got very angry.

3   Arriving at the stadium for the opening game, c. the driver was not much injured.

4   Attacked and kicked by a drunken man,   d. he was punished severely.

5   Not having enough money,   e. the players saw many supporters.

6   Having a meeting with the prime minister,   f. the king expressed his satisfaction.

C   Complete the sentences using the given words.

1   오른쪽 코너를 돌면 너는 그 교회를 발견할 것이다.
    →　　　　*Turning to the right corner*　　　　, you'll find the church. (turn)

2   산에서 보면 그 집은 매우 작아 보일 것이다.
    →　　　　　　　　　　　　　　　　　, the house will look very small. (see)

3   그 책은 쉬운 영어로 쓰여서 베스트셀러가 되었다.
    →　　　　　　　　　　　　　　　　　, the book became a best-seller. (write)

4   그는 혼자 남겨졌을 때 두려움과 당황스러움을 느꼈다.
    →　　　　　　　　　　　　　　　　　, he felt terrified and embarrassed. (leave)

5   그는 멀리 떨어져 살았기에 그를 찾는 방문객이 별로 없다.
    →　　　　　　　　　　　　　　　　　, he has few visitors. (live)

Choose the right words for (A) and (B).

> One special phenomenon happened every full moon in October. We all passed the night watching lightboats (A) <going / to go> slowly up and down the river. We enjoyed eating grilled trout and other delicious food (B) <served / serving> in abundance at the seashore as parties went on there.

 Read and answer the questions in English.

> Crude oil is mostly found in underground areas called reservoirs. (A) <Coming / To come> out of the ground, oil is a thick liquid, brown or greenish-black in color, which is called crude oil. Oil was formed from the remains of tiny sea plants and animals (B) <catching / caught> between layers of rock. Over the years, the remains were covered by layers of mud and sediment. Heat and pressure from these layers helped the remains turn into crude oil. Oil wells are holes (C) <drilled / drilling> down into the oil pools, (D)<allowed / allowing> the crude oil to rise to the surface.

1 Choose the right words for (A), (B), (C) and (D).

2 According to the passage, what is oil made of?
   → Oil is made of _____.

 Read and answer the question in English. 기출 응용

> To be a mathematician you don't need an expensive laboratory. The typical equipment of a mathematician is a blackboard and chalk. It is better to do mathematics on a blackboard than on a piece of paper because chalk is easier to erase, and mathematical research is often filled with mistakes. One more thing you need to do is 수학에 전념하는 클럽에 가입하는 것이다. Not many mathematicians can work alone; they need to talk about what they are doing. If you want to be a mathematician, you had better expose your new ideas to the criticism of others. It is possible to contain hidden assumptions that you do not see but that are obvious to others.

1 Rearrange the words to have the same meaning as the underlined part.
   → One more thing you need to do is <a club / devoted to / mathematics / to join>
   _____.

Ⓐ phenomenon 현상 trout 송어 abundance 풍부 Ⓑ crude oil 원유 liquid 액체 remains 유해, 유물 sediment 퇴적물 layer 겹, 층
Ⓒ laboratory 실험실 equipment 장비 expose 노출시키다 criticism 비판 assumption 가정, 가설

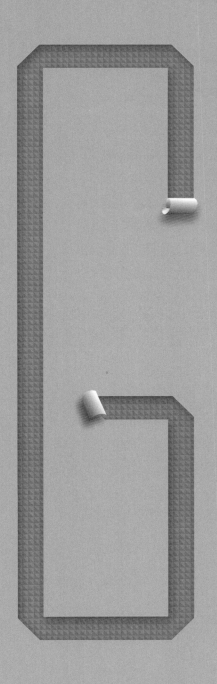

Unit 21

-ing/-ed의 형용사
- -
1 -ing와 -ed 형태의 형용사 Ⅰ
2 -ing와 -ed 형태의 형용사 Ⅱ

Questions
1 감정을 나타내는 동사는 정말 모두 타동사인가요?

2 사람이 주어이면 -ing를, 사물이 주어이면 과거분사가 오나요?

3 감정동사로 분류된 것들을 다 외워야 하는지?

Answers
1 주어의 감정이나 기분은 외부의 무엇이 그렇게 만드는 것이다. 그래서 '~하게 하다'의미의 타동사로만 사용된다.

2 아니다! 무엇이든지 주어(主語)가 직접 그렇게 만드는 경우이면 능동인 현재분사를, 주어가 당하는 내용이면 수동인 과거분사를 사용한다.

3 그냥 단어 외우듯 동사를 기억하면 된다. 현재분사인가 과거분사인가는 문맥에 맡겨두자!

-ing와 -ed 형태의 형용사(감정동사) Ⅰ

1 감정동사는 타동사!

These were some examples of how to **annoy** your roommate.
Her musical gift **impressed** quite a few teachers.

An earthquake shock **was terrifying** the inhabitants of the village.
She **was surprising** me. She pushed me back down.

> **1**
> 감정동사는 반드시 목적어를 필요로 하는 타동사로만 쓰이며, 능동과 수동적 의미에 따라 -ing와 -ed의 형태로 바뀐다.

2 -ed와 -ing로 끝나는 형용사

	감정동사	수동(S+be+pp)	능동(현재분사) .	
1	please 기쁘게 하다	I am pleased	It is pleasing	
2	satisfy 만족시키다	satisfied	satisfying	
3	excite 열광시키다	excited	exciting	
4	interest 관심있게 하다	interested	interesting	
5	delight 기쁘게 하다	delighted	delighting	
6	amuse 재미나게 하다	amused	amusing	
7	touch 감동시키다	touched	touching	= move
8	amaze 놀라게 하다	amazed	amazing	= astonish
9	concern 관심있게 하다	concerned	concerning	
10	encourage 용기를 주다	encouraged	encouraging	
11	confuse 혼란케하다	confused	confusing	
12	irritate 짜증나게 하다	irritated	irritating	
13	bore 지루하게 하다	bored	boring	
14	frighten 놀라게 하다	frightened	frightening	
15	disappoint 실망시키다	disappointed	disappointing	
16	surprise 놀라게 하다	surprised	surprising	
17	fascinate 매혹시키다	fascinated	fascinating	= charm
18	attract 매혹시키다	attracted	attracting	
19	exhaust 지치게 하다	exhausted	exhausting	
20	embarrass 당황케하다	embarrassed	embarrassing	
21	depress 낙담시키다	depressed	depressing	
22	bewilder 당황케하다	bewildered	bewildering	
23	upset 뒤집다,당황케하다	upset	upsetting	
24	annoy 귀찮게 하다	annoyed	annoying	
25	terrify 겁나게 하다	terrified	terrifying	= horrify
26	impress 감동시키다	impressed	impressing	
27	worry 걱정케하다	worried	worrying	
28	scare 겁주다	scared	scaring	
29	frustrate 좌절시키다	frustrated	frustrating	
30	shock 충격을 주다	shocked	shocking	
31	trouble 난처하게 하다	troubled	troubling	

EXERCISE

A Choose the right words.

1 People were <disappointed / disappointing> to see the bad results.

2 I find it very <exciting / irritating> to watch actors needlessly smoking.

3 We are all <exhausted / bored> in the storm and don't have enough food left.

4 When night comes, Karen is very cold and <impressed / scared> to death.

5 You're going to be so <tired / tiring> when you get home after a soccer game.

6 It's <embarrassing / boring> to send an e-mail carelessly to the wrong person.

7 When he taught world history, I became <confused / fascinated> and tired.

B Complete the sentences using the given words.

1 bore   a) I had nothing to do. I was ___*bored*___ and lonely.
          b) I haven't read the book you gave me. It was so ___*boring*___ .

2 interest a) She is an _____ speaker. She certainly held our attention.
          b) She was _____ in dieting and working out.

3 depress   a) The bad news was very _____ .
          b) They feel lonely and _____ when they have no one to love.

4 terrify   a) My mother's anger rose up like a _____ wave in my mind.
          b) She felt _____ and helpless, so she wanted to run away.

5 disappoint a) I feel _____ to have lost the match.
          b) He's been very _____ in this season. He should be dismissed.

6 embarrass a) He was dreadfully late. It was very _____ .
          b) They're feeling _____ , scared, or stressed.

C Complete the sentences so that they mean the same as the first sentence.

1 The results surprised us.   - It was ___*surprising*___ results.
2 He was delighted at receiving many letters. - He was a _____ man.
3 The film has bored audiences.   - It is a _____ film.
4 The entire world was horrified by the attack. - It was a _____ attack.
5 The false fact frustrates the students.   - They are _____ students.
6 My puppy irritated me sometimes.   - It was an _____ puppy.

2 ▶ -ing/-ed 형태의 형용사(감정동사) Ⅱ

1 능동(active)과 수동(passive)의 구분

The news **disappointed** my father.
The report **satisfied** my professor.
I found the results **disappointing**.

My father **was disappointed** by the news.
My professor **was satisfied** with the report.
The results were found **disappointing**.

> 1
> 감정동사는 주로 사물이 주어로 등장하는 타동사이다.
> 주어+동사의 관계가 능동인가 수동인가에 따라 분사의 종류(현재분사와 과거분사)가 바뀐다.

2 감정동사의 형용사형+명사

(1) 능동적 의미

Spend your holiday with fun and **exciting games**.
He stands outside while I sit in **the boring class**.
Thank you for your wonderful, **amazing, touching, and fascinating** music and sound.

> 2
> (1) 의미상 주어인 명사가 동작의 주체인 경우 현재분사를 사용한다.
> – 주어: games
> – 주어: class

(2) 수동적 의미

He was one of many **delighted students** at the Maryport school.
The bored students have stopped listening to the teacher.
Our school's success is measured by **the satisfied parents**.
Sometimes the **embarrassed** person tries to mask embarrassment with smiles or nervous laughter.

> (2) 의미상 주어인 명사가 동작을 당하는 경우에는 과거분사를 사용한다.
> – 주어: students
> – 주어: students
> – 주어: parents
> – 주어: person

3 보어

(1) 능동적 의미

Indeed she shouldn't drink! She was **embarrassing**!
Holiday season seems **exciting** and festive to me.
I found the book **interesting** and logical.
You will find the lesson **boring** and won't concentrate.

> 3
> (1) 주어가 사물과 사람에 관계없이, 능동적인 의미에는 현재분사를 사용한다.

(2) 수동적 의미

They were **embarrassed** at the sight.
Everyone thought it was funny, but she was not **amused**.
It's the only time I ever saw my mother **frightened**.
His failure in exam made me **disappointed**.

> (2) 사람의 기분과 감정은 '~놀라게 된다', '기쁘게 된다' 처럼 주로 수동적의미로 표현된다.
> 주어가 사물과 사람에 관계없이, 수동의 의미에는 과거분사를 사용한다.

E EXERCISE

A Choose the right words.

1 <Compared / Comparing> with other teas, the quality is indeed higher.

2 The panda developed very slowly, <comparing / compared> with other animals.

3 Jack stopped reading the novel because he found it very <bored / boring>.

4 After an <exhausting / exhausted> day, we returned home, tired and thirsty.

5 Jane won three gold medals in the Olympics. We were really <amazing / amazed>.

6 It is very <surprising / surprised> that Korean people can't speak English well.

7 Do you ever feel sick, confused, or very <tiring / tired> after a long plane ride?

B Complete the sentences using the given words.

1 I received a ___confusing___ notice from my landlord that is difficult to follow. (confuse)

2 Ryan was so badly ill that he simply has the look of an _____ man. (annoy)

3 A _____ worker has usually given up searching for a job. (discourage)

4 Helping a _____ friend takes some care and lots of planning. (depress)

5 Everyone has experienced a few _____ stories in person. (scare)

6 An _____ bride comes back to the booth to book her wedding. (excite)

7 I can't really give you a _____ answer to the question. (satisfy)

C Complete the sentences.

1 The novel fascinated me. For me, the novel was ___fascinating___ . I was ___fascinated___ .

2 The novel shocked Harry. He was _____ . For him, the novel was _____ .

3 The game bored me. I was _____ . To me, the game was _____ .

4 The game excited Rosa. She was _____ . To Rosa, the game was _____ .

5 The TV show delighted me. I was _____ . To me, the TV show was _____ .

6 The TV show didn't satisfied Mary. To Mary, the TV show wasn't _____ .

7 The player discouraged supporters. Supporters were _____ .

8 The player satisfied supporters. Supporters were _____ .

9 The drama entertained Mark. Mark was _____ . To Mark, the drama was _____ .

10 The drama didn't amuse me. I _____ . To me, the drama _____ .

Further Study

A Choose the right words for (A), (B) and (C).

I was very (A) <disappointed / disappointing> with Jackie. He was smaller and thinner than I had expected from the advertisement I had seen. His voice had an (B) <annoyed / annoying> accent, which my son started to copy. There were not many changes in his performance and my kid got (C) <bored / boring> very quickly with him.

B Read and answer the questions in English.

A man went into a new fruit shop in New York. He picked some oranges but he was (A) <shocked / shocking> when the shop assistant asked him for $19.50. He gave the girl a $20 bill and said, "Your prices are (B) <shocked / shocking>." Then he left the shop. The assistant ran after him and said, "Sir, you've forgotten your change." The man turned around and said, "Oh, you'd better keep it. I stepped on a grape on the way out."

1 Choose the right words for (A) and (B).

2 Complete the sentence so that the meaning is similar to the above passage.
 → The expensive orange _____ him. It had a _____ price. (shock)

C Read and answer the question in English.

I am delighted to introduce you to this exciting piece of land. From the largest dinosaur park to the most majestic mountains, Kariba offers charming attractions for everyone. ① A little more exploration uncovers fascinating cultural attractions and an exciting shopping scene. ② Perhaps surprisingly, most of the city's most appealing tourist sites offer free admission. ③ All across Kariba, people are preparing for delighting annual festivals and events that expect to draw large and delighted crowds. ④ Nearby you can shop, hike, golf, ski, climb, bike or fish for trout in a tumbling stream. ⑤ Kariba has fields of fluffy snow for skiing, frozen lakes for skating, and more winter activities than imaginable.

1 Where would the following sentence best fit in ①~⑤?

Who says you can't do it all in one place?

Ⓐ performance 연기, 연주, 수행 Ⓑ assistant 보조원 bill 청구서 Ⓒ dinosaur 공룡 majestic 장엄한 attraction 매력, 인기거리 annual 연간의 fluffy 푹신한

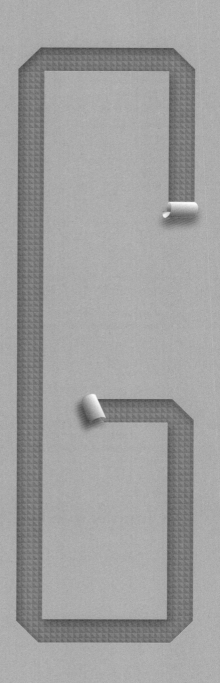

Unit 22

수동태 문장-1

1 be+과거분사
2 주의할 수동태 표현

Questions

1 수동태를 왜 사용해야 하는 것이지?

2 be+과거분사의 해석은 무조건 '되어지다'인가?

3 복잡하다! 정말 중요한 것이 무엇인지 알 수 없나?

Answers

1 주어가 가해자인가 피해자인가를 구분해보자는 것이다. 항상 주어를 중심으로 판단하는 것이 중요하다. 그러므로 수동태 문장으로 바꾸는 연습보다 수동 형태의 문장을 활용하고 이해하는 것이 중요하다.

2 주어(subject)가 동작을 가하는 입장이면 능동이고 당하는 입장이면 수동이므로, 무조건 '되어지다'가 아니라 '가하다'와 '당하다'는 의미를 이해해야 한다.

3 수동태(be+과거분사)의 표현을 적절하게 사용하고 빨리 이해하는 연습이 더 중요하다. 수동태로 사용되는 표현 자체에 익숙해야 한다.

1 ▶ be+과거분사(Past Participle)

1 능동과 수동의 관계(active and passive)

(1) 수동태 문장

He **saw** the bird flying high from tree to tree. (주어가 '직접 보았다')
The bird **was seen** flying high in the sky. (주어가 '목격되었다')

My father **broke** the door open. (주어가 '문을 부수고 열었다')
The door **was broken** open on the left side. (주어가 '부수어졌다')

(2) 누가 주어인가?

It is necessary <u>for the dog</u> **to be trained** for the test.
We want <u>the game</u> **to be cancelled** because of rain.
<u>The number</u> **is expected** to increase steadily.

(3) 수동태를 해석할 때

Actress Brooke **was seen** shopping in Malibu the other day.
I don't know if the watch **was stolen** or not.
I **was shown** a picture of my aunt Jean in an exhibition.

2 수동태의 핵심 – 동사의 형태

(1) 자동사(intransitive verb)

주요 자동사	*appear, seem, lie, die, rise, sit, arise, look, fall *disappear, occur, happen, exist, remain, stay, wait 등

Water might **disappear** into the air by evaporating quickly.
More important debates may **arise** about school work.

(2) 구동사(2어 동사)의 수동태

The basketball player was **laughed at** because of his short height.
He was **brought up** by an aunt in his youth.
My mother was **taken good care of** and she is fine now.

(3) 수동태(passive)의 시제(tense)

The hotel tax **has been increased** from 7% to 9%.
Ellie **is being taken** by ambulance to the nearest hospital.
Every sin of every man can **be punished and forgiven**.

1

(1) 능동은 주어가 직접 동작을 하며, 수동은 주어가 동작을 당하는 경우이다.
* 수동태의 동사형태는 **be+과거분사**이며, 행위자인 **by**+목적격은 생략할 수 있다.

(2) 주어가 동작을 당하면 수동태(**be**+과거분사)가 되며, 주어가 '~당하다, ~되어지다'로 해석.
– 주어는 the game
– 주어는 The number

(3) 주어는 '동작을 당하다, ~되어지다'로 해석된다.
– 목격되다
– 도난당하다
– 보다 – 동작의 반대

2

(1) 자동사는 주어가 직접 동작을 하므로 수동태(**be**+과거분사)로 쓰이지 않는다.

수동태 표현이 어색한 타동사(have, resemble, lack, suit 등)는 능동표현만 사용한다.

(2) 2어 동사와 3어 동사는 수동태에서 하나의 동사로 취급하여 분리되지 않는다.
– 비웃다
– 기르다
– 잘 돌보다

(3) 수동태에서도 단순, 완료, 진행 등 모든 시제가 등장할 수 있다.

EXERCISE

A   Choose the right words.

1   It appears the phone bill has not <been paid / paid>.

2   The telephone has <been disconnected / disconnected>.

3   We want the results to <be remained / remain> on the page.

4   No one knows why the dinosaur <disappeared / was disappeared>.

5   Smoking is not <permitted / permitting> anywhere on this campus.

6   Since then nothing has really <been happened / happened> to Mark.

7   The old stone house is <operated / operating> as a historical center.

8   That vast army <divided / got divided> into groups and attacked the enemy.

B   Complete the sentences using the given words.

1   explain   a. The results were ___explained___ in terms of evolutionary theory.
             b. A Turkish man was ___explaining___ to me about the joys of massage.

2   prepare   a. Syria was _____ for a large-scale Israeli attack.
             b. The report was _____ for the benefit of the bank.

3   invent   a. Mr. Toshiaki has been _____ a new puzzle game for the blind.
             b. No effective method has been _____ to deal with the disease.

4   recognize a. The UFO phenomenon in Mexico has been _____ as a fact.
             b. Our community has _____ the rights of the children.

5   postpone   a. A girl whose heart operation was _____ died yesterday.
             b. A court _____ the hearing till January 15 due to the earthquake.

6   expose   a. Your personal data has been _____ due to the stolen computers.
             b. Many people were _____ to radiation and other toxic substance.

C   Match the sentences on the left with one on the right.

1   *He lives in a small house.* ———————   *a. It was built about forty years ago.*

2   Chinese is worth learning.   b. She is known for composing songs.

3   My niece is a musician.   c. It is being shown at our local cinema.

4   The Virginia film is marvellous.   d. It is spoken in a lot of Asian countries.

5   The airport was too small for visitors. e. They had to be taken to the hospital.

6   The students stopped breathing.   f. The walls and ceilings had to be repaired.

7   I had a severe leak from the roof.   g. A new airport is being built now.

2 ▶ 주의할 수동태 표현 (수동태의 동사 형태)

1 수동태의 해석

| 주어 + | be told~ 듣다 | be shown~ 보다 | be taught~ 배우다 |
| | be lent~ 빌리다 | be given~ 받다 | be heard~ 말하다 |

We **gave** the police the information.
→ The police **were given** the information by us.
→ The information **was given** to the police by us.

I **was told** a ghost story by my grandmother.
I have **been taught** English by my own mother.
Students **were shown** a picture of an African boy.

> 1
> 수동태는 주어인 사람이나 사물이 동작을 '~당하다, ~되어지다, ~받다'로 해석된다.
> * S+V+간접목적어+직접목적어의 문장에서 직접목적어가 주어로 오는 수동태 해석에 주의한다.
>
> – 경찰은 ~를 받았다
>
> – 정보가 ~에게 주어진다
>
> – ~듣다
>
> – ~배우다
>
> – ~보다

2 동사+to be+과거분사

> His colleagues started to respect Tim.
> → Tim started to be respected (by his colleagues).

She came to **be recognized** / as the best violinist in our school.
She tends to **be frustrated** / because of her current condition.
The tin opener seems to **be designed** / for left-handed people.

> 2
> 수동태를 포함한 동사 뒤에 끊어읽기
> seem to, appear to, begin to, come to, continue to, tend to 등의 경우에 나타나는 형태이다.
>
> 동사+to 동사원형을 하나의 동사로 간주하여, 수동태에서 동사+to be+과거분사가 된다.

3 be+과거분사+~ing

> They saw him climbing over the fence.
> → He **was seen** climbing over the fence.

She **was heard** / saying : "Please call the police."
He **was noticed** / making a little movement and getting up.
He **was found** / sleeping in a neighbours' garage.

> 3
> 분사 앞에서 끊어읽기
> 주어+동사+목적어+보어에서 보어 위치에 현재분사가 오는 문장이 수동태로 표현되었다.

4 be+과거분사+to~

> Mr. Price taught Peter to sing.
> → Peter **was taught to sing** (by Mr. Price).

At the clinic, I **was advised** / to bring my child for testing.
He **was allowed** / to return to the Philippines.
We **were supposed** / to perform Korean music and dance.

> 4
> 부정사 앞에서 끊어읽기
> 동사+목적어+to부정사 형태의 문장이 수동태로 나타난 경우이다.

E EXERCISE

A

Match the beginning of each sentence with the most appropriate ending.

1 Pam has her own car
Pam has her own chauffeur

   a. because she likes driving.
   b. because she likes being driven.

2 To advertise my products, I gave
To advertise my products, I was given

   a. everybody's address.
   b. everybody my address.

3 Today this tiger killed
Today this tiger was killed

   a. by two hunters.
   b. two hunters.

4 Before the storm everyone
Before the storm the weatherman

   a. was told to stay inside their homes.
   b. told people to stay inside their homes.

5 Tony is a music student now;
Dick is a music teacher now;

   a. he's teaching the piano.
   b. he's being taught the piano.

B

Complete the sentences using the given words.

1 notice
  a. She ___*was noticed*___ coming into class late.
  b. I ___*noticed*___ her carrying a yellow bag.

2 catch
  a. I _____ them taking apples from my garden.
  b. They _____ stealing apples from the farmer's fields.

3 hear
  a. As he fell into the pool, he _____ himself shouting for help.
  b. Jones _____ shouting at Mrs. Markham before the robbery.

4 find
  a. We _____ the bills waiting for us when we got home.
  b. They _____ entering the building with knives.

C

Complete the sentences using the given words.

1 The children ___*were seen playing football in the park this morning.*___ (play)
〈아이들이 오늘 아침 공원에서 축구하는 모습이 목격되었다.〉

2 It is said that Barry _____ (allow)
〈Barry는 예일 대학에 입학을 허락받았다고 한다.〉

3 The door appears _____ (make)
〈그 문은 플라스틱을 재료로 만들어진 것 같다.〉

4 Bell said he _____ (tell)
〈Bell은 그가 그 프로그램에 관한 정보를 들었다고 말했다.〉

A Choose the right words for (A), (B) and (C).

A man tried to sell a painting that had (A) <been stolen / robbed>. At first the painting was owned by Christine Jones, aged 85. She had (B) <been owned / owned> it since 1926, when it (C) <gave / was given> to her as a wedding present.

B Read and answer the questions in English.

Restless legs syndrome is a common sleep disorder affecting about 1 in 10 adults. The disorder is caused by an uncontrollable desire to move the legs. Ten years ago, I fractured my ankle. My leg (A) <placed / was placed> in a cast and I was told to keep the leg suspended for at least a month. What I can never forget is that my dreams (B) <filled / were filled> with unstable movements, which would wake me up. Moreover, when trying to sleep, my limbs become prickly and this disorder could only (C) <be relieved / relieve> by getting up and moving around. Needless to say, sleeping when you have this syndrome is next to impossible. Restless legs syndrome <is said / to be / causes / of / one of the most common / insomnia>.

1 Choose the right words for (A), (B) and (C).

2 Rearrange the words to complete the sentence.
→ Restless legs syndrome _____ .

C Read and answer the question in English.

How can you obtain hydrogen from water? Since water is made up of 2 hydrogen atoms and 1 oxygen atom, water can be broken down and separated into hydrogen and oxygen supplying a lot of energy. To obtain hydrogen from water, you need to build a device that can electrolyze water. This device can be easily made with a few tools you can get in any hardware store. First, you have to apply enough energy to break its atomic bonds. A battery is connected to two electrodes, which are submerged in water. Hydrogen bubbles from one of the electrodes, and oxygen from the other. This is a major way to obtain hydrogen. The hydrogen <can be / acquired / as an energy source / from this process / used>.

1 Rearrange the words in the bracket to complete the sentence.
→ The hydrogen _____ .

A own 소유하다 wedding present 결혼선물 **B** restless 불안정한, 활동적인 fracture 부러뜨리다 suspend (매)달다 prickly 따끔따끔 아픈 syndrome 증후군 **C** hydrogen 수소 atom 원자 submerge 물속에 잠그다 electrode 전극(電極) bubble 거품, 기포

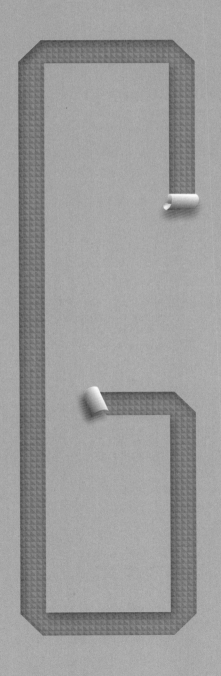

Questions

1 영어에는 be+과거분사 형태의 문장이 많다. 왜 그렇지?
2 be+과거분사+전치사의 표현들을 모두 외워야 하나요?

Answers

1 동사를 이용해 다양한 표현을 만드는 방법이 바로 수동태 문장이다. 우리는
  숙어라고 외웠던 be+과거분사+전치사의 문장도 사실은 동사의 다양한 표현
  이다.
2 영어는 동사가 매우 중요하다. 동사를 알면 절반을 이해했다고 할 수 있다.
  be+과거분사+전치사도 하나의 동사표현이라고 할 수 있다.

수동 형태의 동사구 Ⅰ

1 steal과 rob

□ 주어 + **steal** + 목적어(물건)	~을 훔치다
주어 + **be stolen** (by목적격)	~을 도난당하다
□ 주어 + **rob A of B**	A에게서 B를 빼앗다
A + **be robbed of** B (by목적격)	A는 B(물건)를 빼앗기다

1
− 주어+훔치다
− 주어+도난당하다
− 주어+빼앗다
− 주어+빼앗기다

Jane **stole** my book.
→ My book **was stolen** by Jane.
A lady **robbed** me **of** my purse.
→ I **was robbed of** my purse by a lady.

2 '~라고들 한다'

□ It is said(believed, thought, reported) that S+V~.
□ S+is said(believed, thought, reported) to 부정사~.

People say that Barbara traveled to Uganda last month.
=**It is said that** Barbara traveled to Uganda last month.
=Barbara **is said to** have traveled to Uganda last month.

3 동사+목적어(A)+of+명사(B)

* rob A of B (A에게서 B를 빼앗다)	→ be robbed of
* deprive A of B (A에게서 B를 빼앗다)	→ be deprived of
* accuse A of B (A에게서 B(죄목)를 고소하다)	→ be accused of
* remind A of B (A에게 B를 상기시키다)	→ be reminded of
* convince A of B (A에게 B를 확신시키다)	→ be convinced of
* notify A of B (A에게 B를 통보하다)	→ be notified of
* inform A of B (A에게 B를 알리다)	→ be informed of
* persuade A of B (A에게 B를 설득하다)	→ be persuaded of

3
'A에게서 B를 ~하다'의 형태로 해석이 된다.
− ~을 빼앗기다
− ~을 빼앗기다
− ~로 고소당하다
− ~가 생각나다
− ~를 확신하다
− ~를 통고받다
− ~을 알고 있다
− ~을 확신하고 있다

Mr. Peter **was convinced of** the effectiveness of the music.
After watching the film, I **was reminded of** the people I loved.

4 know의 변신

The secret **was known to** plenty of individuals.
A man **is known by** the company he keeps.
Simone **was known for** her civil right songs.
Mary has **been known as** a doctor in our village.

4
− ~에 알려져 있다
− ~로 판단되다
− ~로 유명하다
− ~로서 알려져 있다

E EXERCISE

A **Write the right prepositions.**

1 She was informed _____*of*_____ the threat to her life.

2 A female student was robbed _____ her purse.

3 Alice was convinced _____ her husband's genius.

4 This cigar was known _____ its strong tobacco taste.

5 Pythagoras was known _____ "The Father of numbers".

6 Ireland was deprived _____ over $400 billions in natural gas.

7 Jesus Christ was accused _____ being a murderer in his time.

B **Change the sentences into the passive forms.**

1 Someone stole her pen.   Her pen _____*was stolen*_____ .

2 Someone robbed the bank.   The bank _____ .

3 A judge sent the bank robber to jail. The bank robber _____ .

4 The storm destroyed dozens of trees. Dozens of trees _____ .

5 People speak Arabic in many countries. Arabic _____ .

6 Edison invented the electric light bulb. The electric light bulb _____ by Edison.

7 He is taking the child to a camp.   The child _____ .

C **Complete the sentences using the given words.**

1 Two teenagers _____ a cell phone and an MP3 player. (say, rob)
   〈10대 두 명이 휴대폰과 MP3를 빼앗겼다고 한다.〉

2 The committee have _____ the earth's global warming. (convince)
   〈그 위원회는 지구의 온난화를 확신했다.〉

3 She carefully _____ her good intentions. (persuade)
   〈그녀는 조심스럽게 그에게 자신의 좋은 의도를 설득시켰다.〉

4 The man _____ his own approaching death. (persuade)
   〈그 사람은 자신이 죽음에 가까워졌다고 믿고 있다.〉

5 My brother _____ a robbery that never happened. (accuse)
   〈내 남동생은 발생하지도 않은 강도 사건으로 고소되었다.〉

2 ▶ 수동 형태의 동사구 Ⅱ

1 기억해야 할 be+과거분사+전치사

How do I prove that I **was qualified for** the promotion?

Florida State **is known for** its athletic programs during summer.

1
be+과거분사 형태에 목적어가 오기 위해 목적어 앞에 전치사가 오는 경우이다.
* be+과거분사+전치사가 하나의 동사 역할을 하게 되는 경우이다.

a. ☐ be **made** of   ～를 재료로 만들어지다
   ☐ be **made up** of   ～로 구성되어있다
   ☐ be **possessed** of   ～를 소유하다
   ☐ be **ashamed** of   ～를 부끄러워하다
   ☐ be **composed** of   ～로 구성되어 있다

b. ☐ be **employed** in   ～에 종사하다
   ☐ be **lost** in   ～에 빠져있다
   ☐ be **absorbed** in   ～에 열중하다   = be engaged in
   ☐ be **involved** in(with)   ～와 관계있다
   ☐ be **dressed** in   ～를 차려입다
   ☐ be **located** in   ～에 위치하다   = be situated on

c. ☐ be **faced** with   ～에 직면하다
   ☐ be **associated** with   ～와 연합하다, ～와 관계있다
   ☐ be **afflicted** with   ～로 시달리다
   ☐ be **provided** with   ～를 공급받다
   ☐ be **occupied** with(in)   ～에 몰두하다
   ☐ be **acquainted** with   ～를 잘 알다
   ☐ be **equipped** with   ～가 장착되어 있다
   ☐ be **compared** with   ～와 비교되다
   ☐ be **crowded** with   ～로 혼잡하다

* 자주 등장하는 수동태 표현

* be located ～에 위치하다
* be seated ～에 앉다
* be placed ～위치해 있다
* be situated ～에 위치해 있다
* be supposed to ～하기로 되어있다

d. ☐ be **known** for   ～로 유명하다
   ☐ be **qualified** for   ～에 적격이다
   ☐ be **renowned** for   ～로 유명하다
   ☐ be **suited** for   ～에 적합하다

e. ☐ be **devoted** to   ～에 바치다(～에 열중하다)
   ☐ be **related** to   ～와 관계있다
   ☐ be **based** on   ～를 근거로 하다
   ☐ be **married** to   ～와 결혼하다
   ☐ be **accustomed** to   ～에 익숙해있다   = be used to+명사
   ☐ be **addicted** to   ～에 중독되다

EXERCISE

A Choose the right words.

1 Water is composed <of / with> hydrogen and oxygen.

2 He was dressed <in / to> a robe reaching down to his feet. *robe: 길고 품이 넓은 겉옷

3 My son was addicted <to / with> a certain online video game.

4 My daughter was married <to / with> a worker of the same age.

5 An empty stomach is connected <in / with> a feeling of hunger.

6 The Korean soccer team was accustomed <on / to> the climate of Korea.

7 Yellow was associated <of / with> the idea of royalty and majesty in China.

B Complete the sentences using the given words.

1 occupy   a. She ___was occupied___ with Alaskan fishery investigations.
            b. They ___are occupying___ most of the forest areas.

2 know   a. A man _____ by the company he keeps.
            b. The government _____ for a long time that UFOs exist.

3 equip   a. The soldier _____ with a variety of different weapons.
            b. The auto manufacturer should _____ the car with airbags then.

4 addict   a. Tobacco companies intentionally have _____ smokers to nicotine.
            b. A lot of politicians and soldiers _____ to drinking.

5 suit   a. The light blue _____ you the best, better than the grey lenses.
            b. This program _____ for athletes at the beginning level.

6 qualify   a. He _____ for the job that he applied for.
            b. His computer skills will _____ him for this position.

C Complete the sentences using the given words.

1 The store ___was crowded with___ customers and employees. (crowd)

2 A few technicians _____ their work and felt happy. (absorb)

3 I _____ basketball when I was younger. (devote)

4 Coffee drinking _____ with tea drinking in 18th century. (compare)

5 The garden _____ with weeds which need to be taken out. (cover)

6 She was a good cook and was _____ cooking for her parents. (use)

7 The disease _____ with a shortage of feed. (associate)

A Choose the right words for (A) and (B).

A cab driver was (A) <accusing / accused of> spying with no evidence. After arrest he was brought to the CIA, where he (B) <was stolen / was robbed of> his belongings, deprived of food, severely threatened and beaten. Finally he confessed his spying activities out of fear of being beaten more.

B Read and answer the questions in English.

Parental involvement in reading achievement has been a concern since the 1980's for both educators and parents. Reading aloud to children is a most important factor in developing reading. Parental involvement at home is consistently associated (A) <to / with> higher student achievement. Reading at home protects a child from getting addicted to television or computers. Also it actively monitors a child's time, helps with homework and provides space to discuss school matters. Parents are able to get (B) <involved / involving> in their child's education positively in many ways. What matters is to do it consistently and stick with it because it will make an important difference in a child's life.

1 Choose the right words for (A) and (B).

2 According to the passage, what can parents do to help in children's reading success?
   → Parents can _____ for their reading success.

C Read and answer the question in English.

What is the content of the universe? Murphy, a scientist associated with NASA, explains that only a small percentage of matter of the universe is composed of what we call ordinary matter. Around 70 percent of the universe is dark energy, and about 22 percent is made up of dark matter, which makes up a substantial part of the universe's material. Although astronomers don't know what composes dark matter, they say that it is related to supersymmetry. To know what it is would answer a crucial question about the universe. Whoever solves the dark matter problem would certainly win a Nobel Prize.

*NASA: 미국 항공 우주국(National Aeronautics and Space Administration)

1 According to the passage, what composes the universe substantially?
   → The universe _____ .

A evidence 증거 belongings 소유물, 소지품 confess 고백하다 beat 때리다, 이기다 **B** consistently 시종일관하게 achievement 업적, 성적 stick 달라붙다 **C** content 내용 make up 구성하다 substantial 실질적인 crucial 결정적인, 중대한

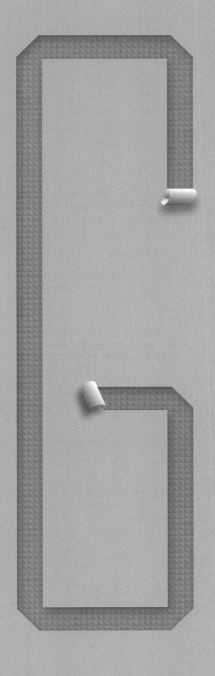

Questions

1 왜 우리는 to+동사원형을 '부정사'라고 부르지?
2 그 많은 부정사의 용법을 어떻게 하라고?
3 그렇다면 to부정사를 빠르게 해석하는 방법은?

Answers

1 다양한 의미로 사용되도록 만든 것이 부정사(不定詞)이다. 이름도 '의미를 정해두지 않고 사용하는 품사'를 의미하며, 영어로도 to-infinitive(무한적인 의미)라고 한다.

2 to부정사는 의미가 다양하여 문장의 주어, 목적어, 보어 등으로 사용되는데, 이러한 것을 「명사적 용법」으로 이름 붙이는 것은 '매를 버는 짓'이다. 주어 위치에 오면 '~은,는,이,가'로 해석하고, 목적어로 오면 '~를'로 해석하는 수준으로도 충분하다. 단, 습관적으로 to부정사와 함께 쓰이는 표현에 주의해야 한다.

3 항상 to부정사와 함께 쓰이는 표현을 제외하고는 to부정사 앞에서 끊어 읽어 보자. to부정사는 문맥에 따라 의미를 달리하므로, 앞에서 끊어 읽으면 문맥을 정리하는 기회가 된다.

to부정사와 동명사 - 닮은점

1 문장의 주어(Subject)와 보어(Complement)

To know yourself is important for success.
Fishing in a boat used to be my favorite sport.

All we can do is **to stay and wait** for the ship.
My favorite pastime is **playing** video and computer games.
The doctor asked the patient **to bend** his body forward.

2 문장의 목적어로 온다.

(1) to부정사가 목적어(Verb+to-Infinitive)

> hope, wish, agree, want, plan, expect, decide, intend 등

Nonsmokers want **to escape** the pollution of smokers.
In the spring we expect **to see** hummingbirds in Kentucky.

(2) 동명사가 목적어(Verb+Gerund)

> finish, stop, escape, avoid, help(피하다), enjoy, mind(꺼리다), deny 등

Don't avoid **answering** any questions the patient may ask.
The pilot insisted on **landing** the plane under bad weather.

3 의미상의 주어

(1) to부정사의 의미상 주어

It is impossible **for me** to carry the heavy books.
This made it difficult **for him** to see words correctly.

It is very kind **of him** to help me with the bag.
Do you think it's wise **of you** to use it without asking her?

I expected **Mary** to accept the invitation to dinner.
Online shopping allowed **us** to acquire food, and even pets.

(2) 동명사의 의미상 주어

We couldn't stand **Tom('s)** being rude to us.
We appreciate **your** helping us in our struggles.

4 부정표현 방법 - not의 위치

I was driving on the highway so I tried **not** to drink.
He was sure of his son **not** being ill.

1
to부정사와 동명사는 공통적으로 문장의 주어(~하는 것은)와 보어 역할을 한다.

- 주격 보어
- 주격 보어
- 목적격 보어

2
(1) to부정사를 목적어로 취하는 동사 : 주로 희망, 기대, 선호, 결심 동사들이 많다.
* 습관적으로 'hope to'처럼 to~ 를 붙여 사용하면 기억하기 쉬워진다.

(2) 동명사를 목적어로 취하는 동사 : 주로 중단, 회피, 탈출 등의 회피성 동사가 많다.

- 동사의 목적어
- 전치사의 목적어 : 전치사 뒤에는 반드시 명사형태가 와야 하므로, 동사는 동명사의 형태가 된다.

3
(1) 부정사의 의미상 주어는 to부정사 앞에 for(또는 of)+목적격으로 표시
* to부정사 앞에 of+목적격: 문장의 보어가 사람의 성격, 특성의 형용사일 때이다.

> * polite, kind, wise, smart, cruel, rude, considerate, silly, selfish 등

- 목적어가 to부정사의 의미상 주어

(2) 동명사의 의미상 주어는 동명사 앞에 소유격이나 목적격(명사의 경우)으로 표시한다.

4
부정표현은 공통적으로 to부정사의 앞과 동명사의 앞에 not을 둔다.

EXERCISE

A Complete the following sentences using the words in the box.

| answer | attend | walk | help | borrow | excel | stop | change |

1 He tried to avoid _____answering_____ my questions.

2 We should run five kilometers without _____.

3 Her parents always encouraged her _____ in school.

4 I won't get a bicycle. I don't mind _____ to the lake.

5 Diane may get in trouble by _____ too much money.

6 Mary has decided not _____ the conference next week.

7 We appreciated your _____ us over the past six months.

8 It would be selfish of her _____ her mind for personal reasons.

B Match the beginning of each sentence with the most appropriate ending.

1 The thief strongly denied   a. filming a gangster movie.

2 I feel cold. Would you mind   b. taking part in the marathon.

3 As a movie star, I've just finished   c. accepting returns on opened and used products.

4 The shop owner has the right to deny   d. breaking into that shop.

5 Father, a heavy smoker, stopped   e. teaching and learning.

6 Most singers try to avoid   f. smoking for at least one week.

7 He got a cold and gave up   g. closing the window for me?

8 I place value in education and I enjoy   h. singing through their nose.

C Complete the sentences using 'to-infinitive'.

1 I don't want to speak to the players. → I want _____you to speak to them._____

2 He doesn't want anyone to eat it. → He wants somebody _____

3 Cathy doesn't want to go alone. → Cathy wants me _____

4 He said I shouldn't believe what she says. → I was warned _____

5 The police said I shouldn't say anything. → The police advised me _____

6 I found the ball returned to its original shape. → I found the ball _____

7 I expect he'll increase his fluency in French. → I expect him _____

2 ▶ to부정사와 동명사—다른 점

1 stop + ┌ to 동사원형 : ~하기 위해 걸음을 멈추다
      └ V-ing 동명사 : ~하는 것을 중단하다

He stopped **to smoke** while walking to the library.
He stopped **smoking** for his health all his life.

> **1**
> stop동사는 동명사만을 목적어로 취하므로,
> 뒤의 to부정사는 '~하기 위하여'가 된다.

2 기억동사 ┌ remember ┐ + ┌ to 동사원형 : ~할 내용을 기억하다(잊다)
      └ forget   ┘   └ V-ing(동명사) : ~했던 것을 기억하다(잊다)

We remember **to meet** again 10 years after graduation.
We remember **meeting** again 10 years after graduation.

> **2**
> to부정사는 앞으로의 예정 상황을, 동명사는
> 과거의 상황(~한 것)을 나타낸다.

3 regret + ┌ to 동사원형 : (앞으로) ~하게 되어 유감스럽다
        └ V-ing(동명사) : (과거에) ~한것을 후회하다

I regret **to say** that the house was destroyed completely.
We did not regret **accepting** your proposal.

> **3**
> 일반적으로 to부정사는 동작(~할, ~하게되
> 어)을 나타내며, 동명사는 명사적 의미(~한
> 것)를 나타낸다.

4 주의할 표현들

(1) use 관련 표현

S(주어) +		
used to + 동사 :	~하곤 했었다	
be used to + 동사 :	~하기 위해 이용되어 진다	
be used to + -ing :	~하는 데에 익숙해 있다.	

There **used to be** a church on the hill in my childhood.
Nuclear power **is used to make** electricity in many countries.
People in Seoul **are used to riding** a crowded subway.

> **4**
> 해당문맥에서 동사원형과 동명사 중 어느 표
> 현이 적당한 표현인지 정해야 한다.

(2) to + -ing(동명사)

* object to -ing	~에 반대하다 (= be opposed to)
* What do you say to -ing	~하자 (= Let's~.)
* devote to -ing	~에 바치다 (= dedicate to-ing)
* look forward to -ing	~하기를 기대하다 (= expect)
* when it comes to -ing	~에 관한 이야기라면
* be accustomed to -ing	~에 익숙해있다 (= be used to -ing)

I am looking forward **to seeing** you again.
I object **to sailing** during a violent storm.

> (2) to가 전치사이므로 뒤에 (동)명사가 오는
> 경우이다.
>
> > * ~하지 않을 수 없다
> > cannot help + ing
> > = cannot but 동사원형
> > = have no choice but to + 동사원형
>
> We cannot help laughing to hear it.
> = We cannot but laugh to hear it.
> = We have no choice but to laugh to
> hear it.

EXERCISE

A

Match the beginning of each sentence with its ending.

1 I am used to driving on the left   a) because I've lived in Japan for a long time.
2 I used to drive on the left   b) when I lived in England in my childhood.

3 I used to get up early   a) and I make it a rule to get up early.
4 I'm used to getting up early   b) but those good days are over now.

5 I got used to the hot weather   a) after I'd been here for a few years.
6 I'm used to the hot weather   b) because I am from Uganda.

7 Allah is used to mean any god   a) and Christians say they've used it for centuries.
8 Allah used to mean any god   b) but the term now means muhammad.

9 I used to smoke while driving   a) and I have smoked 30 cigarettes a day.
10 I am used to smoking while driving   b) but I stopped smoking after an accident.

B

Write the correct forms of the given verbs.

1 I remember _____dressing_____ as a pirate for Halloween 2005 or 2006. (dress)

2 Please remember _____to feed_____ the birds tomorrow morning. (feed)

3 I shall never forget _____ the Swiss Alps for the first time. (see)

4 Don't forget _____ the women who helped us in the past. (remember)

5 Have you ever stopped _____ and forgotten to start again? (think)

6 Why has he stopped _____ my calls and e-mails? (answer)

7 I now regret _____ what I said. I shouldn't have said it. (say)

8 I regret _____ you that I am unable to accept your invitation. (inform)

C

Complete the sentences with your opinion using gerund(-ing).

1 I don't want to have other people around. I'm used to _____doing everything by myself_____ .

2 I got a lot of free time. What do you say to _____ ?

3 There are enough people out there to do it. I object to _____ .

4 He'll come home from the war. He looks forward to _____ .

5 He is a vegetarian. That's why he draws the line when it comes to _____ .

6 I used to go to the beach in the summer. I was accustomed to _____ .

7 He tries to master a computer. He devoted his free time to _____ .

Further Study

A Choose the right words for (A), (B) and (C).

I met Damon in Boston at a mall a year or so ago. I was staring at the actor being asked for an autograph. I forgot (A) <asking / to ask> for the autograph. Soon he came through to order food and I was amazed at how polite and friendly he was. He stopped (B) <signing / to sign> autographs, gave me one, told me (C) <take / to take> it easy, and walked away.

B Read and answer the questions in English.

(A) <Take / Taking> a kid's temperature generates emotional extremes. The sudden increase in temperature may scare parents. A majority of parents frequently check a feverish child's temperature and give a child fever-reducing medication. However, excessive concern about a kid's fever can lead parents to make some wrong moves. If a child is running around a room, it's better (B) <not to visit / to not visit> an emergency room no matter what the temperature. If you can't hold down a child to get a temperature, then chances are that he or she's not seriously sick. It's OK <for him or her / to calm down / to wait / to take> his or her temperature.

1 Choose the right words for (A) and (B).

2 Rearrange the words in the bracket to complete the sentence.
   → It's OK _____ his or her temperature.

C Read and answer the questions in English.

Recently some research suggest that young animals fed diet food tend to overeat regular food. This research tells us that children who are fed low-calorie meals will end up eating much more when they grow up – thus increasing their risk of obesity. Though the experiments were done on rats, it means that the more low-calorie food one consumes, the more one's body demands payback for the calories it was deprived of. Thus, before feeding your children diet food you should think it over carefully. When it comes to dieting, most Americans are willing to resort to a shortcut to help eat less, such as opting for artificial sweeteners instead of sugar. Yet, research suggests that sugar substitutes are no key to weight loss.

1 Complete the sentence to represent what the author intended.
   → Perhaps _____ are helping to explain why Americans are heavier than ever.

Ⓐ stare 지켜보다 autograph 서명   Ⓑ medication 약물치료 excessive 과도한 emergency 비상, 응급 calm down 진정시키다
Ⓒ obesity 비만 payback 회수, 보복 resort to ~에 가다, 의지하다 opt 선택하다 substitute 대용(代用)하다, 대용물

156

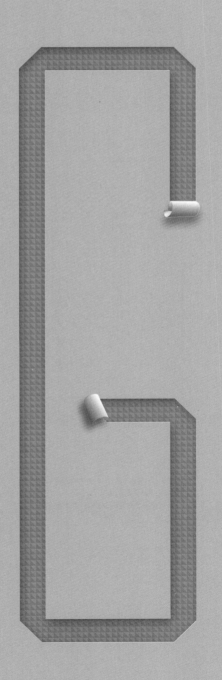

to부정사가 만드는 표현

1 to+동사원형의 문장
2 형용사+to부정사, 명사+to부정사

Questions

1 to부정사는 동사 뒤에만 올 수 있나요?

2 to부정사는 어떻게 만들어졌을까?

Answers

1 to부정사는 명사나 형용사 뒤에도 올 수 있다.

2 동사를 변형시켜 형용사 형태로 사용하는 것이 분사, 그리고 명사로 사용하기 위해 만든 것이 동명사이다. 그 중간 즈음에서 이 두가지의 의미로 사용하기 위해 부정사를 발명했다고나 할까!

to+동사원형의 문장

1 의문사(question-word)+to부정사의 표현

how to~	「~하는 법」	: how to drive, how to read
when to~	「~할 때」	: when to start, when to study
where to~	「~할 장소」	: where to go, where to live
what to~	「~할 것」	: what to eat, what to sell
who to~	「~할 사람」	: who to go, who to call
whom to~	「~할 사람」	: whom to go with, whom to believe
which to~	「~할 것」	: which to choose, which to buy

I don't know **which one to** choose for the project.
Which one to choose is purely a matter of taste.
The problem is **when to** begin the work.
I don't know **whether to** laugh or cry.

> **1**
> 「의문사+to부정사」는 명사의 역할(주어, 목적어, 보어)을 한다. (<u>why+to부정사</u>는 쓰지 않는다.)
> – 언제 ~할지
> – 어디에 ~할지
> – 무엇을 ~할지
> – 누가 ~을 할지
> – 누구를 ~할지
> – 어느 것을 ~할지
>
> – 접속사+to부정사

2 to부정사와 함께 쓰이는 표현

seem to ~인 것 같다	happen to 우연히 ~하다
appear to ~인 것 같다	manage to ~그럭저럭 해내다
mean to ~할 의도이다	fail to ~을 못하다
seek to(=try to) ~하려 애쓰다	afford to ~할 여유가 있다
intend to ~할 의향이 있다	prove to ~ 판명되다
tend to ~하는 경향이 있다	pretend to ~인 체하다
deserve to ~를 받을 자격 있다	but to ~하는 것을 제외하고

She **failed to** come to the party.
He **never fails to** keep his word.
He cannot **afford to** buy his own car.

> **2**
> to부정사와 함께 사용되는 표현이므로, to부정사를 붙여 기억해야 한다.

3 반드시 동사원형이 필요하다!

* would rather+동사원형	차라리 ~하는 것이 낫다
* may as well+동사원형	~하는 편이 좋다
* may well+동사원형	~하는 것도 당연하다
* had better+동사원형	~하는 편이 좋다(명령적 의미)
* do nothing but+동사원형	~하기만 한다

We **would rather** watch it than read it.
You **may as well** not waste your time.
The new baby **may well** cry every 2-3 hours.

> **3**
> 하나의 조동사로 취급하기 때문에 뒤에는 반드시 동사원형이 온다.
> – 부정어(not)는 동사원형 앞에 붙는다.

EXERCISE

A Complete the sentences using 'infinitive phrases'.

1 I'm looking for a used car. Can you tell me where ____*to buy a used car*____ ?

2 There are two standards. Users get confused and can't decide which _____.

3 I don't have any specific plans about my stay in the UK. I don't know where _____.

4 Writing a resume in English is confusing. Help me with how _____.

5 There is no one to blame for the mistakes. How do we decide whom _____ ?

6 Bad smells on fish! You have no lemon. Guess what _____.

7 A robber hid in the cave. Nobody dares to go in. The problem is who _____.

B Complete the sentences using the example as a model.

1 Smoking should be banned. Cigarettes do nothing but ____*harm one's health*____ .

2 He needs a laptop, but he can't afford it. He _____.

3 My computer broke down and he helped me out. He managed _____.

4 Exercise is better than a diet. You'd better _____.

5 They tried hard to win the game. They deserved _____.

6 The US hired many engineers from Canada. Canada may well _____.

7 A bear is said not to harm a dead body. Facing a bear, you'd better pretend _____.

8 Heavy snow blocked our path, so I quit climbing. I have no option but _____.

C Rearrange the words to complete the sentences.

1 I <would / rather / for the next bus / walk / than wait>.
   → I _____.

2 There is <on where / to go / and / whom / to go with / no idea>.
   → There is _____.

3 Baseball players <more than / get paid / to / football players / don't deserve>.
   → Baseball players _____.

4 You <may / not / anything / say / as well / at all>.
   → You _____.

5 Every politician <had better / listening to / start / their voters>.
   → Every politician _____.

2 ▶ 형용사+to부정사, 명사+to부정사

1 형용사+to부정사(adjective+to-infinitive)

be ready to ~할 준비가 되어 있다	be eager to ~하기를 갈망하다
be sorry to ~해서 미안하다	be willing to 기꺼이 ~하다
be apt to 자칫 ~하기 쉽다	be inclined to ~하는 경향이 있다
be likely to ~할 것 같다	be liable to 흔히 ~하기 쉽다
be available to ~하는 데 쓰이다	be adequate to ~하기에 적절하다
be free to 마음대로 ~하다	be anxious to ~하기를 갈망하다
be sure to 반드시 ~하다	be reluctant to ~하기를 꺼리다

They **are likely to** travel around the country.
She **is anxious to** take a piano lesson.

> **1**
> to부정사의 해석은 함께 쓰이는 형용사에 따라 달라질 수 있다.

2 명사+to부정사(noun+to-infinitive)

the last man to ~하지 않을 사람	the ground to ~할 만한 근거
the attempt to ~하려는 시도	the willingness to 기꺼이 ~함
the permission to ~하라는 허가	the request to ~하려는 요청
the decision to ~하려는 결정	the necessity to ~할 필요성
the refusal to ~하는 것의 거절	the instinct to ~하려는 본능
the failure to ~하지 못함	the power to ~하는 권한

He is **the last man to** accept a bribe in our country.
He has the **willingness to** accept their job offer.

> **2**
> to부정사는 명사 뒤에서 앞의 명사를 수식하는 형용사 역할을 한다.
> 일반적으로 추상명사가 자주 사용된다.
>
> – bribe: 뇌물

3 too ~ to부정사

He ran **too** slowly **to** pursue and catch victims.
(=He ran **so** slowly **that** he couldn't pursue and catch victims.)
That hill is **too** steep **to** ride up. You have to walk.
(=That hill is **so** steep that you **cannot** ride up. You have to walk.)

> **3**
> too+형용사/부사+to부정사는 '너무 ~해서 ...할 수 없다'는 부정적인 의미를 나타낼 수 있다.

4 be동사+to부정사

If we **are to** better the future, we must disturb the present.
You must exploit this weakness if you **are to** survive.

Garry announced that he **was to** retire from competitive chess.
He **is to** meet the U.S. president at the White House on Thursday.

The picture **is to** be seen from a distance and **is to** fill space.
Food **is to** be eaten or stored only in designated areas.

> **4**
> be동사 뒤에 to부정사가 오는 경우, 문맥에 맞게 해석을 한다.
> – ~하려면
>
> – ~할 예정이다
>
> – ~할 수 있다

EXERCISE

A Match the sentences on the left with one on the right.

1 *The prime Minister is likely to resign* ——— a. *because he has taken a bribe.*

2 History is inclined to repeat itself   b. because of world troubles, such as disasters.

3 They are reluctant to have children   c. because it would be her first trip to the city.

4 She's anxious to go around the city   d. because human being doesn't change greatly.

5 He is eager to achieve it for himself   e. because I can't attend university due to war.

6 I'm determined to educate myself   f. and he has become a self-starter.

B Rewrite the sentences beginning with a noun phrase.

1 He was eager to win, which encouraged their team.
   → His _____*eagerness to win encouraged their team*_____ .

2 She was willing to care for the babies and this was welcomed.
   → Her _____ .

3 He decided to give up the right to take benefit, which surprised us.
   → His _____ .

4 Our government refused to join the league of nations, which disappointed us.
   → Our government's _____ .

5 Everybody else was scared to see the snake but Jim was not.
   → Jim was the last _____ .

C Rewrite these two sentences into one sentence.

1 Cathy is very foolish. She gives up her job for marriage.
   → Cathy is _____*very foolish to give up her job for marriage*_____ .

2 Jane worked out the answer. It was very clever of her.
   → It was _____ .

3 His cancer spreads too far. It cannot be operated.
   → His cancer _____ .

4 He is eager in nearly everything. He wants to help you work it out.
   → He is _____ .

A Choose the right words for (A) and (B).

Her father said, "I appreciate that you've taken an interest in my daughter. Nevertheless, if you (A) <are to court / will court> her, I ask you to do so in secret." I smiled at him, relieved that he would allow me (B) <to court / court> his daughter. In time, if and when she accepts me, I will make our relationship publicly known.

B Read and answer the questions in English.

Pain is an unpleasant physical and emotional experience. Chronic pain can have negative effects on the parts of the brain responsible for mood and attention. More often, pain can prevent you from doing things that must be done, if you are to survive. Not everyone has the capacity (A) <ignore / to ignore> severe pain. Under such circumstances, pain relief is the only practical alternative, despite any adverse effects. It is important for you to be well informed of medications and dosage you may need. That's why you should know how (B) <to use / use> the emergency medical kit. It is vital <the skill / someone's life / to have / to save>.

1　Choose the right words for (A) and (B).

2　Rearrange the words to complete the sentence.
　　→ It is vital _____ .

C Read and answer the questions in English.

You may think intuition is the capability to see the future and is an inner awareness that goes beyond logical thought. (A) Yet, in fact intuition is the ability to alert you if you are in trouble. (B) Many times we hear from our intuition what we should be doing, but we don't trust it. (C) Your friends or family give contradictory advice, or you are too afraid to follow it. (D) I've learned through experience that my life flows more smoothly if I follow my intuitive voice. (E) Using the logical side of your brain is useful for solving lots of problems, but if you don't use your intuition you are not going to make the best decisions. The core problem <when / is / an action / to / begin>.

1　Where would the following sentence best fit in (A) ~ (E)?

　　Then what's stopping you from listening to that?

2　Rearrange the words to complete the sentence.
　　→ The core problem _____ .

Ⓐ appreciate 감사하다　court 구혼하다　　**Ⓑ** chronic 만성적인　medical kit 의료 상자　pain relief 통증 완화　capacity 능력　severe 심한
adverse effect 역효과　**Ⓒ** intuition 직관　alert 경계시키다　contradictory 모순된, 반박의

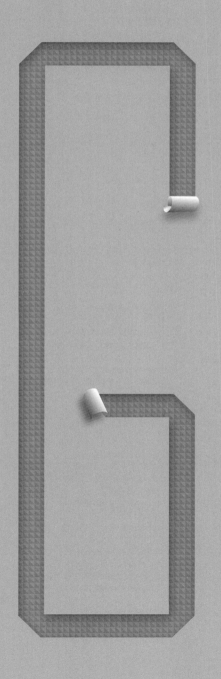

명사–어휘 확장

1 다양한 명사 표현
2 명사를 만드는 접미사

Questions

1 군집명사, 집합명사, 추상명사 등을 구분해야 할까?

2 우리말처럼 여러 개의 명사를 제한없이 연결해도 될까?

Answers

1 명사의 종류별 명칭을 외우는 것이 무슨 의미가 있을까? 우리말의 명사 종류를 파악하기도 버거운데… 단, 셀 수 있는 명사(Countable)와 셀 수 없는 명사(Uncountable)를 구분하는 것은 꼭 필요하다. 왜냐하면 그토록 까다로운 관사(the, a)와 복수표현을 붙이는 데 필요하기 때문이다.

2 '할머니 옆집 과수원 주인 아들 학교 선생님께서…'하면 명사가 7개 등장한다. 영어에서도 명사를 나열하여 연결할 수 있기는 하지만, 소유관계를 표시하는 표현('s 또는 of)을 사용한다. 이러한 규칙들에 주의하고, 다양한 명사표현들을 암기하는 것이 더 중요하다. 특히, 명사를 만드는 접미사를 알면 많은 어휘를 기억할 수 있다.

다양한 명사 표현

1 복합명사(compound noun)를 만드는 방법

1. a living room	drinking water	a sleeping pill
2. life-saving	risk-taking	shop-lifting
3. a shoe store	a book store	a gold watch
4. clothes shop	a glasses frame	the arms trade
5. looker-on	hanger-on(부하)	passer-by
6. outcome	intake	outbreak
7. my mom's bag	the boys' school	the lady's hat

1
복합명사(명사+명사)에서 앞의 명사는 단수형으로 온다.
1. 동명사+명사
2. 명사+-ing
3. 명사+명사
4. 복수형 명사+명사
5. 명사복수+전치사
6. 전치사+동사
7. 단수형과 복수형의 소유격
사람이나 생명체의 경우 소유격(명사's+명사)을 사용하며, 복수명사인 경우 the girls' car처럼 나타낸다.

2 남녀(gender)를 구분하는 표현

actor – actress	bachelor – spinster	bridegroom – bride
bull – cow	male – female	hero – heroine
prince – princess	nephew – niece	widower – widow
waiter – waitress	cock – hen	horse – mare
god – goddess	monk – nun	lion – lioness

It is easy to make a huge difference in the life of a **monk** or **nun**.
I'm an actor. I feel like a **hero** and she is my **heroine**.

3 항상 복수형으로 쓰는 동사(nouns with a plural form)

a pair of **glasses**	a pair of **spectacles**	a pair of **jeans**
a pair of **pants**	a pair of **scissors**	a pair of **trousers**
a pair of **shoes**	a pair of **socks**	a pair of **gloves**
a pair of **boots**	a pair of **compasses**	a pair of **shorts**

3
안경처럼 2개가 있어야 하나의 물건이 되는 명사 표현은 a pair of~로 나타낸다.

a pair of glasses가 주어이면 단수 취급,
my glasses가 주어이면 복수 취급을 한다.

4 셀 수 없는 명사(uncountable noun)

a bar of chocolate	a bottle of milk	a flock of birds
a cube of ice	a pot of beer	a cattle of horses
a cattle of horses	a herd of lambs	a sheet of paper
a splash of water	a pinch of salt	a jar of jam

4
'물'처럼 셀 수 없는 명사를 표현할 때는 'a bottle of water'처럼 단위표현을 이용한다.
– flock : 떼, 무리
– cube : 입방체, 정육면체
– sheet : 얇은 판, 종이장
– splash : 물 튀김, 한 잔의 물

> * 빵의 다양한 단위 표현
> a loaf of bread(큰 덩어리)
> a slice of bread(얇게 자른 덩어리)
> a piece of bread(떼어낸 작은 덩어리)

I decided to buy **a bottle of milk**.
I got **a sheet of paper** from my teacher.
A cattle of half-wild **sheep** is the only sign of life.

E EXERCISE

Answers P.38

A Rewrite the phrases into the form of a compound noun or 's.

1 The fish hasn't seen <u>the surface of water</u>. → *the water surface*

2 He made himself <u>a lamp for reading</u> in bed. → _____

3 I'm proud to be <u>the mother of twins</u>. → _____

4 <u>The door of the garage</u> has been partially opened. → _____

5 I tried to put myself in <u>the position of the children</u>. → _____

6 Tell me how to clean <u>the keyboard of the computer</u>. → _____

7 He saw a note on <u>the table of the kitchen</u>. → _____

8 Steve was <u>the husband of my sister</u>. → _____

B Choose and write the right words for the blanks.

1 A: Where _____ my spectacles I bought yesterday? (are / is)

   B: _____ are in the first drawer on the left. (It / They)

2 A: How much did you pay for _____ shoes? (a / a pair of)

   B: _____ were very expensive. (It / They)

3 A: How many lookers-on _____ speaking English? (are / is)

   B: Most of _____ can speak English. (it / them)

4 A: I am sorry my clothes _____ dirty. (are / is)

   B: Please put _____ in the laundry basket. (it / them)

5 A: Four bottles of milk _____ frozen in the freezer. (was / were)

   B: It's better to take _____ beer. (a / a pot of)

C Supply the missing words.

1 A _____ is an adult female of a large animal species, such as cattle.

2 A _____ refers to the son of your sister or brother.

3 A _____ is a male of any member of the birds, specifically a male adult chicken.

4 A _____ is a woman whose spouse has died.

5 A _____ is an unmarried man who is beyond the normal age for marriage.

6 A _____ is a woman of courage and self-sacrifice in the face of danger.

7 A _____ is a female who is about to be married, currently being married.

2 ▶ 명사를 만드는 접미사

1 명사형 접미사 – ure

* procedure [prəsíːdʒər]   * pressure [préʃər]   * moisture [mɔ́istʃər]
* failure [féiljər]   * signature [sígnətʃər]   * exposure [ikspóuʒər]
* enclosure [enklóuʒər]   * pleasure [pléʒər]   * departure [dipáːrtʃər]
* expenditure [ikspénditʃər]   * creature [kríːtʃər]   * mixture [míkstʃər]

1
동사나 형용사에 접미사를 붙여 명사를 만든다.
– 절차, 압력, 습기
– 실패, 서명, 노출
– 동봉, 기쁨, 출발
– 지출, 창조물, 혼합

2 명사형 접미사 – hood

* brotherhood [brʌ́ðərhùd]   * falsehood [fɔ́ːlshùd]
* neighborhood [néibərhùd]   * livelihood [láivlihùd]
* likelihood [láiklihùd]   * adulthood [ədʌ́lthùd]

2

– 형제애, 거짓
– 이웃, 생계
– 있음직한 일, 성인임

3 명사형 접미사 – th

* breath [breθ] 호흡   * width [widθ] 폭   * breadth [bredθ] 넓이
* depth [depθ] 깊이   * strength [streŋkθ] 힘   * length [leŋkθ] 길이
* truth [truːθ] 진실   * growth [grouθ] 성장   * warmth [wɔːrmθ] 따뜻함

3

– 통 breathe   형 wide   형 broad
– 형 deep   형 strong   형 long
– 형 true   형 grow   형 warm

4 명사형 접미사 – age

* bondage [bándidʒ]   * salvage [sǽlvidʒ]   * heritage [héritidʒ]
* homage [hámidʒ]   * leakage [líːkidʒ]   * shortage [ʃɔ́ːrtidʒ]
* orphanage [ɔ́ːrfənidʒ]   * hostage [hástidʒ]

4

– 구속, 억압 / 해난구조 / 상속, 유산
– 존경, 누출(동. leak), 부족
– 고아 / 볼모, 저당

5 명사형 접미사 – ant, eer, ar(or, er), ive

* assistant, attendant, applicant, participant, descendant,
  protestant, servant, consultant, defendant
* beggar, engineer, volunteer, politician, actor, singer
* detective, relative, executive, representative, captive

5
사람의 접미사
* 조수, 참석자(수행원), 지원자, 참여자, 후손, 항의자(신교도), 하인, 의논상대, 피고

* 거지, 기술자, 지원자, 정치가, 연기자, 가수

* 탐정, 친척, 경영진, 대표자, 포로

6 명사형 접미사 – al

* denial [dináiəl] 부정   * approval [əprúːvəl] 승인
* burial [bériəl] 매장   * appraisal [əpréizəl] 평가
* trial [tráiəl] 시도   * proposal [prəpóuzəl] 제안
* survival [sərváivəl] 생존   * revival [riváivəl] 재생

6

– 통 deny   통 approve
– 통 bury   통 appraise
– 통 try   통 propose
– 통 survive   통 revive

EXERCISE

A Choose the one whose suffix has different meaning from the others.

1 ① boredom ② seldom ③ kingdom ④ freedom ⑤ wisdom

2 ① boyhood ② neighborhood ③ robinhood ④ falsehood ⑤ sisterhood

3 ① arrival ② denial ③ survival ④ spiritual ⑤ proposal

4 ① participant ② attendant ③ descendant ④ pleasant ⑤ assistant

5 ① truth ② path ③ width ④ breadth ⑤ depth

6 ① engineer ② marketeer ③ volunteer ④ foreseer ⑤ career

7 ① actress ② waitress ③ stewardess ④ lioness ⑤ access

8 ① respective ② detective ③ relative ④ executive ⑤ representative

B Choose the one which is not related to the others.

1 ① deep–depth ② broad–breadth
③ long–length ④ strong–strength ⑤ wild–width

2 ① deny–denial ② propose–proposal
③ appraise–appraisal ④ approve–approval ⑤ appear–appeal

3 ① assist–assistant ② attend–attendant
③ apply–applicant ④ distance–distant ⑤ descend–descendant

4 ① short–shortage ② ever–average
③ bond–bondage ④ orphan–orphanage ⑤ leak–leakage

C Choose and write the correct words in the box.

assistant	attendant	applicant	participant	descendant
consultant	defendant	protestant	servant	

1 _____ : a person or animal that is descended from a specific ancestor.

2 _____ : a person who helps another person with his or her work.

3 _____ : a member of the Christian churches that separated from the Roman Catholic.

4 _____ : someone who is privately employed to perform domestic services.

5 _____ : a person who gives professional or expert advice.

6 _____ : a person who is present and participates in a meeting.

7 _____ : a person who seeks something such as assistance or employment.

Further Study

A **Choose the right words for (A), (B) and (C).**

How is the (A) <breadth / height> of a huge area like an ocean measured? I wonder how the (B) <length / strength> of a country, the height of a mountain or the (C) <deepth / depth> of a sea is measured. Of course, the answer is that we have satellite data on which we can accurately measure the relative distances between faraway points.

B **Read and answer the questions in English.**

If a child lives with criticism, he learns to blame. If a child lives with (A) <hospitality / hostility>, he learns to fight. If a child lives with ridicule, he learns to be shy. But do not despair. If a child lives with tolerance, he learns to be (B) <impatient / patient>. If a child lives with encouragement, he learns confidence. If a child lives with applause, he learns to appreciate. If a child lives with fairness, he learns justice. If a child lives with acceptance and friendship, he learns to find love in the world. <Children Learn What They Live — Dorothy Law Nolie>

1 Choose the right words for (A) and (B).
2 Rearrange the words so that the sentence represents the main idea of the passage.
   *Children learn <how to do / adults / do / as / around them>.
   → Children learn _____.

C **Read and answer the question in English.**

When Richard died, I kept in contact with his dad, his brothers, his wife and their children. I'm not close to his mother. His parents have been divorced for years and my relationship with mother-in-law is a long, complicated story. Although I still call Richard's dad my '_____' and I'm still "Aunt" Rosa to those nieces and nephews, I know that legally I'm not related to them anymore. My kids, however, will always be related to them. Emotionally I will always feel that connection to them. For me, that won't go away; at least, it hasn't yet.

1 Complete the sentence, inferring from the family connections in the passage.
   → I still call Richard's dad my '_____'.

A measure 재다 satellite 위성,인공위성 faraway 먼 **B** hostility 적대감 despair 절망하다 tolerance 인내,관용 confidence 신용,자신 appreciate 감사하다 **C** divorce 이혼하다 legally 법적으로 at least 적어도

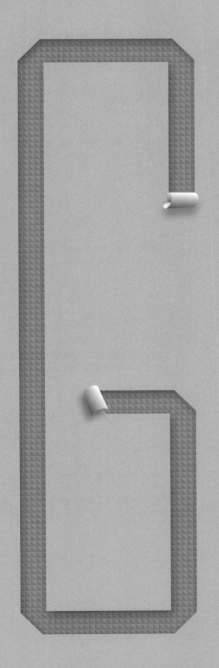

Unit 27

대명사—1

1 It/There 관련 문장
2 대명사

Questions

1 대명사를 사용할 때 정해진 원칙이 있나요?

2 대명사 it만 나오면 무슨 용법으로 사용되었는지 겁나요.

Answers

1 누구나 같은 말을 반복하기 싫어한다. 대명사는 it과 **one**, **one**과 **the other**, **every**와 **each** 등을 구분하여 사용한다. 이들을 어떤 경우에 사용하는지 정해진 원칙이 있다.

2 대명사 it은 다양한 역할을 한다. 주어로 사용되면 대부분 별 의미가 없다. 가주어, 비인칭주어, 강조, 대명사 등의 다양한 의미를 지니지만 중요한 역할이 없으므로 허수아비 주어로 이해하면 된다. 목적어로 나오는 it은 가목적어, 또는 명사를 대신하는 대명사 역할을 한다는 것을 알고 있으면 된다.

It/There 관련 문장

1 There V+S

There remains a risk of a nuclear accident.
There are a lot of ways to make toast.
There will be a solution to the tax crisis.

1
문장을 유도하는 There(유도부사)는 <u>There V+S</u>의 순서로 쓰인다.
– 주어 : a risk
– 주어 : ways
– 주어 : a solution

2 명사를 대신하는 대명사 it

I bought the book, but I haven't finish reading **it**.
She learned to speak English before she learned to read **it**.
The old postage never loses **its** face value.

2
it은 특정한 명사(the+명사)를 대신하는 대명사로 사용된다.
– the book
– English
– the old postage

3 가주어 it

It takes a lot of effort / **to play** the flute well like Mary.
It is certain / **that** he will come tomorrow.
It happened / **that** one of the tourists lost his wallet.

3
가주어 It은 본래의 주어가 너무 길어서, 가주어와 진주어를 나누기 위해 제시하는 것이다.

4 가목적어 it

I make **it** a rule / **to read** one chapter of the Bible every day.
Do you find **it** pleasant / **to live** in a small village?
I took **it** for granted / **that** you would participate in the project.

4
진목적어가 너무 길 때 <u>S+V+it+목적보어 + 진목적어</u>의 형태로 사용한다.

5 It~ that... 〈강조표현〉

It was the computer / **that** I bought when I was a sophomore.
It was Monica / **that** absented herself from work today.
It is during the harvest / **that** farm workers have to work hard.

5
It과 that의 사이에 강조하고 싶은 표현(주어, 목적어, 부사, 부사구 등)을 둔다.

6 막연한 의미의 it

What time is **it** by your watch?
It is one mile from here to the school.

6
시간, 거리, 가격, 날씨 등을 나타낼 경우 주어로 It을 내세우며, 별도로 해석하지 않는다.

* 아무 의미 없는 it을 넣어 사용하는 표현이 있다.

---

* Take **it** easy. 「마음 편히 먹어라」
* You can't miss **it**. 「그렇게 가면 찾을 수 있다」
* **It** is all over with my business. 「만사 끝장이다」
* What time shall we make **it**? 「언제 만날까요?」
* How is **it** going? 「요즈음 어때?」
* **It** is up to you. 「그것은 네게 달려 있다」

EXERCISE

A Complete the sentences using 'it' or 'there'.

1 _____ are many ways to say 'I love you'.

2 I am learning Spanish, but _____ is very difficult to understand.

3 She was very scared to see the snake, so she tried not to look at _____ .

4 I found _____ difficult to maintain my balance and fell down after a few steps.

5 _____ takes time and effort to find the type of advertising that is best for you.

6 This town seems hotter than the equator because _____ is no mountain nearby.

7 I have complained about barking dogs but _____ has been no improvement.

B Match the sentences on the left with one on the right.

1 *You can see the cloud in the sky.* ————————— a. *There will be a storm.*

2 I jumped up and down to keep warm.　　b. It is located near Edmonton, Alberta.

3 I visited the restaurant she runs in Canada.　　c. It was terribly cold and I was freezing.

4 Is there any supermarket here?　　d. There should be a change to the law.

5 The government admits the law was wrong.　　e. It is completely dark outside.

6 I wonder what the weather is like today.　　f. There is one, but it closed.

7 Recently I heard noise in the engine.　　g. I thought it was a waste of money.

8 He bought too many pencils.　　h. There is something wrong with the car.

C Rearrange the words to complete the sentences.

1 It is <appearance / that / is / very important / certain>.
　→ It is _____ .

2 He made it <get rich / by playing / possible / to / the game>.
　→ He made it _____ .

3 Do you know it was <that / Napoleon / canned food / invented>?
　→ Do you know it was _____ ?

4 It can be boring <with / outside / to do / to go / nothing>.
　→ It can be boring _____ .

5 There seems <be / the best / answer / to / a disagreement / over>.
　→ There seems _____ .

2 ▶ 대명사–one, another, the other, others

1 one

(1) 막연한 사람

One has to rely on **oneself** for everything in the mountains.

I never found **one** who'd been in the park more than 2 hours.

(2) a(an)+명사

I like this kind of hat. Please show me **one**.

We'd like to buy a new car, but we cannot afford **one**.

I don't want to wear my old shoes. I want to wear new **ones**.

Their marriage was a wonderful and happy **one**.

1
(1) 막연한 일반 사람들을 나타낸다.
   (= everyone, anyone, people)

(2) 정해져 있지 않고 막연한 대상(a+명사)
   을 나타내며, 앞에 형용사가 올 수 있다.
   * 복수명사를 대신할 때 ones로 표현한다.

2 one / another / the other / others

* One~, the other~	(둘 중)하나 ~, 나머지 하나 ~
* One~, another~, the other~	(셋 중)하나 ~, 또 하나 ~, 나머지 하나 ~
* One~, the others~	(다수 중)하나 ~, 나머지 모두 ~
* Some~, others~	(다수 중)몇몇 ~, (막연한)다른 것들 ~

One is a music book and **the other** is an art book.

One player's gain is the **other player's** loss.

One is for you, **another** is for me, and **the other** is for father.

He is a singer and his son is **another**.

One student passed in the exam but **the others** failed.

Some students are very creative, and **others** are not.

2
one은 막연한 '하나'를 나타내며, another
는 막연한 '또 하나의 다른 것'을 나타낸다.
* the other는 '나머지 하나'를 나타내며,
others는 막연한 '다른 것들'을 나타낸다.

= a singer, too.

– the other = the third

3 No(=not any), None(=no one)

There isn**'t any** milk here.　　(=There's **no** milk here.)

She did**n't** give me **any** help at all.　(= She gave me **no** help at all.)

People have **no** food to eat.　　(=People have **none** to eat.)

I phoned Mary at home, but there was **no answer**.

He seems very lonely at school, and has **no friends**.

None of the food we had was particularly helpful.

Of the ten most popular cars, **none** were produced in Korea.

3
not~any를 의미하는 부정어 no~ 뒤에는
단수명사나 복수명사가 올 수 있다.

EXERCISE

A Complete the sentences using 'it(them)' or 'one(ones)'.

1 I'm looking for a used car. But just a small _____ .

2 I've got the stamp. I put _____ in the envelope by mistake.

3 He lives near a big shopping center. _____ must be very noisy.

4 Put away the dirty food and get some clean and fresh _____ .

5 His family is a small one. _____ consists of himself, his wife, and a son.

6 I planted some small sized trees but he planted lots of large _____ .

7 He would sell that old house and build a new _____ .

B Complete the sentences using 'another', 'the other', 'the others', or 'others'.

1 We'll need _____ five minutes to serve everything.

2 Some people chose the smaller pumpkins. _____ chose the larger ones.

3 Jane has only two hats. One is a blue one and _____ is a black one.

4 We have five fingers. One is our thumb and _____ is our index finger.
   The third one is our middle finger and the fourth finger is the ring finger.
   And _____ finger is our little finger.

5 We have many means of transportation. The bus is one means of transportation.
   The airplane is _____ .

6 Six of us fell into the water but _____ managed to jump across the water.

C Complete the sentences with your opinions.

1 Some students are very tall; others are ___*very short*___ .

2 Only two of the boys like classical music, but the others _____ .

3 Some people like to have straight hair, but _____ .

4 Some students in our class are lazy, but others are _____ .

5 Some of us are morning people; others are _____ .

6 Some people like to go for long walks in a forest. Others prefer to _____
   _____ .

7 Some old palaces have fallen. Others disappeared because of _____ .

A Choose the right words for (A) and (B).

People frequently talk about having an angel on (A) <one / the one> shoulder and the devil on (B) <the other / the others>. The devil is the thoughts telling you to do something wrong in order to gain short term personal satisfaction. The angel is your conscience telling you not to listen to the devil.

B Read and answer the questions in English.

Why is it that some people are fortunate enough to succeed with seemingly no effort, while (A) <others / the other> struggle all their lives to make ends meet? The main cause can't be a physical one; otherwise only good looking people would be successful and other people would be subjected to slave labor. Yet there are countless examples that plain-looking people are insanely successful. We know (B) <it / one> is a mental ability that determines your success. Success blossoms from your mind: your mental outlook impacts the way you live. In other words 당신의 삶을 통제하는 것은 바로 당신의 마음이다.

1 Choose the right words for (A) and (B).

2 Rearrange the words to have the same meaning as the underlined part.
In other words, it <your mind / that / controls / is / your life>

→ In other words, it _____.

C Read and answer the question in English.

Tips-for-Travel has completely renewed its website! (A) It's got not only small changes but an entirely new concept. We think that (B) it looks more professional than the previous one. (C) It will give us the chance to expand our programs to several more countries, and (D) it'll be easier to find out and use our new site. However, we also fear that the changes in our colors and logo make the frequent visitors not recognize us. So, we are sending this newsletter to all our contacts to assure you that we are the same company and the same people. Please take a look at our new site!

1 Choose one of the above (A) ~ (D) whose meaning is different from the others.

A conscience 양심 devil 악마 short term 단기간 **B** otherwise 그렇지 않으면 be subjected to ~를 받다, ~에 시달리다 insane 미친, 제정신이 아닌 **C** professional 전문적인 expand 확장하다 assure 확신시키다

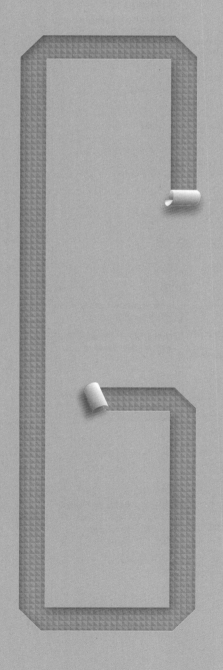

Unit 28

대명사-2

1 수량표현의 대명사
2 재귀대명사

Questions

1 무조건 단수로 취급해야 하는 대명사가 있나요?
2 "너 자신을 알라!"를 영어로는 어떻게 표현할까?

Answers

1 every와 each는 무조건 단수로 취급해야 하고 all이나 helf는 경우에 따라
  달라진다. 이렇듯 무조건 단수로 취급해야 하는 대명사와 경우에 따라 달라지
  는 대명사를 정리하면 고민이 해결된다.
2 "Know you!"가 아니라 "Know yourself!"가 된다. 왜냐하면 주어와 목적어
  가 동일인이기 때문이다. 주어와 목적어가 동일인이면 목적어를 재귀대명사
  (-self)로 써야 한다.

1 ▶ 수량표현(Quantity)의 대명사(Pronoun)

1 either와 neither / both와 all / each와 every

종류	의미	특징
either	둘 중 하나	* There are two eggs. **Either** is too old. * **Either** he or I am wrong. * Can we trust **either** of them?
neither	둘 다 아닌	* There are two eggs. **Neither** is too old. * **Neither** I nor she is wrong. * I like **neither** of them.
each	각각	* **Each** student in the class reads novels. * **Each** of students has a blue shirt.
every	(전체)모든	* Do something new **every** month. * **every** two months: 2개월마다 　(=**every** second month, **every** other month)
both	둘 다	* **Both** of us can help you. * **Both** my sons(=Both of my sons) are asleep.
all half	모두 절반	* **All** my friends(=All of my friends) live here. * **Half** this money(=Half of this money) is his.

Either of them is a major threat to human life or health.
Neither of them is planning to go to the dance.

1
– 단수 취급
– B에 동사일치(either A or B)

– 단수 취급
– B에 동사일치(neither A nor B)

– 단수 취급

– 단수 취급

2 few와 little / much와 many

* not a little (=no little, quite a little)	=much
* not a few (=no few, quite a few)	=many

I just need a **little** of your attention.
Only a **few** of them recognized me.

We felt **not a little** pride on this occasion.
Not a few schoolboys have laptop computers.

2
수(數)에는 few와 many, 양에는 little과 much를 사용한다.

관사(a) 없이 단순한 few와 little은 '거의 없는'의 부정적인 의미를 나타낸다.

– 대명사
– few는 부정적 의미이지만 복수의 의미를 지닌다.
– 형용사

3 most / most of

□ the most(가장) - This is **the most** beautiful scene.
□ most of(대부분의) - **Most of them** are high school students.
□ most(대부분의) - **Most people** are Korean.
□ most(부사:가장) - I like him **most**.
□ mostly(부사:대부분) - These cars are **mostly** made in Korea.
□ almost(부사:거의) - He comes here **almost** every day.

3
최상급의 의미에는 the가 붙는다.
'대부분의'를 나타내는 most of는 명사 앞에서 of를 생략(most+명사)하는 것이 보통이다.

176

EXERCISE

A Complete the sentences using the words in the box.

| either | neither | both | all | most | few |

1 I tried two hotels yesterday, but _____neither of_____ them had any rooms.

2 Hannah hasn't been abroad. She has lived here _____ of her life.

3 I asked the two boys for directions, but _____ ran away without any reason.

4 I sent invitation cards to Tim and Cathy and _____ of them have come.

5 A big storm is coming. _____ the horses I had for training were shipped home.

6 We were both so excited, because _____ of us had seen a buffalo in the wild.

B Complete the sentences using 'every' or 'each'.

1 The plant generally flowers _____ other year.

2 Twins can look the same, but _____ one has his own personalities.

3 If you got paid _____ two weeks, you'd get 26 paychecks in the year.

4 I had to switch cars 3 times because _____ car had a different problem.

5 We are open 'til midnight _____ day so there's plenty of time to browse.

6 Our homepage picture will be updated _____ few hours with a new image.

7 The six players are diverse in age and _____ one has his own strengths.

C Match the beginning of each sentence with the most appropriate ending.

1 *The work brings me great pleasure,* ———— a. *and it gives not a little pride.*

2 It was difficult to learn African languages,   b. so he enjoys nature almost every day.

3 He works two jobs to support his family   c. so he has little time for anything else.

4 Hurry up, or we'll miss the train   d. because we have few visitors from Africa.

5 My husband works at South Park   e. and there is little time to spare.

6 Presently every teacher doesn't get paid   f. so most citizens are not able to attend.

7 They schedule the meeting at 8 a.m.,   h. because most of them are volunteers.

2 ▶ 재귀대명사(Reflexive Pronoun)

1 재귀대명사(Reflexive Pronoun)

(1) 용도와 위치(usage and position)

He described **himself** as an engineer.

Heaven helps those who help **themselves**.

Would you tell me a little bit about **yourself**?

(2) 재귀대명사의 정확한 사용

Children need those who believe in **themselves**.   (×)

→ Children need those who believe in **them**.   (○)

(3) 강조하기 위한 재귀대명사

The president announced the news **himself**.

They painted the house and fence **themselves**.

Mary **herself** doesn't have much to say today.

2 재귀대명사 표현

(1) by oneself(=by one's own)

Children can start eating their meals **by themselves**.

The beginners are not allowed to canoe **by themselves**.

Four girls are staying **on their own** in an isolated farmhouse.

(2) 동사+재귀대명사

* adapt(적응시키다)	adapt oneself to : ~에 적응하다
* suit(적합시키다)	suit oneself : 자신이 원하는대로 하다
* devote(바치다)	devote oneself to : ~에 몰두하다
* apply(열중케하다)	apply oneself to : ~에 전념하다
* lose(잃어버리다)	lose oneself in : 몰두하다, 길을 잃다
* seat(앉히다)	seat oneself : 자리에 앉다

(3) 자주 사용하는 표현

* Pride yourself on your health.	당신의 건강을 자랑스럽게 여기세요.
* Help yourself to this.	이것 많이 드세요.(맘껏~하다)
* Make yourself at home.	편히 쉬세요.
* Be yourself!	진정하라, 정신차려라.
* He comes to himself.	의식을 되찾다, 제정신이 들다.
* Enjoy yourself!	재미있게 놀아!

1

(1) 주어와 목적어가 동일인이면 목적어를 재귀대명사(-self)로 써야 한다.

– 동사의 목적어

– 동사의 목적어

– 전치사의 목적어

(2) 재귀대명사는 '주어+동사+목적어'에서 주어와 목적어가 동일인인 경우에만 사용한다.

– who와 them은 동일인이 아님

(3) 주어나 목적어 뒤에 쓰여서 '직접, 친히, 혼자'를 나타낸다.

2

(1) '혼자힘으로(without others' help)', '홀로, 외로이(alone)'를 나타낸다.

(2) 스스로에게 동작을 하는 경우 재귀대명사를 주로 사용한다.

= be proud of, take pride in

– at home=comfortable

EXERCISE

A   Choose the right words.

1   Come in and make \<oneself / yourself> comfortable.

2   He applied \<him / himself> to the study of English.

3   I found \<me / myself> sleeping in a stranger's yard.

4   One should adapt \<himself / oneself> to circumstances.

5   Help \<you / yourself> to the hot tea before it gets cold.

6   When he touched the lock, the door opened of \<himself / itself>.

7   Suit \<you / yourself>. But you're really missing out good chances.

8   Pay attention to the warning sound, or you may hurt \<yourself / you>.

9   She kept telling \<himself / herself> that she would scold him someday.

B   Complete the sentences using 'reflexive pronouns'.

1   You don't have to worry about them. They can look after _*themselves*_ .

2   I think it's not your fault. Please don't blame _____.

3   In fact, I have lied about my age. I'm ashamed of _____.

4   He doesn't rely on others. He prides _____ on being a self-starter.

5   For safety, never put _____ behind the wheel when you are drunk.

6   We had a great holiday. We enjoyed _____ very much at the party.

7   This site provides excellent software. Help _____ to this free software.

C   Complete the sentences using the given words in the box.

introduce	look at	make	devote	take care of	defend	blame

1   Our new neighbors knocked at our door and _*introduced themselves*_ .

2   Jimmy seems self-confident. He knows how to _____.

3   Nobody can help you. You should _____ against danger.

4   He did his best. He has no reason to _____.

5   Susan headed to the bathroom and _____ in the mirror.

6   My cat, Tommy, became friends with our other cats, and _____ at home.

7   Mary was a loyal Buddhist. She _____ to the temple services.

 Choose the right words for (A) and (B). 기출 응용

When you attempt to do something and fail, you have to ask (A) <you / yourself> why you have failed to do what you intended. Answering this question in a new, unexpected way is the essential creative act. (B) <It / They> will improve your chances of succeeding next time.

 Read and answer the questions in English.

Moreno's twinkling eyes and thin beard gave (A) <him / himself> a natural pride and arrogance but he always <himself / described / as / humble / a shy / and innocent man>. Moreno was one of only nine entertainers to win all four major entertainment awards: the Tony, the Oscar, the Emmy and the Grammy. Moreno also won all four awards in the shortest amount of time: within a 16 year period. Although he described (B) <him / himself> as 'an ordinary character actor', British people have described (C) <him / himself> as 'the greatest gift.'

1 Choose the correct words for (A), (B) and (C).

2 Rearrange the words to complete the sentence.
→ but he always _____.

C **Read and answer the question in English.**

Most plants must hold their leaves above those of competitors in the environment. Without access to sunlight, they can't gather energy. Most of the plants in nature need many hours of sunshine daily in order to grow satisfactorily. Leaves must create a broad enough area of photosynthetic tissue to capture as much sunlight as possible. A large surface area means greater chances of gaining light. A good general rule to remember is that less sun just means slower growth, or may ultimately result in a smaller and less vigorous plant. Usually mornings provide the most intense sunlight for maximum plant growth. Thus the east side <for every plant / position / of your house / is / favored / the most>. *photosynthetic: 광합성의

1 Rearrange the words in the bracket to complete the sentence.
→ Thus the east side _____.

A attempt to 시도하다 essential 꼭 필요한 **B** twinkling 반짝반짝하는 arrogance 거만함 entertainment 연예, 연회 **C** vigorous 원기왕성한 maximum 최대

180

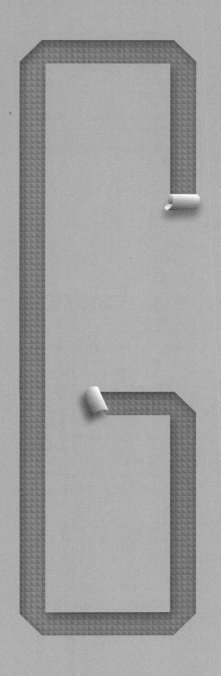

Unit 29

형용사 – 어휘 확장

1 까다로운 형용사
2 파생어

Questions

1 어떤 순서로 단어와 그 단어의 파생어를 외워야 하나요?

2 파생어나 까다로운 어휘를 외우는 비결은 없나요?

Answers

1 쉬운 단어를 먼저 외우고 나서 어렵거나 까다로운 파생어(명사형, 형용사형, 동사형, 부사형)를 추가하여 외우는 것이 효과적이다.

2 까다로운 형용사를 외우기 어렵다면 어구를 만들어 덩어리 형태로 기억하는 것이 효과적이다. 예를들어, industrial revolution(산업혁명)과 industrious ants(부지런한 개미)로 구분하다면 혼동을 피할 수 있다.

1 ▶ 까다로운 형용사

1 형용사+명사(adjective+noun)

* the **whole** story
* the **main** theme
* the **only** solution
* the **absolute** beginner
* the **chief** leader
* the **entire** world
* the **mere** fact
* the **utter** failure

Negotiations are **the only solution** for the Middle East.
Many of you won't acknowledge **the utter failure** of this war.

> 1
> 형용사는 명사를 수식하거나 보어로 사용되지만, 〈형용사+명사〉 형태로 한정적인 역할만 하는 형용사가 있으므로 해석에 유의한다.

2 위치에 따른 의미 변화

* a **present** chairman 현재의   the chairman **present at** ~에 참석한
* a **concerned** doctor 담당의   the doctor **concerned about** ~에 대해 걱정하는
* a **responsible** girl 신뢰할만한   the girl **responsible for** ~에 대해 책임이 있는
* an **involved** question 복잡한   the person **involved in** ~에 관련된

He is a **responsible** man who is sincere about love and marriage.
We do not know the person **responsible for** this death.

> 2
> 하나의 형용사가 다양한 의미를 지니며, 위치에 따라 의미가 구분된다.
>
> 명사 뒤에서 수식하는 형용사의 경우 전치사를 수반한다.

3 형용사와 부사로 쓰이는 enough

I was foolish **enough to** think so.
I could see well **enough to** know we were losing.

We have **enough** information to write a story.
How can I make **enough** money to buy a Ferrari 360?

> 3
> enough는 부사(충분히)로 쓰일 때와 형용사(충분한)로 쓰일 때 그 위치가 각각 정해져 있다.
>
> > 부사의 위치: 형용사/부사+enough to~
> > 형용사의 위치: enough+명사+to~

4 a-로 시작하는 형용사

Do you believe Sam is still **alive**?
Why do people believe we are **alone**?
Police found him **asleep** inside his sport utility vehicle.

> 4
> a-로 시작하는 형용사는 반드시 보어로만 사용되며, 명사를 수식하지 않는다.
>
> > * a-로 시작하는 형용사
> > afraid, alike, alive, alone
> > awake, aware, asleep 등

5 -en/-y로 끝나는 형용사

* wood – a **wooden** table
* stone – a **stony** path
* steel – a **steely** door
* gold – a **golden** sunset
* wool – a **woolen** pullover
* thorn – a **thorny** tree
* silk – a **silken** dress
* earth – an **earthen** jar

> 5
> 형용사+명사로만 사용되며, '~로 만든, ~를 재료로 만든'의 의미이다.
> – 목재로 만든   양털의
> – 돌이 많은   가시가 많은
> – 강철로 만든   비단으로 만든
> – 황금빛의   흙으로 만든

EXERCISE

A Change the word order using adjectives.

1 The UFO looked like a large jar made of earth. → *a large earthen jar*

2 He was riding on a horse made of wood. → _____

3 The wires are covered with thread made of silk. → _____

4 There is a crack in a part of the wall made of stone. → _____

5 She put on a sweater made of wool from Australia. → _____

6 A robot is a man-like machine made of steel. → _____

B Write the given words in the right place.

1 My father is a hard working and _*responsible*_ man _____. (responsible)

2 He appointed the _____ officers _____ for the safety equipment. (responsible)

3 Most of the _____ people _____ in the struggle are now dead. (involved)

4 This _____ process _____ takes long time. It's very complex. (involved)

5 There were over thirty _____ people _____ at the meeting. (present)

6 There is no need to change the _____ law _____. (present)

7 Please tell me the _____ doctor _____ and cost. (concerned)

8 I met many _____ people _____ about the quality of our environment. (concerned)

C Rearrange the words to complete the sentences.

1 He is <master / industrious / enough to / them all / in a week>.
→ He is _*industrious enough to master them all in a week*_ .

2 You'll <after lunch / falling / see / asleep / people>.
→ You'll _____ .

3 There were <involved / a few / people / in the union movements>.
→ There were _____ .

4 Don't forget to <something / take time / to make / special / for your father>.
→ Don't forget to _____ .

5 Micky understands <enough / to teach / it / math / well / to her sister>.
→ Micky understands _____ .

2 ▶ 파생어

주요 파생어 Ⅰ

economy [ikánəmi]
- economic [í:kənámik] 형 경제의, 경제학의
- economical [ì:kənámikəl] 형 절약하는 (= thrifty, frugal)

child [tʃaild]
- childish [tʃáildiʃ] 형 유치한, 어른답지 못한
- childlike [tʃáildlàik] 형 어린애 같은, 귀여운

sense [sens]
- sensible [sénsəbəl] 형 분별력 있는 (명 sensibility 감각력)
- sensitive [sénsətiv] 형 민감한 (명 sensitivity 민감성)
- sensory [sénsəri] 형 감각의

memory [méməri]
- memorable [mémərəbəl] 형 기억할 만한, 잊기 어려운
- memorial [məmɔ́riəl] 형 기념의, 추도의

respect [rispékt]
- respectful [rispéktfəl] 형 존경하는, 예의바른
- respective [rispéktiv] 형 각각의 (부 respectively 각각)

confide [kənfáid]
- confident [kánfidənt] 형 자신이 있는 (명 confidence 자신감)
- confidential [kànfidénʃəl] 형 은밀한, 기밀의

industry [índəstri]
- industrial [indʌ́striəl] 형 산업의
- industrious [indʌ́striəs] 형 부지런한

* 기억하기 쉬운 표현을 만들어 의미를 연상
  하는 방법을 활용한다.
~ housewife
~ adult
~ baby
~ choice
~ skin
~ organ
~ gift
~ day(현충일)
~ behavior
~ role
~ player
~ information
~ revolution
~ student

주요 파생어 Ⅱ

moment [móumənt]
- momentary [móuməntèri] 형 순간적인
- momentous [mouméntəs] 형 중요한

practice [præktis]
- practical [præktikəl] 형 실질적인, 실용적인
- practicable [præktikəbəl] 형 실천할 수 있는

favor [féivər]
- favorable [féivərəbəl] 형 호의적인, 유리한
- favorite [féivərit] 형 가장 좋아하는 (명 좋아하는 것)

succeed [səksí:d]
- successful [səksésfəl] 형 성공적인 (명 success 성공)
- successive [səksésiv] 형 잇따른, 연속적인 (명 succession 연속)

consider [kənsídər]
- considerable [kənsídərəbəl] 형 상당한, 중요한
- considerate [kənsídərit] 형 사려깊은, 동정심 많은

imagine [imædʒin]
- imaginable [imædʒənəbəl] 형 상상할 수 있는
- imaginary [imædʒənèri] 형 상상의
- imaginative [imædʒənətiv] 형 상상력이 풍부한

vary [véəri]
- variable [véəriəbəl] 형 변하기 쉬운 (명 variation 변화)
- various [véəriəs] 형 다양한 (명 variety 다양성)

~ pause
~ decision
~ clothes
~ plan
~ deal
~ poem
~ businessman
~ victory
~ amount
~ behavior
~ result
~ animal
~ poet
~ weather
~ species

EXERCISE

Answers P.42

A **Choose the right meaning of the words.**

1 sensitive   a. having or showing reasonableness or good judgement
2 various   b. feeling or responding readily, strongly, or painfully
3 memorial   c. operating with little waste
4 economical   d. serving to preserve the memory of a person or an event
5 sensible   e. working energetically and devotedly; hard-working; diligent
6 industrious   f. approving or pleasing
7 favorable   g. several different

B **Choose the right words.**

1 You should grow up. You're so <childish / childlike>.
2 His parents were frugal and <industrial / industrious> farmers.
3 When it comes to pain, women are in fact more <sensitive / sensible>.
4 O'Neill won 10 gold medals at three <successful / successive> games.
5 It is very <considerable / considerate> of you to respond to people's questions.
6 I'm <confidential / confident> of the guilt of the person who committed the crime.
7 Any <sensible / sensitive> person must see that violence doesn't change the world.

C **Choose the right words for the blanks.**

1 All contents of this site belong to their _____ authors.

   Later on, athletes from both countries will compete under their _____ flags.

   All other trademarks are the property of their _____ owners.

   ① respective   ② favorite   ③ economical

   ④ sensitive   ⑤ memorial

2 If you could invent your own _____ city what would it be like?

   Children will dismiss the _____ friend once they find real ones.

   What is the _____ animal living on the moon?

   ① favorable   ② imaginary   ③ industrious

   ④ childish   ⑤ memorial

 Choose the right words for (A) and (B).

Generally, a citizen who has resided for five (A) <successive / successful> years will obtain the right of permanent residence. In order to obtain the right of (B) <temporary / contemporary> residence, a citizen must contact the local government authorities. The applicant can be granted the right to reside five years.

 Read and answer the questions in English. 기출 응용

Falling in love is (A) <alike / like> being wrapped in a magical cloud. The air feels fresher, the flowers smell sweeter, food tastes more delicious, and the stars shine more (B) <brilliant / brilliantly> in the night sky. You feel light and happy as though you are sailing through life. Your problems and challenges suddenly seem insignificant. Your body feels (C) <alive / lived>, and you jump out of bed each morning with a smile on your face. <u>You are in a state of supreme delight.</u>

1 Choose the right words for (A), (B) and (C).

2 Rewrite the underlined part into another one using '-ed adjective'.
  → You feel _____ _____.

C **Read and answer the questions.**

Aloe vera has been used externally to heal various skin conditions, such as burns and eczema. The lower leaves of the Aloe vera plants are used for medicinal purposes, protecting the immune system and improving digestive function. Its multiple beneficial properties may come from the (A) <present substances / substances present> in the gel of the plant's leaves. The light gel cream is (B) <valuable / variable> in soothing the eye area, reducing swellings and removing little wrinkles. Aloe gel is also useful for dry skin conditions, especially (C) <sensible / sensitive> facial skin. One should always use the inner gel of the plant and not the aloe latex which is the yellow substance that comes from the inner side of the skin of the plant.

1 Choose the right words for (A), (B) and (C).

2 According to the passage, mostly for what part of the body is aloe good?
  → Aloe is mostly good for _____.

Ⓐ reside 거주하다 permanent 영구적인 grant 주다, 수여하다   Ⓑ wrap 감싸다 challenge 도전 supreme 최고의   Ⓒ digestive 소화의 beneficial 유익한, 이익을 가져오는 property 재산, 성질, 특성 substance 물질 wrinkle 주름

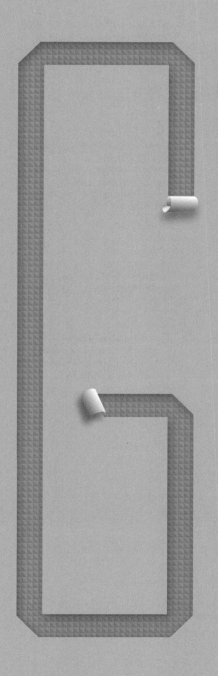

Unit 30

형용사와 부사

----

1 다양한 부사
2 혼동하기 쉬운 형용사와 부사

Questions

1 -ly로 끝나는 단어는 모두 부사인가요?

2 hard(힘든, 단단한, 열심히)처럼 다의어들은 어떻게 외우나요?

3 부사의 위치는 정해져 있나요?

Answers

1 friendly, lovely와 같은 단어는 -ly로 끝나지만 형용사이다. 따라서 -ly로 끝나는 단어는 모두 부사라고 생각하면 안된다.

2 가장 좋은 것은 다의어가 들어간 문장을 기억하는 것이지만, 그렇게 하려면 시간이 오래 걸리므로, hard work(힘든 일), hard board(단단한 판), work hard(열심히 일하다)처럼 어구를 만들어 덩어리로 외우는 방법이 효과적이다.

3 우리말에서 부사의 위치가 특별히 정해져 있지 않은 것처럼, 영어에서도 원칙대로 사용되지 않아도 큰 문제는 없다. 하지만, 빈도부사, 부정부사, yet 등은 문장 구성상 정해진 위치를 지켜야 한다.

1 ▶ 다양한 부사

1 부사구(adverb phrase)

I was really lucky to live **with British students for a year**.
He explained to me **with great patience** that he was in trouble.
She asked me **in such a nice manner** that I couldn't refuse.

2 부사(adverb), 전치사(preposition), 접속사(conjunction)

Fiona saw Chelsea win the game. She called me shortly **after**.
Our nuclear policy has changed two times **since** World War II.
After he took the watch apart, he couldn't put it together again.

3 문장 앞의 부사

Beyond the house / lies the open field.
Just down the hill / was the resort center.

Unfortunately, I had an aisle seat three rows from the back.
Last year I collected 50 cans and **this year** I collected 35 cans.

4 빈도부사의 위치(adverb of frequency)

I'm so excited that I can **hardly** stand it.
Eating too much **often** results in illness.
He's **always** trying to do the best he can.

5 자주 등장하는 부사 – still, already, yet

still	여전히 아직도	I'm **still** waiting for the bus. (긍정문) He wouldn't **still** leave. (부정문)
already (문장 뒤나 중간)	이미 벌써	I have **already** finished it. (긍정문) Have you **already** finished it? (의문문)
yet (문장 뒤)	아직 벌써	He has not arrived **yet**. (부정문) Has he finished the work **yet**? (의문문)

6 다양한 연결 부사(connecting adverb)

* **to be brief** = briefly, in brief, in a word, in short

* **to summarize** = in brief, in conclusion

* **to add something** = in addition, besides, moreover, furthermore

* **to express one's/my opinion** = as far as I'm concerned, in my opinion

---

1
부사는 하나의 단어나 부사구(전치사+명사)
의 형태를 띤다.

2
since, before, after는 용도에 따라 전치사,
부사, 접속사로 사용되기도 한다.
– 부사

– 전치사

– 접속사

3
장소의 부사를 문장 앞에 두면, 동사+주어
의 순서로 도치된다.
* 단, 동사가 자동사이며, 또 다른 부사가 없
  을 때 이러한 도치가 나타난다.
* 부사의 의미를 강조하고 싶을 때 문장 앞
  에 부사를 두어 문장 전체를 수식할 수 있
  다.

4
빈도부사는 부정문의 not 위치와 같다. be
동사와 조동사의 뒤에, 일반 동사의 앞에 위
치한다.

> – 빈도부사
> * always, often, generally,
>   usually, frequently, sometimes
> * seldom, hardly, ever, never,
>   scarcely, rarely, barely

EXERCISE

A **Write the right adverbs in the blanks.**

1 He is a sincere worker. He works _____sincerely_____.

2 Harry is an eager dancer. He dances _____.

3 The fire fighters were brave. They acted _____.

4 Mac delivered a careful speech. He spoke _____.

5 The bus was late. It came _____ by sixteen minutes.

6 He is one of the early risers. He always gets up _____.

7 My teacher made a quick answer. He answered _____.

B **Complete the sentences using 'yet', 'already', or 'still'.**

1 It's nine o'clock and Dick is _____ working.

2 We have had enough but we are _____ hungry.

3 Have you joined the tennis club _____? Welcome!

4 I have _____ answered the rest of the questions.

5 Have you _____ got that information from the media?

6 I haven't got the tickets _____. I will wait until midnight.

7 You have to tell Jimmy. He doesn't know the truth _____.

C **Complete the sentences by choosing the right words in the box.**

fortunately	obviously	generally	personally	unbelievably	frankly

1 It is unfortunate that your claim is worthless.

→ _____Unfortunately_____, your claim is worthless.

2 To say what I really think, you've not been much help to me.

→ _____, you've not been much help to me.

3 It is fortunate that it was not too cold this year.

→ _____, it was not too cold this year.

4 I'm sure we've seen him somewhere before.

→ _____, we've seen him somewhere before.

5 In my opinion, I object to people abusing their freedom of speech.

→ _____, I object to people abusing their freedom of speech.

2 ▶ 혼동하기 쉬운 형용사와 부사

1 형용사인가, 부사인가! 다의어(multi-sense word)

fast	형 빠른, 단단한	My watch is 5 minutes **fast**.
	부 빨리, 곤하게	The baby sleeps **fast**.
slow	형 느린	The guests are **slow** in arriving.
	부 천천히	Please drive **slow** here.
last	형 마지막의	He is my **last** hope.
	부 마지막으로	We met **last** ten days ago.
pretty	형 귀여운	Everyone is very **pretty** in the mirror.
	부 꽤, 상당히	He plays tennis **pretty** well.
well	형 건강한(서술적)	You'll soon get **well**.
	부 알맞게, 잘	She speaks English **well**.
long	형 오랜, 긴	How **long** is it from here?
	부 오래, 길게	He has stayed here **long**.
ill	형 나쁜, 아픈	She is **ill** in bed.
	부 나쁘게	Everyone speaks **ill** of him.

1
- 통 단식하다 –
  He fasted for seven days.

- 통 지속하다 –
  The storm lasted for three days.

- 부 prettily 예쁘게

- look well 건강해보이다

- 통 갈망하다
  I longed for him to say something.

2 부사로 착각하기 쉬운 형용사

Navigator can give the driver **timely** advice on efficient driving.
In the past, sugar was a **costly** food enjoyed by the wealthy.

* costly	형 값비싼	* elderly	형 나이 많은
* lively	형 생기있는, 활기찬	* lovely	형 사랑스러운
* silly	형 어리석은	* friendly	형 친숙한
* timely	형 시기적절한	* quarterly	형 1년에 4번의
* manly	형 남성다운	* worldly	형 세속의

2
일반적으로 <u>명사+ly</u> = 형용사,
<u>형용사+ly</u> = 부사가 된다.
* 파생어가 아니라 원래 -ly로 끝나는 어휘도
  있으므로 주의한다.

* 시간의 형용사
daily 매일의   weekly 매주의
monthly 월간의   yearly 연간의
hourly 매시간의

3 의미를 바꾸는 부사 -ly

* high	형 높은 부 높이	highly	부 매우 (예: think highly of)
* late	형 늦은 부 늦게	lately	부 최근에 (예: until lately)
* near	형 가까운 부 가까이	nearly	부 거의 (예: nearly dead)
* hard	형 단단한, 힘든 부 열심히	hardly	부 거의 ~않는
* direct	형 직접의 부 똑바로	directly	부 즉시
* short	형 짧은 부 짧게	shortly	부 곧 (예: shortly after)

The government thinks **highly** of foreign investment.
Love and marriage came **late** in life for Cole Palen.

3
접미사 -ly가 와서 본래 의미와는 다른 부사
를 만드는 경우에 주의해야 한다.

–예: Do it directly.

EXERCISE

A Choose the right words.

1 I'm afraid I don't feel very <live / lively> today.

2 It is very <cost / costly> to produce the first copy of papers.

3 He has been feeling very lonely <late / lately>, so he needs friends.

4 Don't go too <near / nearly> the edge of the cliffs. It's too dangerous.

5 He was a very proud man and thought very <high / highly> of himself.

6 Most teenagers can <hard / hardly> earn enough to pay their cellphone bills.

7 There are increasing numbers of <elder / elderly> people in western societies.

8 The training is very <hard / hardly>, but I'm trying very hard to get used to it.

B Match each sentence on the left with one on the right.

1 *I completed the assignments nearly.* a. I'll be there soon.

2 An assistant gets paid weekly. b. It is published four times per year.

3 She has hardly worn the coat. c. Too many students are late for school.

4 'Poetry Wales' is a quarterly magazine. d. She will be paid every Friday.

5 My teacher has been upset lately. e. It no longer fits so she has to sell it.

6 He passed away shortly after war. f. Thank you for your good advice.

7 Your advice was timely and invaluable. g. He was buried in National Cemetery.

C Choose the right words and change the form if necessary.

fast	slow	last	pretty	well	long

1 These insects are _____ high on the nutrition scale.

2 Maybe the thing he _____ for so long is a new hat.

3 He is getting _____ and thank you for the caring of him.

4 I've walked so _____ . I can't remember where my home is.

5 My computer _____ down considerably. How can I speed it back up?

6 This paper is dried so _____ after printing and ink does not run over it.

A Choose the right words for (A) and (B).

For the first 2 weeks of my ownership of the N95, I was (A) <prettily / pretty> unhappy. I was a very heavy mobile phone user, but the battery lasted only 7 hours per day. Now, though, I get well over 2 days from the battery. So everything is (B) <very / well> now.

B Read and answer the questions in English.

Dick would show up in Florida a lot and (A) <always feel / feel always> so zealous and happy. He'd travel with his little backpack that was still smaller than my purse. Lately I have been thinking about how he (B) <hard / hardly> ever had any baggage. I think that his free spirit and his curiosity enabled him to travel lightly with little baggage. He didn't hesitate to touch hundreds of lives and was willing to stay in contact with everyone. He not only created relationships with people all over the world, but he maintained them. My friend once said that in a relationship there is the gardener and there is the flower. Dick was a gardener.

1 Choose the right words for (A) and (B).
2 Why does author say 'Dick was a gardener.'?
→ 'Dick was a gardener.' means that he _____.

C Read and answer the question in English.

When you think about diabetes you usually think it has something to do with sugar. But sadly, that's not all to it. A patient is diagnosed as having prediabetes when glucose called blood sugar is higher than normal but not high enough to be diagnosed as diabetes. Our body needs glucose to function properly, but occasionally it becomes incapable of processing the sugar that it gets from foods. Once the body can't process sugar efficiently, it is diagnosed as diabetes. Knowing that the symptoms are in the early stages can aid in getting the proper treatment. This is why <on a regular basis / a diabetic patient / his or her blood sugar levels / frequently / tests>.

1 Rearrange the words to complete the sentence.
→ This is why _____.

Ⓐ ownership 소유자 자격, 소유권 last 지속하다 standby 대기, 예비 Ⓑ backpack 배낭 curiosity 호기심 Ⓒ diabetes 당뇨 glucose 포도당 occasionally 이따금, 때때로 process 처리하다 diagnose 진단하다

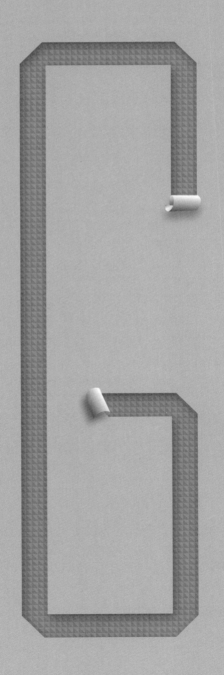

Unit 31

관사와 전치사

1 아 다르고, 어 다르다! – 관사
2 아 다르고, 어 다르다! – 전치사

Questions

1 영어를 모국어로 하지 않는 외국인에게 가장 취약한 부분이 관사라는데!

2 뒤에 붙는 전치사에 따라 의미가 다른 표현들이 있던데!

Answers

1 관사(the)의 사용은 정말 까다로워 원어민도 정확하지 않을 정도라고 한다. 하지만, 기본적인 원칙만은 적용할 줄 알아야 한다. 수식 받는 명사 앞에, 정해진 대상의 명사 등에는 반드시 **the**를 붙인다.

2 그래서 전치사에 따라 의미가 바뀌는 표현들을 모아서 정리해 두었다.

Unit 31

1 ▶ '아'다르고 '어'다르다 – 관사(Article)

1 명사 앞의 정관사 the(definite article)

(1) 특정한 명사 앞의 the(the+particular noun)

The young man began to run towards **the** boy.

I had a sandwich for breakfast. **The** sandwich was good.

Young people usually don't like **these** operas.

(2) 수식어가 있는 명사 앞의 the (the+modified noun)

The gift you gave me is so valuable it must be guarded.

This is a good way of getting **the** mobile phone you wanted.

What is **the** name of that woman we met at the church?

1

(1) 정해진 명사를 지칭하는 경우 일반적으로 명사 앞에 the를 붙인다.

* 지칭하는 명사 앞에 this(these)나 that (those)을 붙이기도 한다.

(2) 명사에 수식어가 따를 경우 특정 명사이므로 명사 앞에 the를 붙인다.

2 the가 있느냐 없느냐!

1	out of question	확실한, 확실히 (= without question)
	out of the question	불가능한 (= impossible, uncertain)
2	behind time	지각한, 늦은 (= late)
	behind the time	시대에 뒤진 (= out of date)
3	time	시간 (Do you have time?)
	the time	시대, 기간 (Do you have the time?)
4	take place	발생하다 (= happen)
	take the place (of)	대신하다 (= substitute)

Her marriage with Brad is **out of question**.

Military action against Iran is **out of the question**.

2

– 시간 있니?

– 몇시니?

3 a number of / the number of

* a number of the number of	많은 (= many) ~의 수	+복수동사 +단수동사
* a kind of the kind of	일종의 (= a sort of) ~의 종류 (= the sort of)	+단수동사
* a variety of the variety of	다양한 ~의 다양성	+단수동사
* a range of the range of	일정 범위의 ~의 범위	+단수동사

A variety of tools are used to gather information.

The variety of cultures offers great experience for the travelers.

Whales are **a kind of** animals that live in the water.

The kind of animals isn't limited to mammals, reptiles, and amphibians.

3

the는 수식받는 명사에 붙이므로 the+명사 of~는 뒤에서부터 해석하며, a+명사 of~는 앞에서부터 해석을 한다.

194

EXERCISE

A **Complete the sentences using 'the' only when necessary.**

1 This event will take _____ place of our October meeting.

2 Marriage is out of _____ question when neither has objection.

3 Auditions will take _____ place throughout the weekend at the W Hotel.

4 "Excuse me, Miss, do you have _____ time?" "See, I don't wear a watch."

5 It is difficult to work well if you're behind _____ time with your work schedule.

6 In the future, I really want to drive, which is not entirely out of _____ question.

7 Do you have _____ time to keep up with the latest movies, books, and design?

B **Complete the sentences using 'is' or 'are'.**

1 A number of trees ___*were*___ removed for cattle grazing.

2 The number of trees per acre _____ 30 or fewer.

3 There _____ a range of services that customers can take advantage of.

4 The kind of flowers you use _____ based on the event you plan.

5 A variety of cultures _____ on display in the form of music and food.

6 The variety of foods _____ less on islands than on mainland.

C **Rearrange the words to complete the sentences.**

1 Experts say <with diabetes / the number / cats / of / is increasing>. *diabetes: 당뇨병
   → Experts say ___*the number of cats with diabetes is increasing*___.

2 A car crashed into <the driver / the car / a tree / and / of> wasn't hurt.
   → A car crashed into _____ wasn't hurt.

3 I stayed at a hotel. But I <at / near / ate / the / hotel / a / restaurant>.
   → I stayed at a hotel. But I _____.

4 There are <variety / of / a / throughout / events / the / year>.
   → There are _____.

5 Wood burning is <of / the / question / apartment buildings / in / out>.
   → Wood burning is _____.

2 '아'다르고 '어'다르다 – 전치사(Preposition)

1 전치사 + 명사 = 접속사 + 주어 + 동사

* because of+명사 = because S+V	~ 때문에
* according to+명사 = according as S+V	~ 에 따르면, ~ 에 따라서
* in spite of(=despite)+명사 = though S+V	~ 에도 불구하고
* in case of+명사 = in case S+V	~ 할 경우에
* in proportion to+명사 = in proportion as S+V	~ 에 비례하여

According to a Gallup Poll, 67% say they disapprove the law.
We see things differently, **according as** we are rich or poor.

접속사 뒤에는 완전한 문장이 오며, 전치사 뒤에는 반드시 명사가 온다.

2 전치사에 따라 의미가 다르다

(1) 형용사 뒤의 전치사(adjective+preposition)

be angry about	~ 에 관해 화내다
be angry with	~ (사람)에게 화를 내다
be anxious about	~ 에 관해 걱정하다
be anxious for	~ 를 열망하다 (= be anxious to + 동사)
be good at	~ 에 능숙하다 (≠be bad at)
be good for	~ 에 좋다 (≠be bad for)
be concerned about	~ 에 관해 걱정하다
be concerned with	~ 와 관계있다
be sorry about	~ 에 대해 미안하다
be sorry for	~ 에 대해 유감스럽다 (동정심을 느끼다)

Everyone **was anxious for** the last of the events-fireworks.
Lora **was anxious about** leaving friends and meeting new ones.

(2) 동사 뒤의 전치사(verb+preposition)

* consist in	~에 놓여있다	consist of	~로 구성되어 있다
* attend to	~에 주의를 기울이다	attend on	~의 시중들다, 간호하다
* succeed in	~에 성공하다	succeed to	~ 을 계승하다
* result in	~란 결과를 가져오다	result from	~의 결과이다
* deal with	~을 다루다	deal in	장사하다

(3) 명사 앞의 전치사(preposition+noun)

* in the way	방해되는	on the way	도중에
* on duty	당번인	off duty	비번인
* in behalf of	~을 위하여	on behalf of	~을 대표하여
* in time	제 시간에	on time	정각에

 **EXERCISE**

A Complete the sentences using the words in the box.

consist	attend	succeed	result	deal

1 Scientist showed that water ___*consists of*___ hydrogen and oxygen.

2 Queen Elizabeth II _____ the throne in 1952.　　　*throne: 왕좌

3 Anyway, you can _____ life without going to college.

4 Floods that occurred in early August _____ heavy rain.

5 The citizenry _____ my words and believed them.

6 Snowfalls in China _____ the reduced exports of fruit and vegetables.

B Choose the right words.

1 <Because / Because of> the Internet, we have won the election.

2 <Because / Because of> the Internet never sleeps, these are available 24 hours a day.

3 According <as / to> an expert cook, low-fat food is tasteless but healthy.

4 According <as / to> the weather is calm or windy, the temperature varies.

5 <Despite / Though> the large tax cuts, the current economic expansion is weaker.

6 <Despite / Though> exam results are important for you, they are not everything.

7 <In case / In case of> danger, your responsibility is to yell 'Man the lifeboats!'

8 <In case / In case of> there's something wrong with this CD player, can I return it?

C Complete the sentences using the words in the box.

about	with	for	into

1 I think God was concerned _____ man's thoughts.

2 Investors should not be concerned _____ short-term losses.

3 When you get angry _____ something, here are some ways to calm down.

4 He was angry _____ her because she had hurt his pride.

5 He was anxious _____ peace and recognition from the pope.

6 As a mom, I was anxious _____ every physical change in my baby's body.

UNIT 31 **197**

 Choose the right words for (A) and (B).

> When Ben's family moved into a white neighborhood, the kids would tease Ben (A) <because / because of> his terrible Spanish accent. The move was good for him (B) <despite / in spite> the culture shock, because now Ben could only speak English. Little by little, Ben learned to speak and write the English language.

 Read and answer the question. 기출 응용

> Many people keep big cats (A) <as / like> pets across U.S., in spite of risk. How would you feel if you discovered that a tiger is living next door in your suburban neighborhood? Like puppies, big cats are quite appealing when they're young and playful. In fact, the country may have more pet tigers than there are estimated to be remaining in their wild habitats in Asia, (B) <according to / according as> research done for the National Geographic Ultimate Explorer television documentary. Acquiring large cats is legal and surprisingly easy in many states in the United States. But most owners end up with trouble and damage.

1 Choose the right words for (A) and (B).

C **Read and answer the question.**

> Wessex is one of the kingdoms of Anglo-Saxon Britain. According to the documents pertaining to its origin, Ethelwulf succeeded to the throne of Wessex at his father's death in 839, while the eastern provinces went to his son or brother. A similar division took place on Ethelwulf's death between his two sons Ethelbald and Ethelberht. Later, the former was succeeded in 865 by Ethelred and the latter by Alfred in 871. This was the period of the great Danish invasion. Shortly afterwards Ethelred accepted Alfred's overlordship. By 886 Alfred's authority was recognized in all the provinces of England which were not under Danish rule. From this time onwards the history of Wessex is the history of England.

1 Complete the following sentence to represent the main idea of the passage.
  → The history of England originated in the kingdom of _____.

Ⓐ tease 놀리다 Ⓑ suburban 교외의 puppy 강아지 appealing 애원적인; 매력적인 habitat 서식지, 주거지 legal 법적인 Ⓒ origin 기원, 유래 succeed to ~를 계승하다 throne 왕좌 province 지방, 지역(district) the former 전자(前者) the latter 후자 overlordship 대군주의 지위

부록

1. 동사의 변화

1 형태상 혼동하기 쉬운 동사변화

현재형	과거형	과거분사 (PP)	의미 (Meaning)
lie	lay	lain	자 눕다, 놓여있다
lay	laid	laid	타 ~을 놓다, 눕히다
lie	lied	lied	자 거짓말하다
rise	rose	risen	자 (해, 달이)뜨다
raise	raised	raised	타 재배하다, ~을 올리다
arise	arose	arisen	자 발생하다, (일이)생기다
arouse	aroused	aroused	타 발생시키다, 불러일으키다
set	set	set	타 ~을 두다, 배치하다
sit	sat	sat	자 앉다
seat	seated	seated	타 앉히다
hang	hung	hung	타 ~을 걸다, 매달다
hang	hanged	hanged	타 교수형에 처하다
see	saw	seen	타 ~을 보다
sow	sowed	sown	타 씨를 뿌리다
sew	sewed	sewn	타 꿰매다, 바느질하다
find	found	found	타 발견하다
found	founded	founded	타 설립하다, 기초하다
wind	wound	wound	타 ~을 감다
wound	wounded	wounded	타 상처를 입히다
fly	flew	flown	자 날아가다
flow	flowed	flowed	자 (물이) 흐르다
blow	blew	blown	자 불다 타 불어대다
bear	bore	born	타 (아이를) 낳다, 간직하다
bore	bored	bored	타 지루하게 하다
shine	shone	shone	자 빛나다
shine	shined	shined	타 비추다
hurt	hurt	hurt	타 해치다
upset	upset	upset	타 뒤집다
hit	hit	hit	타 때리다, 치다
shut	shut	shut	타 닫다, 닫히다

2 쉽지만 주의해야 할 동사변화

현재형	과거형	과거분사 (PP)	의미 (Meaning)
bring	brought	brought	가져오다, 초래하다
buy	bought	bought	사다, 구입하다
catch	caught	caught	잡다, 따라잡다
fight	fought	fought	싸우다
seek	sought	sought	찾다, 추구하다
drive	drove	driven	운전하다, 몰다
ride	rode	ridden	타다, 타고 가다
rise	rose	risen	일어서다, 기상하다, 오르다
draw	drew	drawn	끌다, 당기다
fly	flew	flown	날다, 비행하다
throw	threw	thrown	던지다, 팽개치다
blow	blew	blown	불다, 바람에 날리다
grow	grew	grown	성장하다, 자라다
know	knew	known	알다, 알고 있다
break	broke	broken	깨다, 부수다
choose	chose	chosen	선택하다, 고르다
freeze	froze	frozen	얼다
speak	spoke	spoken	이야기하다, 말하다
steal	stole	stolen	훔치다, 몰래 빼앗다
do	did	done	하다
begin	began	begun	시작하다
drink	drank	drunk	마시다
eat	ate	eaten	먹다
fall	fell	fallen	떨어지다, 낙하하다
go	went	gone	가다, 향하다
beat	beat	beaten	치다, 때리다
bite	bit	bitten	깨물다
bear	bore	born(e)	나르다, 몸에 지니다
see	saw	seen	보다, 바라보다, 관찰하다
show	showed	shown	보이다, 제시하다, 나타내다
sing	sang	sung	노래하다
swim	swam	swum	수영하다
take	took	taken	손에 잡다, 쥐다, 가져가다
wear	wore	worn	입고 있다, 몸에 지니고 있다

2. -ing(동명사) 형태의 문장 ○ ○ ○

1. **There is no ~ing** ～을 할 수 없다
=It is impossible to~=We cannot~

There is no telling what may happen. ⇒ It is impossible to tell what may happen.

2. **It is no use(good) ~ing** ～해도 소용없다
=It is of no use (useless) to~
=What is the use of~ing? ～하는 것이 무슨 소용이 있겠는가?

It is no use [no good] crying over spilt milk. ⇒ It is of no use [useless] to cry over spilt milk.
⇒ What is the use of crying over spilt milk?

3. **cannot help ~ing** ～하지 않을 수 없다
=have no choice but to 동사원형 ～

She couldn't help laughing to hear the news. ⇒ She had no choice but to laugh to hear the news.

4.
prevent
keep
stop   A from B   A가 B하는 것을 막다
prohibit

The rain prevented me from starting. ⇒ Because of the rain, I could not start.

5. **have difficulty (in) ~ing** ～하느라 고생하다
=have a hard time (in) ~ing
=have trouble (in) ~ing

I had difficulty (in) finding her. ⇒ I had a hard time (in) finding her.

6. **on+ ~ing =as soon as S+V** ～하자마자
in+~ing =When S+V ～할 때에

On hearing the news, he burst into tears. ⇒ As soon as he heard the news, he burst into tears.
I had no difficulty in persuading him. ⇒ When I persuaded him, I had no difficulty.

7. **make a point of ~ing** ～하는 것을 규칙(습관)으로 생각하고 있다
=be in the habit of ~ing
=make it a rule to

He makes a point of getting up early. ⇒ He makes it a rule to get up early.

3. 혼동하기 쉬운 어휘 ○ ○ ○

1 어원을 기억하라!

1. -fer　　운반하다(carry)

defer v. 연기하다	= postpone
infer v. 추리하다, 추론하다	inference n. 추론
prefer v. ~을 더 좋아하다	preference n. 선호

2. -pel　　밀다

expel v. 쫓아내다	= dismiss, drive out
propel v. 추진하다, 몰아대다	propeller n. 프로펠러, 추진기
compel v. 강제하다	compulsion n. 강요, 강제

3. -cede -ceed　　경과

proceed v. 나아가다, 가다	process n. 진행,
recede v. 물러나다, 퇴각하다	recession n. (일시적) 경기 후퇴
exceed v. 넘다, 초과하다	excess n. 초과　excessive adj. 과다의

4. -ceive　　받다

deceive v. 속이다	deceit n. 사기, 기만
perceive v. 지각하다, 감지하다	perception n. 감지, 인지

5. -tribute　　주다, 공유하다

attribute v. ~탓으로 돌리다	attribution n. (~탓으로) 돌림
contribute v. 기여하다	contribution n. 기부, 기여
distribute v. 분배하다	distribution n. 분배

6. -rupt　　깨다

corrupt adj. 부정한, 타락한	corruption n. 타락
abrupt adj. 돌연한, 갑작스러운	abruptly adv. 갑자기
interrupt v. 가로막다, 저지하다	interruption n. 방해

7. -dict　　말

contradict v. 반박하다	contradiction n. 부정, 반박
predict v. 예언하다	prediction n. 예언

8. -scribe　　쓰다

prescribe v. 규정하다, 처방하다	prescription n. 처방
subscribe v. 기부하다, 구독하다	subscription n. 기부, 구독

9. -form　　　형태, 형성

perform v. 실행하다, 이행하다　　　performance n. 실행
reform v. 개혁하다　　　reformation n. 개혁
transform v. 변형시키다　　　transformation n. 변형

10. -scend　　　가다

ascend v. 올라가다　　　ascent n. 상승
descend v. 내려가다　　　descendant n. 후손　descent n. 하강

11. -pose　　　놓다

oppose v. 반대하다　　　opposition n. 반대
compose v. 구성하다, 작문하다　　　composition n. 구성, 작문
expose v. 노출시키다　　　exposure n. 노출

12. -quire　　　묻다, 요청

acquire v. 손에 넣다, 획득하다　　　acquirement, acquisition n. 취득, 습득
inquire v. 묻다, 문의하다　　　inquiry n. 문의
require v. 필요로 하다, 요구하다　　　requirement n. 요구, 필요

13. -ject　　　던지다

project v. 입안하다, 계획하다　　　project n. 계획, 설계
reject v. 거절하다　　　rejection n. 거절
inject v. 주사하다, 주입하다　　　injection n. 주사, 주입

14. -sume　　　갖다(take)

assume v. 떠맡다, 추정하다　　　assumption n. 추정, 가정
resume v. 회복하다, 다시 시작하다　　　resumption n. 회복
presume v. 추정하다, 상상하다　　　presumption n. 추정

15. -tain　　　갖다(hold)

obtain v. 얻다, 획득하다　　　= gain
retain v. 보유[유지]하다　　　= keep
sustain v. 떠받치다, 유지하다　　　= support

16. -volve　　　돌다

evolve v. 발전시키다, 진화시키다　　　evolution n. 진화, 전진
revolve v. 회전하다, 돌다　　　revolution n. 회전, 혁명
involve v. 말아 넣다, 관련시키다　　　involvement n. 관련

17. -fine   제한, 끝

confine   v. 제한하다, 감금하다

define   v. 규정짓다, 정의를 내리다

confinement   n. 감금, 구금

definition   n. 정의, 한정

18. -live   살다

alive   adj. 살아 있는

live   adj. 살아 있는, 생생한

lively   adj. 생기 넘친, 활기찬

He's alive. 그는 살아있다.

a live program 생방송 프로

lively music 활기찬 음악

19. lone   혼자

alone   adj. 다만 홀로, 고독한

lone   adj. 혼자의

lonely   adj. 외로운, 고독한

Leave me alone. 혼자 있게 해줘요.

a lone house 외딴집

a lonely road 사람이 거의 다니지 않는 길

20. -tract   당기다

distract   v. 흩뜨리다

extract   v. 추출하다, 발췌하다

attract   v. 끌다, 매혹시키다

distraction   n. 주의 산만

extraction   n. 발췌

attraction   n. 매력

2 철자의 혼동에 주의하라

1. **conscious** adj. 의식적인   **consciousness** n. 의식
   conscientious adj. 양심적인   **conscientiousness** n. 양심

2. **valuable** adj. 귀중한, 값비싼   ⇔ **valueless** adj. 가치 없는
   invaluable adj. 매우 귀중한   = **priceless** adj. 매우 귀중한, 값을 매길 수 없는

3. **affectionate** adj. 애정 깊은, 다정한   **affection** n. 애정
   affectation n. ~인 체함, 짐짓 꾸밈

4. **application** n. 신청(서)   **apply for** 신청하다
   appliance n. 가전기기

5. **physical** adj. 육체의, 물질적인   ⇔ **spiritual** a. 정신의, 정신적인   **mental** a. 마음의, 정신의
   physiological adj. 생리학의   **physiology** n. 생리학

6. **physician** n. 의사, 내과의(사)   **surgeon** n. 외과의사
   physicist n. 물리학자, 유물론자   **physics** n. 물리학

7. **psychology** n. 심리학   **psychological** adj. 심리학의
   psychiatry n. 정신병학   **psychiatric** adj. 정신병학의

8. **objection** n. 반대
   object n. 물체, 목표   v. 반대하다
   objective n. 목표   adj. 객관적인

9. **alternation** n. 교대, 교체   **alternate** v. 교대하다
   alternative n. 양자택일, 대안   adj. 대신의, 양자택일의

10. **sometime** adv. 언젠가 후일
   sometimes adv. 때때로, 때로는

11. **board** n. 판자
   aboard adv. 배에[로], 배를 타고
   abroad adv. 외국으로, 해외로   I want to live abroad. 나는 해외에서 살고 싶다.

3 철자의 혼동에 주의하라.

1. **temper** n. 기질, 성질
   tempo n. 빠르기, 박자

   lose one's temper 화내다(≒lose one's head)
   temporal adj. 시간의, 순식간의(↔ eternal 영원한)
   *contemporary adj. 동시대의

2. **mass** n. 덩어리, 집단, 다량
   mess n. 혼란, 난잡

   massive adj. 거대한   a mass of iron 쇳덩이
   What a mess! 이런 엉망이군!

3. **scar** n. 상처, 자국
   scare v. 겁을 주다
   scarce adj. 부족한

   a vaccination scar 우두 자국
   a scared look 겁에 질린 표정
   scarcity n. 부족   a job scarcity 취직난

4. **serious** adj. 진지한, 중대한
   sincere adj. 성실한, 진실한
   severe adj. 심한, 가혹한

   Are you serious? 진담이세요?
   sincere thanks 진심에서 우러나오는 감사
   severe illness 중한 병

5. **soar** v. 날아오르다, 치솟다
   sore adj. 아픈
   soak v. (물에 쏙) 젖다

   The jet soars. 제트기가 치솟다.
   sore throat 아픈 목
   soak bread in milk 빵을 우유에 적시다

6. **jealous** adj. 질투하는
   zealous adj. 열정적인

   jealousy n. 질투
   zeal n. (일반적인)열정, 열의

7. **duel** n. 결투
   dual adj. 둘의, 이중의

   fight a duel with a person 아무와 결투하다.
   dual flying 동승 비행

8. **tiny** a. 작은, 조그마한
   tidy a. 말쑥한, 단정한

   a tiny hint 작은 힌트   a tiny clue 작은 실마리
   a tidy room 잘 정돈된 방

9. **adopt** v. 양자삼다, 채택하다
   adapt v. 적용시키다

   adopt a proposal 제안을 채택하다
   an adapter n. 어댑터, 연결관

10. **desert** n. 사막
    　　　adj. 사막의, 불모의
    　　　v. 버리다, 돌보지 않다 (=abandon)
    dessert n. 디저트(식후의 푸딩 · 파이 따위)

    the Sahara Desert 사하라 사막
    a desert island 무인도 (= barren)

11. **bald** adj. 대머리의, 꾸밈없는
    bold adj. 대담한, 굵은

    a bald man 대머리
    a bold description 힘찬 묘사

12. **loyal** adj. 충성스러운   a loyal dog 충성스런 개
    royal adj. 왕의   the royal family 왕실

13. **staff** n. 막대, 지휘봉, 간부, 직원   the teaching staff 교수[교사]진
    stuff n. 원료   building stuff 건축 자재

14. **realty** n. 부동산   = real estate
    reality n. 진실, 현실   in reality 실은, 실제는

15. **leap** v. 뛰다, 도약하다   Look before you leap. 뛰기 전에 보라.
    reap v. 수확하다   As you sow, so shall you reap. 뿌린대로 거둔다.

16. **principal** n. 교장, 원금   adj. 제 1의, 주요한
    principle n. 원리   the principle of relativity 상대성 원리

17. **complement** n. 보어
    compliment v. 칭찬하다   the compliments of the season 계절의 인사

18. **low** adj. 낮은 adv. 낮게   low temperature 저온
    row n. 열, 줄, (배의)노   in rows 줄지어, 여러 줄로 늘어서서
    row n. 법석, 소동, 싸움   make a row 소동을 일으키다

19. **wander** v. 배회하다   wander about 어슬렁 돌아다니다
    wonder n. 놀라움 v. 궁금하다   It is no wonder. 당연하다

20. **conscience** n. 양심,   conscientious adj. 양심적인
    consciousness n. 의식   be conscious of ~를 의식하다

21. **pray** v. 기도하다   prayer n. 기도
    prey n. 먹이, 희생   make a prey of ~을 먹이로 삼다

22. **eminent** adj. 저명한   an eminent scholar 저명한 학자
    imminent adj. 절박한   an imminent danger 임박한 위험

23. **sow** v. 씨앗 뿌리다   (sow-sowed-sown)
    sew v. 꿰매다   (sew-sewed-sewn)
    saw v. 톱질하다   (saw-sawed-sawn)

24. **effective** adj. 유효한, 효과적인   an effective speech 효과적인(감명적) 연설
    efficient adj. 능률적인   an efficient machine 효율적인 기계

25. **fun** n. 장난, 놀이, 재미   What a fun! 참 재미있는데, 거 참 좋다.
     funny adj. 익살맞은, 재미있는   a funny fellow 별스러운 놈.

26. **terrible** adj. 무서운   a terrible crime 무서운 범죄
     terrific adj. 대단한, 아주 좋은   terrific speed 맹렬한 속도

27. **hospitable** adj. 환대하는   hospitality n. 환대
     hostile adj. 적의 있는   hostility n. 적대적임

28. **moss** n. 이끼   A rolling stone gathers no moss.
     moth n. 나방   the difference between a butterfly and a moth

29. **pace** n. 걸음걸이, 걷는 속도   a fast pace in walking 빠른 걸음
     phase n. (발달·변화의) 단계, 국면   a new phase 새로운 국면

30. **altitude** n. (산·천체) 높이   mountain altitudes 높은 산마루
     attitude n. 태도   attitude of mind 마음 가짐
     aptitude n. 경향, 적성   an aptitude for mathematics 수학의 재능

31. **gem** n. 보석   gem cutting 보석 연마(술)
     germ n. 미생물, 병원균   a germ disease 세균병
     gene n. 유전자   genetics n. 유전공학

32. **beside** prep. 곁[옆]에, ～와 나란히   He sat beside me. 그는 내 옆에 앉았다.
     besides prep. 그 밖에, 따로   We know no one besides him. 우리는 그 외에 아무도 모른다.

33. **cite** v. 인용하다
     site n. 위치, (사건 따위의) 장소   historic sites 사적

34. **council** n. 회의   a family council 친족 회의
     counsel v. 의논하다, 조언하다   counselling n. 조언, 상담

35. **flash** v. 번쩍이다, 빛나다   a flash of lightning 전광의 번득임, 번개
     flesh n. 살, 육체   all flesh 모든 생물, 인류

36. **gross** adj. 큰, 총계의   the gross amount 총계
     grocery n. 식료품, 식품점

37. conceive v. 마음에 품다, 고안하다 　　　**conception** n. 생각, 고안
　　conceit n. 자부심, 자만 　　　　　= **pride** n. 자존심, 자긍심

38. thrive v. 번창하다, 번영하다 　　　　(thrive-throve-thriven)
　　thrift n. 검약, 검소 　　　　　　　**thrifty** adj. 검소한

39. meditate v. 명상하다 　　　　　　　**meditation** n. 명상
　　mediate v. (분쟁 등을) 중재하다 　　**mediation** n. 중재

40. moral adj. 도덕(상)의 　　　　　　　**morality** n. 도덕
　　mortal adj. 죽을 운명의 　　　　　　**mortality** n. 죽어야 할 운명

41. pat n. 가볍게 두드리기
　　pet n. 애완 동물 　　　　　　　　　a pet shop 애완 동물 상점

42. stripe n. 줄무늬, 줄 　　　　　　　　the Stars and Stripes 성조기
　　strip v. (겉껍질 따위를) 벗기다, 까다 　strip off the skin of a banana 바나나 껍질을 벗기다

43. vain adj. 헛된, 보람없는 　　　　　　　vain efforts 헛수고
　　vein n. 정맥

44. flight n. 비행 　　　　　　　　　　　a night flight 야간 비행
　　fright n. 공포, 두려움 　　　　　　　a stage fright 무대공포증
　　freight n. 화물 　　　　　　　　　　by freight 보통 화물편으로

45. lock n. 자물쇠 v. 잠그다 　　　　　　a locker room (사물함 있는) 탈의실
　　rock n. 바위 v. 흔들다, 흔들리다 　　a rocking chair 흔들의자

46. moral n. 도덕 adj. 도덕의 　　　　　moral hazard 도덕적 해이
　　morale n. 사기, 의욕 　　　　　　　high morale 높은 사기

47. robber n. 도둑, 강도, 약탈자 　　　　a bank-robber 은행 강도
　　rubber n. 고무, 문지르는 사람 　　　rubber boots 고무 장화

48. personal adj. 개인의 　　　　　　　a personal history 이력
　　personnel n. 인원, 요원 　　　　　a personnel department 인사부[과]

49. defend v. 막다, 방어하다 　　　　　defense n. 방어
　　depend v. 의지하다, ～에 달려있다 　dependence n. 의지

50. **plain** adj. 간단한, 쉬운   in plain Japanese 쉬운 일본어로

                  adj. 솔직한   a plain manner 꾸밈없는 태도

                  adj. 검소한   plain living 검소한 생활

                  adj. 편평한 n. 평원   a plain land 평지

     plane n. 평면, 면, 수평면, 비행기   a plane crash 비행기 추락

                  adj. 편평한, 평탄한, 평면 도형의   a plane surface 평면

51. **quite** adv. 아주, 완전히, 꽤   quite a lot of people 매우 많은 사람들

     quiet adj. 조용한, 고요한   Be quiet! = Be silent! 조용히 하시오!

     quit v. 그만두다, 중지하다   Quit that! (그것을 하는 것을) 그치시오!

52. **command** v. 명령하다, 내려다보다

     commend v. 칭찬하다, 추천하다

     commence v. 시작하다

4. 다양한 전치사 ○ ○ ○

1 on, over, under, above, below

1. on　　　「~의 표면에, ~위에」의 의미로 쓰인다.

He stands **on his one foot**.	한 쪽 발을 딛고서
She put a bell **on her cat**.	몸에 지닌
My son is **on the baseball team**.	속하다
I bought a book **on history**.	역사에 관한
I watched the soccer game **on TV**.	TV로

2. over　　　「위로, 넘치는」의 의미로 쓰인다.

A lamp is hanging **over the table**.	테이블 위에
She put her hands **over her face**.	얼굴을 덮어
He stayed in Paris **over a month**.	한 달 넘게
We talked **over the matter**.	그 문제에 관하여

3. under　　　「아래, 못미치는」의 의미로 쓰인다.

She stood **under the umbrella**.	우산 아래에
We welcome children **under 16 years of age**.	16세 미만인
The road is **under repair**.	수리중
The soldier marched **under heavy load**.	무거운 짐을 지고

4. above　　　「저 위로, 거리가 먼」의 의미로 쓰인다.

The birds fly **above the ocean**.	바다 위 높이
He lives **above his income**.	수입에 초과하여
He is **above telling a lie**.	거짓말 하지 않는
He is **above all others** in originality.	누구보다 뛰어난

5. below　　　「아래에, 못미치는」의 의미로 쓰인다.

It was sold **below cost**.	원가 이하로
She is **below me in the class**.	나보다 성적이 못한
There is a waterfall **below the bridge**.	다리 아래에

2 through, from, about, off, across

1. through 「관통하여, 처음부터 끝까지」의 의미로 쓰인다.

We can go **through the room** to the kitchen.	방을 통해
They went **through a red light**.	빨간 신호를 무시하고
We camped there **through the summer**.	여름 내내
He has got **through the examination**.	시험을 끝마친
I could succeed **through his help**.	그의 도움 덕택으로

2. from 「~에서, ~부터」의 의미로 쓰인다.

How far is it **from here** to the station.	여기서부터
The mountain is 5 miles away **from here**.	5마일 떨어져
Many people die **from hunger**.	굶주림 때문에
I received a letter **from my uncle**.	삼촌으로부터

3. about 「관하여, 이리저리, 대략」의 의미로 쓰인다.

What is it **about**?	관하여
He came **about four o'clock**.	약 4시경에
I have no wallet **about me**.	내몸에
There have been a bird **about the tree**.	나무 주변에

4. off 「떼내어, 떨어져」의 의미로 쓰인다.

The town is five miles **off** the main road.	떨어져
You must take **off your hat**.	모자를 벗어
She is **off cigarettes**.	담배를 끊어
He is **off duty**.	비번인, 근무하지 않는
Keep **off the grass**.	잔디에 들어가지 마세요.

5. across 「가로질러, 건너서」의 의미로 주로 쓰인다.

They hurry **across the river**.	강을 건너
There are many over weight people **across the world**.	전 세계에
It rained heavily in every town **across the country**.	전국에 걸쳐
Tom lives **across the river**.	맞은편에

3 for, against, beyond, by, with

1. **for**   「위하여, 찬성, 대신하여, 때문에」가 기본적인 의미이다.

He gave his life **for his country**.	조국을 위해
I spoke **for another**.	다른 사람을 대신하여
I waited **for the answer**.	답을 얻기 위해
He is crying **for many reasons**.	많은 이유 때문에
Are you **for or against the plan**?	찬성 또는 반대인
For me, the plant will die out.	나로서는, 내 입장은
He looks young **for his age**.	나이에 비해
I gave up the money **for lost**.	잃어버린 상태로

2. **against**   「반대, 저항, 부딪혀」의 의미를 지닌다.

I leaned **against the wall**.	벽에 기대어
Are you **against the plan**?	계획에 반대하여
We are standing **against the setting sun**.	지는 태양을 배경으로
Passengers were warned **against pickpockets**.	소매치기에 대비하여
Everything was **against her**.	그녀에게 불리한

3. **beyond**   「넘쳐, 너머로, 닿지 않는」의 의미를 지닌다.

It is **beyond the appointed time**.	약속시간 지난
It is **beyond me**.	내 능력이 닿지 않는
The scenery is **beyond description**.	말로 다 묘사할 수 없는
He lives **beyond the river**.	강건너에

4. **by**   「옆에, 어떤 기준으로」의 의미를 지닌다.

Mary was standing **by her brother**.	그녀의 오빠 옆에
Finish this work **by the end of the week**.	주말까지
He was paid **by the week**.	주 단위로
I missed the train **by five minutes**.	5분 차이로
He caught me **by the arm**.	팔을 잡고서
He solved the problem **by consulting his brother**.	형과 상의함으로써

5. **with**   「~와 함께, ~에 대하여, ~을 가지고」의 의미를 지닌다.

James lives **with his brother**.	동생과 함께
I have nothing to do **with the matter**.	그 문제와 관련이
They want a room **with an ocean view**.	바다가 보이는
Don't speak **with your mouth full**.	음식물을 문 채로

5. 말하기 주요 표현 ○ ○ ○

1 부정어를 사용하는 표현

It couldn't be worse.	최악이야.
= Terrible!; Awful!; Pretty bad!	
It couldn't be better.	더할 나위 없이 좋아.
I don't mind.	상관없어 난 괜찮아.
It doesn't matter.	상관없어.
It doesn't make any difference.	상관없어.
= It makes no difference.	
Definitely not.	절대 안돼.
You can't miss it.	틀림없이 찾으실 거에요.
I'm afraid, it's out of the question.	죄송하지만, 안되겠는데요.
Sorry, but I won't be able to make it that day.	죄송하지만, 그날은 안될 것 같습니다.
I'm afraid I can't.	죄송하지만…할 수가 없군요.
By no means! = Absolutely not!	절대로 안돼!
Why not?	물론이죠.
Not at all. = Certainly not. = Of course not.	천만에요. 괜찮아요.
= I don't mind.	
Not much. = Nothing much.	그저 그래.
I really can't thank you enough.	너무 너무 고맙습니다.
I can't stand ~.	~ 하는 것 못 참아.
No (more), thank you.	그만 하겠어요, 고마워요.
I can't afford it.	난 감당하지 못해.
Why don't you mind your own business?	너나 잘 해.
= None of your business.	간섭하지 마세요.

2 의문문 형태의 표현

What does it matter? = What's the difference?	무슨 상관이야?
Who knows?	그걸 어떻게 알아. (= Nobody knows.)
What's new with you?	별일 없니?
Are you with me? = Do you follow me?	내말 이해하겠니? (= Have you got that?)
What is he like?	그 사람 어떻게 생겼는데?

Who cares? 알게 뭐야!
What are you up to? 오늘 뭐 할거니?
Cash or charge? 현금으로 하시겠습니까, 카드로 하시겠습니까?
Can I take a rain check on the invitation? 이 초대를 다음기회로 미루면 안될까요?
When will you be available? 언제 시간이 나시겠어요?

May I ask a favor? 부탁 좀 드려도 될까요?
How(What) about going shopping? 쇼핑하러 가는 것이 어때요?
What time shall we make it? 몇 시로 할까요?
What's a good time for you? 언제가 좋을까요?
= When is it convenient for you?

What seems to be the problem (matter)? 뭐가 문제입니까?
What's bothering you? 불편한 것이 있나요?
Can you give me a discount? 할인 좀 해 주실 수 있나요?
Can you do me a favor? 부탁 하나만 들어줄래?
What time do you call it a day? 몇 시에 퇴근해요?

What has brought you here? 무슨 일로 여기 왔습니까?
Are you hiding something? 뭐 찔리는 거라도 있는 거야?

3 질문에 대한 반응의 표현

You bet. 당연하지!
That's exactly what I have in mind. 동감이야.
Just so so. 그저 그래.
Same here. 저도 그렇습니다.
You said it! = You can say that again. 맞는 말이야!

With pleasure. 기꺼이(그렇게 하겠어요).
It's my pleasure. 천만에요.
Why? You feel guilty? 왜 너 찔리는 데가 있니?
Sure. That would be fun. 물론이지. 재미있겠다.
Let's make it another time. 다음 기회에 하기로 하죠.

It's none of your business. 남의 일에 참견하지 마.
It depends. 상황에 따라서 달라.
I'm afraid so. 유감스럽지만 그런 것 같아요.

What a shame!	저런 그것 참 안됐다.
What a pity!	저런 그것 참 안됐다.
Are you out of your mind?	너 제정신이니?
What a waste!	아까워라!
= Good for you!	그것 참 잘됐군요!
(You've done a) good job! = Well done!	잘했군요!
That's great(terrific)!	아주 잘됐네요!
I mean it!	정말이야!
That's it.	바로 그거야.
I can't tell you how sorry I am.	대단히 죄송합니다.
I'm sorry, but I couldn't help it.	죄송하지만, 어쩔 수 없었어요.
Don't get me wrong.	오해 하지 마세요.
Suit yourself.	네 맘대로 해.
Absolutely.	정말이야.

4 소개, 인사, 만남

It's a pleasure to meet you.	만나 뵙게 되어서 반갑습니다.
I think we'd better be going.	이제 가봐야 할 것 같아요.
Would you mind if I ask for a ride?	차 좀 태워 주시겠어요?
Let's keep in touch.	연락하고 지내자.
You look familiar to me.	상당히 낯이 익군요.
May I call on you today?	오늘 잠깐 찾아뵈어도 될까요?
Take care. = Take it easy.	잘가.
Haven't we met before?	우리 전에 만난 적이 있지 않던가요?
I'd better be going now. = I must be off now.	이제 가봐야겠어요.
You'd better hurry up.	서두르는 것이 낫겠다.
Come on in. I've been expecting you.	들어오세요. 기다리고 있었습니다.
Make yourself at home.	편히 하세요.
Sorry. I'm on my way.	미안해. 지금 가고 있어.
Be punctual, please.	시간 맞춰 오세요.
Who's calling, please?	누구세요?

This is he(she) speaking. = Speaking.   전데요.
Spare me a few minutes.   시간 좀 내주세요.
Hold the line, please. = Hold on, please.   끊지 말고 기다리세요.
You're wanted on the phone.   전화왔습니다.
The line is busy.   통화중입니다.

May I take your message?   전하실 말씀이 있습니까?
= Would you like to leave a message?
I'm afraid I have the wrong number.   전화 잘못 걸었나 봅니다.
Go straight ahead. = Follow your nose.   곧장 앞으로 가세요.
How about 10 o'clock at your place?   네 집에서 10시 정각에 만나는 게 어때?

5   친근한 표현―쇼핑, 여행

Please let me off here.   여기에서 내려 주세요.
Do you have any vacancies tonight?   오늘밤에 빈 방이 있습니까?
It's raining cats and dogs.   비가 억수같이 퍼붓고 있다.
Put me through to extension 144, please.   내선 144번 연결해 주시기 바랍니다.
Hold on, let me transfer your call.   기다리십시오. 전화를 돌려 드리겠습니다.

What's the round-trip fare for children?   아이들 왕복 요금은 얼마입니까?
I want this parcel insured.   이 소포를 보험에 들고 싶습니다.
How long will it take by surface mail?   보통해상우편으로 부치면 얼마나 걸릴까요?
Be my guest this time.   이번에는 제가 내겠습니다.
I'll take care of the bill.   제가 계산을 하겠습니다.

Let's go fifty-fifty on the bill.   계산을 반반 합시다.
Help yourself.   마음껏 드세요.
Please help yourself to the steak.   스테이크를 마음껏 드세요.
Let's grab a bite.   뭐 좀 먹으러 가자.
I've had enough. = I'm full.   많이 먹었어요.

That's better than nothing.   그게 어딘데? 없는 것보다 낫지.
It's out of my budget.   예산을 벗어난 금액이네요.
Here is ten dollars. Keep the change.   여기 10달러요. 잔돈은 가지세요.
This wrist watch is waterproof.   이 손목 시계는 방수입니다.
This curtain is fireproof.   이 커튼은 내화성이 있습니다.

These blue jeans are durable.   이 청바지는 내구성이 있습니다.
That's a good deal.   싸게 잘 샀다.
That hat looks good on you.   그 모자가 당신에게 잘 어울리는군요.
I've never eaten better.   음식 잘 먹었습니다.
Today, it's on me!   오늘은 내가 한 턱 낸다.

6 Listening 대비 표현

I'd appreciate it.   (그렇게 해주시면)고맙겠어요.
Good job! = Well done!   잘 했다!
I feel heavy.   몸이 찌뿌둥하다.
It's up to you.   그건 너한테 달려 있어.
It slipped my mind.   깜박했어.

It's six o'clock. Let's call it a day.   벌써 6시야. 오늘은 그만 하자.
I live a stone's throw away from here.   여기서 지척에 살아
You can't be serious! = You don't mean that!   설마, 진정은 아니겠지!
What a nerve!   참 뻔뻔스럽기도 하군.
Calm down. = Slow down.   진정해.

Stop it! = Cut it out!   그만해!
This is too much. = This is going too far.   이거 너무한다!
You're kidding(joking)! = No kidding!   농담마! 설마!
Keep it up!   계속 잘해!
It serves him right./He deserves it.   그 사람 참 잘 됐다.(쌤통이다.)

Put yourself in my shoes.   너는 상대편 입장이 되어 봐야 돼.
That's a good point.   일리 있는 말이야.
Shame on you!   창피한 줄 좀 알아라.
I got a crush on her!   나는 그녀에게 반했어.
Let it be!   그대로 놔둬!

You have my condolence.   삼가 조의를 표합니다.
Are you mad at me? Are you pissed off?   너 삐졌니?
Come on, what are friends for?   야, 친구 좋다는 게 뭐야?
I didn't want to let you down.   당신을 실망시켜 드리고 싶지는 않았어요.
I'm freezing to death.   얼어 죽을 것처럼 추워.

Concise and Core Grammar Points!

The Grammar

Nexus Contents Development Team

3
Level

Workbook

NEXUS Edu

Contents

어휘와 어휘의 결합

A 다음 괄호 안에서 알맞은 말을 고르시오.

1 I love her (in spite / in spite of) her faults.

2 The festival was held (despite / despite of) the bad weather.

3 A cheer went up from the crowds (watch / watching) the game.

4 The chemicals slow the growth of (egg-laid / egg-laying) moths.

5 Oh, what a (frightened / frightening) Christmas present I've received!

6 Why would you want to vote for (somebody strange / strange somebody)?

7 I'm trying to figure out (something special / special something) to do on a trip.

B 다음 문장에서 잘못된 부분을 찾아 바르게 고치시오.

1 The children are playing happy in the garden.

2 We can buy cheap something in the supermarket.

3 I would like to make a speech fluent without hesitation.

4 Her name was neat written at the top of the application.

5 Six students share a rest room, a shower room, and a dined room.

6 We want somebody tall and friend enough to get us out of here.

C 다음 괄호 안의 말을 알맞게 배열하여 문장을 완성하시오.

1 (are / or / for / against / you) stem cell research?
→ _____ stem cell research?

2 The weather (been unusually / has / cold / year / this).
→ The weather _____.

3 There (something / was / about / strange) the way he acted.
→ There _____ the way he acted.

4 (heavily / smoking / influenced / is / quitting) by spouses and friends.
→ _____ by spouses and friends.

5 The old lady next door always wears a (furry / black / big) hat.
→ The old lady next door always wears a _____ hat.

Further Study

1 다음 〈보기〉에서 알맞은 것을 골라 문장을 완성하시오.

| Word Bank | injured | surrounding | missing | participating | driving |

1 Smoking gives bad effects to _____ people.

2 A man claims to have invented a device for finding _____ people.

3 The authors wish to express their gratitude to the _____ people.

4 After the accident, the _____ people were carried away in the ambulance.

5 When beggars run across the busy roads, they put the _____ people at risk.

2 다음 중 어법상 어색한 문장을 고르시오.

① A social enterprise gets unemployed people back to work.

② All participants must sign up in the book located in the music room.

③ Most of the factories building in 1960s were destroyed by the hurricane.

④ We decorated the living room and prepared a surprise party for his birthday.

⑤ According to the weather forecast, the rainy season will start next week.

3 다음 글을 읽고, (A)와 (B)에 알맞은 말을 고르시오.

As we checked out of the hotel, the town was quite nice on the outside but dirty and (A) (bad / badly) maintained. It was crammed with Chinese tourists and pilgrims. The pilgrims were dressed in the traditional way, and that was a nice contrast to the regular Chinese tourists who had their pictures taken on every corner. The air was (B) (clear / clearly), cool and crispy. Autumn was definitely here.

4 다음 주어진 단어를 이용하여 문장을 완성하시오.

1 두 마을을 연결하는 그 도로는 매우 좁다. (join, village)
The road _____ is very narrow.

2 이 공장에서 생산된 상품의 대부분은 수출된다. (make, factory)
Most of goods _____ are exported.

3 그 게으른 판매원은 일주일 내내 그들의 전화를 고장인 채로 방치해 두었다. (leave, out of order)
The lazy agent _____ for a whole week.

4 그 세기의 중반쯤에는 그 바다에서는 낚을 수 있는 것이 아무것도 남아 있지 않을 것이다. (nothing)
There _____ left to fish from the seas by the middle of the century.

1 단순 문장-주어의 형태

A 다음 괄호 안에서 알맞은 말을 고르시오.

1 He kept (silent / silently) at all times.

2 The fact that he is a doctor (make / makes) him different.

3 What you saw here (is / are) not what we like to present.

4 (Taking / Take) a walk after dinner is one of my favorite pastimes.

5 Whether he succeeds or not (depend / depends) on his willingness.

6 (To stay / Stay) in this country is (to destroy / destroy) our valuable lives.

B 다음 문장의 주어를 찾아 밑줄을 그으시오.

1 Either Sally or John can attend the meeting.

2 No one in the earth will know how to solve this problem.

3 The importance of luck in achieving one's goals tends to be ignored.

4 One of the most important steps you must take is to believe in yourself.

5 To forget about the most embarrassing moment in your life is never easy.

6 With his best seller, *The Road*, the world is turning its attention to this writer.

7 Excluding those from voting who are already socially isolated destroys our democracy.

8 Introducing a new management style and overcoming its huge losses brought a great success.

C 다음 괄호 안의 말을 알맞게 배열하여 문장을 완성하시오.

1 (you / what / know / you / and / what / do) don't often agree.
→ _____ don't often agree.

2 (one / the apples / third / of) were damaged by the latest typhoon.
→ _____ were damaged by the latest typhoon.

3 (serious disease / smoking / the most / connected / with) is cancer of the lungs.
→ _____ is cancer of the lungs.

4 (containing / sewage / human waste) is piped directly into lakes and rivers.
→ _____ is piped directly into lakes and rivers.

5 (where / I / the company / work) offers everyone 30 days of paid vacation each year.
→ _____ offers everyone 30 days of paid vacation each year.

Further Study

1 다음 문장의 구성요소에 밑줄을 긋고, S(주어), V(동사), O(목적어), C(보어)로 표시하시오.

1 Different ways of speaking are found between men and women.

2 Overall, getting up early and going to bed early is good for health.

3 Following these simple guidelines will have a good effect on the environment.

4 Maintaining friendship with anybody requires a lot of patience and understanding.

5 Taking pictures and collecting old paintings as a student made your pocket empty.

6 Doing things together such as camping and traveling is an important part of friendship.

2 다음 중 어법상 어색한 문장을 고르시오.

① Give direct commands to your children is not a good way.

② Dental visits are a very necessary part of preventive dental care.

③ Modern technology doesn't always make people comfortable.

④ Many of the gases that pollute the air come from the burning of fossil fuels.

⑤ No country in the world has enough resources to satisfy completely its people's wants.

3 다음 글을 읽고, (A)와 (B)에 알맞은 말을 고르시오.

The idea of spending two months on the Argentine Pampas (A) (was / were) not exciting. I had never been very far from New England, and I had been homesick during my first two weeks at college. What would it be (B) (as / like) in a strange country? And what about the language?

4 다음 주어진 단어를 이용하여 문장을 완성하시오.

1 의심할 나위 없이, 제주도 여행은 너에게 도움이 될 것이다. (do ~ good)
Undoubtedly, a trip to Jeju Island _____.

2 인구에서 노령인구 비율이 꾸준히 증가하고 있다. (proportion of, older people, increase)
The _____ in the population is _____ steadily.

3 소형자동차의 편리함과 경제성이 그들의 인기를 설명해준다. (economy, account for)
The convenience and _____ of small cars _____ their popularity.

4 세 명의 남자가 우리 집으로 걸어 들어가고 있는 것을 보자, 이상한 느낌이 나를 사로잡았다. (creep over)
A _____ me as I watched three men walking into my house.

2 단순 문장–동사의 형태

A 다음 괄호 안에서 알맞은 말을 고르시오.

1 These movies seem (popular / popularly) with the teenagers.

2 My boss remained (quiet / quietly) about the new project.

3 I love it when a cat (lies / lays) in front of the fire on its back!

4 She (lay / laid) the book on the table and kept silent for a long time.

5 How old was Prince Charles when he (married / married with) Princess Diana?

B 다음 〈보기〉에서 알맞은 것을 골라 문장을 완성하시오. (필요 없는 경우 Ø표 하시오.)

Word Bank	at	to	for	in	about	with

1 Mary discussed _____ the movie she saw last night with her friends.
  Scarlet and I talked _____ how pretty she looked on her wedding day.

2 By the time I arrived _____ my office, people had all gone out for lunch.
  Taking Highway 14, we could reach _____ the office faster than ever.

3 Opening the door, they heard _____ the clock on the wall strike twelve.
  Clare listened _____ the sound very carefully and tried figure out what it was.

4 I looked _____ my watch and discovered that it was only two.
  Tom saw _____ a scar on the old man's face and wondered where it had come from.

5 Peter said _____ me, "You shouldn't go there without permission."
  My mother had always told _____ me that I should never trust in everlasting love.

6 He provided us _____ a lot of useful information.
  My science teacher lent _____ me the textbook, so I don't have to buy one.

C 다음 괄호 안에서 알맞은 말을 고르시오.

1 Her friends (envied / envied about) her weight loss.

2 Mary promised (me / to me) that she won't tell anyone.

3 Her problem is that she (worries / worries about) money too much.

4 I entirely (agree / agree with) you that our school needs to be renovated.

5 We were confused to see that all the babies (resembled / resembled with) each other.

6 How you (answer / answer to) the phone says a great deal about your personality.

Further Study

1 다음 문장에서 <u>잘못된</u> 부분을 찾아 바르게 고치시오.

1　The company located on its headquarters in Sydney.

2　Joanna wants to meet a guy who resembles like her father.

3　All my children seemed happily with their Christmas presents.

4　With great effort, he completed with the project in two years.

5　James didn't mention about the title of the statue, but everybody knew what he meant.

6　A group of environmentalists gathered to discuss about ways to save vanishing wetlands.

2 다음 중 어법상 <u>어색한</u> 문장을 고르시오.

① The children helped the old men get on the train safely.

② You can't enter the building without permission from the police.

③ They approached to me asking if I had been using the computer.

④ The leaders will discuss the political crisis in Ivory Coast this Friday.

⑤ The man, who was wearing a black jacket, remained conscious after the shooting.

3 다음 글을 읽고, (A)와 (B)에 알맞은 말을 고르시오.

Mr. Brown, the owner of an antique store, (A) (lay / laid) awake for a long time wondering if his money was really safe, and it was well after midnight before he fell asleep. Almost immediately, he was awakened by the loud ringing of the doorbell downstairs. He (B) (sat / seated) up in bed. The doorbell rang again, echoing through the two-story building.

4 다음 주어진 단어를 이용하여 문장을 완성하시오.

1　그 상관은 그들에게 즉시 이라크로 출발할 것을 명령했다. (order)
The boss _____ for Iraq immediately.

2　그들에게 그 일의 나쁜 점에 관해서 충분히 알려지지 않았다. (poorly, inform)
They _____ about the disadvantages of the job.

3　많은 단어는 문맥에 따라 다양한 의미를 갖는다. (multiple)
Many words _____, depending on the context.

4　나는 신문에서 흥미로운 광고를 보았고, 그 일에 응시하기로 결정했다. (apply, the job)
I saw an interesting ad in the newspaper and decided _____.

1 단순 문장–목적어의 종류

A 다음 문장의 목적어를 찾아 밑줄을 그으시오.

1 I used to envy him his well-shaped figure.

2 The news surprised many market observers.

3 I believe that animal intelligence can be measured.

4 We are enjoying hearing all about your adventures.

5 This training program gave me what I really needed.

6 I wonder how to send videos from this camera to an e-mail address.

B 다음 두 문장이 같은 뜻이 되도록 할 때 빈칸에 알맞은 말을 쓰시오.

1 Mom ordered me a special meal.
→ Mom ordered a special meal _____ me.

2 My grandmother made me a nice blue sweater.
→ My grandmother made a nice blue sweater _____ me.

3 Fiona gave me a dirty look when I asked her out.
→ Fiona gave a dirty look _____ me when I asked her out.

4 The stranger asked him the directions to the drugstore.
→ The stranger asked the directions to the drugstore _____ him.

C 다음 주어진 말을 알맞게 배열하여 문장을 완성하시오.

1 Scott / doll / her / at Christmas / a pretty / gave
→ _____

2 pizza / ordered / some / for us / they
→ _____

3 she / me / wanted / I / really / gave / what
→ _____

4 I / know / to do / after / what / don't / graduation
→ _____

5 cost / the brand-new / an arm and a leg / car / me
→ _____

6 me / of / teacher / my / asked / a question
→ _____

Further Study

1 다음 문장에서 <u>잘못된</u> 부분을 찾아 바르게 고치시오.

1 I expected Jim coming to the concert that night, but he never showed up.

2 This photograph reminds me for having a miserable birthday all by myself.

3 Susan thanked Mr. Thomson to teaching her how to swim without a life jacket.

4 She criticized the newspaper company for have a political bias against Muslim countries.

5 The government's new law clearly prohibits teenagers from buy lottery tickets as well as cigarettes and alcohol.

2 다음 빈칸에 들어갈 알맞은 말을 고르시오.

1 My father can make everything with his hands, and he made a bike _____ me.

　① for　　　　　② of　　　　　③ with　　　　　④ by　　　　　⑤ to

2 She always tells a lie _____ me, so I don't believe her.

　① for　　　　　② of　　　　　③ with　　　　　④ by　　　　　⑤ to

3 다음 글을 읽고, (A)와 (B)에 알맞은 말을 고르시오.

I received a call from Bob. "Hey. I'm calling from Taji bus stand, and please (A) (tell / say) me how far I am from it," he asked. Hearing this, I asked him to disconnect and (B) (to wait / waited) for me. After a while, I told him to take a taxi and to give my phone number to the driver. I gave the location to the driver when he called up. About ten minutes later, Bob showed up with his fingernails painted black, and I stood there saying nothing, just looking at him.

4 다음 주어진 단어를 이용하여 문장을 완성하시오.

1 Sally는 취업면접 준비를 잘 하였다. (prepare, well)

Sally _____ her job interview.

2 지금 그는 많은 친구와 함께 인생을 아낌없이 즐기고 있다. (enjoy, every moment)

Now he _____ of his life with many friends.

3 그 연극은 가난한 외판원인 Willy의 삶과 죽음을 다루고 있다. (deal with)

The play _____ of a poor salesman named Willy.

4 학생들은 다음 학기에 누가 자신들의 선생님이 될지 궁금해 한다. (who, will)

Students wonder _____ in the following semester.

2 단순 문장-보어의 형태

A 다음 괄호 안에서 알맞은 말을 고르시오.

1 His intention is (to make / make) the area a ball park.

2 The weather caused us (bond / to bond) with each other.

3 She looked (surprise / surprised) when she heard the news.

4 The teacher didn't allow us (shout / to shout) in the classroom.

5 Her music sounds (good / well) and should not be heard alone.

6 I heard my name (called / calling) out on the radio this morning.

7 One of my hobbies is (make / making) dollhouses and decorating them.

B 다음 문장에서 잘못된 부분을 찾아 바르게 고치시오.

1 The accident caused her be changed so much.

2 His dream came truly when he got first prize.

3 My mother always encourages me doing my best.

4 My wife looked so beautifully in that red dress.

5 They were busy talking about the coming election, but Paul remained silently.

6 The doctor said my overweight would cause a big problem and advised me doing exercise.

C 다음 두 문장이 같은 뜻이 되도록 빈칸에 알맞은 말을 쓰시오.

1 Elizabeth was young when she married.
   → Elizabeth married _____.

2 The book proved a little difficult for me.
   → I found _____.

3 He was dismissed because he was idle.
   → His idleness caused _____.

4 To my great relief, I learned that the danger was gone.
   → I felt greatly _____.

5 Why did they turn down his job application?
   → What made _____?

6 He became very unpopular with the staff because of the decision.
   → The decision made _____.

Further Study

1 다음 괄호 안에서 알맞은 말을 고르시오.

1 The report finally turned out to be (true / truly).

2 She felt tears (run / to run) down her cheeks.

3 The researcher found it very (hard / hardly) to do without help.

4 He lived (happy / happily) in the southeastern part of the country.

5 Peter got up, leaning on his stick, and looked (shy / shyly) at the prince.

2 다음 빈칸에 들어갈 알맞은 말을 고르시오.

1 Let that misinformation _____ in one ear and out the other.

① go   ② to go   ③ going

④ gone   ⑤ to be gone

2 The committee persuaded me _____ its offer to help my children.

① accept   ② accepting   ③ to accept

④ accepted   ⑤ to be accepted

3 다음 글을 읽고, (A)와 (B)에 알맞은 단어를 고르시오.

> Water pollution is also serious because we all rely on a supply of pure water to live. River pollution has become so (A) (bad / badly) that fish and plants can hardly survive. In some countries, local government authorities add to the pollution problem by allowing sewage (B) (flow / to flow) into the rivers and seas.

4 다음 주어진 단어를 이용하여 문장을 완성하시오.

1 가을에 단풍과 같은 나뭇잎들이 붉게 물든다. (such as, turn, maple leaves)
In autumn, the leaves of trees, _____.

2 나이가 들면 너는 내가 지금 말하고 있는 진리를 깨닫게 될 것이다. (grow, the truth of)
When you _____, you will realize _____ what I'm saying now.

3 의사는 며칠 후면 그가 좋아질 것이라고 말했다. (get better, in, few)
The doctor said he would _____.

4 이런 바람 속에서 따뜻하게 유지하는 것은 어렵다. (keep, warm)
With this wind, it is _____.

1 복합 문장—접속사

A 다음 괄호 안에서 알맞은 말을 고르시오.

1 Hurry up, (and / or) you'll arrive there in time.

2 He phoned (and / but) left a message yesterday.

3 Yesterday they didn't eat, (nor / or) did they sleep.

4 I can either leave now (nor / or) stay for another hour.

5 He was both training them in theater (and / or) acting with skills.

6 We were bored yesterday, (but / for) there was nothing to do.

7 Jim not only built his own house (and / but) also designed it.

B 다음 괄호 안의 단어가 들어갈 위치를 고르시오.

1 He found ① it difficult ② to read the newspaper, ③ his eyes were ④ failing. (for)

2 We must not only end the era of ① strife ② open ③ an era of ④ friendship. (but also)

3 Iron and nickel have ① great resistance ② to the passage of electricity, ③ they become ④ hot. (so)

4 Ultimately, we'll ① have ② peace of mind ③ or worry about ④ what other people think. (either)

5 When asked "How's it going?", ① he said ② he was doing okay ③ could have ④ been better. (but)

6 Cyber.Com had neither the equipment ① the employees ② to link ③ all of its subscribers ④ to the Internet. (nor)

C 다음 괄호 안의 말을 알맞게 배열하여 문장을 완성하시오.

1 Aesop's Fables (both / are / and / interesting) instructive.
→ Aesop's Fables _____ instructive.

2 Albert Schweitzer (but also / not only / was / a doctor) a musician.
→ Albert Schweitzer _____ a musician.

3 Do you (school / by / go / or / bus / to) by subway?
→ Do you _____ by subway?

4 My father is healthy because (smokes / he / nor / neither) drinks.
→ My father is healthy because _____ drinks.

5 I felt very tired, (to / I / went / so / bed) early.
→ I felt very tired, _____ early.

6 She did all the shopping and cooking, (mother / for / was / her / sick).
→ She did all the shopping and cooking, _____.

Further Study

1 다음 〈보기〉에서 알맞은 것을 골라 문장을 완성하시오. (단, 한 번씩만 사용하시오.)

Word Bank	so	for	but also	and	or	but

1 Spring has come, _____ it is still cold.

2 I went to Paris _____ bought some postcards.

3 The dogs are hungry, _____ I must feed them now.

4 We stayed at school, _____ it was raining hard.

5 You can either boil some eggs _____ make some sandwiches.

6 China is famous for not only its huge population _____ the Great Wall.

2 다음 중 어법상 어색한 문장을 고르시오.

① Both milk and orange are nutritious food.

② Some books are both boring and uneducational.

③ Sports give us health physically as well as spiritually.

④ He either plays tennis nor goes hiking on weekends.

⑤ Not only the snake but also the scorpion has venom.

3 다음 글을 읽고, (A)와 (B)에 알맞은 말을 고르시오.

When I went to a souvenir shop in London, I wanted to buy some postcards. I chose several cards, took them to the assistant who was standing behind the counter (A) (and / but) held them out to her. I waited, (B) (and / but) she remained bent over her work.

4 다음 주어진 단어와 접속사를 이용하여 문장을 완성하시오.

1 19세기에는 텔레비전도 라디오도 없었다. (there)
   In the 19th century, there _____.

2 매 식사가 끝나면 칫솔질을 해라, 그렇지 않으면 치통을 겪게 될 것이다. (get, toothache)
   Brush your teeth after every meal, _____.

3 내 안경이 깨져서 나는 무슨 일이 벌어지는지 볼 수 없었다. (happen)
   I had my glasses broken, _____.

4 우리 부모님께서는 나를 사랑하실 뿐만 아니라, 나를 신뢰하신다. (love, trust)
   My parents _____ but also _____.

2 병렬 구조

A 다음 괄호 안에서 알맞은 말을 고르시오.

1 Neither he nor I (are / am) interested in science.

2 Neither my brothers nor my father (are / is) a doctor.

3 My teacher as well as my classmates (are / is) in the gym.

4 Bob not only met Tom but also (had / have) dinner with him.

5 Both diligence and (sincere / sincerity) are required in this job.

6 My hobby is reading books and (watching / to watch) action movies.

7 They don't take life seriously, either dancing (nor / or) playing sports.

B 다음 괄호 안에 주어진 말을 이용하여 빈칸에 알맞은 말을 쓰시오.

1 Neither my kids nor my husband _____ early. (get up)

2 Not only my sister but also my cousins _____ ballerinas. (be)

3 I'm fond of exploring ancient relics and _____ old coins. (collect)

4 My elder brother as well as my younger brothers _____ to play tennis. (like)

5 Either boys or girls _____ allowed to wear skirts during the festival. (be)

6 She not only entered Harvard University but also _____ a scholarship. (get)

C 다음 괄호 안에 주어진 말을 이용하여 주어진 문장을 다시 쓰시오.

1 Fish is good for our health. Milk is good for our health. (both A and B)
   → _____

2 I saw Susie at the shopping mall. I saw her sister at the shopping mall, too. (B as well as A)
   → _____

3 Thomson has an electric guitar. He has a classical guitar, too. (not only A but also B)
   → _____

4 They play basketball or they play computer games after school. (either A or B)
   → _____

5 He does not like fishing. He does not like swimming, either. (neither A nor B)
   → _____

6 His speech is boring. His speech is difficult. (both A and B)
   → _____

Further Study

1 다음 문장에서 <u>잘못된</u> 부분을 찾아 바르게 고치시오.

1 He finished his work easily and skillful.

2 He heard an explosion and calling the police.

3 Speaking slowly is as important as to speak clearly.

4 She not only passed the test but also receives the highest score.

5 The quizzes help you practice grammar and building your vocabulary.

6 Both gratitude and honest are required for the improvement of our society.

2 다음 중 어법상 <u>어색한</u> 문장을 고르시오.

① Neither his brothers and he has been to Japan.

② You have to either clean the room or mow the lawn.

③ Both she and her son were rescued from the rollover accident.

④ Not only Tom but also his friends like taking a walk in the morning.

⑤ His goal is not only to give the homeless food but also to give them hope.

3 다음 글을 읽고, (A)와 (B)에 알맞은 말을 고르시오.

My job consisted of sitting on a stool and (A) (watching / to watch) empty bottles pass by for eight or nine hours a day. A light behind the conveyer belt helped me spot the cracked bottles. I was supposed to grab such bottles with my hooked cane and (B) (break / breaking) them before they went into the washer.

4 다음 주어진 단어와 접속사를 이용하여 문장을 완성하시오.

1 영어를 배울 때 우리는 언어뿐만 아니라 문화도 배우는 것이다. (learn, as well as)
   When we study English, _____.

2 과식은 당신이 음식을 낭비하게 할 뿐만 아니라, 당신의 건강도 해친다. (waste, damage)
   Excessive eating not only makes you _____.

3 TOEFL 시험은 고용주, 대학, 그 밖의 다른 기관들에서 종종 필요로 한다. (required by)
   TOEFL tests _____ employers, universities _____ other institutions.

4 네가 용돈으로 10달러를 벌려면 잔디 깎기와 세차 둘 중 하나를 해야 한다. (mow the lawn)
   You must _____ to get $10 for pocket money.

1 주어와 동사의 일치

A 다음 괄호 안에서 알맞은 말을 고르시오.

1 There (was / were) a big church on the hill.

2 Most of the water in the basket (has / have) gone.

3 There (has / have) been a few hurricanes in the region recently.

4 One third of the students in the classroom (are / is) from Korea.

5 A number of chances (are / is) available for enhancing your reputation.

6 The number of the tourists (are / is) increasing due to the mild weather.

7 Why (was / were) one of the students excluded from the exam?

B 다음 문장에서 <u>잘못된</u> 부분을 찾아 바르게 고치시오.

1 There remains few potatoes in the sack now.

2 Half of the oranges sent by the farmer was bad.

3 The movements of the dancer was very graceful.

4 The waitress who served us dinner were friendly.

5 What keep you from going to the movies tonight?

6 A number of the wounded was carried to the hospital.

7 The number of cars in Seoul are much larger than before.

8 Few girls has passed the company's entrance examination.

9 The subject of these lectures have been announced by Mr. Kim.

10 There seem nowadays to be little optimism about economic growth.

C 다음 괄호 안에 주어진 말을 이용하여 빈칸에 알맞은 말을 쓰시오.

1 Usually half of my spare time _____ spent in reading. (be)

2 Three fourths of the earth's surface _____ water. (be)

3 There _____ a big problem for us to solve. (remain)

4 A number of people _____ present at the meeting yesterday. (be)

5 The number of students in the class _____ limited to fifteen. (be)

6 Who _____ the cooking at your house when your mother goes away? (do)

7 There _____ to be a connection between pollution and cancer. (seem)

8 In old times, people never knew what _____ happening on the other side of the world. (be)

Further Study

1 다음 괄호 안에서 알맞은 말을 고르시오.

1 There (is / are) little milk left in the refrigerator.

2 That girl with blue eyes (is / are) my younger sister.

3 There (was / were) few people in Seoul during the Korean War.

4 There (have / has) been only two major political parties in America.

5 The boy playing basketball with his classmates (is / are) my brother.

6 What (makes / make) you think so about the current problem of low birthrates?

2 다음 중 어법상 올바른 문장을 고르시오.

① The fastest way to go to the beach is to take the highway.

② There were a terrible hurricane in Thailand last summer.

③ Thirty percent of the people in the area lives on a pension.

④ Half of the students doesn't want to wear the school uniform.

⑤ About two thirds of the furniture in the shop were destroyed due to the earthquake.

3 다음 글을 읽고, (A)에 알맞은 말을 고르시오.

The wartime use of penicillin was instrumental in saving thousands of lives. For example, in World War I, eighteen percent of all deaths in the United States Army (A) (was / were) due to pneumonia. In World War II, however, the rate of pneumonia-related deaths dropped to less than one percent.

4 다음 주어진 단어를 이용하여 문장을 완성하시오.

1 자신의 지식을 업무에 응용하는 그의 능력이 그의 주요 자산이다. (ability, apply)
His _____ to his work is his chief asset.

2 상당한 수의 승객들이 지난밤에 발생한 사고에서 부상당했다. (a number of, injured)
_____ in the accident that happened last night.

3 항구도시 부산행 열차가 출발하기까지는 아직 몇 분이 남아 있다. (still, left)
There _____ before the train leaves for the port city of Busan.

4 그 지역의 약 3분의 2가 최근의 태풍 때문에 피해를 입었다. (been damaged)
Approximately, two thirds of the area _____ by the recent typhoon.

2 주어+단수동사

A 다음 괄호 안에서 알맞은 말을 고르시오.

1 Each country (has / have) its own traditional dress.

2 Every one of my coworkers (has / have) lunch at twelve o'clock.

3 Thirty dollars (is / are) enough to get a nice shirt or a pair of jeans.

4 Statistics (are / is) the study of how to summarize and analyze data.

5 Ten kilograms (is / are) the maximum weight limit allowed for a package.

6 Listening to classical music before going to bed (make / makes) me feel comfortable.

7 To learn other cultures (are / is) very important to understand various ideologies.

B 다음 문장에서 <u>잘못된</u> 부분을 찾아 바르게 고치시오.

1 Boiling water prevent sickness.

2 Thirty miles are a long distance for me to walk every day.

3 Most of my pocket-money are spent for buying books.

4 One of the trees that thrive in the cold weather are a maple tree.

5 Mathematics were my most favorite subject when I was young.

6 Each of these hundreds of students are eager to study English.

7 Diabetes have become a serious disease as the number of obese people has increased.

C 다음 〈보기〉와 같이 괄호 안에 주어진 지시에 따라 문장을 고쳐 쓰시오.

> **Example**　You lose ten pounds. It makes you feel more attractive to others. (동명사)
> → <u>Losing ten pounds makes you feel more attractive to others.</u>

1 You nod your head up and down. It means "yes" in this country. (동명사)
　→ _____

2 We learn a foreign language. It is a process that takes a lifetime. (동명사)
　→ _____

3 You earn the respect of your children. It is a real success in life. (부정사)
　→ _____

4 You laugh often and much. It brings you a healthier life. (부정사)
　→ _____

1 다음 문장에서 <u>잘못된</u> 부분을 찾아 바르게 고치시오.

1 Every possible means have to be tried.

2 To speak English well require practicing every day.

3 Two million dollars are a large sum of money.

4 Playing with ducks in the pond were my greatest pleasure.

5 Linguistics are what I want to major in at the university.

6 Every member of this Boy Scout group perform his duty well.

7 One of Hemingway's most interesting works are "A Farewell to Arms."

2 다음 빈칸에 알맞은 말을 고르시오.

1 _____ of the students has his/her own computer in the classroom.

① A number   ② Each   ③ Most   ④ Both   ⑤ Every

2 To learn foreign languages _____ important for your future.

① is   ② are   ③ has   ④ have   ⑤ holds

3 다음 글을 읽고, (A)와 (B)에 알맞은 말을 고르시오.

I'm confused about strategies for the long run in marathon training. I've read that three hours (A) (is / are) the maximum time for an expert like me. But I've also read that two and a half hours (B) (is / are) moderate, and mileage should be between 18 and 22 miles. I'm never sure how far or how long I should run.

4 다음 주어진 단어를 이용하여 문장을 완성하시오.

1 각각의 주가 가뭄으로 인한 전력부족에 직면하고 있다. (state, face)

Each _____ a power shortage because of the drought.

2 12년은 시골 외딴 곳에서 지내기에는 긴 시간이다. (spend)

Twelve years _____ in a remote corner of the country.

3 의술의 발전에도 불구하고 당뇨병은 여전히 완치가 어려운 질병으로 간주된다. (diabetes, regarded)

Despite medical progress, _____ as an incurable disease.

4 한국전쟁 중에 많은 어린 소년들이 나라를 지키기 위하여 무기를 들었다. (a number of, take up arms)

During the Korean War, _____ to defend the country.

1 부정의 문장

A 다음 괄호 안에서 알맞은 말을 고르시오.

1 (Neither / Nothing) politician has read my book.

2 He didn't want (any / no) advice on how to do it.

3 (Nobody / Nowhere) in her office wants extra work.

4 They don't know (anything / nothing) about the accident.

5 We haven't got (any / no) clue about the missing jewelry box.

6 No one could find the missing boy (anywhere / nowhere) on the mountain.

B 다음 주어진 우리말과 같은 뜻이 되도록 빈칸에 알맞은 말을 쓰시오.

1 그 소년들 둘 다 그곳에 가지 않았다.
→ _____ of the boys didn't go there.

2 나는 그의 친구들 중 아무도 좋아하지 않는다.
→ I don't like _____ of his friends.

3 자이언츠 팀은 두 경기 중 어느 것도 지지 않았다.
→ The Giants didn't lose _____ game.

4 그 소년들 둘 다 거기에 가지 않았다.
→ _____ of the boys went there.

5 우리 반 급우들 모두가 방과 후에 축구를 하는 것은 아니다.
→ _____ _____ of my classmates play soccer after school.

C 다음 〈보기〉의 단어를 이용하여 문장을 다시 쓰시오.

Word Bank	never	none	nowhere	neither

1 I don't know any of the girls sitting there.
→ I know _____.

2 I haven't read either of these books.
→ I have read _____.

3 I have not ever experienced this problem before.
→ I have _____.

4 There is not anywhere to get some drinking water.
→ There is _____.

Further Study

1 다음 〈보기〉에서 알맞은 것을 골라 문장을 완성하시오. (단, 한 번씩만 사용하시오.)

Word Bank	anything	nobody	no	anybody	none	neither

1 _____ wants to go out in this weather.

2 I haven't done _____ special this week.

3 Since I arrived, I haven't seen _____ in the house.

4 _____ of the club members is interested in the plan.

5 _____ of the two students was eligible for scholarships.

6 A "_____ trespassing" sign means people should not enter the area.

2 다음 중 어법상 <u>어색한</u> 문장을 고르시오.

① I have never seen such an amazing view in my life.

② None of the soldiers was seriously injured, and all were back on duty.

③ We went to a convenience store because there wasn't anything in the refrigerator.

④ The police looked everywhere for the boy, but they couldn't find him anywhere.

⑤ The students who attended the seminar could hardly not understand what he was saying.

3 다음 글을 읽고, (A)와 (B)에 알맞은 말을 고르시오.

> Marriage, traditionally, was arranged by parents or parental representatives such as a family elder or a matchmaker. Young people themselves had (A) (any / no) choice in the matter, and sometimes the couple met for the first time on their wedding day. They were not allowed to take (B) (any / no) initiative on their marriage.

4 다음 주어진 단어를 이용하여 문장을 완성하시오.

1 그의 가족 모두가 대학교육을 마친 것은 아니다. (everyone)
   Not _____ finished college education.

2 모든 사람이 기회를 붙잡을 준비가 되어 있는 것은 아니다. (grab chances)
   Not all of the people are _____ when they come.

3 안락한 생활을 위하여 건강보다 내가 중히 여기는 것은 없다. (there, none)
   For a comfortable life, _____ I would place above health.

4 돈이 항상 행복을 가져다주는 것은 아니라는 사실은 인정된 진리이다. (bring, always)
   It is an accepted truth that _____.

2 도치의 문장

A 다음 괄호 안에서 알맞은 말을 고르시오.

1 Never (will I / I will) do that again.

2 Here (the bus comes / comes the bus) which we are waiting for.

3 They (could barely / barely could) see the top of the mountain in the fog.

4 Not until yesterday (did I know / I knew) the fact that he had skipped the class.

5 Only in Africa (can we / we can) see animals such as a lion, a zebra and a giraffe.

6 A: He likes volleyball.   B: So (do / does) my father.

7 A: Cathy isn't a doctor.   B: Neither (is / isn't) Mary.

B 다음 밑줄 친 부분을 어법에 맞게 고쳐 쓰시오.

1 Not until years afterwards <u>did</u> he able to understand it.

2 Little <u>was</u> I dream of having such a luxury in my own home.

3 Rarely <u>he has</u> been away for a few days and nights at a time.

4 Hardly <u>he could</u> finish his test paper when the school bell rang.

5 Honestly speaking, <u>never were</u> I see such an excellent language school.

C 다음 주어진 단어로 시작하는 도치 문장으로 바꿔 쓰시오.

1 We have received complaints about her.
   → Rarely _____.

2 She knew that her boyfriend had a twin sister.
   → Little _____.

3 I can believe what he said about the incident.
   → Hardly _____.

4 I will leave the office before it gets dark.
   → Never _____.

5 The city has developed since we moved three years ago.
   → Scarcely _____.

6 The weather changes in some parts of the world.
   → Seldom _____.

Further Study

1 다음 문장을 도치의 문장을 바꿔 쓸 때 빈칸에 알맞은 말을 쓰시오.

1 They rarely go for a walk.
→ Rarely _____.

2 I have never seen such a splendid sight.
→ Never _____.

3 She could hardly understand what the book was about.
→ Hardly _____.

4 Mr. Jones seldom spent money buying clothes and shoes.
→ Seldom _____.

2 다음 중 어법상 어색한 문장을 고르시오.

① Next to the hill was a small house.
② Not until this morning did I realized that I lost my wallet.
③ Rarely did they go out for dinner when they owed me a debt.
④ Never did I expect such a misfortune that would befall my family.
⑤ Little had I known of his death before I came across his son last Sunday.

3 다음 글을 읽고, (A)와 (B)에 알맞은 말을 고르시오.

When it comes to getting older, people often think of only bad aspects of aging, such as physical pain and memory loss. However, not (A) (all / either) elderly people suffer from these conditions. Not only (B) (do / does) many senior citizens live in good health condition, but also they enjoy their old age without any kind of worries.

4 다음 주어진 단어를 이용하여 문장을 완성하시오.

1 우리 선생님께서 오신다. (come)
Here _____.

2 나는 어머니가 화내는 것을 거의 본 적이 없다. (chance)
Hardly _____ to see my mother getting angry.

3 그는 좀처럼 자신의 동료와 문제를 일으키지 않는다. (have trouble)
Rarely _____ with his coworkers.

4 나는 조국으로의 귀환이 실현되리라고는 꿈도 꾸지 못했었다. (dream)
Little _____ that returning to my motherland would become reality.

1 명사절

A 다음 괄호 안에서 알맞은 말을 고르시오.

1 (If / That) she became a doctor is unbelievable.

2 The problem is (that / whether) they can help us or not.

3 (That / Whether) he will come or not depends on his father.

4 The problem is (if / that) the cost of living is increasing recently.

5 I recommended that Michele (will / should) attend the annual meeting.

6 We proposed that he (be allowed / is allowed) to return to Canada.

B 다음 빈칸에 whether만 쓰이면 'a', whether와 if 둘 다 쓰이면 'b'라고 쓰시오.

1 I wonder _____ dogs are color-blind or not.

2 Please ask him _____ he can speak English.

3 _____ we go or not depends on the weather.

4 It matters very little to us _____ he goes or not.

5 I don't know _____ he will apply for the job or not.

6 _____ he loves her or not is not a big deal to her.

7 Did he tell you _____ he submitted his history report on time?

8 _____ he will become a successful president or not remains to be seen.

C 다음 문장을 주어진 'if' 또는 'whether'를 포함하는 문장으로 바꿔 쓰시오.

1 Did he buy the car on the installment plan?
   → I don't know if _____ the car on the installment plan.

2 Do many Japanese people celebrate Chinese New Year?
   → Can you tell me if _____ Chinese New Year?

3 Did I lock the front door?
   → I can't remember whether _____ the front door or not.

4 Will Jennifer get married next month?
   → Do you know if _____ next month?

5 Does Canada have two official languages?
   → I wonder whether _____ two official languages.

Further Study

1 다음 괄호 안에서 알맞은 말을 고르시오.

1 He ordered that the goods (are / be) sent by air.

2 The doctor insisted that he (give / gives) up smoking.

3 I demanded that Mr. Kim (is / be) expelled from the club.

4 It is necessary that one (save / saved) for a rainy day.

5 The students requested that exams (be / are) postponed.

2 다음 밑줄 친 <u>that</u>의 쓰임이 다른 것을 고르시오.

① He demanded <u>that</u> he be allowed to enter the army.

② The problem is <u>that</u> he is not accustomed to our culture.

③ They insisted <u>that</u> we should participate in the opening ceremony.

④ Their claim <u>that</u> they should be paid for extra work was accepted.

⑤ The hotel <u>that</u> is located at the center of the town is very expensive.

3 다음 글을 읽고, (A)와 (B)에 알맞은 말을 고르시오.

Every year, it seems that more and more people are going on holiday abroad. This means that more and more people are also experiencing the discomfort and frustration of foreign travel. Therefore, it is always a relief (A) (of / that) we return home, and we are often left wondering (B) (about / if) travel is really worth the effort. Next year, however, we will find ourselves at the airport again.

4 다음 주어진 단어를 이용하여 문장을 완성하시오.

1 당신이 우리 동아리의 규율을 따르는 것은 중요하다. (critical, that)
It is _____ all the rules of our club.

2 아들이 입학시험에 실패했다는 소식이 그녀를 무척 놀라게 하였다. (had failed)
The news that _____ shocked her very much.

3 한국 사회가 급속히 노령화 되고 있다는 사실을 누구도 부인하지 못할 것이다. (deny)
No one _____ that Korea is fast becoming an aging society.

4 농부는 닭에게 모이를 먼저 줘야 하는지 젖소의 우유를 먼저 짜야 하는지 알지 못했다. (feed, first)
The farmer didn't _____ he would _____ or milk the cows.

2 that S+V

A 다음 괄호 안에서 알맞은 말을 고르시오.

1 I'm sorry (that / to) give you all this trouble.

2 We insisted (on / that) her turning the volume down at night.

3 I never heard (of / that) his doing a dishonest thing.

4 I'm sorry (for / that) he had to leave his family behind.

5 We were pleased (at / that) you were able to get it done in time.

6 I was disappointed (at / that) nobody recognized me in Korea.

B 다음 문장에서 잘못된 부분을 찾아 바르게 고치시오.

1 I'm happy to taking you in my car.

2 He is convinced to succeeding in the business.

3 She was aware to being in a dangerous situation.

4 Your remarks are likely of hurt her feelings.

5 We are confident of get higher profits next year.

C 다음 문장을 that절을 이용하여 다시 쓰시오.

1 She is proud of having an expensive necklace.
  → She is proud that _____.

2 There was no doubt of his being a spy.
  → There was no doubt that _____.

3 He insisted on my going out in the rain.
  → He insisted that _____.

4 We are glad to know your being healthy.
  → We are glad to know that _____.

5 I was relieved to find her returning home safe.
  → I was relieved to find that _____.

6 He complained of the room being too cold.
  → He complained that _____.

7 I was sorry to hear of your father's death.
  → I was sorry that _____.

Further Study

1 다음 빈칸에 알맞은 말을 쓰시오.

1 We were sorry _____ miss your concert.

2 I was happy _____ hear about your success.

3 I'm sure _____ he will win first prize.

4 She is afraid _____ going out alone late at night.

2 다음 빈칸에 들어갈 말이 바르게 짝지어진 것을 고르시오.

I'm anxious _____ know the result of the test.
We are sure _____ his sister's coming here.

① of - for   ② for - to   ③ to - of
④ to - for   ⑤ for - of

3 다음 글을 읽고, (A)와 (B)에 알맞은 말을 고르시오.

Everyone has a cell phone these days, but I don't. At first, I didn't feel the necessity. Moreover, I thought it would somewhat disturb my privacy. I was even proud (A) (of / that) not having a cell phone. However, now I'm worried if I'm not informed about something important. A few days ago, I drove myself 100 miles to attend a conference, but it wasn't held. I was not aware (B) (of / that) it was canceled because I didn't have an instant contact number.

4 다음 주어진 단어를 이용하여 문장을 완성하시오.

1 내 맏아들은 어린애처럼 대우받는다고 불평을 털어 놓았다. (be treated)
My oldest son _____ that _____ like a child.

2 그는 영어로 의사소통을 할 수 없어서 불안했다. (make oneself understood)
He was afraid that _____ in English.

3 오늘날 많은 젊은이들은 가난이 어떤 것인가를 알지 못한다. (be aware of)
Many young people today _____ what it is like to be poor.

4 여름방학이 임박했으므로 학생들은 즐거워한다. (please)
The students _____ summer vacation is just around the corner.

1 형용사절-관계대명사 I

A 다음 괄호 안에서 알맞은 말을 고르시오.

1 Joe is one of the best actors (that / whose) I've ever seen.

2 I know a guy (whose / that) height is too tall for his bed.

3 Most people (living / lived) in the city go to work by subway.

4 He was the new manager (appointed / appointing) by the city.

5 This is the gentleman (whom / whose) we have wanted to meet.

6 There lived a man (who / whom) had no intention of being a supportive husband.

B 다음 중 밑줄 친 관계대명사를 생략할 수 있으면 ○ , 생략할 수 없으면 ×표 하시오.

1 What is the language that is spoken in Brazil? _____

2 A woman has just bought the scarf that I want to buy. _____

3 The man who is painting a picture under the tree is my uncle. _____

4 This is the most difficult problem that I have ever had to face. _____

5 The men and horses that were killed at the battle were innumerable. _____

6 I will make some cookies for the boy who is reading a book in the room. _____

7 Even the student whom I thought to be clever could not solve the problem. _____

C 다음 〈보기〉와 같이 두 문장을 관계대명사를 이용하여 한 문장으로 만들 때 빈칸에 알맞은 말을 쓰시오.

Example   Bring me the dictionary. + I left it on the desk.
→ Bring me the dictionary which/that I left on the desk.

1 Her son often sends her a lot of money. + He is now in New York.
→ Her son _____ often sends her a lot of money.

2 Mike is working at the car company. + It is located in the suburbs.
→ Mike is working at the car company _____.

3 Pavarotti was a famous tenor. + He performed with many other artists.
→ Pavarotti _____ was a famous tenor.

4 The banjo became a popular music instrument. + It was first used in Africa.
→ The banjo _____ became a popular music instrument.

5 The picture is a masterpiece. + Many tourists are looking at it.
→ The picture _____ is a masterpiece.

Further Study

1 다음 〈보기〉에서 알맞은 것을 골라 문장을 완성하시오.

| Word Bank | who | which | whom | whose |

1 The novel is about a spy _____ wife betrays him.

2 I can lend you this book _____ I talked about yesterday.

3 Do you see the mountain _____ top is covered with snow?

4 The people _____ migrated from Asia brought their cultures with them.

5 A man with _____ I work perfectly matches your Mr. Right descriptions.

6 Her latest performance _____ attracted thousands of people was a success.

2 다음 중 어법상 어색한 문장을 고르시오.

① The man attending the seminar is my boss.

② Have you seen my glasses I put on the table?

③ Did you see the boy lay on the grass yesterday?

④ Do you know the children playing baseball over there?

⑤ The novel she wrote is not so interesting as we expected.

3 다음 글을 읽고, (A)에 알맞은 말을 고르시오.

Governments are facing many problems, and most of the problems are international ones. Take traffic, for example. All the major cities of the world are trying to find ways of dealing with too many vehicles and the congested roads (A) (who / which) they cause.

4 다음 주어진 단어를 이용하여 문장을 완성하시오.

1 나의 형이 사랑에 빠졌던 그 소녀는 우리 형을 냉대했다. (fall in love with)
   The girl _____ turned a cold shoulder to him.

2 문 옆에 앉아 있는 그 신사는 강연에 지각하였다. (sit next to)
   The gentleman _____ came to the lecture late.

3 많은 유명한 노래를 불렀던 앨비스 프레슬리는 영화에도 출현했다. (sing, many)
   Elvis Presley _____ also acted in movies.

4 그 지역에서 사용되는 언어는 아프리카 토착민의 언어이다. (spoken, province)
   The language _____ is an African aboriginal one.

2 형용사절-관계대명사 II

A 다음 괄호 안에서 알맞은 말을 고르시오.

1 We have ten dogs, (one of which / two of which) are very big.

2 This is the book (about which / which) we talked the other day.

3 He said he was a famous singer, (that / which) proved to be true.

4 I'm working at the shopping mall, (that / which) is just over the road.

5 There is lots of information available here, (much / many) of which I don't understand.

6 There are many signs along the street, (of which / which) the meanings I don't know.

B 다음 문장에서 <u>잘못된</u> 부분을 찾아 바르게 고치시오.

1 You have the book which I've been looking.

2 The bed on that I slept last night was not very comfortable.

3 My grandfather made the armchair which you are sitting.

4 We can see many tourists here, much of whom are from Japan.

5 He didn't watch the action movies which he had once been fond.

6 The magazine, that my father is reading, is published once a month.

7 She invited lots of people to her wedding, some of whom was foreigners.

C 다음 문장을 관계대명사를 이용하여 완성하시오.

1 그녀는 자식이 셋 있는데, 아무도 대학을 다니지 않았다.
   → She has three children, _____ attended college.

2 나는 어제 양말을 열 켤레 샀는데, 그 중 몇 개는 흰색이다.
   → I bought ten pairs of socks yesterday, _____ are white.

3 나의 삼촌은 책을 많이 저술했는데, 나는 그 중 한 권도 아직 읽지 않았다.
   → My uncle wrote many books, _____ I have read yet.

4 아프리카에는 많은 나라가 있는데, 대부분 빈곤에 시달리고 있다.
   → There are many countries in Africa, _____ suffer from poverty.

5 나의 할아버지에게는 열두 명의 손자와 손녀가 있는데, 대부분 서울에 살고 있다.
   → My grandfather has twelve grandchildren, _____ live in Seoul.

6 버스에는 상당한 수의 승객이 있었는데, 그들 중 일부는 사고를 모면했다.
   → There were a number of passengers on the bus, _____ escaped the accident.

Further Study

1 다음 괄호 안에서 알맞은 말을 고르시오.

1 I said nothing, (that / which) made him angrier.

2 I tried to open the door, (which / of which) was impossible.

3 It is hard to break a habit (to / on) which one has grown accustomed.

4 Tom has a lot of friends, many of (whom / which) like playing basketball.

5 The most striking example of a canal is the Suez Canal, (that join / which joins) the Mediterranean and the Red Sea.

2 다음 문장 중 어법상 어색한 문장을 고르시오.

① The house which he lives in is very elegant but not large.

② My secretary, who is good at English, is on vacation now.

③ He read many novels, most of which was about detectives.

④ They are all my classmates, some of whom came from China.

⑤ Jack was very smart, which was a great pleasure for his mother.

3 다음 글을 읽고, (A)와 (B)에 알맞은 말을 고르시오.

My uncle, Jim likes traveling and meeting people. For this reason, his house is like a museum. It is filled with exotic stuff, (A) (that / which) he collected while traveling, and pictures showing famous places. He also has lots of foreign friends. Once I visited him, I met his friends, most of whom (B) (was / were) speaking German.

4 다음 주어진 단어와 관계대명사를 이용하여 문장을 완성하시오.

1 우리 학교 최고의 테니스 선수는 Jack인데, 그는 하얀 색 옷을 입는 것을 좋아한다. (wear, clothes)
The best tennis player in my school is Jack, _____.

2 Jessica와 이야기를 나누고 있는 남자를 아니? (talk)
Do you know the man _____?

3 그 백만장자에겐 20대의 차가 있는데, 대부분은 새 자동차이다. (brand-new)
The millionaire has 20 cars, _____.

4 평창은 강원도에 위치해 있는데, 동계 올림픽을 유치하려고 애쓰고 있다. (locate)
Pyungchang, _____ Kangwon Province, is seeking to host the winter Olympic Games.

1 형용사절–관계부사

A 다음 괄호 안에서 알맞은 말을 고르시오.

1 This is the box (where / which) I keep my jewelry.

2 We found (the way / the way how) Millet made the cake.

3 The volcano erupted in 1979, (when / which) I was thirteen.

4 She remembered the day (when / which) she first met his parents.

5 There are several reasons (why / which) I can't finish the project.

B 다음 주어진 문장과 같은 뜻이 되도록 관계부사를 이용하여 문장을 완성하시오.

1 I don't know the reason for which she dislikes me.
→ I don't know the reason _____.

2 An intersection is the point at which roads meet.
→ An intersection is the point _____.

3 March is the month in which the new school year begins.
→ March is the month _____.

4 Do you know the reason for which Mr. Kim is absent from work for a few days?
→ Do you know the reason _____?

5 The party, at which I was the guest of honor, was extremely enjoyable.
→ The party, _____, was extremely enjoyable.

C 다음 두 문장을 관계부사를 이용하여 한 문장으로 만드시오.

1 Beijing is the capital of China. + The Olympic Games took place there in 2008.
→ Beijing is the capital of China _____.

2 The Beatles toured America. + And there they had many devoted fans.
→ The Beatles toured America, _____.

3 Nobody knows the way. + The young boy made a million dollars in that way.
→ Nobody knows _____.

4 I was married in 2002. + The World Cup soccer tournament took place in Korea then.
→ I was married in 2002, _____.

5 That is the reason. + I cannot agree with you therefore.
→ That is the reason _____.

Further Study

1 다음 〈보기〉에서 알맞은 것을 골라 문장을 완성하시오. (단, 한 번씩만 사용하시오.)

Word Bank	where	when	why	how	which

1 The guide took us to the museum, _____ we enjoyed ourselves.

2 Please tell me the reason _____ you majored in history.

3 Monday is the day _____ I have a lot of work to do.

4 Could you teach me _____ you solve the problem?

5 Africa is one of the places _____ I would like to visit.

2 다음 중 어법상 <u>어색한</u> 문장을 고르시오.

① I will never forget the day when we won the championship.
② He came back to the town which he spent his childhood.
③ She is not going to tell you why she broke up with him.
④ We went to the Chinese restaurant where he worked as a manager.
⑤ I visited the building at which I worked before I was transferred to Seoul.

3 다음 글을 읽고, (A)와 (B)에 알맞은 말을 고르시오.

Of course, parking space is not always available. Some firms provide car parks, (A) (which / where) at least some of their employees can leave their cars. Most people, however, have to rely on public car parks. Since they are usually highly restricted, some people ignore lines painted down the edge of the road which (B) (indicate / indicates) parking restrictions.

4 다음 주어진 단어를 이용하여 문장을 완성하시오.

1 나는 호숫가에서 그림을 그리곤 했던 그 마을로 나는 돌아가고 싶다. (village)
   I would like to return to _____ by the lake.

2 내가 이 회사에 지원했던 이유는 의료영상기기에 관심을 갖고 있기 때문이었다. (reason, apply for)
   _____ was that I was interested in the medical image system.

3 부산은 외국에서 들어온 물건들이 하역되는 항구이다. (foreign, goods from)
   Busan is the port _____ are unloaded.

4 그는 고객의 욕구에 맞춘 것이 아니라, 자신이 원하는 방식대로 그림을 그렸다. (the way)
   Instead of painting what his customers wanted, he painted exactly _____.

2 관계사절의 다른 형태

A 다음 괄호 안에서 알맞은 말을 고르시오.

1 This is not (that / what) I want to have.

2 I'll give it to (whoever / wherever) comes first.

3 (However / Whatever) hard he may try, he can't do it.

4 (Whatever / Whenever) I get homesick, I go to the beach.

5 (Whoever / Whomever) gets the job will earn a lot of money.

6 These books are just (that / what) we've always wanted to read.

B 다음 두 문장이 같은 뜻이 되도록 빈칸에 알맞은 말을 쓰시오.

1 At any time when it rains, the roof leaks.
   → _____ it rains, the roof leaks.

2 You can set up a tent at any place where you like.
   → You can set up a tent _____ you like.

3 You must obey anything that he tells you.
   → You must obey _____ he tells you.

4 No matter what you do, don't keep him waiting.
   → _____ you do, don't keep him waiting.

5 I will give this picture to anyone whom you call an art-collector.
   → I will give this picture to _____ you call an art-collector.

6 No matter how hard I try, it is too far for me to swim to shore.
   → _____ hard I try, it is too far for me to swim to shore.

C 다음 밑줄 친 that이 관계대명사이면 a, 관계부사이면 b, 접속사이면 c라고 쓰시오.

1 This is the reason that I respect my father.   _____

2 The police have found the gun that she was shot with.   _____

3 The day that my father died, I was on holiday in France.   _____

4 There are lots of things that I need to buy before the trip.   _____

5 The trouble with you is that you are quick to become angry.   _____

6 The rules state that only the goal keeper can handle the ball.   _____

7 The fact that he is your brother-in-law should not affect your decision.   _____

Further Study

1 다음 괄호 안에서 알맞은 말을 고르시오.

1 (Whatever / Whenever) I have is yours.

2 You may invite (however / whomever) you like.

3 Do not put off until tomorrow (that / what) you can do today.

4 I will buy a cup of coffee for (whoever / whomever) comes first.

5 From (what / which) I hear, he seems to be a very kind person.

2 다음 빈칸에 공통으로 들어갈 말을 고르시오.

_____ you choose, you will regret your choice.
You can take _____ book you like.

① whenever   ② wherever   ③ whichever
④ however   ⑤ whoever

3 다음 글을 읽고, (A)와 (B)에 알맞은 말을 고르시오.

(A) (That / What) matters is that, as the number of old people is increasing, the number of young people is decreasing. The combination of a falling birth rate and an increase in life expectancy is likely to cause problems for government. It is the young and the middle-aged (B) (who / which) do most work and pay most taxes. In other words, it is they who keep the country going, for it is the revenue from taxes that pays for public services.

4 다음 주어진 단어를 이용하여 문장을 완성하시오.

1 어디를 가도 집과 같은 곳은 찾을 수 없다. (may)
   _____, you will never find a place like home.

2 내가 너를 신뢰하므로 네가 추천하는 사람 누구든 고용하겠다. (recommend)
   I trust you, and I will employ _____ to me.

3 내가 말하고 싶은 것은 너 자신을 신뢰해야 한다는 것이다. (say)
   _____ is that you should have faith in yourself.

4 내가 계획된 일정이 없고 한가하므로, 그녀가 시간이 있을 때마다 우리는 만날 수 있다. (have)
   Because I have no plans and lots of free time, we can meet _____ free time.

1 의문사 의문문

A 다음 괄호 안에서 알맞은 말을 고르시오.

1 (Why / What) are you wearing sunglasses?

2 Who (did take / took) the cake in the refrigerator?

3 (Where / What) did you get the chair made of plastic?

4 Whom (did you see / saw you) at the opening ceremony?

5 (From whom / Whom) did you get the idea for your exhibit?

6 (For what reason / What reason) do you decide to join the club?

B 다음 〈보기〉에서 알맞은 것을 골라 문장을 완성하시오. (단, 한 번씩만 사용하시오.)

Word Bank	who	whose	whom	what	why

1 _____ music do you like best? → I like the Beatles' music best.

2 _____ is your favorite subject? → My favorite subject is history.

3 _____ did you talk to before class? → I talked to Jack before class.

4 _____ won't you come to the party? → Because I have a lot of homework to do.

5 _____ is wearing jeans today? → Our music teacher is wearing jeans today.

C 다음 주어진 말을 알맞게 배열하여 문장을 완성하시오.

1 there / the auditorium / how many / are / students / in
→ _____

2 showed / to / her / the way / who / the station
→ _____

3 choose / book / they / did / which
→ _____

4 did / for / you / pay / your hat / how much
→ _____

5 has / your / where / gone / father
→ _____

6 better / do / like / you / which / spring / autumn / or
→ _____

Further Study

1 다음 문장에서 <u>잘못된</u> 부분을 찾아 바르게 고치시오.

1 How are her parents like?

2 Where color do you like best for the dress?

3 What reason was he charged and fined?

4 How day of the week is it the cheapest to fly?

5 From what did you get my phone number?

2 다음 빈칸에 알맞은 말을 고르시오.

1 _____ advice will you follow for more desirable campus life?

　① What　　　　② Who　　　　③ Whom　　　　④ How　　　　⑤ When

2 _____ long have you stayed away from your family living in Jeju Island?

　① What　　　　② Who　　　　③ Whom　　　　④ How　　　　⑤ Whose

3 다음 글을 읽고, (A)와 (B)에 알맞은 말을 고르시오.

　Suppose the business pays for its client's free lunch. Suppose the government pays for the free lunch at the schools. The source of income the business has is (A) (which / what) it earns from selling goods just as the major source of income the government has is taxes. So the more a business gives away for free, the more it has to charge for its goods. The more a government gives away for free, the more taxes it has to raise. (B) (Who / What), then, pays for this lunch and pays taxes? It may be you.

4 다음 주어진 단어와 의문사를 이용하여 문장을 완성하시오.

1 우리 방과 후에 해변에 수영하러 가는 게 어떨까? (how, for a swim)
　_____ after school?

2 오늘 아침 학교 강당에서 너는 누구 옆에 앉았니? (sit next to)
　_____ in the school auditorium this morning?

3 자유와 기회의 나라인 이곳에 너와 함께 이민 온 사람은 누구니? (immigrated)
　_____ with you to this country freedom and opportunity?

4 한국 사람들이 8월에 기념하는 국경일은 어떤 날이니? (national holiday)
　_____ celebrate in August?

2

간접 의문문

A 다음 괄호 안에서 알맞은 말을 고르시오.

1 Nobody knows (is which / which is) the best apple.

2 I don't know (will who / who will) be our next president.

3 Please tell me when (did you go / you went) to the park.

4 (Where do you think / Do you think where) they will visit?

5 Can you tell me (what does / what) your father looks like?

6 Could you tell me how long (will it / it will) take to finish the project?

B 다음 문장을 괄호 안의 말을 이용하여 간접의문문으로 바꿔 쓰시오.

1 Who will help me cut the wheat field today? (do you think)

　→ _____

2 How does your father make a living? (I wonder)

　→ _____

3 What is the population of Seoul? (I asked her)

　→ _____

4 Whom is he looking for? (do you suppose)

　→ _____

C 다음 문장을 〈보기〉처럼 바꿔 쓰시오.

Example	Could you tell me when you met her?
	→ When did you meet her?

1 Who do you suppose broke the window?

　→ _____

2 Do you know when their train will arrive?

　→ _____

3 Could you tell me where your brother lives?

　→ _____

4 How far do you think it is from Seoul to Busan?

　→ _____

1 다음 문장에서 <u>잘못된</u> 부분을 찾아 바르게 고치시오.

1　I wonder who is the mayor of the town.

2　Do you suppose which way was the shortest?

3　What do you know would happen the next moment?

4　Could you tell me what color does she like best?

5　Why do you know the giraffe has such a long neck?

6　Could you tell me what is the best title of this passage?

2 다음 중 어법상 <u>어색한</u> 문장을 고르시오.

① Let's ask her in which direction she will go.

② Do you guess how long does this movie run?

③ Can you tell me what you usually do in your spare time?

④ Tell me what the weather will be like on the coming weekend.

⑤ Do you remember when Korea was liberated from Japan's colonial rule?

3 다음 글을 읽고, (A)와 (B)에 알맞은 말을 고르시오.

　　Yesterday I went to a bookstore to buy a book about computers. I asked a clerk (A) (where did they have / where they had) books about computers. She said that they were on the second floor. I was surprised that there were a large number of books. It took me a long time to find one (B) (what / that) was for beginners like me.　　　　*수능기출

4 다음 주어진 단어를 이용하여 문장을 완성하시오.

1　너는 세계에서 두 번째로 큰 나라가 어디라고 생각하니? (what, the second)
　　_____ in the world is?

2　당신이 현재의 직업에 종사한 기간을 말해 주세요. (work)
　　Please _____ in your present job.

3　너는 저녁 몇 시에 은행이 문을 닫는지 알고 있니? (close)
　　Do you have any idea _____ in the evening?

4　나는 보수가 낮은데도 왜 네가 그 일에 지원하였는지 알고 싶다. (apply for)
　　I want to know _____ in spite of the low salary.

1 시간의 문장 I

A 다음 괄호 안에서 알맞은 말을 고르시오.

1 He wonders when Addie (will pay / pays) me back.

2 Ever since you arrived, you (are / have been) sleeping.

3 I (have been / was) interested in biology since I was ten.

4 After he (will finish / finishes) writing the letter, he will take a shower.

5 Gomez will go to the gym when his wife (will come / comes) back home.

6 The plane will take off by the time we (arrive / will arrive) at the airport.

B 다음 괄호 안에 주어진 단어를 이용하여 빈칸에 알맞은 말을 쓰시오.

1 I did my homework and _____ to bed. (go)

2 I have no idea when the film _____ _____ finished. (be)

3 He'll do the dishes after he _____ the dog. (walk)

4 We were playing in the garden when supper _____ _____. (cook)

5 While I _____ _____ at the bus stop, I met my ex-boyfriend. (wait)

6 She began to talk after she _____ _____ silent for three hours. (keep)

7 I haven't had a good night's sleep since I _____ a baby. (have)

8 You look very familiar. _____ we _____ before? (meet)

C 다음 우리말과 같은 뜻이 되도록 빈칸에 알맞은 말을 쓰시오.

1 오래 기다린 뒤에야 그가 왔다.
→ I had waited long _____ he came.

2 나는 그 영화를 전에 본 적이 있다.
→ I have seen the movie _____.

3 해가 비추는 동안 건초를 말려라.
→ Make hay _____ the sun shines.

4 나는 사랑에 빠진 이후로 공부에 집중할 수가 없다.
→ I haven't been able to concentrate on my studies _____ I fell in love.

5 네가 거기에 도착할 때면 날이 어두울 것이다.
→ _____ _____ _____ you get there, it will be dark.

Further Study

1 다음 〈보기〉에서 알맞은 것을 골라 문장을 완성하시오. (단, 한 번씩만 사용하시오.)

Word Bank	before	after	while	since

1 _____ you are sleeping, your heart is not resting, but it is still beating.

2 He hasn't decided what to do _____ he graduates from university.

3 I have had several complaints from my neighbors _____ I bought a dog.

4 It will not be long _____ our company captures the whole game market.

2 다음 빈칸에 들어갈 말이 바르게 짝지어진 것을 고르시오.

I have been living in Dallas _____ I retired in 2002.
My cousin will take care of my pets _____ I'm away on vacation.

① after - since   ② since - while   ③ before - while
④ after - while   ⑤ since - till

3 다음 글을 읽고, (A)와 (B)에 알맞은 말을 고르시오.

In many countries, more and more people are working longer hours. People used to be able to leave behind the tension and anxiety of the workplace (A) (when / before) they went on holiday. Unfortunately, (B) (ever since / by the time) modern communication systems, such as mobile phones and e-mail, were invented, they have made this a thing of the past. We find it almost impossible to leave our work behind.

4 다음 주어진 단어를 이용하여 문장을 완성하시오.

1 내가 여기 온 지 한 달이 지났다. (since)
A month has passed _____.

2 그가 나를 방문했을 때 나는 신문을 읽고 있었다. (newspaper)
_____ when he visited me.

3 내가 오늘 저녁 슈퍼에 갈 때 빵을 좀 사올게. (go to the supermarket)
I will buy some bread _____ this evening.

4 우리가 영화관에 도착 할쯤이면, 영화는 이미 시작했을 것이다. (start)
By the time we get to the cinema, the film _____.

2 시간의 문장 II

A 다음 괄호 안에서 알맞은 말을 고르시오.

1 He ran away (as soon as / while) he saw me.

2 You can lose weight (since / while) sleeping at night.

3 Not until this morning (did I know / I knew) that he was injured.

4 We'll never forget your kindness (as soon as / as long as) we live.

5 (Once / Whenever) he completed his military service, he got a job.

6 (While / So) we were young, we were not allowed to watch the movie.

B 다음 〈보기〉와 같이 「접속사+분사」의 문장으로 바꿔 쓰시오.

> **Example**   We got the receipt after we paid the bill.
> → We got the receipt after paying the bill.

1 We talked about the economic problems while we were having dinner.
→ We talked about the economic problems _____.

2 We stopped suddenly when we heard a child crying softly.
→ We stopped suddenly _____.

3 I finished my homework before I went out to ride a bike.
→ I finished my homework _____.

4 After he spent all his money, he asked me to send him some more.
→ _____, he asked me to send him some more.

C 다음 문장이 같은 의미가 되도록 문장을 완성하시오.

1 She did not return home until midnight.
→ Not until _____.
→ It was not until _____.

2 People do not know the blessing of health until they lose it.
→ Not until _____.
→ It is not until _____.

3 Scott didn't realize he was wrong until last week.
→ Not until _____.
→ It was not until _____.

Further Study

1 다음 〈보기〉에서 알맞은 것을 골라 문장을 완성하시오. (단, 한 번씩만 사용하시오.)

| Word Bank | as long as | as soon as | once | whenever |

1 Call me _____ you need a ride.

2 You may keep the book _____ you like.

3 _____ he went to Seoul, he called on his aunt.

4 _____ my father sees my report card, I'll be grounded for a month.

2 다음 빈칸에 들어갈 말이 바르게 짝지어진 것을 고르시오.

_____ this morning did I receive the letter of resignation.

_____ children are about six months old, they become more mobile.

① Until - Once ② Not until - While ③ Not until - Once

④ After - While ⑤ Since - As soon as

3 다음 글을 읽고, (A)와 (B)에 알맞은 말을 고르시오.

Not all children are capable of achieving academic success. This does not matter (A) (as long as / as soon as) parents are willing to accept this, but it is quite common for parents to think (B) (that / which) all their children have to do is to study hard and they will pass their exams. Parents just succeed in causing too much stress in their offspring.

4 다음 주어진 단어를 이용하여 문장을 완성하시오.

1 그녀는 70대가 되어서야 비로소 그림 그릴 시간을 갖게 되었다. (be, in her 70's)
She didn't have time for painting _____.

2 사고 소식을 듣자마자, 그는 현장으로 달려갔다. (hear of)
_____, he hurried to the scene.

3 우리가 응접실 문을 열었을 때 안에는 아무도 없었다. (open, door)
_____ to the reception room, we found no one inside.

4 늙어감에 따라 그들은 더욱 완고해졌고 말싸움은 더욱 심해졌다. (grow older)
_____, they became more stubborn and their quarreling got worse.

1 조건 · 가정의 문장

A 다음 괄호 안에서 알맞은 말을 고르시오.

1 If I (tell / will tell) him the truth, will he keep it secret?

2 If I (had / have) enough money, I would travel by air.

3 If it (is / were) not for your help, I could not complete the work.

4 If I had saved money in my youth, I (would be / would have been) rich now.

5 I took a taxi to go home. (However / Otherwise) I would have arrived too late.

6 If Jina (had taken / have taken) his advice, she would have recovered from the illness.

B 다음 두 문장이 같은 뜻이 되도록 문장을 완성하시오.

1 As I don't know how to drive a car, I can't take you home.
   → If _____.

2 As I followed your advice, I was not deceived.
   → If _____.

3 It rained hard last night, so the road is very muddy.
   → If _____.

4 Thanks to my mother's tender care, I am strong and healthy.
   → Without _____.

5 My mother's illness prevented me from attending the meeting.
   → If my mother _____.

C 다음 문장을 직설법 문장으로 전환하시오.

1 If I had had the book, I could have lent it to you.
   → As _____.

2 If he had had open-heart surgery, he might be alive.
   → As _____.

3 If he were a man of sense, he would not do such a thing.
   → As _____.

4 If I got up early, I could eat breakfast with my family.
   → As _____.

1 다음 괄호 안에서 알맞은 말을 고르시오.

1 (Have / Had) I seen you, I would have said hello.

2 We will go on a picnic if it (does / will) not rain.

3 If it (were not / had not been) cold today, I could go swimming.

4 If I had had enough money, I would (buy / have bought) the car.

5 If it (were not / had not been) for your help, I could not have succeeded.

2 다음 빈칸에 들어갈 말이 바르게 짝지어진 것을 고르시오.

> If I _____ breakfast this morning, I _____ not be hungry now.

① have - will ② have - could ③ had had - would
④ had have - will ⑤ had had - will

3 다음 글을 읽고, (A)와 (B)에 알맞은 말을 고르시오.

> People today have a completely different attitude to debt from previous generations. Formerly, debt was often regarded as something shameful. (A) (If / While) they could not afford to buy something, they either gave up hopes of buying it, or else saved up for it. Nowadays, we tend to speak more of credit than of debt, and it is increasingly easy to obtain such credit. (B) (As / If) the number of credit cards available increases, more and more of us are paying for our purchases by credit cards.

4 다음 주어진 단어를 이용하여 문장을 완성하시오.

1 내가 너의 입장이라면 경찰을 불렀을 텐데. (be in one's position)
_____, I would call the police.

2 네가 조심해서 운전했더라면 그 사고는 일어나지 않았을 텐데. (drive carefully)
_____, the accident would not have happened.

3 그 소년이 작년에 부모님 말을 들었더라면 지금 곤란을 겪지 않을 텐데. (be in trouble)
If the boy _____ his parents last year, he _____ now.

4 나는 즉시 출발했다. 그렇지 않았다면 기차를 놓쳤을 텐데. (miss)
I started off at once. _____ the train.

2 소망 · 가정의 문장

A 다음 괄호 안에서 알맞은 말을 고르시오.

1 I wish you (can / could) join us.

2 It is time that I (will go / went) to bed.

3 I wish I (told / had told) him the truth then.

4 We will play outside (if / unless) it's really cold.

5 If it (were not / had not been) for water, we all would die.

6 He studied hard. Otherwise, he (could not pass / could not have passed) the exam.

B 다음 문장을 「I wish~」를 사용하여 가정법 문장으로 바꾸시오.

1 I'm sorry I could not go with him.
→ _____

2 I'm sorry I don't have a car.
→ _____

3 It is a pity that he cannot visit us more often.
→ _____

4 To my regret, I was not there yesterday.
→ _____

C 다음 문장을 같은 의미를 가진 가정법 문장으로 바꾸시오.

1 We must leave here now.
→ It is high time that _____.

2 He is not a baby, but he cries like one.
→ He cries _____.

3 Born in better times, he would have been known all over the world.
→ If _____, he would have been known all over the world.

4 A true Christian would have acted differently.
→ If _____, he would have acted differently.

5 I owed my success to your kind help.
→ Without _____, I could have succeeded.
→ If _____, I could have succeeded.

Further Study

1 다음 괄호 안에서 알맞은 말을 고르시오.

1 They treat him as if he (is / were) a king.

2 It is time you (went / have gone) to school today.

3 Milk quickly turns sour (if / unless) it is refrigerated.

4 I wish I (have taken / had taken) your advice yesterday.

5 (With / Without) his continued effort, he would not have succeeded.

2 다음 빈칸에 들어갈 말로 알맞지 <u>않은</u> 것을 고르시오.

> Without his support, our plan to set up a new branch office would have failed.
> = _____, our plan to set up a new branch office would have failed.

① If it were not for his support ② If it had not been for his support

③ Had it not been for his support ④ If he had not supported us

⑤ But for his support

3 다음 글을 읽고, (A), (B), (C)에 알맞은 말을 고르시오.

> It's time that we (A) (stop / stopped) complaining and arguing over things that won't matter to any of us. It's time we (B) (are realizing / realized) that life is too short to be upset with the people we love. It's time we all (C) (appreciate / should appreciate) the fact that we are still alive. Please, let's all do our best to live better lives now, because we don't know how long that opportunity may last.

4 다음 주어진 단어를 이용하여 문장을 완성하시오.

1 그는 마치 미국에 살았던 것처럼 미국에 대하여 얘기한다. (live, the U.S.A.)
He talks about America _____.

2 공해를 줄이기 위하여 정부가 의미 있는 조치를 취해야 할 때다. (time)
_____ something significant to reduce pollution.

3 너의 시기적절한 조언이 없었다면 우리는 파멸했을 것이다. (without, timely)
_____, we would have been ruined.

4 너의 생각을 바꾸려 하지 않는다면 너는 성공할 수 없을 것이다. (be willing to)
You will never be successful _____ your thinking.

1 원인 · 이유의 문장

A 다음 괄호 안에서 알맞은 말을 고르시오.

1 He was absent from school, (so / for) he was very ill.

2 (Because / Due to) the house is expensive, he can't afford to buy it.

3 She is very fat, and this is (because / why) she likes to eat fast food.

4 (Because / Because of) the heavy traffic, they were late for the meeting.

5 Jim can't speak Japanese. That is (because / why) he doesn't read the book.

6 The hurricane (resulted from / resulted in) severe river flooding in the area.

7 His death (resulted from / resulted in) a head injury he received at the accident.

B 다음 문장에서 잘못된 부분을 찾아 바르게 고치시오.

1 Due to night approached, the street became hushed.

2 He could not come, so he was seriously wounded in the leg.

3 Because his father's sudden illness, he could not attend the meeting.

4 There is no horse in the amusement park. This is because the children are disappointed.

5 The Great East Japan Earthquake resulted from more than 10,000 of deaths and incalculable property loss.

C 다음 두 문장이 같은 뜻이 되도록 괄호 안의 주어진 말을 이용하여 문장을 완성하시오.

1 The gasoline was out, so the car stopped. (for)
→ The car stopped, _____.

2 She could not see far because her sight was weak. (due to)
→ She could not see far _____.

3 His behavior is leading me to a lot of problems. (cause)
→ His behavior _____.

4 The final match was canceled because it rained heavily. (because of)
→ The final match was canceled _____.

5 The end of the 2nd World War resulted in the independence of many countries. (result from)
→ The independence of many countries _____.

6 Because some people believe meat is not good for their health, they stop eating it. (because)
→ Some people stop eating meat and this is _____.

1 다음 괄호 안에서 알맞은 말을 고르시오.

1 Sadly, poverty led him (to / for) crime.

2 He had to retire (because / because of) his ill health.

3 I'm sure it will snow, (so / for) the barometer is falling.

4 His pain resulted (in / from) a blow while playing football.

5 He lost his wife recently. That's (because / why) he is so depressed.

2 다음 중 어법상 어색한 것을 고르시오.

① Since I didn't understand what they said, I stayed calm during the meeting.

② Alice was an honest leader, and that is because she was elected three times.

③ All the flights for Busan were canceled, and that is because it snowed heavily.

④ The Gulf War resulted in the serious destruction of the oil fields in Kuwait.

⑤ Due to the storm, the political rally scheduled for tomorrow has been canceled.

3 다음 글을 읽고, (A)와 (B)에 알맞은 말을 고르시오.

It began in 1860 (A) (when / which) Abraham Lincoln was elected president. Lincoln wanted to end slavery. But the Southern states did not. One by one, they seceded from the United States. They announced that they were starting their own country. It was called the Confederate States of America. President Lincoln was bitterly opposed to the South's actions. He was determined to keep the United States together. However, the Confederates attacked a United States fort. That's (B) (because / why) Lincoln declared the war.

4 다음 주어진 단어를 이용하여 문장을 완성하시오.

1 나는 옷차림이 초라하다고 해서 그를 깔보지는 않는다. (despise)
_____ because he is poorly dressed.

2 지방과 당분 함유가 많기 때문에 사람들은 초콜릿을 먹을 때 죄의식을 느낀다. (has, fat, sugar)
People feel guilty when they eat chocolate _____.

3 올해 추운 날씨로, 천연 가스비가 증가했다. (due to, weather)
_____, the price of natural gas has increased.

4 어젯밤 발생한 심각한 교통사고의 결과 세 명의 사망자가 발생하였다. (result, the death of, passenger)
A serious car accident last night _____.

2 결과 · 목적의 문장

A 다음 괄호 안에서 알맞은 말을 고르시오.

1 She kept silent (so as not to / result in) bother me.

2 He noted everything I said (lest / do that) he should forget.

3 He was (so / such) frightened that he couldn't move at all.

4 He was (so / such) a selfish man that we all didn't like him.

5 Everybody works hard (in order to / so as not to) fail again.

6 I was in (such / so) a great mood that I slept well last night.

7 Jason moved to the city (in order to / in order that) get a better job.

B 다음 두 문장이 같은 뜻이 되도록 괄호 안에서 알맞은 말을 고르시오.

1 He ran very fast lest he should be overtaken.
→ He ran very fast (in order / so as not) to be overtaken.

2 I'm so young that I cannot do such work.
→ I'm so young as to be (able / unable) to do such work.

3 I moved to Seoul so that I might get a job.
→ I moved to Seoul (in order / so as) that I might get a job.

4 Do you have a telephone number where I can reach you, Jenny?
→ Do you have a telephone number (for / so that) I can reach you, Jenny?

5 She is wise enough to understand the article of the newspaper.
→ She is (so wise / too wise) that she understands the article of the newspaper.

C 다음 두 문장이 같은 뜻이 되도록 빈칸에 알맞은 말을 쓰시오.

1 It was very hot. We could not sleep.
→ It was _____ _____ that we could not sleep.

2 So great was her sorrow that she became ill.
→ She was in _____ _____ sorrow that she became ill.

3 He was a very nice fellow. Everybody liked him.
→ He was _____ a nice fellow _____ everybody liked him.

4 The blizzard continued, and consequently they were forced to remain in their tents.
→ The blizzard continued, _____ _____ they were forced to remain in their tents.

Further Study

1

다음 〈보기〉에서 알맞은 것을 골라 문장을 완성하시오. (단, 한 번씩만 사용하시오.)

Word Bank	such	so	in order	lest	so that

1 I kept quiet _____ I should wake my sister.

2 I hurried, _____ I almost forgot my umbrella.

3 She is _____ a good girl that everybody loves her.

4 Catherine saved money _____ she might buy a beautiful dress.

5 My mother drove me to the school _____ for me to not be late.

2

다음 빈칸에 들어갈 말이 바르게 짝지어진 것을 고르시오.

> She set the alarm clock _____ get up in the morning.
> He was trying to speak very slowly _____ he could be understood.

① so that - in order to　　② in order that - so that　　③ so as to - so that

④ in order that - therefore　　⑤ lest - in order to

3

다음 글을 읽고, (A)와 (B)에 알맞은 말을 고르시오.

> The earth is hot inside. It is (A) (so / such) hot that some rocks melt. They become a thick liquid called magma. Magma is lighter than the solid rock around it, (B) (so / for) it rises. As it nears the surface, bubbles form. The gas bubbles create a lot of pressure. Scientists think volcanoes are the earth's way of releasing underground heat.

4

다음 주어진 단어를 이용하여 문장을 완성하시오.

1 아이들이 길을 건널 수 있도록 그 기사는 차를 멈췄다. (order, cross the road)
   The driver stopped the car _____ that the children _____.

2 꽤 작은 부엌이라서 청소하는 데 별로 힘들지 않다. (tiny)
   It is _____ I don't have to do much to keep it clean.

3 Mary는 지난주에 결석하였다. 그 결과 중요한 테스트를 치르지 않았다. (miss, as a result)
   Mary wasn't at school last week. _____.

4 전쟁터의 전사자들을 잊지 않기 위해서 우리는 기념식을 갖는다. (lest)
   We have a memorial service _____ those who died in battle.

1 대조의 문장–양보절

A 다음 괄호 안에서 알맞은 말을 고르시오.

1 (In spite / In spite of) the difficulty, he decided to continue his walk.

2 (Despite / Despite of) their effort, they failed to find the missing boy.

3 (Even though / Despite) he was handicapped, he never gave up his dream.

4 (However / Whichever) rich he may be, he can't buy love and happiness.

5 (Frighten / Frightened) as they were, they decided to walk into the darkness.

6 (However / Whatever) fast you may run, you will never reach the school in time.

B 다음 문장에서 잘못된 부분을 찾아 바르게 고치시오.

1 However an old man may be, he may learn.

2 Parents love their children, however roughly children are.

3 Though it is raining, yet he is still working in the field.

4 Strange so it may seem to you, his remark encouraged me.

5 As they work hard, they are not paid enough or even not paid at all.

6 They decided to get married in spite the huge differences in their ages.

7 Despite of the fact that the doctor had told her to rest, she went to Spain.

C 다음 두 문장이 같은 의미가 되도록 빈칸에 알맞은 말을 쓰시오.

1 He is rich, but I don't envy him.
= _____ _____ he is rich, I don't envy him.

2 Despite their poverty, they are generous.
= _____ _____ of their poverty, they are generous.

3 Though she is tired, she tried to help him.
= _____ _____, she tried to help him.

4 No matter how hard you would try, you could not solve the problem.
= _____ hard you would try, you could not solve the problem.

5 Although she is poor, she is envied by everyone.
= _____ _____ of her poverty, she is envied by everyone.

6 However cold it is outside, he goes for a walk every day.
= _____ _____ _____ cold it is outside, he goes for a walk every day.

Further Study

1 다음 주어진 문장이 같은 뜻이 되도록 빈칸에 알맞은 말을 쓰시오.

1 No matter how painful it is, you should not take any painkillers.
= _____ _____ it is, you should not take any painkillers.

2 Though she is young, she occupies an important position in the company.
= _____ _____ she is young, she occupies an important position in the company.

3 Even though she is sick, she never loses her smile.
= Sick _____ _____ _____, she never loses her smile.

4 Despite his lack of experience, he was hired as a manager.
= _____ _____ _____ his lack of experience, he was hired as a manager.

2 다음 중 어법상 <u>어색한</u> 문장을 고르시오.

① Despite working hard, they didn't submit the term paper in time.
② Even if it rains tomorrow, the concert will be held as scheduled.
③ Though he lived in Japan for five years, he can't speak Japanese.
④ However difficult the task may be, I will finish it within two months.
⑤ Poorly as she was, she tried to find a way to help him out of his troubles.

3 다음 글을 읽고, (A)와 (B)에 알맞은 말을 고르시오.

(A) (Despite / Although) our belief that human beings are created equal, there are innumerable people who still suffer destitution, disease and even hunger in the world. This is true, (B) (so that / even though) there are people who are enjoying a highly civilized mode of life, with material abundance owing to their efforts for modernization.

4 다음 주어진 단어를 이용하여 문장을 완성하시오.

1 힘든 일이라 하더라도 연습하면 쉬워진다. (difficult, a thing)
_____, it becomes easy by practice.

2 비록 그 결정이 마음에 안 든다 할지라도 너는 그것을 웃으며 받아들여야 한다. (even if, like)
_____, you should accept it with a smile.

3 그들의 제안이 명백히 불공정했지만, 우리는 그것을 받아들이지 않을 수 없었다. (offer, obviously)
_____, we were forced to accept it.

4 학교를 존속시키려는 우리의 노력에도 시 당국은 학교 폐쇄를 결정했다. (effort)
_____ to save the school, the county decided to close it.

2

대조의 문장–연결사

A 다음 괄호 안에서 알맞은 말을 고르시오.

1 She is tall, (whereas / still) her sister is very short.

2 We have no milk. Would you like juice (instead / instead of)?

3 You think him idle, but (on the contrary / while), he is very busy.

4 (Like / Instead of) most artists, he has got through many difficulties.

5 I've watched the movie three times. (Nevertheless / Instead), I want to watch it again.

6 He is good at math, but (on the other hand / therefore) he is bad at science.

B 다음 빈칸에 알맞은 말을 〈보기〉에서 골라 쓰시오. (단, 한 번씩만 사용하시오.)

| Word Bank | like | instead of | yet | nevertheless | instead |

1 We should do something striking _____ just talking about it.

2 She runs a shoe store, _____ she always wears old worn out shoes.

3 Suddenly there was a terrible noise. It was _____ a bomb exploding.

4 Benjamin did not join the army; _____ he decided to become an actor.

5 He had not slept that night; _____ he led the rally with his usual vigor.

C 다음 밑줄 친 부분과 바꿔 쓸 수 있는 것을 고르시오.

1 Don't talk to me like you talk to a child.
   ① when   ② as   ③ if   ④ while   ⑤ so

2 I went to the conference instead of my father.
   ① along with   ② without   ③ in place of   ④ because of   ⑤ in spite of

3 That region has plenty of natural resources, while this one has none.
   ① as   ② if   ③ though   ④ because   ⑤ whereas

4 She has a big house and a nice car, yet she always says she has no money.
   ① if   ② but   ③ while   ④ as   ⑤ instead

5 Unlike previous years, we have had much snow this year.
   ① As   ② Considering   ③ Different from   ④ Due to   ⑤ Instead of

6 Sarah was short and plump. On the contrary her mother was tall and willowy.
   ① Like   ② Instead   ③ In fact   ④ Nevertheless   ⑤ On the other hand

Further Study

1 다음 괄호 안에서 알맞은 말을 고르시오.

  1 You may be right, (so / yet) you cannot influence me.

  2 It's (like / unlike) him to be late; he's usually on time.

  3 It is raining heavily. (Still / On the other hand), we have to go out.

  4 (In spite of / Instead of) my repeated advice, he did not stop drinking.

  5 He had made a constant effort. (While / However), he could not complete his work.

2 다음 빈칸에 알맞지 <u>않은</u> 것을 고르시오.

Everyone attended the meeting. _____, we could not make a decision.

① Instead   ② Even so   ③ Therefore

④ Nonetheless   ⑤ Still

3 다음 글을 읽고, (A)와 (B)에 알맞은 말을 고르시오.

> Education is a very important part of a child's life, (A) (so / yet) an increasing number of children are showing reluctance to attend school. It is not because they find the work too difficult or are afraid of the teachers. No. It is because they are being bullied. School bullies can make other children's lives a misery. They threaten their victims with a beating if they don't do (B) (as / so) they say, and steal possessions from them by force.

4 다음 주어진 단어를 이용하여 문장을 완성하시오.

  1 그녀의 어머니와는 달리, Sharon은 좋은 목소리를 가지고 있다.
     _____, Sharon has a very good voice.

  2 그녀는 공항을 향해 매우 빨리 차를 몰았지만, 비행기를 놓치고 말았다. (yet)
     She drove very fast to the airport, _____ her plane.

  3 교통 혼잡이 지금 완화되고 있지만, 그것은 여전히 신경 쓰이는 문제이다. (a matter of concern)
     The traffic congestion is reducing now, _____.

  4 인생은 불행의 연속이다. 그럼에도 우리는 삶의 긍정적인 면을 봐야 한다. (bright)
     Life is a chain of misery. Nevertheless, we should _____ of it.

1 원급의 비교

A 다음 괄호 안에서 알맞은 말을 고르시오.

1 He is taller than (I / mine) by three inches.

2 This river is three times longer (as / than) that one.

3 The building is about twice as large (as / than) my house.

4 The speed of a bus is not so fast (as / than) that of a train.

5 Mars never appears to be as (large / larger) as the full Moon.

6 The size of the island is similar to (that / this) of my town.

B 다음 문장에서 잘못된 부분을 찾아 바르게 고치시오.

1 Rumors spread as fast than lightning.

2 This year's profits are the same like last year's.

3 Ralph earns three times much money than his brother.

4 China's population is ten times bigger than Japan.

5 The story of the movie is very different from the original book.

6 My house covers an area two times as larger than my cousin's.

7 An eagle's eye is about four times as sharper as that of a human.

C 다음 두 문장이 같은 뜻이 되도록 원급 비교를 이용하여 빈칸에 알맞은 말을 쓰시오.

1 My father is 70 years old, and my son is ten years old.
   → My father is _____ as my son.

2 This cheese cake is delicious, and the chocolate cake is equally delicious.
   → This cheese cake is _____ the chocolate cake.

3 This building is 200 feet tall, and that building is 50 feet tall.
   → This building is _____ as that building.

4 The speed of the subway is fast, but that of the bus is not fast.
   → The speed of the bus is _____ that of the subway.

5 The delivery service of K-mart is quick, but that of C-mart is not quick.
   → The delivery service of C-mart is _____ that of K-mart.

6 The vegetables at the Kim Market are fresh, and those at the Lee Market are equally fresh.
   → The Kim Market's vegetables are _____ the Lee Market's.

Further Study

1 다음 괄호 안에서 알맞은 것을 고르시오.

1 Silva's rent is as (cheap / cheaper) as Rachel's.

2 The human heart is roughly the same size (as / like) a fist.

3 Rich's neighbors are not so friendly (as / than) Jane's.

4 The venom of spiders is as dangerous as (that of snakes / snakes).

5 The interviewer thought she was more qualified than (I / mine) for the position.

2 다음 빈칸에 공통으로 들어갈 말을 고르시오.

You can make mistakes, but try to make _____ possible.
This room can be furnished to seat _____ five people and as many as ten.

① as many as   ② as little as   ③ as much as
④ as few as   ⑤ as hard as

3 다음 글을 읽고, (A)와 (B)에 알맞은 말을 고르시오.

Rainforests take up only six percent of the Earth's surface, yet more (A) (than / as) half of the world's plant and animal species live there. The climate of rainforests is very hot and humid with normal annual rainfall between 1750–2000mm, so the animals and plants living there have to adapt to this. Scientists estimate that as (B) (many / much) as 30 million species of plants and animals live in tropical rainforests.

4 다음 주어진 단어와 원급 비교를 이용하여 문장을 완성하시오.

1 의사는 내게 가능한 한 적게 먹으라고 권했다. (advise, little)
The doctor _____.

2 내 아파트는 삼촌 아파트보다 방의 수가 2배이다. (many)
My apartment has _____.

3 Elizabeth는 작년에 남동생보다 두 배 많은 수입을 올렸다. (earn, much)
Last year, Elizabeth _____ her brother.

4 도쿄의 대중교통요금은 내가 생각했던 것만큼 비싸지는 않았다. (not, expensive)
The public transportation fare in Tokyo was _____ I thought.

2 비교의 문장

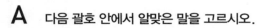

A 다음 괄호 안에서 알맞은 말을 고르시오.

1 I like the (later / latter) part of the movie.

2 It is much (hot / hotter) than last year.

3 Tommy arrived here (later / latter) than planned.

4 It was (by far / very) the worst novel I had ever read.

5 This is (most / the most) wonderful lake in the world.

6 We have a (much / very) more serious problems than this one.

7 The higher your credit scores, (the less / the little) you'll pay for the loan.

B 다음 문장에서 <u>잘못된</u> 부분을 찾아 바르게 고치시오.

1 The more you talk, the least I hear.

2 This puzzle is less complicated as I thought.

3 She talks as if she were the happyest girl in town.

4 Thomas is many younger than any other boy in the class.

5 If you want any farther information, please contact us via e-mail.

6 Kevin is my oldest brother, who is fifteen years elder than I.

C 다음 문장을 최상급을 이용하여 바꿔 쓰시오.

1 I have never eaten such a delicious apple as this.
→ This is _____.

2 I have never seen more beautiful scenery than this.
→ This is _____.

3 No other animal in the world is as big as the blue whale.
→ The blue whale is _____.

4 No other river is longer than the Missouri River in the U.S.A.
→ The Missouri River is _____.

5 I like Rome better than any other European city.
→ Of all the European cities I like _____.

Further Study

•점수 _____

1 다음 괄호 안에서 알맞은 말을 고르시오.

1 Mt. Halla is less (high / higher) than Mt. Baekdu.

2 Seoul is one of the largest (city / cities) in the world.

3 Alexander is the (brightest / most bright) boy in his class.

4 He spent the (later / latter) half of his vacation in Hawaii.

5 We want to get (farther / further) details of the charity event.

6 The job took us (many / much) longer than we had expected.

2 다음 빈칸에 들어갈 말이 바르게 짝지어진 것을 고르시오.

The job took us _____ longer than we had expected.
The more you give, _____ you will get.

① even, the most   ② very, the less   ③ many, the least
④ much, the more   ⑤ so, the less

3 다음 글을 읽고, (A)와 (B)에 알맞은 말을 고르시오.

When the news reached Mrs. Bennet's ears, she got (A) (even / very) more excited than Jane. Even Mr. Bennet couldn't help being happy about the (B) (later / latest) turn of events. A few weeks before, the Bennets were nearly ruined; now, they were thought to be the luckiest family in the world.

4 다음 주어진 단어를 이용하여 문장을 완성하시오.

1 세계에서 두 번째로 큰 대륙이 어디라고 생각하니? (continent, big)
What do you think _____ in the world?

2 날씨가 더워지면 더워질수록 바닷가는 더욱 심하게 붐빈다. (crowded)
_____ the weather is, _____ the beaches get.

3 중고차 값은 새 차보다 훨씬 싸기 때문에, 나는 중고차를 선호한다. (cheap)
Because used cars are _____, I prefer them.

4 나는 우리 동생보다 적게 먹는데 왜 동생보다 살이 찔까? (eat)
Why am I heavier than my sister even though _____?

1 동사의 단순시제

A 다음 괄호 안에서 알맞은 말을 고르시오.

1 I wonder when she (will drop / drops) by my office.

2 We will wait here until you (come / will come) back.

3 When (did you finish / have you finished) the assignment?

4 If it (rains / will rain) tomorrow, the game will be canceled.

5 Steven (has gone / has been) to the funeral, so he is not here.

6 I'm not sure whether she (comes / will come) to my wedding tomorrow.

7 He (has been / was) in the hospital for two months. He is not in the hospital now.

B 다음 괄호 안에 주어진 말을 이용하여 빈칸에 알맞은 말을 쓰시오.

1 Mac _____ _____ a loved one. He is very alone. (lose)

2 We have all been taught that the sun _____ in the east. (rise)

3 They _____ television while I was cooking in the kitchen. (watch)

4 I'm not saying that everyone in the group _____ all the time. (agree)

5 Richard _____ from kidney cancer all his life. He is now dead. (suffer)

6 Richard _____ _____ from kidney cancer all his life. He is still alive. (suffer)

7 A burglar _____ into the nuns' residence at Holy Family University yesterday. (break)

8 We _____ _____ until we succeed in mixing the right color. (experiment)

9 If it is cold tomorrow, it _____ _____ necessary to distribute warm clothing to the soldiers. (be)

C 다음 문장에서 <u>잘못된</u> 부분을 찾아 바르게 고치시오.

1 Let us start as soon as he will come back.

2 I wonder whether she visits again tomorrow night.

3 If you will start now, you will catch up with them soon.

4 I have been interested in becoming a vet when I was a child.

5 He said that Jupiter was the largest planet in the solar system.

6 If it will rain tomorrow, our school trip will be put off until next Tuesday.

7 Teddy is working as a counselor at the school since he was thirty.

Further Study

1 다음 〈보기〉에서 알맞은 것을 골라 문장을 완성하시오. (필요하면 동사의 형태를 바꾸시오.)

| Word Bank | stay | take | teach | finish | attend |

1 Please wait in the school library until I _____ mowing the lawn.

2 Jonathan _____ science at a middle school since 2008.

3 The new students _____ the orientation which was held yesterday.

4 We _____ him to the general hospital near the express bus terminal last Friday.

5 On Sunday evenings, people usually _____ home and prepare for the week ahead.

2 다음 중 어법상 <u>어색한</u> 문장을 고르시오.

① I often went fishing with my dad when I was young.

② We don't know if he will change his mind tomorrow.

③ Morris told us that the Sun is very important to life on Earth.

④ I have lost my wallet, so I don't have money to pay for lunch now.

⑤ Ronald was in jail for two years, so he can't go to your wedding.

3 다음 글을 읽고, (A)와 (B)에 알맞은 말을 고르시오.

"Necessity is the mother of invention." You may have heard that old saying (A) (ago / before). In many cases, it's probably true. Recognizing a need, a resourceful inventor (B) (is jumping / jumps) in to create something to fill the gap. While some inventions are created after years of experimentation, many others can come about by accident. Some inventions improve the way we live, while others, such as weapons of war, can do us harm.

4 다음 주어진 단어를 이용하여 문장을 완성하시오.

1 Tommy는 매일 두 번 이를 닦는다. (brush)

Tommy _____ twice a day.

2 네가 떠나기 전에 너희 부모님께 전화를 드리는 게 낫겠다. (leave)

_____, you'd better call your parents.

3 소년은 너무 피곤해서 침대에 누웠다. (lie down)

The boy was so tired that _____.

4 요전 날 나는 미국인 선장을 칵테일파티에서 만났다. (meet)

The other day _____ at a cocktail party.

2 동사의 완료시제

A 다음 괄호 안에서 알맞은 말을 고르시오.

1 She has taught at the university (for / since) ten years.

2 Carl seems to (be / have been) a famous singer in his twenties.

3 I (have been / have gone) to Japan only once in my life.

4 I'm sorry, but she (has already left / has already been) for London.

5 Many strange things (had happened / have happened) to me since March.

6 I lost the cellular phone that John (had bought / has bought) for me last year.

B 다음을 두 문장이 같은 뜻이 되도록 빈칸에 알맞은 말을 쓰시오.

1 Robert went to Canada. He is not here now.
→ Robert ＿＿＿＿＿＿＿ ＿＿＿＿＿＿＿ to Canada.

2 I forgot her name, and I can't remember it now.
→ I ＿＿＿＿＿＿＿ ＿＿＿＿＿＿＿ her name.

3 It is nearly five years since they married.
→ They ＿＿＿＿＿＿＿ ＿＿＿＿＿＿＿ ＿＿＿＿＿＿＿ for nearly five years.

4 Mary went to Hawaii, but now she has come back.
→ Mary ＿＿＿＿＿＿＿ ＿＿＿＿＿＿＿ to Hawaii.

C 다음 문장을 〈보기〉처럼 바꿔 쓰시오.

Example	Scarlet seems to have been rich.
	→ It seems that Scarlet was rich.

1 There is no doubt of his having been a spy.
→ There is ＿＿＿＿＿＿＿＿＿＿＿＿＿＿＿＿＿＿＿＿.

2 He seems to have been ignorant of the fact.
→ It seems ＿＿＿＿＿＿＿＿＿＿＿＿＿＿＿＿＿＿＿.

3 He is ashamed of having done such a thing.
→ He is ashamed ＿＿＿＿＿＿＿＿＿＿＿＿＿＿＿＿＿＿.

4 Having forgotten my instructions, I couldn't solve the problem.
→ As I ＿＿＿＿＿＿＿＿＿＿＿＿＿＿＿＿＿＿＿＿＿, I couldn't solve the problem.

Further Study

1 다음 괄호 안에서 알맞은 말을 고르시오.

1 I (had known / have known) her for almost four years.

2 When I called on him, he (has already gone / had already gone) out.

3 Richard has owned his own business (for / since) he moved to Ohio.

4 Mary (has been / has gone) to Paris, and she is not here now.

2 다음 〈보기〉에 주어진 단어를 이용하여 문장을 완성하시오. (필요하면 동사의 형태를 바꾸시오.)

Word Bank   do   visit   belong   be

1 Sam _____ his military service for one year.

2 She seems to _____ an actress about twenty years ago.

3 Henry _____ to the volunteer fire department since 1996.

4 We are enjoying our trip. We _____ four countries so far.

3 다음 글을 읽고, (A)와 (B)에 알맞은 말을 고르시오.

Harry S. Truman (A) (has been / had been) vice president for less than 90 days when President Franklin D. Roosevelt died suddenly in April 1945. As the new president, Truman faced many challenges. World War II was almost over when he became president of the United States. Germany surrendered in May 1945, but war with Japan continued. Truman made the difficult decision to drop atomic bombs on two cities in Japan. This brought the war that (B) (has / had) begun in 1939 to an end. Truman believed this saved millions of American lives.

4 다음 주어진 단어를 이용하여 문장을 완성하시오.

1 Sarah는 심장발작을 겪은 이후로 매일 2마일씩 걷고 있다. (two miles)
Sarah _____ since she had a heart attack.

2 서울에 산 지 2년도 되지 않아서 그는 부산으로 전근되었다. (transfer to)
He had not lived in Seoul two years when _____.

3 세계 곳곳의 사람들이 영화를 관람하는 방식은 최근 몇 년에 변화가 있었다. (change, recent years)
The way in which people all over the world watch movies _____.

4 Anna는 관록 있는 세일즈우먼일 것이다. 왜냐하면, 5년 동안 생명보험을 판매했으니까. (life insurance)
Anna may be a veteran saleswoman, for _____ for five years.

1 조동사의 다양한 의미

A 다음 괄호 안에서 알맞은 말을 고르시오.

1 He used to (cook / cooking) for his wife.

2 You (must / may) not drive while intoxicated.

3 You (had better not / had not better) go out for a walk.

4 I'm really hungry. (May / Must) I have this chocolate cake?

5 Your flight will be delayed, so you (don't have to / have to) hurry up.

6 We (ought not to / ought to not) lose this chance to find a solution to our problem.

B 다음 두 문장이 같은 뜻이 되도록 〈보기〉에서 알맞은 말을 골라 빈칸에 쓰시오.

| Word Bank | must | must not | may | doesn't have to | may not |

1 It is not necessary for a learner to own a car.
→ A learner _____ own a car.

2 It is against the law for you to leave the scene of an accident.
→ You _____ leave the scene of an accident.

3 Perhaps scientists will find a cure for AIDS.
→ Scientists _____ find a cure for AIDS.

4 It is the law that you register your car.
→ You _____ register your car.

5 It is possible that Jane will not come to the party tonight.
→ Jane _____ come to the party tonight.

C 다음 우리말과 같은 뜻이 되도록 괄호 안에 주어진 단어를 이용하여 문장을 완성하시오.

1 내일 몇 시에 만나기로 할까요? (shall, make it)
→ What time _____ _____ _____ _____?

2 어머니는 세탁기가 아니라 손으로 빨래하곤 하셨다. (wash clothes)
→ My mother _____ _____ _____ _____ by hand instead of by washing machine.

3 훗날 우주여행을 하고 싶으세요? (would)
→ _____ _____ _____ _____ take a space trip in the future?

4 그가 의사일 리 없다. 그를 믿지 않는 것이 낫겠다. (would)
→ He _____ _____ a doctor. You _____ _____ _____ trust him.

Further Study

1 다음 〈보기〉에서 알맞은 것을 골라 문장을 완성하시오.

Word Bank   used to   had better   must   can't be

1   Liz is the best player. She _____ be the first-prize winner.
2   Gerald has a slim build now. He _____ be a big, fat guy.
3   If possible, you _____ not take pictures in the shade.
4   Susie didn't know anything about farming. She _____ a farmer.

2 다음 빈칸에 들어갈 말이 바르게 짝지어진 것을 고르시오.

Drivers with small children _____ put them in the back seat.
He is a ruthless dictator. Nobody _____ to disobey him.

① may - used to   ② must - used to   ③ would - may
④ had better - can   ⑤ ought to - dares

3 다음 글을 읽고, (A)와 (B)에 알맞은 말을 고르시오.

It takes a lot of time and effort to produce a first-rate animated movie. A studio (A) (can / must) find a brilliant story and script. Then, to bring that story to life, it (B) (has to / used to) gather a huge team of directors, illustrators, animators, and voice actors. These professionals spend years working away at the drawing board, on the computer, or behind the camera.

4 다음 주어진 단어와 조동사를 이용하여 문장을 완성하시오.

1   너는 운전 중에 술을 마시면 안 된다. (alcoholic beverages)
    You _____ while driving.

2   잠깐 일을 멈추고 쉬는 게 좋겠습니다. (take a break)
    You _____ from work for a while.

3   차 양 쪽 모두에 커다란 에어백이 당신에게 필요치 않다. (need)
    _____ air bags on both sides of your car.

4   나는 자주 영화 보러 가곤 했지만, 지금은 시간이 없다. (go to the cinema)
    I often _____, but I never have the time now.

2

까다로운 조동사

A 다음 괄호 안에서 알맞은 말을 고르시오.

1 When he was young, he (can / could) jump very high.

2 I thought you and your family (will / would) immigrate to America.

3 The restaurant is always crowded. The food (cannot be / must be) great.

4 You (need have watched / should have watched) the movie. It was very fun.

5 They (must have been / cannot have been) shocked by the bomb explosion sound.

B 다음 두 문장이 같은 뜻이 되도록 〈보기〉에서 알맞은 말을 골라 쓰시오.

| Word Bank | must have | cannot have | need not have |
| | should have | shouldn't have | may have |

1 I wonder whether he has taken the wrong bus.
→ He _____ taken the wrong bus.

2 You wrote to him again, but it was not necessary.
→ You _____ written to him again.

3 It is certain that he has forgotten the promise.
→ He _____ forgotten the promise.

4 It is not right that you laughed at his mistakes.
→ You _____ laughed at his mistakes.

5 It is silly of you to have neglected the messenger's warning.
→ You _____ paid attention to the messenger's warning.

6 It is impossible that the little boy wrote the letter by himself.
→ The boy _____ written the letter by himself.

C 다음 괄호 안에 주어진 단어를 이용하여 문장을 완성하시오.

1 You _____ _____ _____ me about it. Why didn't you? (tell)

2 It's a sunny day. I _____ _____ _____ _____ this umbrella. (bring)

3 It is impossible that he wrote the essay. He _____ _____ _____ it. (write)

4 He didn't buy anything for his wife. He _____ _____ _____ her birthday. (forget)

5 She is angry. You _____ _____ _____ _____ her computer without her permission. (use)

Further Study

1 다음 문장에서 <u>잘못된</u> 부분을 찾아 바르게 고치시오.

1 All the laundry was all wet on the rack. It cannot have rained.

2 Until three years ago, I can run one hundred meters in thirteen seconds.

3 I'm not sure where my wallet is. I need have left it at home or at work.

4 You cannot have joined the farewell party last night. It was your last chance to see her.

2 다음 빈칸에 들어갈 말이 바르게 짝지어진 것을 고르시오.

> You look worse today. You _____ the medicine last night, but you didn't.
> Ralph is very sleepy. He _____ computer games until midnight.

① must have taken - may have played
② can have taken - must have played
③ should have taken - can't have played
④ should have taken - must have played
⑤ should not have taken - should have played

3 다음 글을 읽고, (A)와 (B)에 알맞은 말을 고르시오.

> For years, my friends have told me that I (A) (cannot have been / should have been) a comedian, but that's impossible because I suffer stage fright. I can't stand speaking in public! So, I'll just (B) (don't have to / have to) end up writing humor in my blog.

4 다음 주어진 단어와 조동사를 이용하여 문장을 완성하시오.

1 당신의 집은 여기서 멀리 있지 않으므로 그렇게 서둘러 떠날 필요가 없었다. (leave, in such a hurry)
As your home is not far from here, _____.

2 그녀가 외국에 있을 때 그가 적어도 한 달에 한 번은 그녀에게 편지를 썼을지도 모른다. (write)
_____ at least once a month when she was abroad.

3 너는 잡지에 나오는 주식 추천내용을 따랐어야만 했다. (follow)
_____ the stock recommendations in the magazine.

4 나는 그곳에 나의 집을 짓지 말았어야 했다. 왜냐하면, 직장에서 너무 멀기 때문이었다. (build)
I _____ there, for it was far away from my work.

1 사역동사

A 다음 괄호 안에서 알맞은 말을 고르시오.

1 My mom helped me (finish / finished) my essay.

2 Scott got the waiter (bring / to bring) some water.

3 I let her (use / to use) my car during the holiday.

4 She had her computer (repair / repaired) yesterday.

5 I was made (tell / to tell) the secret to my teacher.

6 Mary had her son (play / to play) soccer after school.

B 다음 괄호 안에 주어진 말을 이용하여 빈칸에 알맞은 말을 쓰시오.

1 My parents don't let us _____ food out. (leave)

2 The man is helping his son _____ his backpack. (pack)

3 He made the children _____ their own rooms. (clean up)

4 I had my pocket _____ while getting off the subway. (pick)

5 Charles got his students _____ their instruments. (practice)

6 I got my car _____, and there was no problem. (check up)

C 다음 괄호 안의 말을 알맞게 배열하여 문장을 완성하시오.

1 I (my / had / painted / room) blue last June.
   → I _____ blue last June.

2 Sam (the waiter / to / got / clean up) the table.
   → Sam _____ the table.

3 Don't (control / anyone / let) your life.
   → Don't _____ your life.

4 I (made / was / shed / to) a tear by the movie.
   → I _____ a tear by the movie.

5 Sean (the repairman / had / fix) the roof leaks.
   → Sean _____ the roof leaks.

6 He (made / to / move into / was) another apartment.
   → He _____ another apartment.

Further Study

1 다음 괄호 안에서 알맞은 말을 고르시오.

1 He got his eyes (test / tested).

2 I got the man (paint / to paint) the house.

3 Jack had his nose (break / broken) in a fight.

4 You had better have that tooth (pull / pulled) out.

5 I was made (kneel / to kneel) down in front of the altar.

6 Have the next patient (come / to come) in please, nurse.

2 다음 빈칸에 들어갈 말이 바르게 짝지어진 것을 고르시오.

I had my secretary _____ the documents this morning.
The room was so messy. I need to get the room _____.

① bring - cleaned　　② bring - to clean　　③ brought - clean
④ brought - to clean　　⑤ brought - cleaned

3 다음 글을 읽고, (A)와 (B)에 알맞은 말을 고르시오.

　　Eating chocolate often makes us (A) (feel / to feel) good. Moreover, some doctors have now discovered some benefits in chocolate. Recent research suggests that chocolate, like aspirin, can delay blood clotting, making it potentially useful in preventing thrombosis. That helps (B) (prevent / preventing) heart attacks and strokes.

4 다음 주어진 단어를 이용하여 문장을 완성하시오.

1 그 집 중 몇몇은 폭발로 말미암아 그 집들의 유리창이 깨졌다. (break)
Some of the houses _____ by the explosion.

2 그녀는 항상 수술 전에 자신의 환자들의 긴장을 풀어주려고 노력한다. (make, relax)
She always tries to _____ before an operation.

3 제가 이 MP3 플레이어의 몇몇 특별기능에 대하여 설명해 드리겠습니다. (let, point out)
_____ some of the special features of this MP3 player.

4 저희는 지급액을 나눠서 낼 수 있도록 좋은 할부 제도를 제공합니다. (spread out, the payment)
We offer a very good installment plan to help you _____.

2 지각동사

A 다음 괄호 안에서 알맞은 말을 고르시오.

1 He felt something (crawling / crawled) on his back.

2 I saw a young boy (painting / to paint) on the wall.

3 I noticed the thief (running / to run) away from the store.

4 A telephone pole was seen (knock / knocked) down by a truck.

5 They were seen (wait / waiting) for the bus to the stadium.

6 The artist wants to see his works (displaying / displayed) in the exhibit.

7 I perceived the storm (approaching / approached) apace from the South.

B 다음 괄호 안에 주어진 말을 이용하여 빈칸에 알맞은 말을 쓰시오.

1 I heard a mosquito _____ around my ear last night. (fly)

2 Clare saw a thief _____ out of the house and called the police. (run)

3 People make a wish when they watch a shooting star _____. (fall down)

4 I haven't seen any fish _____ in this river since the last bank construction. (catch)

5 They felt amazed when they saw the Statue of Liberty _____ on a small island. (stand)

C 다음 두 문장이 같은 뜻이 되도록 빈칸에 알맞은 말을 쓰시오.

1 I saw a man who was writing at the desk.
→ I saw a man _____ at the desk.

2 He was crossing the road when I saw him.
→ I saw him _____ the road.

3 I saw George, and he was playing the guitar.
→ I saw George _____ the guitar.

4 You will see a tall building that stands on a hill.
→ You will see a tall building _____ on a hill.

5 Nobody saw Mr. Brown entering his house last night.
→ Mr. Brown was not seen _____ his house last night.

6 We noticed a boy, and he was holding a sign saying "Free Hug."
→ We noticed a boy _____ a sign saying "Free Hug."

Further Study

1 다음 〈보기〉에 주어진 단어를 이용하여 문장을 완성하시오. (필요하면 동사의 형태를 바꾸시오.)

| Word Bank | call | beat | strike | walk | sing |

1 He heard a song _____ in the forest.

2 Brian could feel his heart _____ wildly.

3 I feel the cold air _____ against my face.

4 The thief was heard _____ around the house.

5 I heard somebody _____ my name at the mall.

2 다음 중 어법상 올바른 문장을 고르시오.

① The boy was noticed broken a window.

② Eric watched the rain to drop from the sky.

③ I heard you saw a woman arrested by the police.

④ They felt their house to shake right after dinner.

⑤ Linda observed the full moon risen above the sky scrapers.

3 다음 글을 읽고, (A)와 (B)에 알맞은 말을 고르시오.

Demetrius ran through the grove, still looking for Hermia. It was dark, and he moved so quickly that he didn't see her (A) (to sleep / sleeping) under a nearby tree. He went deeper into the forest. Meanwhile, Hermia had a terrible dream that a large snake was seen (B) (approaching / approach) her. It scared her so much she woke up crying. She realized that she was entirely alone in the dark woods.

4 다음 주어진 단어를 이용하여 문장을 완성하시오.

1 한 소년이 급히 교실 밖으로 뛰어나오는 것이 눈에 띄었다. (notice, run out of)
   A boy _____ the classroom in a hurry.

2 내가 학교 가는 길에 나는 한 가엾은 남자가 사고로 부상당하는 것을 보았다. (injure)
   I _____ in the accident on my way to school.

3 작년에 유럽 방문했을 때 이 오페라가 이탈리어로 불리는 것을 들었니? (sing)
   Did you hear _____ when you visited Europe last year?

4 나는 빗줄기가 숲 속 오두막의 지붕을 두드리는 소리를 들었다. (the rain, patter)
   I _____ on the roof of my hut in the forest.

1 구동사

A 다음 괄호 안에서 알맞은 말을 고르시오.

1 Everything depends (on / in) what they think of the plan.

2 Jimmy gave me a hat, and I (put it on / put on it) my head.

3 She forgot to (put off / turn off) the light before she went out.

4 I will help you learn how to (cope with / stay with) the problem.

5 World War II (broke out / broke in) when my grandfather was young.

6 Could you (call me up / call up me) at six o'clock tomorrow morning?

7 They have to (put off / turn off) their trip due to a contagious disease.

B 다음 밑줄 친 부분을 주어진 철자로 시작하는 한 단어로 바꿔 쓰시오.

1 He takes after his father in everything.   r _____

2 Mr. Brown had a maid wait on him.   s _____

3 The theory cannot account for this fact.   e _____

4 I'm here to talk about the school fair on Friday.   d _____

5 The speaker referred to his personal experience.   m _____

6 How do I get rid of the wrinkles around my eyes?   r _____

7 Never put off until tomorrow what can be done today.   p _____

8 They called off the meeting scheduled for this Thursday.   c _____

C 다음 괄호 안의 말을 알맞게 배열하여 문장을 완성하시오.

1 Don't (wake / up / me) before ten o'clock.
   → Don't _____ before ten o'clock.

2 It's often easier to make plans than it is to (out / carry / them).
   → It's often easier to make plans than it is to _____.

3 That's nonsense. Who would (a car / away / give) to a stranger?
   → That's nonsense. Who would _____ to a stranger?

4 A hearing was scheduled for Wednesday, but the committee (off / it / put).
   → A hearing was scheduled for Wednesday, but the committee _____.

Further Study

1 다음 〈보기〉에 주어진 단어를 이용하여 문장을 완성하시오. (필요하면 동사의 형태를 바꾸시오.)

Word Bank	run out	get through	break up	work out	turn out

1 The money he had _____ to be counterfeit.

2 I will _____ to lose weight and gain strength for sports.

3 As the batteries _____, I coudn't take any pictures.

4 My boyfriend and I _____ last year, but I still like him a lot.

5 You should show yourself that you have the strength to _____ the hardship.

2 다음 중 어법상 어색한 것을 고르시오.

① The phone is useless. You can throw away it.

② Can you put off the presentation until next Friday?

③ Do you mind if I call you back in a few minutes?

④ We have to take off our shoes when we enter the room.

⑤ I don't know why Jackson gave up his dream to become an actor.

3 다음 글을 읽고, (A)와 (B)에 알맞은 말을 고르시오.

(A) (Turn down it / Turn it down) — it's Energy-Saving Week. Camden Council is asking residents to cut down on the energy they use during this year's Energy-Saving Week. Simple energy-saving measures at home include making sure that appliances are (B) (switched off / put off) on standby and buying energy-saving light bulbs.

4 다음 주어진 단어를 이용하여 문장을 완성하시오.

1 그 홍수는 여러 날 동안의 폭우로 말미암아 야기되었다. (flood, bring about)
_____ by several days of heavy rain.

2 강한 토네이도 때문에 전기가 여러 시간 동안 단전되었다. (electricity, cut off)
_____ for hours due to the strong tornado.

3 그 토의는 7시부터 11시까지 4시간 동안 진행되었다. (carry on)
The discussion _____ from seven o'clock to eleven.

4 그 소년은 그 나라의 가장 가난한 지역 중 한 곳에서 자라났다. (bring up)
_____ in one of the poorest district of the country.

2 다양한 구동사

A 다음 괄호 안에서 알맞은 말을 고르시오.

1 What helped the fire fighters (put out / figure out) the fire efficiently?

2 The singer (turned down / let down) an offer to pose for a magazine.

3 L.E.D. traffic signals don't (give off / drop off) enough heat to melt snow.

4 The fire (broke out / keep out) in the chemical lab on the third floor of the building.

5 The man was suspected as the driver who (ran away / keep away) from the accident.

6 We (made up for / got through with) lost time by taking an airplane instead of a train.

B 다음 밑줄 친 부분을 주어진 철자로 시작하는 한 단어로 바꿔 쓰시오.

1 She passed away peacefully.   d _____

2 I finally picked out the book.   s _____

3 He cannot get over his shyness   o _____

4 Too much work leads to illness.   c _____

5 She has gone through all her money.   s _____

6 Our trip to Hawaii calls for lots of money.   r _____

7 He promised to look into my father's affairs.   i _____

8 I can no longer put up with noisy neighbors.   e _____

C 다음 〈보기〉에 주어진 단어를 이용하여 문장을 완성하시오. (필요하면 동사의 형태를 바꾸시오.)

Word Bank	stand by	stand for	figure out	put on
	go with	come into	run after	

1 The dove _____ peace.

2 White wine doesn't _____ meat.

3 His wife _____ him through all his difficulties.

4 He _____ a large fortune when his father died.

5 I cannot _____ what is wrong with my computer.

6 The policeman _____ the pickpocket but lost him.

7 Jacob _____ rain boots and went out to play in the rain.

Further Study

1 다음 밑줄 친 동사와 바꿔 쓸 수 있는 숙어를 고르시오.

1 You should <u>abolish</u> such evil customs.
　① go back on　② stand up for　③ do away with　④ go on with

2 I ran as fast as possible to <u>overtake</u> him.
　① make away with　② catch up with　③ get down to　④ come up to

3 I can't <u>endure</u> the noise any longer.
　① go in for　② keep away from　③ keep abreast of　④ put up with

4 I'm <u>anticipating</u> seeing you again.
　① running out of　② making little of　③ speaking well of　④ looking forward to

2 다음 빈칸에 들어갈 말이 알맞게 짝지어진 것을 고르시오.

> I still can't _____ why Jason quit his job.
> You are obligated to _____ all debts by the end of the month.

　① make out - keep away　② figure out - pay off　③ take away - go on
　④ turn on - give up　⑤ go over - get over

3 다음 글을 읽고, (A)와 (B)에 알맞은 말을 고르시오.

> For the longest time, European explorers and traders took the same route to get (A) (on / to) Asia–sailing east across the Mediterranean Sea and then traveling by caravan across deserts and mountains. This was a long and troublesome route, so many explorers dreamed (B) (of / on) finding a direct sea route.

4 다음 주어진 단어를 이용하여 문장을 완성하시오.

1 솔직히 말해서 이 그림은 우리의 기대에 차지 않는다. (come up to)
　Frankly speaking, this picture _____.

2 생소한 단어를 만났을 때 사전을 참고하는 것을 잊지 마라. (look up)
　When you meet a new word, never _____ in the dictionary.

3 그 과학자들은 소아마비를 예방하는 그 어려움을 해결하였다. (work out)
　The scientists _____ about preventing polio.

4 나는 다락방 상자에서 어머니의 오랜 사진 몇 장을 우연히 발견했다. (come across, some)
　I _____ of my mother in a box in the attic.

1 현재분사와 과거분사

A 다음 괄호 안에서 알맞은 말을 고르시오.

1 I wish you the best in the (coming / come) year.

2 We found many students (lying / laying) on the grass.

3 She was looking at the boy (playing / played) the piano.

4 They don't want to disturb the (sleeping / slept) baby.

5 On arriving at the house, we found the door (locked / locking).

6 People wish for (long-lasting / long-lasted) batteries for mobile phones.

B 다음 괄호 안에 주어진 말을 이용하여 빈칸에 알맞은 말을 쓰시오.

1 He stared at the guest _____ to be seated. (wait)

2 They won the championship _____ at Liverpool. (hold)

3 There are piles of books _____ with dust in the attic. (cover)

4 SRS is an advanced _____ system for students with disabilities. (educate)

5 It was great fun to see lots of colorful kites _____ above the sky. (fly)

C 다음 두 문장이 같은 뜻이 되도록 빈칸에 알맞은 말을 쓰시오.

1 They danced, as they sang merrily.
   → They danced _____ _____.

2 Her children sat surrounding her.
   → She sat _____ by her children.

3 You should express your views.
   → You should make your views _____.

4 I have an uncle. He lives in Japan.
   → I have an uncle _____ in Japan.

5 This is a poem. Mr. Brown wrote it.
   → This is a poem _____ by Mr. Brown.

6 She sat there. She was staring at the wall.
   → She sat there _____ at the wall.

7 He found that the horse was tied to a tree.
   → He found the horse _____ to a tree.

Further Study

1 다음 괄호 안에서 알맞은 말을 고르시오.

1 He kept his eyes (fixing / fixed) on the table.

2 She does not look (well-dressing / well-dressed).

3 Please have my luggage (carry / carried) to the station.

4 The castle (building / built) in the 16th century has stood empty.

5 He jumped into the river and saved the (drowning / drown) man.

6 The shepherd stood (wondered / wondering) what to do next to keep the sheep safe.

2 다음 중 어법상 어색한 문장을 고르시오.

① He is in the habit of leaving his work half-done.

② Those cars made in Korea are very popular in Europe.

③ They wanted the project finished by the end of this month.

④ The room filling with toys has been cleaned by my sister.

⑤ My dad decided to sell his car due to the soaring price of gas.

3 다음 글을 읽고, (A)와 (B)에 알맞은 말을 고르시오.

In 221 B.C., China became a (A) (unifying / unified) country for the first time. The Qin Dynasty began at this time. Qin Shi Huang became the country's first emperor. When Qin Shi Huang was emperor, he decided to join the (B) (existing / existed) sections of the Great Wall. He also ordered new sections to be built. A large part of the Great Wall was also built during the Ming Dynasty.

4 다음 주어진 단어와 분사를 이용하여 문장을 완성하시오.

1 그 사고에서 부상을 당한 소녀는 지금 병원 중환자실에 있다. (injure)
_____ is in the intensive care unit now.

2 그 지역에서 사용되는 언어는 스페인어이다. (speak)
_____ in the province is Spanish.

3 TV에서 허리케인이 몰고 온 재앙의 광경을 보고 Peter는 공포에 질렸다. (terrify)
Peter _____ at the sight of the hurricane disaster on TV.

4 버스 안에서 줄곧 서 있었기 때문에 Frank는 매우 피곤함을 느꼈다. (remain)
Frank felt tired because _____ all the way in the bus.

2 분사구문

A 다음 괄호 안에서 알맞은 말을 고르시오.

1 They always watch TV while (eating / eaten) dinner.

2 (Taking / taken) the taxi, you will arrive there in time.

3 Sally was sitting on the chair with her right leg (crossed / crossing).

4 (Written / Writing) in Japanese, the book was difficult to understand.

5 (Seeing / Seen) the police, the boys holding cans in their hands ran away.

6 (Not knowing / Knowing not) what to do, she wrote to Carl asking for his advice.

B 다음 빈칸에 알맞은 분사구문을 쓰시오.

1 As I did not know what to say, I remained silent.
→ _____, I remained silent.

2 As there was no bus service, we had to walk all the way.
→ _____, we had to walk all the way.

3 Tom and Jimmy came in, and they were followed by their wives.
→ Tom and Jimmy came in, _____.

4 A few good books, if they are carefully read, will be of great use to you.
→ A few good books, _____, will be of great use to you.

5 Since this book is written in easy English, it will be useful for beginners.
→ _____, this book will be useful for beginners.

C 다음 문장이 올바른 의미가 되도록 문장을 연결하시오.

1 Not having received a reply,   •   • a. I went to bed early.

2 The elevator being out of order,   •   • b. the dog began to bark.

3 Feeling tired,   •   • c. she had to do the housework.

4 Living next door,   •   • d. this is better than that.

5 Wounded seriously,   •   • e. I wrote again.

6 Her mother being away,   •   • f. everyone had to walk.

7 Seeing the guest,   •   • g. I seldom see him.

8 Other conditions being equal,   •   • h. he still tried to fight.

1 다음 괄호 안에 주어진 단어를 이용하여 빈칸에 알맞은 말을 쓰시오.

1 _____ with her sister, she is not so beautiful. (compare)

2 _____ of her purse on the way, she could buy nothing. (rob)

3 _____ from a distance, the snowman looked like a human. (see)

4 All things _____ into consideration, my father's life was a happy one. (take)

5 The boy ran into the room, with his face and hands _____ with mud. (cover)

2 다음 중 어법상 <u>어색한</u> 문장을 고르시오.

① Hit by the car, Sandra was taken to the hospital.

② Leaving alone in the woods at night, he felt terrified.

③ Seen from the sky, the buildings look like match boxes.

④ Jacob stood still with his eyes fixed on something strange.

⑤ Sick of living in a big city, she wants to move to the suburbs.

3 다음 글을 읽고, (A)와 (B)에 알맞은 말을 고르시오.

(A) (Situated / Situating) at an elevation of 1,350m, the city of Kathmandu, which looks out on the sparkling Himalayas, enjoys a warm climate year-round. Kathmandu sits almost in the middle of a basin, (B) (formed / forming) a square about 5km north-south and 5km east-west. It was the site of the ancient kingdom of Nepal. * 수능기출

4 다음 주어진 단어와 분사구문을 이용하여 문장을 완성하시오.

1 수영을 잘하지 못해서 그는 급류에 휩쓸려 익사했다. (able)
_____, he was drowned in the strong current.

2 자주 속기 때문에 나는 그가 하는 말은 믿지 않는다. (deceive)
_____, I cannot believe what he says.

3 가진 돈을 모두 써버리고, 그는 나에게 돈을 좀 보내 줄 것을 요청하였다. (spend)
All his money _____, he asked me to send him some.

4 거리나 공원에서 개를 산책시킬 때에는 목줄을 걸고 개를 이끌어야 한다. (walk a dog)
_____, you should lead it by the leash.

1 -ing와 -ed 형태의 형용사 I

A 다음 괄호 안에서 알맞은 말을 고르시오.

1 I was very (touching / touched) by his kind letter.

2 My first day in the university was rather (boring / bored).

3 Jane was (disappointed / disappointing) to hear the news.

4 The way a spider weaves its web is (fascinating / fascinated).

5 The result of the soccer game was (pleasing / pleased) to both of us.

6 Finally, they found her (scared / scaring) half to death in the woods.

B 다음 주어진 표현과 같은 뜻이 되도록 빈칸에 알맞은 말을 쓰시오.

1 a game that excites you   → an _____ game

2 a girl who is excited   → an _____ girl

3 a meeting that tires you   → a _____ meeting

4 a man who is tired   → a _____ man

5 a story that bores you   → a _____ story

6 a boy who is bored   → a _____ boy

7 a rumor that surprises you   → a _____ rumor

8 a woman who is surprised   → a _____ woman

C 다음 주어진 단어를 이용하여 빈칸에 알맞은 말을 쓰시오.

1 please   a) The painting is very _____ to the eye.

              b) Alice seems _____ with her new car.

2 annoy   a) He was _____ by her apparent indifference.

              b) It's _____ that we didn't know about this before.

3 satisfy   a) I'm not really _____ with the way he cut my hair.

              b) It was very _____ to see him mowing the lawn earnestly.

4 irritate   a) She has an _____ habit of interrupting everything you say.

              b) Tom was _____ by the necessity for polite conversation.

5 confuse   a) If you try to learn too many things at the same time, you may get _____.

              b) Betty's brother married a girl named Betty, and it is very _____ to have two

                 Bettys in the family.

Further Study

1 다음 괄호 안에서 알맞은 말을 고르시오.

1 The children were (pleasing / pleased) when they got a present.

2 The results of the survey have been very (encouraging / encouraged).

3 The experiment we conducted yesterday was really (exciting / excited).

4 He left the room apparently (satisfying / satisfied) with my explanation.

5 The face of an (embarrassed / embarrassing) person usually turns red.

2 다음 중 어법상 <u>어색한</u> 문장을 고르시오.

① It's frustrated for me to eat food like this.

② I was so bored because his lecture was boring.

③ We were very impressed by your customer service.

④ I'm very irritated by the use of mobile phones in public places.

⑤ Mr. Brown felt depressed when he found that his watch was an imitation.

3 다음 글을 읽고, (A)와 (B)에 알맞은 말을 고르시오.

Have you ever thought about how (A) (amazing / amazed) the human body is? The body is actually a very impressive machine. There are some bodily functions we can control, but others we can't. A bodily function is considered uncontrollable if we don't have to think about it to make it happen. Even if we want to, we cannot stop an uncontrollable bodily function. Uncontrollable bodily functions can happen to all of us. They can be uncomfortable, or (B) (embarrassing / embarrassed).

4 다음 주어진 단어를 이용하여 문장을 완성하시오.

1 그녀가 나에게 이야기한 것은 정말로 놀라운 소식이었다. (very, surprise)
   What she told me was _____.

2 대학의 분위기가 매우 흥미로웠다. (enormously, excite)
   The atmosphere of the college _____.

3 나는 빈집에 혼자 남는다는 점이 두려웠다. (frighten)
   I _____ by myself in the empty house.

4 혼동되는 부분이 있으면 주저하지 말고 사무실로 전화해 주세요. (confuse)
   If _____ about anything, don't hesitate to phone my office.

2 -ing와 -ed 형태의 형용사 II

A 다음 괄호 안에서 알맞은 말을 고르시오.

1 It was a very long and (tiring / tired) day for me.

2 We found the movie (interested / interesting) and creative.

3 Spend your holiday with fun and (exciting / excited) games.

4 The (bored / boring) audience has stopped listening to his speech.

5 One of the most (interesting / interested) sports in the world is baseball.

6 My coworkers were (satisfied / satisfying) with the health care reform.

7 His foolish behavior at the party made me (disappointed / disappointing).

8 Thank you for your (fascinating / fascinated) and emotional presentation at our convention.

B 다음 문장에서 잘못된 부분을 찾아 바르게 고치시오.

1 We are easily disillusioning with TV advertising.

2 The girl found the documentary very intrigued.

3 Michael looked troubling when he heard the news.

4 Mary will visit other interested parts of the city tomorrow.

5 The film was so bored, and I was dozing off the whole time.

6 Ashley received a very touched letter, and she was moved to tears.

7 I was amazing when I saw Niagara Falls. It was the most amazed sight I had ever seen.

8 Jennifer was pretty exhausting with the trip, but most people didn't think it was exhausting at all.

C 다음 괄호 안에 주어진 말을 이용하여 빈칸에 알맞은 말을 쓰시오.

1 We found the situation very _____. (confuse)

2 I was very _____ to hear of your mother's death. (shock)

3 She felt _____ by the many letters of support. (encourage)

4 It is an _____ experience to travel through the African rainforest. (excite)

5 We were very _____ with the standard of the children's work. (impress)

6 The firm wants to avoid any _____ questions about its finances. (embarrass)

7 He told of _____ events that had taken place in his hometown. (frighten)

8 Understanding the cultural habits of another nation is a _____ task. (bewilder)

Further Study

1 다음 괄호 안에서 알맞은 말을 고르시오.

1 I don't find his jokes (amusing / amused) at all.

2 The end of the movie was (disappointing / disappointed).

3 I found the whole experience very (depressing / depressed).

4 You may rest (assuring / assured) that we will do our best.

2 다음 빈칸에 들어갈 말이 바르게 짝지어진 것을 고르시오.

He will get _____ when he can't win.
It is very _____ that you don't know anything about the project.

① frustrating - amazing   ② frustrated - amazed   ③ frustrated - amazing

④ frustrate - amazed   ⑤ frustrating - amazing

3 다음 글을 읽고, (A)와 (B)에 알맞은 말을 고르시오.

Imagine taking a final exam, and you're so nervous that you start sweating. All of a sudden, you start to hiccup! Being too nervous can cause you to hiccup. So why does this happen? It happens when the diaphragm becomes (A) (irritating / irritated). This irritation can be caused by many things, such as eating or drinking too fast or too much or from feeling (B) (exciting / excited).

4 다음 주어진 단어를 이용하여 문장을 완성하시오.

1 너는 그 남자가 지루하다는 것을 알게 되면 그를 다시 만나고 싶지 않을 거야. (find)
If you _____ the man _____, you don't want to meet him again.

2 그 사원이 본래의 상태 그대로인 것을 발견하고 우리는 깜짝 놀랐다. (astonished)
We _____ to find that the temple was still in its original condition.

3 비교적 사소한 일에 흥분한 것에 대해 George는 부끄러웠다. (ashamed)
George _____ that he had lost his temper over a relatively trivial affair.

4 내가 초청을 거절한다고 해서 존이 기분 나빠하지 않기를 바랍니다. (feel, insult)
I hope John will not _____ if I turn down his invitation.

1 be+과거분사

A 다음 괄호 안에서 알맞은 말을 고르시오.

1 The car (was disappeared / disappears) into the darkness.

2 The wounded soldier (took / was taken) to the hospital.

3 These problems may (arise / be arisen) from global warming.

4 It is necessary that the bills should (be paid / pay) within five days.

5 They want the concert (to cancel / to be canceled) due to the storm.

6 The new teacher (laughed at / was laughed at) because of his strange accent.

B 다음 괄호 안에 주어진 말을 이용하여 빈칸에 알맞은 말을 쓰시오.

1 She has never _____ to cry. (see)

2 What language _____ in Canada? (speak)

3 His dictionary was nowhere to _____. (find)

4 By whom will the children _____? (look after)

5 A new school is _____ in the village now. (build)

6 I hope your first report will _____ by others. (follow)

7 When was the door _____ by your father? (paint)

8 The paper _____ and handed to the secretary yesterday. (sign)

C 다음 주어진 말을 이용하여 문장을 완성하시오.

1 mend　　a) My father used to _____ our shoes.

　　　　　　b) The main gate in question _____ now.

2 observe　a) She _____ her brother meeting Margaret yesterday.

　　　　　　b) Children's Day _____ as a general holiday.

3 change　a) Emma refused to _____ her name when she married.

　　　　　　b) It is high time for the subject to _____.

4 scold　　a) He hasn't told me why he _____ by the teacher.

　　　　　　b) I hate to _____ you, but you shouldn't stay out so late at night!

5 ascribe　a) He always _____ his failure to ill-health.

　　　　　　b) The country's difficulties should not _____ to the last government's

　　　　　　　 policies.

Further Study

1 다음 괄호 안에서 알맞은 말을 고르시오.

1 We want the question to (answer / be answered).

2 What cannot be cured must (endure / be endured).

3 As he is so selfish, he deserves to (scold / be scolded).

4 Water (consists / is consisted) of hydrogen and oxygen.

5 You (mistake / are mistaken) if you think that he is wrong.

6 Climatic changes have (occurred / been occurred) throughout the world.

7 Thanks to vaccination, some diseases have now (disappeared / been disappeared).

2 다음 중 어법상 어색한 문장을 고르시오.

① There are still some problems for us to solve.

② About half of those arrested appeared in court last week.

③ Typhoons usually occur in the western Pacific in summer.

④ We didn't know whether the car you bought had been stolen or not.

⑤ My father has been invited to the seminar, which will be held this Sunday.

3 다음 글을 읽고, (A)와 (B)에 알맞은 말을 고르시오.

The town (A) (is located / located) in Yellowstone National Park, which is beautiful with its forests and rocky mountains. The city (B) (hides / is hidden) in a narrow valley of a small mountain river, and even the road to it is a curvy lane that is a lot of fun to drive.

4 다음 주어진 단어를 이용하여 문장을 완성하시오.

1 너에게 말을 걸기 전까지는 낯선 사람에게 말하지 마라. (speak)
Don't speak to a stranger until you _____.

2 그의 연설은 변호사로서의 다년간의 경험에 근거하고 있다. (base)
His speech _____ from many years as a lawyer.

3 먼지가 한 겹 쌓인 것이 이 방이 수년 동안 사용되지 않았음을 나타낸다. (have, use)
A film of dust shows that this room _____ for years.

4 탁월한 재능과 꾸준한 근면함이 그의 야망을 뒷받침하고 있었다. (ambition, support)
_____ great talents and untiring diligence.

2 주의할 수동태 표현

A 다음 괄호 안에서 알맞은 말을 고르시오.

1 I was advised to (stop / stopping) eating fast food.

2 He (was found / found) playing basketball in the park.

3 We are supposed (to have / having) a warmer weekend.

4 The car seems (to be made / to make) for the handicapped.

5 English has been taught (of / to) me by my own mother.

6 She tends (to be frustrated / to frustrate) because of her current condition.

B 다음을 수동태로 바꿀 때 빈칸에 알맞은 말은 쓰시오.

1 We heard him say so.
  → He _____ say so.

2 They elected him captain of the team.
  → He _____ of the team.

3 We saw him entering the building.
  → He _____ the building.

4 They made her wait for over an hour.
  → She _____ for over an hour.

C 다음 주어진 말을 이용하여 문장을 완성하시오.

1 consider a) I _____ it a great honor to be here with you today.
           b) She came to _____ as the greatest actress in Bollywood.

2 discuss   a) The committee will _____ the plans for the new school.
           b) What to do and where to go should _____.

3 judge   a) Students tend to _____ by their exam grades.
           b) Why can't they _____ me on my brains, not my looks?

4 tell   a) My father _____ me myths about constellation when I was young.
           b) He looked depressed when he _____ by doctor that he had a problem with
              his heart.

5 catch   a) I _____ a man sneaking into my house.
           b) The boy _____ stealing one hundred dollars worth of clothes from the store.

Further Study

1 다음 괄호 안에서 알맞은 말을 고르시오.

1 It (forbids / is forbidden) to bring a pet into the subway.

2 He has never been seen (smile / to smile) in her presence.

3 Picasso came to (recognize / be recognized) as the world's most famous painter.

4 A woman who suffered from a backache (advise / was advised) to take hot baths.

5 A great deal of harm has (done / been done) to our environment since the Industrial Revolution.

2 다음 중 어법상 어색한 문장을 고르시오.

① She was shown a picture of a beautiful island.

② They were allowed to participate in the Olympics.

③ We were told to stay outside and play before dinner.

④ They were found enter the building a few minutes ago.

⑤ Karl was noticed standing alone in the dark empty hallway.

3 다음 글을 읽고, (A)와 (B)에 알맞은 말을 고르시오.

David Hill – a genuine, honest, and trustworthy person. He has never (A) (been heard / heard) to speak a wrong word against anybody. His relationship with both of his parents-in-law is admirable. The charges against him are completely wrong. I (B) (am believed / believe) David Hill is totally innocent of these charges.

4 다음 주어진 단어를 이용하여 문장을 완성하시오.

1 추운 겨울 다음에는 항상 따뜻한 봄이 따른다. (follow, invariably)
The cold winter _____ a mild spring.

2 그는 과실치사 혐의로 재판에 부쳐졌다. (put on trial)
_____ for killing a person accidentally.

3 임금분쟁을 해결하기 위하여 또 다른 제안이 필요할 것이다. (have to, make)
Another suggestion will _____ to settle the dispute about wages.

4 너는 이 빌딩의 중앙난방시스템을 조작하는 법을 배운 적 있니? (have, teach)
_____ how to operate the central heating system of this building?

1 수동 형태의 동사구 I

A 다음 괄호 안에서 알맞은 말을 고르시오.

1 His car (was stolen / was robbed of) by the man.

2 Mike has been known (as / by) a lawyer in our club.

3 My hometown is known (by / for) its beautiful scenery.

4 James (is said / says) to have worked at a hospital as a nurse.

5 Thomson (was stolen / was robbed of) his wallet by a pickpocket.

6 The media box (was situated / situated) directly in front of the sole entrance.

B 다음을 수동태 문장으로 바꿀 때 빈칸에 알맞은 말을 쓰시오.

1 Her family persuaded him of her innocence.
→ He _____ by her family.

2 The guide informed me of some changes in the schedule.
→ I _____ in the schedule.

3 They say that she has twelve children.
→ It _____ she has twelve children.
→ She _____ twelve children.

4 Someone stole my money last night.
→ My money _____ last night.

5 Erin accused Jimmy of giving her a fake watch on her birthday.
→ Jimmy _____ her a fake watch on her birthday.

C 다음 주어진 우리말과 같은 뜻이 되도록 주어진 단어를 이용하여 문장을 완성하시오.

1 나무는 그 나무의 열매로 알 수 있다. (know)
→ A tree is _____ its fruit.

2 그는 영리하지만, 정직하지는 않은 것으로 여겨진다. (think)
→ He _____ clever but dishonest.

3 Peter가 체포되었는데, 나는 그의 유죄를 확신하고 있었다. (convince)
→ Peter was placed under arrest; I _____ his guilt.

4 사람들은 그녀가 시험에 합격할 것이라고 믿는다. (believe)
→ It _____ she will pass the examination.

Further Study

1 다음 문장을 수동태 문장으로 전환할 때 빈칸에 알맞은 말을 쓰시오.

1 He accused me of lying.
→ I _____.

2 The accident deprived him of sight.
→ He _____.

3 The doctor informed me of the risks of the surgery.
→ I _____.

4 People say that the council has decided to demolish the old community center.
→ It _____.

2 다음 빈칸에 들어갈 말이 바르게 짝지어진 것을 고르시오.

This home remedy is known only _____ people of that region.
Bruce Lee is known _____ an action movie star in Hong Kong.

① of - of   ② of - to   ③ to - as   ④ as - to   ⑤ to - of

3 다음 글을 읽고, (A)와 (B)에 알맞은 말을 고르시오.

A man, 39, was putting air into one of the tires of his car at a gas station at 9:30 p.m. Sunday when two men grabbed him around the neck and threw him to the ground. The victim was (A) (stolen / robbed of) much money and a cell phone. A bag containing groceries was (B) (stolen / robbed of), too.

4 다음 주어진 단어를 이용하여 문장을 완성하시오.

1 그는 그 약속이 생각났다. (remind, appointment)
He _____.

2 그들은 건강의 소중함을 확신한다. (persuade)
They _____ of the value of health.

3 시스템의 어떤 변화도 당신에게 통보될 것입니다. (notify)
You will _____ of any changes in the system.

4 사람들은 그가 미국의 45대 대통령이 될 것이라고들 한다. (say, be)
It _____ the 45th President of the United States.

2 수동형태의 동사구 II

A 다음 괄호 안에서 알맞은 말을 고르시오.

1 Henry is devoted (to / for) the study of brain functions.

2 I (am not acquainted with / am accustomed to) the man in black.

3 I don't think that he (is qualified for / is faced with) the position?

4 My brother (was absorbed in / was made of) thinking about the exam.

5 He told me that he (was addicted to / was equipped with) online games.

6 About 70 percent of the human body (is made up of / is made up) water.

7 The street was (crowded with / renowned for) people who wanted to see the parade.

B 다음 〈보기〉에 주어진 단어를 이용하여 문장을 완성하시오.

Word Bank	on	in	with	for	to	of

1 He was ashamed _____ asking such a simple question.

2 Many people are employed _____ gardening and voluntary work.

3 The president is faced _____ the difficult task of restoring the economy.

4 The heart attack could be related _____ his car crash last year.

5 It is important that your opinions should be based _____ facts.

6 It seems to me that you are qualified _____ unemployment benefits.

C 다음 주어진 단어와 시제를 이용하여 문장을 완성하시오.

1 dismay   a) I _____ at the maintenance cost for my car last year. (과거)

   b) His unexpected remarks _____ the viewers at his last interview. (과거)

2 situate   a) The apartments _____ on a steep hill. (현재)

   b) The old man _____ a dirty tent in the center of the park. (과거)

3 cover   a) In the winter months, the village _____ with snow and ice. (현재)

   b) Seeing the lightning hit, the boy _____ his eyes with his hands. (과거)

4 fill   a) The next drawer _____ with neat piles of shirts. (현재)

   b) The man _____ the car with enough fuel to make it to his destination. (과거)

5 equip   a) They _____ with the skills needed to conduct the experiment. (현재)

   b) Simon _____ himself with up-to-date gear when he went camping for the first time. (과거)

Further Study

1 다음 괄호 안에서 알맞은 말을 고르시오.

1 He is possessed (in / of) great wealth.

2 He is dressed (in / with) the latest fashion.

3 I'm accustomed (on / to) eating this sort of food.

4 Much attention was paid (to / with) the noise from upstairs.

5 The translation should be compared (with / about) the original.

6 The troop was entirely composed (of / with) American soldiers.

7 From his youth, he has been devoted (to / with) the public service.

2 다음 중 어법상 어색한 문장을 고르시오.

① They are occupied with fishing and gardening.

② The plaza was crowded with a lot of protesters.

③ The company is involved to all kinds of cargo shipping.

④ It's unbelievable that she was married to two men at the same time.

⑤ The school is equipped with computer labs and medical laboratories.

3 다음 글을 읽고, (A)와 (B)에 알맞은 말을 고르시오.

At the time, Lincoln's speech which became known as the Gettysburg Address got little reaction from the crowd, but today it (A) (regards / is regarded) as one of the most eloquent in American history. Lincoln (B) (referred / was referred) to the Declaration of Independence and its ideals of liberty and equality.

4 다음 주어진 단어를 이용하여 문장을 완성하시오.

1 그의 딸들은 양질의 교육을 받았다. (provide)

_____ good education.

2 나는 그들의 프로젝트에 관련되고 싶지 않다. (associate)

I wouldn't want to _____ their project.

3 그 연구에 따르면, 아침 식사를 거르는 것이 소아비만과 관련이 있다. (skip, relate)

According to the study, _____ childhood obesity.

4 그 어린 항해사는 세계 항해 일주를 하는 동안 많은 난관에 부딪혔다. (be faced, challenge)

The young sailor _____ many _____ while sailing around the world.

1 to부정사와 동명사의 닮은 점

A 다음 괄호 안에서 알맞은 말을 고르시오.

1 I never mind (to help / helping) someone in need.

2 I fear (being not / not being) able to perform well.

3 It was polite (for / of) him to hold the door for the old ladies.

4 She didn't agree (to seek / seeking) help from a professional.

5 It is impossible (for / of) me to make it to early classes on time.

6 We expect (our son to be / to our son be) back home on Saturday.

7 They've planned (not to have / to not have) any kids for five years.

8 We appreciate (your / yours) supporting us during the election campaign.

B 다음 문장에서 잘못된 부분을 찾아 바르게 고치시오.

1 He hates I wearing short skirts.

2 It is silly of his to turn down their offer.

3 Mom always tells me to not talk with my mouth full.

4 The refugees hope realizing their dreams of freedom.

5 It was difficult of her to finish the test in the given time.

6 My favorite pastime is to watching horror movies by myself.

7 Sandra tried to avoid to meet her ex-boyfriend at the party.

C 다음 짝지어진 두 문장이 같은 의미가 되도록 빈칸에 알맞은 말을 쓰시오.

1 He insisted that I should read the book.
   → He insisted on _____ the book.

2 We were proud that he had won the Nobel Prize.
   → We were proud of _____ the Nobel Prize.

3 He complained that the room was too cold.
   → He complained of _____ too cold.

4 There is no hope that the concert will be a success.
   → There is no hope of _____ a success.

5 The children were disappointed because they had to leave early.
   → The children were disappointed because of _____ early.

Further Study

1 다음 괄호 안에서 알맞은 말을 고르시오.

1 The grass was too wet for us to (sit / sit on).

2 Birds can fly without (teaching / being taught).

3 They warned him (not to / to not) do that again.

4 His illness made it very difficult (for him / of him) to lift his head.

5 Lack of time is the most common excuse (not for / for not) exercising.

6 Despite my repeatedly declining the reward, he strongly insisted on (I / my) accepting it.

2 다음 중 어법상 어색한 문장을 고르시오.

① I made it a rule to take a walk early in the morning.
② We appreciate your helping us find a good hotel during the festival.
③ It's wise for you to find a new job before another big financial crisis comes.
④ They denied knowing anything about the bomb explosion at the shopping mall.
⑤ Getting to work and getting home can be difficult in many places around the world.

3 다음 글을 읽고, (A)와 (B)에 알맞은 말을 고르시오.

Jane could not find her passport. She had gone through all her private papers, but it was not among them. Where could it be? Usually, she was very careful about (A) (putting / to put) things away. However, her passport was definitely not in its proper place. She tried (B) (remembering / to remember) when she had last seen it, but she couldn't.

4 다음 주어진 단어를 이용하여 문장을 완성하시오.

1 나는 너의 이름을 기억하지 못해서 매우 당황했다. (remember)
It felt embarrassed about _____ your name.

2 그가 이 이견에 동조하는 것은 당연하다. (sympathize)
It is natural _____ with this opinion.

3 내 상관은 내가 근무시간에 사무실에서 음식을 먹는 것을 꺼려하지 않는다. (mind, eat)
My boss _____ at the office during work hours.

4 내가 발표 자료를 준비하는 동안 그는 계속 나를 방해했다. (interrupt)
He kept _____ while I was preparing for the presentation.

2 to부정사와 동명사의 다른 점

A 다음 괄호 안에서 알맞은 말을 고르시오.

1 He stopped (driving / to drive) to answer his phone.

2 There used to (be / being) a school near the park.

3 The black blocks are used to (make / making) the fence.

4 I remember (seeing / to see) her at the party last week.

5 We are looking forward to (meet / meeting) you soon.

6 The boss didn't object to (give / giving) the workers a raise.

B 다음 두 문장이 같은 뜻이 되도록 빈칸에 알맞은 말을 쓰시오.

1 I clearly remember that I posted the letter.
   → I clearly remember _____ the letter.

2 Please don't forget to post the letter.
   → Please remember _____ the letter.

3 I forget that I didn't bring my cell phone.
   → I forget _____ my cell phone.

4 People use credit cards to make purchases.
   → Credit cards _____.

C 다음 괄호 안에 주어진 단어를 이용하여 동명사를 포함하는 문장으로 바꿔 쓰시오.

1 I didn't want to stay behind. (be opposed to)
   → _____

2 Let's go out for dinner tonight. (what do you say to)
   → _____

3 I have no choice but to follow her directions. (cannot help)
   → _____

4 I anticipate hearing your positive response. (look forward to)
   → _____

5 He spent his whole life studying the Bible. (devote)
   → _____

6 I was sorry that I didn't say good-bye to my friends at work. (regret)
   → _____

1 다음 문장에서 <u>잘못된</u> 부분을 찾아 바르게 고치시오.

1 We look forward to see you at work on Tuesday.

2 Our car just stopped to run in the middle of the road.

3 I should not forget making a hotel reservation tomorrow.

4 He didn't regret to quit a promising career as a photographer.

5 A built-in flash is used to taking pictures when the light levels are low.

2 다음 빈칸에 들어갈 말이 바르게 짝지어진 것을 고르시오.

People living in the city are used to _____ fast food.
They have no choice but to _____ my decision.

① eat - follow   ② eating - following   ③ eating - follow

④ eat - following   ⑤ eating - be followed

3 다음 글을 읽고, (A)와 (B)에 알맞은 말을 고르시오.

Mrs. Reeser had been a teacher for thirty-two years. When she stopped (A) (teaching / to teach), she decided to do some things that she had never done before. One thing she wanted (B) (doing / to do) was learn how to fly. After taking flying lessons for a few hours, she had another idea—she wanted to jump out of an airplane. *수능기출

4 다음 주어진 단어를 이용하여 문장을 완성하시오.

1 그들은 그 법안이 통과하는 것을 반대하지 않을 것이다. (object to, pass)
_____ the bill.

2 나는 처음으로 그녀를 본 것을 생생하게 기억한다. (see)
I clearly _____ for the first time.

3 아버지는 어젯밤 생일 파티에서의 심한 음주를 후회하신다. (regret)
Father _____ too much at the birthday party last night.

4 그는 잠시 숨을 가다듬기 위해 걸음을 멈춰야만 했다. (walk, catch)
He had to _____ his breath.

1 to+동사원형의 문장

A 다음 괄호 안에서 알맞은 말을 고르시오.

1 You may as well (go / to go) to bed early tonight.

2 Which one (to buy / buy) is mostly a matter of choice.

3 I would rather (watch / watching) TV than play outside.

4 The problem is where (stay / to stay) during the holiday.

5 I don't know (whether / what) to congratulate you or not.

6 Linda happened to (know / knowing) he had a pregnant wife at home.

B 다음 〈보기〉에 주어진 단어를 이용하여 문장을 완성하시오.

| Word Bank | how to | which one to | what to | where to | when to | whom to |

1 They all look delicious. I don't know _____ try.

2 The soup has started boiling. Tell me _____ turn off the stove.

3 Since we don't know _____ get off the bus, we should give her a call.

4 When several things happen at the same time, and you have no idea _____ do, relax and pray.

5 Jay, Joe and Tim asked me to go to the school dance with them. I don't know _____ go with.

6 Just knowing _____ drive a car is not enough. You should learn driving etiquette and manners.

C 다음 괄호 안에 주어진 단어를 이용하여 to부정사를 포함하는 문장으로 바꿔 쓰시오.

1 He couldn't pay the school fees for his daughters. (afford)
   → He _____ for his daughters.

2 I met an old friend in town by accident the other day. (happen)
   → I _____ in town the other day.

3 The government campaign was not able to attract people's attention. (fail)
   → The government campaign _____.

4 He will turn out to be the greatest player in the history of baseball. (prove)
   → He will _____ in the history of baseball.

5 Children are likely to learn from their parents by copying their behavior. (tend)
   → Children _____ by copying their behavior.

Further Study

1 다음 〈보기〉에 주어진 단어를 이용하여 문장을 완성하시오. (필요하면 동사의 형태를 바꾸시오.)

| Word Bank | mean | tend | deserve | fail | prove |

1 I'm sorry. I didn't _____ to hurt your feelings.

2 He is a hardworking person. He _____ to be promoted.

3 People said that Ryan had brain cancer, but it _____ to be false.

4 We don't trust him because he has _____ to fulfill any of his promises.

5 Preschool aged children _____ to depend almost everything on their parents.

2 다음 중 어법상 <u>어색한</u> 문장을 고르시오.

① You may as well apologize to him for your wrongdoing.

② The problem is that she doesn't know how to ride a motorcycle.

③ It is said that she and her husband intend to retiring next year.

④ I would rather have frozen pizza than have a dinner buffet at Dyne.

⑤ I don't know what to do with the money I received from the committee.

3 다음 글을 읽고, (A)와 (B)에 알맞은 말을 고르시오.

When President Franklin Roosevelt convened the first National Nutrition Conference in 1941, the biggest problem was how (A) (help / to help) 45 million Americans who were malnourished because they could not afford (B) (buy / to buy) the right foods. Now, more than seventy years later, obesity has become an all-consuming worry of many health officials.

4 다음 주어진 단어를 이용하여 문장을 완성하시오.

1 내가 지나갈 때 그녀는 나를 못 본 체했다. (see)
She pretended _____ me when I passed by.

2 우리는 어디에 머물지 결정하지 않았다. (stay)
We haven't decided _____.

3 그들이 경기의 결과에 실망하는 것은 당연하다. (may well, disappoint)
They _____ at the result of the match.

4 많은 어려움을 겪은 후, 그녀는 결국 다이빙하는 법을 배웠다. (dive)
After a lot of problems she managed to learn _____.

2 형용사+to부정사, 명사+to부정사

A 다음 괄호 안에서 알맞은 말을 고르시오.

1 He is the last man (to tell / telling) a lie to us.

2 If you have any questions, feel (free / sure) to call me.

3 They are likely (to travel / traveling) around the country.

4 Jenny is so short that she (can / can't) ride a roller coaster.

5 She expressed her (pressure / willingness) to learn Chinese.

6 He has announced that he is to (start / starting) his trip next month.

7 Their attempt to (reach / reaching) the top of the mountain was a failure.

B 다음 〈보기〉에 주어진 단어를 이용하여 문장을 완성하시오. (단, 한 번씩만 사용하시오.)

| Word Bank | reluctant | adequate | available | willing | free | sure |

1 If you are _____ to wait until the last minute, you can get the chance.

2 English classes are _____ to help students with their language study.

3 Although she was confronted with the evidence of her guilt, she was _____ to admit it.

4 They were not _____ to release their new products because of the economic downturn.

5 This insurance is _____ to cover any injuries and property damages that may occur.

6 The membership fee is $ 50 a year, and all the members are _____ to use our facilities.

C 다음 문장을 「명사+to부정사」를 이용하여 다시 쓰시오.

1 He attempted to fulfill his New Years' resolutions, but he failed.
   → _____ his New Year's resolutions failed.

2 She refused to sell her house. That turned out to be a wrong decision.
   → _____ her house was a wrong decision.

3 He failed to win the competition. We were very surprised.
   → We were very surprised at _____.

4 The government permitted to import rice, and a lot of people were opposed to it.
   → A lot of people were opposed to _____.

Further Study

1 다음 문장을 「be+to부정사」를 이용하여 다시 쓰시오.

1 If we intend to get there on time, we should leave now.
→ If we _____, we should leave now.

2 The ship is going to arrive at Busan on December 7th.
→ The ship _____ at Busan on December 7th.

3 You have to stay in the building until the storm passes.
→ You _____ in the building until the storm passes.

2 다음 빈칸에 들어갈 말이 바르게 짝지어진 것을 고르시오.

Finally, she has got the _____ to bring home a cat .
Kevin is _____ to talk about his political views because his friends don't
understand him.

① attempt - ready   ② decision - sure   ③ permission - reluctant
④ lesson - easy   ⑤ necessity - apt

3 다음 글을 읽고, (A)와 (B)에 알맞은 말을 고르시오.

The fax system is still very much in use when copies of documents require to (A) (send
/ be sent), but as a means of fast correspondence people are inclined (B) (to use / using)
e-mail. E-mail is short for electronic mail and is used to describe messages which are sent
by electronic means from one computer user to another.

4 다음 주어진 단어와 to부정사를 이용하여 문장을 완성하시오.

1 그 강은 헤엄쳐서 건너기엔 너무 넓다. (wide, swim across)
The river is _____.

2 그는 그가 원하는 것을 얻기 위해 사람들을 속이는 사람이 아니다. (the last, deceive)
He is _____ people to get what he wants.

3 정부는 아프리카 국가에 대한 원조를 늘릴 예정이다. (increase)
The government is _____ its aid to African countries.

4 그가 누군가를 용서하기를 꺼리는 것은 과거 감정의 상처 때문이다. (unwillingness)
His _____ someone is caused by past emotional wounds.

1 다양한 명사 표현

A 다음 밑줄 친 말을 복합명사로 바꿔 쓰시오.

1 We are running out of <u>paper of toilet</u>. _____

2 He never falls asleep without <u>pills for sleeping</u>. _____

3 It is hard to find <u>water for drinking</u> in the desert. _____

4 I dropped by a bookstore to buy <u>books for children</u>. _____

5 I'm never allowed to enter <u>the room of my brother</u>. _____

6 My brother stepped on my glasses and broke <u>the frame of glasses</u>. _____

B 다음 〈보기〉에 주어진 단어를 이용하여 문장을 완성하시오.

| Word Bank | flock | sheet | cube | jar | bottle | bar |

1 Barbara put a _____ of ice in her glass.

2 I picked enough apples to make a _____ of jam.

3 A _____ of chocolate has about 400 calories.

4 Don't forget to buy a _____ of milk on your way home.

5 I saw a _____ of seagulls which were flying in formation.

6 He grabbed a _____ of paper and a pencil and started writing.

C 다음 주어진 설명에 맞는 단어를 〈보기〉에서 골라 쓰시오.

| Word Bank | spinster | heroine | bull | nephew | cock | monk | mare | widower |

1 _____ : a female horse or donkey

2 _____ : an adult male chicken synonym, rooster

3 _____ : an adult male animal of the cattle family

4 _____ : a woman who is admired for doing something extremely brave

5 _____ : a man whose wife has died and who has not married again

6 _____ : a member of an all-male religious group that lives apart from other people

7 _____ : an unmarried woman, one who is no longer young and seems unlikely to marry

8 _____ : the son of your brother or sister, or the son of your husband's or wife's sibling

1 다음 괄호 안에서 알맞은 말을 고르시오.

1 He'll chase before her just like a (school / herd) of lambs.

2 These objects were meant to look like a (flock / cattle) of birds.

3 To draw a perfect circle, we need a pair of (compass / compasses).

4 The (arm / arms) trade brings in about $1 billion a year for the North Korea.

5 The board of directors wants to change the (boys' / boys's) school to a coed system.

2 다음 중 어법상 어색한 것을 고르시오.

① Can I bring a pair of scissor on the plane?

② I don't know how a sleeping pill affects our body.

③ He lived in Paris before the outbreak of World War II.

④ Eating a bar of chocolate will not make you feel good.

⑤ The boy standing on the left peered at me over his spectacles.

3 다음 글을 읽고, (A), (B), (C)에 알맞은 말을 고르시오.

My uncle remains (A) (a bachelor / a spinster), and what an easy life he's had! Of course, even though as a niece I aspire to remain (B) (a bachelor / a spinster) throughout my life, so that I can gather my wealth and lead a single lifestyle without having to worry about my husband and kids'education. Indeed, I'm certainly not planning to hook up with anyone anytime soon. I just wish that my (C) (relatives / correlations) and mom herself would just stop pressuring me.

4 다음 주어진 단어를 이용하여 문장을 완성하시오.

1 날씨가 몹시 추운데, 그는 반바지와 티셔츠를 입고 있다. (pair)
Even though it's freezing, he is wearing _____.

2 우리는 한 무리의 소에 둘러싸여 도로에 갇혀 있었다. (herd, cow)
We were stuck on the road, surrounded by _____.

3 영웅과 여걸에 관한 영화는 특히 아이에게 인기가 있다. (hero)
Movies about _____ are especially popular among kids.

4 그녀는 Robertson 여자고등학교를 졸업하고 Stanford 대학교에 입학했다. (graduate from)
She _____ and entered Stanford University.

2 명사를 만드는 접미사

A 다음 영영사전의 의미에 해당되는 말을 괄호 안에서 고르시오.

1 the state of having your freedom limited: (bondage / shortage)

2 the act or ceremony of putting a dead body into a grave: (burial / denial)

3 the degree to which something can be expected to happen: (likelihood / livelihood)

4 someone whose job is to help customers in a public place: (attendant / applicant)

5 an opinion judging the worth, value or condition of something: (appraisal / approval)

6 small amounts of water that are present in the air or in a substance: (mixture / moisture)

B 다음 주어진 단어에 접미사를 붙여 명사형을 만드시오.

1 fail – _____ (실패)

2 depart – _____ (출발, 떠남)

3 wide – _____ (폭, 너비)

4 deep – _____ (깊이; 깊숙함)

5 breathe – _____ (숨, 호흡)

6 true – _____ (진리, 참)

7 grow – _____ (성장, 생장)

8 short – _____ (부족, 결핍)

9 long – _____ (길이)

10 engine – _____ (기술자)

11 descend – _____ (자손, 후예)

12 consult – _____ (상의자, 상담자)

13 bond – _____ (속박, 감금)

14 leak – _____ (누출, 새어나옴)

15 apply – _____ (응모자, 신청자)

16 assist – _____ (원조자, 조력자)

17 participate – _____ (참가자)

18 approve – _____ (승인, 시인)

19 save – _____ (구조)

20 revive – _____ (재생)

C 다음 짝지어진 단어의 관계가 나머지와 <u>다른</u> 하나를 고르시오.

1 ① enclose - enclosure ② press - pressure ③ moist - moisture
  ④ create - creature ⑤ depart - departure

2 ① true - truth ② grow - growth ③ warm - warmth
  ④ wide - width ⑤ dead - death

3 ① try - trial ② propose - proposal ③ survive - survival
  ④ arrive - arrival ⑤ addition - additional

4 ① speak - speaker ② interpret - interpreter ③ office - officer
  ④ receive - receiver ⑤ develop - developer

●점수 _____

1 다음 괄호 안에서 알맞은 말을 고르시오.

1 Eric came running into the room, out of (breath / breadth).

2 The town takes great pride in its architectural (heritage / hostage).

3 We measured the (length / strength) and width of the living room.

4 The president has already given his (approval / appraisal) of the plan.

5 I was under (procedure / pressure) from my parents to become a teacher.

6 Fishing is the main source of (livelihood / likelihood) for many people in the area.

2 다음 빈칸에 들어갈 말이 바르게 짝지어진 것을 고르시오.

This increase in oil price will slow the _____ of the economy.
Measure the _____ of the floor which is going to be covered with a rug.

① breath - length   ② growth - width   ③ length - breadth
④ strength - length   ⑤ warmth - width

3 다음 글을 읽고, (A)와 (B)에 알맞은 말을 고르시오.

Instant (A) (approval / approvement) credit card offers may appear in your mailbox or pop up on your computer screen. In the past, you probably had to wait weeks to receive a decision. With the ease and accessibility of the Internet, credit card (B) (applies / applications) are as easy as 1-2-3 and can take only a matter of seconds.

4 다음 주어진 단어를 이용하여 문장을 완성하시오.

1 부모가 되는 기쁨은 내 인생에서 가장 멋진 경험 중 하나이다. (joy, parenthood)
_____ is one of the most amazing experiences of my life.

2 새로 당선된 시장은 따뜻한 환영에 진심으로 감동을 받은 듯했다. (warmth, welcome)
The newly elected mayor seemed genuinely touched by _____.

3 햇빛에 너무 많이 노출되는 것은 우리의 눈에 심각한 손상을 입힐 수 있다. (much)
_____ to the sun can cause serious damage to our eyes.

4 그 방은 거의 비어 있었으며, 연사는 적은 인원이 출석한 것에 대하여 실망하였다. (the poor attendance)
The room being almost empty, the speaker _____.

1 It/There 관련문장

A 다음 괄호 안에서 알맞은 말을 고르시오.

1 She bought the cab, but I haven't seen (it / one) yet.

2 It's time to take (it / them) easy and refresh yourself.

3 It was in the park (that / which) he met Sarah yesterday.

4 It is certain (that / which) they will never acknowledge their fault.

5 (There are / There is) many ways to make money without investment.

6 They (found it / found) pleasant to walk around in the sun for some time.

B 다음 문장을 「It~that…」 강조구문으로 바꿔 쓰시오.

1 Tom went there with Ann yesterday.
　→ It was with Ann _____.

2 I first met her in Rome three years ago.
　→ It was three years ago _____.

3 The game was scheduled to be held yesterday.
　→ It was yesterday _____.

4 Gerald companied about the price of the food in the restaurant.
　→ It was Gerald _____.

5 He didn't come until the meeting was half over.
　→ It was not until _____.

C 다음 문장을 가목적어 it을 이용하여 다시 쓰시오.

1 It is illegal to serve alcohol on campus.
　→ Law made it _____.

2 It is quite natural for you to refuse his offer.
　→ I think it _____.

3 It was hard to untie the package. → He found it _____.

4 It is my duty to protect my family and my country.
　→ I think it _____.

Further Study

1 다음 괄호 안에서 알맞은 말을 고르시오.

1 How goes (it / there) with your first job?

2 (It / There) is no use crying over spilt milk.

3 (It / There) used to be a hotel on that corner.

4 (It / There) is little milk left in the refrigerator.

5 There (was / were) several fights outside the stadium.

6 There (was / were) a large crowd of people at the match.

7 Turn left at the corner and go straight. You can't miss (it / them).

2 다음 중 밑줄 친 It의 쓰임이 나머지와 다른 것을 고르시오.

① It was certain that he could not live much longer.

② It is certain that he will agree to the terms of payment.

③ It was the gold that they discovered on the island that night.

④ It is possible that we learn English without face-to-face contact.

⑤ It is necessary that the room should be cleaned from time to time.

4 다음 글을 읽고, (A)에 알맞은 말을 고르시오.

Recently, a severe disease hit Asian nations hard, causing several hundred deaths. Many people who live in this part of the world are likely to be worried again with the beginning of cold weather. In spite of (A) (its / their) close location to these countries, however, Korea has remained free of the deadly disease. Many people think the secret is kimchi.   * 수능기출

4 다음 주어진 단어를 이용하여 문장을 완성하시오.

1 새로운 언어를 배우는 것은 많은 노력이 필요하다. (learn)
_____ takes a lot of effort _____ a new language.

2 월요일 아침이면 항상 교통이 혼잡하다. (heavy traffic)
There _____ on Monday morning.

3 아버지가 내 생일 선물로 준 것은 낚싯대였다. (a fishing rod)
It _____ my father gave to me as a birthday present.

4 그는 학력 조작과 무관하다는 점을 분명히 밝혔다. (make, clear)
He _____ he had nothing to do with the false scholastic degree.

2 대명사

A 다음 괄호 안에서 알맞은 말을 고르시오.

1 I like this kind of hat around here. Please show me (it / one).

2 I don't want to wear my old shoes. I want to wear new (ones / them).

3 One is a music book, and (the other / the others) is an art book.

4 One student passed the exam, but (the others / others) failed.

5 Some people are very creative, and (the others / others) are not.

B 다음 〈보기〉에 주어진 단어를 이용하여 문장을 완성하시오.

Word Bank	another	none	the other	one	
	the others	no	the one	it	others

1 Some like apples; _____ like oranges.

2 I bought a pen yesterday, but I have lost _____.

3 I wanted some cake, but there was _____.

4 Jane has a camera, but she wants _____.

5 Do you mind having black coffee? There is _____ milk.

6 My family has two cars. One is red, and _____ is white.

7 I don't like this book. Show me a more interesting _____.

8 Three of the twenty competitors won prizes, and _____ got nothing.

9 Our new television set is more expensive than _____ we had before.

C 다음 두 문장이 같은 뜻이 되도록 괄호 안에서 알맞은 말을 고르시오.

1 Be kind to other people.
   → Be kind to (other / others).

2 Knowing is quite different from doing.
   → Knowing is one thing, and doing is (another / other).

3 Mind your own business.
   → It is (no / none) of your business.

4 Will you have one more cup of tea?
   → Will you have (another / other) cup of tea?

Further Study

1 다음 괄호 안에서 알맞은 말을 고르시오.

1 He has bought a new car and sold the old (it / one).

2 Habits are easily formed—especially bad (one / ones).

3 One of his eyes is better than (the other / the others).

4 (No one / None) of them were present at the meeting.

5 Some people like summer, and (other / others) dislike it.

6 We wanted some ice cream, but there was (none / no) left.

2 다음 중 어법상 어색한 문장을 고르시오.

① One is a cat, another is a dog, and the others is a rabbit.

② She told me that to say is one thing, to do is quite another.

③ I wanted some small-sized baskets, but they wanted large ones.

④ Two of the girls like to play the piano, and the others like to play the flute.

⑤ Some people want to see a drama, and others want to see a soccer game.

3 다음 글을 읽고, (A)와 (B)에 알맞은 말을 고르시오.

More and more young people are choosing to take a gap year between finishing school and starting university. Alternatively, they may decide to take a gap year between graduating from university and embarking on a career. (A) (One / Some) of the gap-year students have wealthy parents who can easily subsidize their travel. (B) (Others / The other) have to save up before they go, often taking after-school jobs to do so.

4 다음 주어진 단어와 부정대명사를 이용하여 문장을 완성하시오.

1 사람은 다른 사람의 의견을 존중해야 한다. (should)

_____ the opinions of others.

2 그것이 너의 의견이겠지만, 다른 모든 사람들은 달리 생각한다. (differently)

That may be your opinion, but _____.

3 그 학생들 중 누구도 공무원을 선발하는 시험에 합격하지 못했다. (pass, examination)

_____ of the students _____ for selecting public servants.

4 여기에 공이 다섯 개 있는데, 한 개는 빨강, 한 개는 파랑, 나머지는 하얀 색이다. (red, blue)

Here are five balls; _____, and _____ are white.

1 수량 표현의 대명사

A 다음 괄호 안에서 알맞은 말을 고르시오.

1 He comes here (almost / most) every day.

2 (Either / Most) of them are high school students.

3 (Little / Few) people have asked me whether I'm Korean.

4 (Most / Mostly) of these cars are made in Germany.

5 (Little / Few) water is left behind and so little is used.

6 (Both / Either) of them is a major threat to human life or health.

7 Every member (are / is) required to be respectful to each other.

B 다음 두 문장이 같은 뜻이 되도록 빈칸에 알맞은 말을 〈보기〉에서 찾아 쓰시오.

| Word Bank | every | none | everybody | neither |

1 I haven't read either of the two books.
→ I have read _____ of the two books.

2 All the boys in the class were kind to me.
→ _____ boy in the class was kind to me.

3 I don't know any of your classmates.
→ I know _____ of your classmates.

4 Who does not desire to promote the welfare of society?
→ _____ desires to promote the welfare of society.

C 다음 〈보기〉에 주어진 단어를 이용하여 문장을 완성하시오.

| Word Bank | every | either | none | both | each | neither |

1 Direct flights to Budapest leave _____ other day.

2 _____ but fools would believe such nonsense.

3 _____ my ears ache very badly, so I can't hear you well.

4 We have been looking at _____ other for five minutes.

5 I don't like _____ of them. Can you show me some others?

6 _____ of us had money, so we had to walk all the way back home.

1 다음 괄호 안에서 알맞은 말을 고르시오.

1 Both tried, but (all / neither) of them succeeded.

2 Not a (few / little) people wanted to stay in the hotel.

3 Each (man / men) assembled at the corner of the street

4 (All / Neither) of the machines is in good working condition.

5 I can speak (few / a few) words of French, but I'm not very fluent.

6 Every boy and every girl (is / are) expected to work independently.

2 다음 중 어법상 <u>어색한</u> 문장을 고르시오.

① Only a few of the students got an A in the math test.

② The meeting will be held every two months at the hotel.

③ Jane and Karen like apples, but neither of them likes pears.

④ Most of the people in the square have been looking for a job.

⑤ He has to hand in the report by tomorrow, so he has few time for anything else.

3 다음 글을 읽고, (A)와 (B)에 알맞은 말을 고르시오.

> The tasks that (A) (most / almost) companies are doing with information today would have been impossible several years ago. At that time, getting rich information was very expensive, and the tools for analyzing (B) (it / them) weren't even available until the early 1990s. But now the tools of the digital age give us a way to easily get, share, and act on information in new ways.

4 다음 주어진 단어를 이용하여 문장을 완성하시오.

1 당신 아니면 내가 현안 문제들을 상관에게 보고해야 합니다. (either, should, speak)

_____ current issues to the boss.

2 우리 둘 다 다른 사람들이 생각하는 것에 신경을 쓰지 않는다. (neither, care about)

_____ what other people think.

3 Fred는 음주와 흡연으로 그의 월급 대부분을 탕진했다. (spend, salary)

Fred _____ on alcohol and cigarettes.

4 꽤 많은 사람들이 스트레스를 줄이는 방법에 대한 그의 강의를 듣기 위하여 왔다. (few, come)

Quite _____ to listen to his lecture on how to mitigate stress.

2 재귀대명사

A 다음 괄호 안에서 알맞은 말을 고르시오.

1 You must have faith in (you / yourself).

2 (Suit yourself / Help yourself) to this delicious food.

3 I would rather describe (me / myself) as just a counselor.

4 He lost (himself / itself) in the woods and called for help.

5 They said they were really happy and enjoyed (themselves / them) in the show.

6 Helen wanted to help the poor, so she decided to devote (herself / her) to helping the homeless.

B 다음 두 문장이 같은 의미가 되도록 빈칸에 알맞은 말을 쓰시오.

1 She is proud of her own good looks.
→ She prides _____ on her good looks.

2 I had a pleasant time last evening.
→ I enjoyed _____ last evening.

3 The old man lives alone.
→ The old man lives by _____.

4 I like to do everything without others' help
→ I like to do everything for _____.

5 The door opened naturally.
→ The door opened of _____.

6 Between you and me, that is not a real diamond.
→ Between _____, that is not a real diamond.

C 다음 빈칸에 알맞은 재귀대명사를 쓰시오.

1 She remained silent as she lost _____ in thought.

2 Can you make _____ understood in English?

3 I can handle it _____. It's none of your business.

4 Andrew devoted _____ to writing fairy tales for children.

5 All the audience seated _____, and the performance began.

6 Plants and animals become extinct as they fail to adapt _____ to the new circumstances.

Further Study

1 다음 괄호 안에서 알맞은 말을 고르시오.

1 My little son ate the whole goose (him / himself).

2 Welcome to our place. Please make (you / yourself) at home.

3 My grandmother often gave presents to my sister and (me / myself).

4 The United States (itself / themselves) will play a leading role for the world peace.

2 다음 중 어법상 어색한 문장을 고르시오.

① You should blame you when things go wrong.

② Paul managed to repair his computer by himself.

③ We enjoyed ourselves at the festival last weekend.

④ Between ourselves, she failed to repay the mortgage.

⑤ Be careful when you handle the machine, or you may hurt yourself.

3 다음 글을 읽고, (A)와 (B)에 알맞은 말을 고르시오.

Alex and Julie were preparing to play in the finals of the tennis club mixed doubles. For several years in a row they had won it easily, but last year their opponents in the finals had beaten them soundly and won the cup. Neither Alex nor Julie had played well, and they made (A) (them / themselves) feel embarrassed. They also knew that some people in the club had criticized (B) (them / themselves) because of their poor standard of play.

4 다음 주어진 단어와 재귀대명사를 이용하여 문장을 완성하시오.

1 모든 공연 배우들이 무대에 오르고 한 사람씩 자신들을 소개했다. (introduce, one by one)
   All the performers came on the stage, and _____.

2 개척자 가족들은 노래를 부르고 이야기를 나누며 여행을 즐겼다. (entertain)
   During the journey, pioneer families _____ with songs and stories.

3 농장에서 맡은 일을 끝마친 후에, Tom은 종종 낚시에 몰두한다. (occupy)
   After finishing his duties at the farm, _____ in fishing.

4 테레사 수녀는 가난한 사람들을 돌보는 데 헌신하며 조건 없는 사랑을 실천하였다. (devote)
   Mother Teresa _____ to taking care of the poor, practicing unconditional love.

1 까다로운 형용사

A 다음 괄호 안에서 알맞은 말을 고르시오.

1 We found the lion (asleep / sleep) below a tree.

2 We don't believe the soldiers are still (alive / live).

3 This is the (only / alone) solution for your problem.

4 Her condition is (good enough / enough good) to allow her to go there.

5 I have never met the (people present / present people) at the meeting.

6 They don't have (information enough / enough information) about this matter.

B 다음 두 문장의 빈칸에 공통으로 들어갈 말을 〈보기〉에서 골라 쓰시오.

| Word Bank | certain | late | present |

1 a) A _____ lady came to see you.
   b) She is _____ to achieve her goals.

2 a) My _____ husband was a lawyer.
   b) He is _____ for work due to traffic.

3 a) What is your _____ address and phone number?
   b) Were you _____ at the conference last Friday?

C 다음 괄호 안의 말을 알맞게 배열하여 문장을 완성하시오.

1 (are / enough / to seat / there / chairs) 200 people at least.
   → _____ 200 people at least.

2 I want to talk to (for / the person / customer service / responsible).
   → I want to talk to _____.

3 His speech was (to draw / enough / people's attention / interesting).
   → His speech was _____.

4 (lay / he / all night long / awake), worrying about his first day at work.
   → _____, worrying about his first day at work.

5 (involved / all / the fight / the students / in) were disciplined according to the school rules.
   → _____ were disciplined according to the school rules.

Further Study

1 다음 괄호 안에 주어진 단어가 들어갈 위치를 고르시오.

1 Don't ① disturb ② a(n) ③ child ④ in the cradle. (asleep)

2 All ① the ② people ③ were ④ moved by his eloquent speech. (present)

3 It is a(n) ① sentence ②, and it has a(n) ③ obscure ④ meaning. (involved)

4 Saving water ① is the ② solution to ③ China's water shortages ④. (only)

5 The first fireman ① reached the ② victim and ③ found the man ④. (awake)

2 다음 중 어법상 어색한 문장을 고르시오.

① As soon as Julie was left alone in the room, she started to cry.

② The present regime has failed to improve our lives due to the economic downturn.

③ The involved person in the shooting on the street was arrested by the police.

④ He has saved enough money to buy the car that he has wanted for a long time.

⑤ We are looking for a driver responsible for the accident that happened last night.

3 다음 글을 읽고, (A)와 (B)에 알맞은 말을 고르시오.

Some people think that there is a specific age at which a child is (A) (enough old / old enough) to be at home alone. Not so. Parents need to consider other characteristics about their children. According to Karen Debord, child development specialist, the most appropriate way to make a decision to leave (B) (a child alone / an alone child) is to base it on the child's sense of maturity and responsibility in self-care.

4 다음 주어진 단어를 이용하여 문장을 완성하시오.

1 그는 같은 실수를 반복할 만큼 어리석었다. (stupid, repeat)
He was _____ the same mistake.

2 여행을 간다는 설렘으로 잠을 잘 수가 없었다. (fall)
I couldn't _____ with the excitement of travel.

3 지구의 미래에 대해 걱정하는 사람들이 많다. (many, concerned about)
There have been _____ the future of the earth.

4 Abraham Lincoln은 오래전에 죽었지만, 그의 꿈과 영감은 여전히 살아 있다. (dreams, inspirations)
Abraham Lincoln died long ago, but _____.

2 파생어

A 다음 우리말에 맞는 말을 고르시오.

1 민감한 피부   (sensitive / sensible) **skin**

2 각각의 역할   (respectful / respective) **role**

3 중요한 결정   (momentary / momentous) **decision**

4 기억할 만한 선물   (memorable / memorial) **gift**

5 은밀한 정보   (confident / confidential) **information**

6 산업혁명   (industrial / industrious) **revolution**

7 상당한 량   (considerable / considerate) **amount**

8 어린아이 같은 순진함   (childish / childlike) **innocence**

B 다음 괄호 안에서 알맞은 말을 고르시오.

1 They will fight for their (respectful / respective) **hometowns.**

2 It was (considerate / considerable) of you to give me another chance.

3 Keith was blamed for the leakage of (confidential / confident) information.

4 I think he is one of the most (imaginative / imaginary) writers in the world.

5 I'll stay home today because my nose is very (sensible / sensitive) to cold air.

6 The population of the cities increased due to the (industrial / industrious) revolution.

C 다음 〈보기〉에 주어진 단어를 골라 문장을 완성하시오. (단, 한 번씩만 사용하시오.)

Word Bank	successive	considerate	confident
	sensory	favorable	practical

1 She is a very _____ actor, replying to all his fan mail.

2 You shouldn't be too _____ that you can do everything.

3 Shanghai has a _____ condition to become a global financial center.

4 This text teaches the _____ mathematics essential to the building construction.

5 The eye is not only the most beautiful but also the most important _____ organ.

6 Those who live here for five _____ years are able to apply for Korean citizenship.

Further Study

1 다음 괄호 안에서 알맞은 말을 고르시오.

1 My mother is very (sensible / sensitive) to cold.

2 He comes from a (respectable / respective) family.

3 You didn't really see a ghost - it was only (imaginable / imaginary).

4 The political party was (successive / successful) in passing the bill.

5 More (momentary / memorial) services for the war dead are planned.

2 다음 빈칸에 들어갈 말이 바르게 짝지어진 것을 고르시오.

> The handbook on _____ English emphasizes conversational English.
> _____ numbers of animals in the woods have died due to deforestation.

① practice - Considerate   ② practical - Considerate   ③ practice - Considerable

④ practical - Considerable   ⑤ practical - Considerably

3 다음 글을 읽고, (A), (B), (C)에 알맞은 말을 고르시오.

> If you are interested in getting higher pay and promotion in your job, you should start learning how to be (A) (general / generous) in your job. Most people who remain in their position or the same salary for years are people who are selfish. They try to work less, slower and deliver worse results to get the same pay. In other words, they are trying to work (B) (maximum / minimum) and get (C) (maximum / minimum).

4 다음 주어진 단어를 이용하여 문장을 완성하시오.

1 오트밀은 건강에 좋은 음식이다. (healthy)
Oatmeal is _____.

2 그 하키 팀은 5연승 했다. (successive, victory)
The hockey team has had _____.

3 의사들은 환자들의 기록을 철저하게 비밀로 유지해야 한다. (confidential, completely)
Doctors are required to keep patients' records _____.

4 인간은 눈, 코, 귀, 혀, 그리고 피부 5개의 감각기관을 가지고 있다. (organ)
Human beings have _____: eyes, nose, ears, tongue and skin.

1 다양한 부사

A 다음 괄호 안에서 알맞은 말을 고르시오.

1 It's ten o'clock, and Derek is (still / yet) sleeping.

2 The furniture you ordered has not been delivered (already / yet).

3 I have (already / yet) done my one-year of English course.

4 Thomas finished his dinner. She called him shortly (since / after).

5 They (frequently talk / talk frequently) about their childhood dreams.

6 (Fortunately / Unfortunately), I came down with a cold while I was traveling in Europe.

B 다음 〈보기〉에서 알맞은 것을 골라 문장을 완성하시오. (단, 한 번씩만 사용하시오.)

Word Bank	regularly	suddenly	selfishly	badly	perfectly	patiently

1 I like to be active in my spare time and play tennis _____.

2 He hurt himself quite _____, and his leg was very swollen.

3 I waited _____ for a miracle, but it never happened.

4 I made a quick stop because a traffic light changed _____.

5 You must tell them that you feel very unhappy when they behave _____.

6 I can understand _____ if people speak slowly and clearly.

C 다음 우리말과 같은 뜻이 되도록 빈칸에 알맞은 부사를 쓰시오.

1 Brian은 아버지와 정말 많이 닮았다.
   → Brian resembles his father very _____.

2 조사자들은 멈추지 않고 계속해서 일했다.
   → The researchers worked _____ and never stopped.

3 간단히 말해서 살을 빼는 가장 좋은 방법은 덜 먹고 더 운동하는 것이다.
   → _____, the best way to lose weight is to eat less and exercise more.

4 토요일 오후 사고로 두 자동차는 약간 파손되었다.
   → Two vehicles were _____ damaged in the incident on Tuesday afternoon.

5 흰긴수염고래와 범고래는 겨울에 북극에서 좀처럼 모습을 잘 보이지 않는다.
   → The blue whale and the killer whale are _____ seen in winter in the Arctic.

Further Study

1 다음 괄호 안에서 알맞은 말을 고르시오.

1 Have you read today's paper (still / yet)?

2 You should have told me this (ago / before).

3 The bullet went (clear / clearly) through the door.

4 As it was still early in the morning, the store was not (already / yet) open.

5 The museum is located in the center of a (heavily / hardly) populated district.

6 When we set out at five o'clock in the morning, it was (already / still) dark.

2 다음 중 어법상 <u>어색한</u> 것을 고르시오.

① They think always about what they've achieved.

② Have you already seen the movie directed by James?

③ His lawyer still insists Cameron did not murder Helen.

④ Jackson hardly ever goes to work, and he's at home nearly all the time.

⑤ For many years the auditorium was seldom used, so its condition was poor.

3 다음 글을 읽고, (A)와 (B)에 알맞은 말을 고르시오.

The weather was sunny and comfortable, and we had a moderate amount of passengers. The only problem is that my ankle was not having a good day. For some reason, it has been aching (A) (terrible / terribly) all day to the point where I can hardly stand the pain. My wife (B) (barely helps / helps barely). Maybe it's the drastic change in weather, even though the humidity has dropped. I just hope it's better tomorrow.

4 다음 주어진 단어를 이용하여 문장을 완성하시오.

1 나는 아직 내 요청에 대한 응답을 받지 못했다. (any, response)
   I _____ to my request _____.

2 길을 건널 때, 나는 자동차에 거의 치일 뻔했다. (run over)
   When crossing the street, I was _____ by a car.

3 게다가, 저희 웹사이트에서 물건을 주문하시면 할인을 받으실 수 있습니다. (addition, get a discount)
   _____, you _____ when you order from our website.

4 동남아시아의 지진은 너무 끔찍해서 나는 참을 수가 없다. (hardly, stand)
   The southeast Asia earthquake is so horrifying, I _____ it.

2 혼동하기 쉬운 형용사와 부사

A 다음 괄호 안에서 알맞은 말을 고르시오.

1 The children (nearly / near) fell into the river.

2 This machinery is very (costly / cost) to maintain.

3 He studied as (hard / hardly) as he could to be a lawyer.

4 We are thankful to you for your (timely / time) advice and kind support.

5 (Highly / High) educated men and women are likely to support this financial reform.

B 다음 두 문장이 같은 뜻이 되도록 빈칸에 알맞은 말을 쓰시오.

1 I just don't think she's a terribly fast driver.
→ I just don't think she drives terribly _____.

2 He didn't survive long after the accident.
→ He died _____ after the accident.

3 My brother is too young to go to school.
→ My brother is not old _____ to go to school.

4 Here are some tips that may help you win the game with ease.
→ Here are some tips that may help you win the game _____.

C 다음 문장의 빈칸에 공통으로 들어갈 말을 〈보기〉에서 골라 쓰시오.

| Word Bank | well | long | ill | pretty | last |

1 I couldn't sleep _____ last night, so I'm very tired now.
He's really enjoying the lessons, and he did _____ in his exam.

2 I guess his strategy worked _____ well.
A very _____ girl poses for the photographer at the studio.

3 It is a long time since we _____ met.
His _____ hope is to study abroad and receive a scholarship.

4 How does she know his grandmother was _____ in bed?
I don't like to speak _____ of others, nor do I want to hear bad things.

5 Those who have stayed here _____ can make friends with me.
I wonder how _____ hard-boiled eggs can be kept before they spoil.

1 다음 괄호 안에서 알맞은 말을 고르시오.

1 I have neither drunk nor smoked (late / lately).

2 The ball did not fly (high / highly) in the air.

3 It (rare / rarely) rains in this part of the country.

4 He has (hard / hardly) ever treated his men (harsh / harshly).

5 (Most / Almost) critics spoke highly of his recent work.

6 Don't come (near / nearly). The monkey will hurt you (bad / badly).

2 다음 빈칸에 들어갈 말이 바르게 짝지어진 것을 고르시오.

> They have _____ returned from their Antarctic expedition.
>
> We felt our house shaking _____ after midnight, and we ran out to see what was happening.

① lately - shortly   ② lively - nearly   ③ nearly - directly

④ costly - nearly   ⑤ quarterly - lately

3 다음 글을 읽고, (A)와 (B)에 알맞은 말을 고르시오.

> Patsy used the spare bedroom in her parents' house as a study and, by the end of the college term, it was looking (A) (pretty / prettily) untidy. Patsy, (B) (unlike / unlikely) her mother, was not one of those people who derive satisfaction from cleaning. Indeed, she disliked the task very much.

4 다음 주어진 단어를 이용하여 문장을 완성하시오.

1 이륙 후 곧 저녁 식사가 제공됩니다. (serve, shortly, after)
Dinner will _____ take-off.

2 그는 화재에서 살아남긴 했지만, 오래 살지는 않았다. (live)
He managed to survive the fire, but he _____.

3 올해에 거의 만 명이나 되는 사람들이 첫 해돋이를 보려고 모였습니다. (nearly, gather)
This year, _____ to see the sunrise.

4 모든 것이 잘 짜여 있었고, 방문객들은 우리의 전시에 강한 흥미를 보였다. (organize)
Everything was _____, and visitors showed their keen interest in our exhibits.

1 '아'다르고 '어'다르다!—관사

A 다음 괄호 안에서 알맞은 말을 고르시오.

1 The train was thirty minutes (behind time / behind the times).

2 (A number / The number) of students from Korea increases.

3 I had spaghetti for dinner. (The / A) spaghetti was very good.

4 (A number / The number) of animals were killed by the hunters.

5 (A variety of / The variety of) goods like TVs are displayed at the shop.

6 Buying a new car is (out of question / out of the question) for her. She can't afford it.

B 다음 괄호 안에 알맞은 관사(a, an, the)를 쓰시오.

1 My parents live in _____ old house in a small city.
   Mac has a car. He would like to sell _____ car.

2 This villa is very small, but it has _____ garden.
   The villa has a garden, but _____ garden is very small.

3 Meri waited at _____ airport for her plane to start boarding.
   There is _____ airport close to where you would like to travel.

4 You can ask me _____ question if you'd like.
   The proposal is out of _____ question because we don't have enough budget.

5 Sometimes I wish I could just stay away for _____ week or so.
   We will leave next week on a visit to Australia and come home _____ week after next.

6 We had a great stay in _____ good hotel with kind services.
   Memberships mean that they can get _____ best hotel rates around the world.

C 다음 괄호 안에 주어진 단어를 이용하여 빈칸에 알맞은 말을 쓰시오. (단, 현재시제로 쓰시오.)

1 The number of people who want 3D jobs _____ decreasing. (be)

2 A variety of trees _____ found along the tropical beaches. (be)

3 A number of people _____ concerned about the safety of nuclear facilities. (be)

4 The kind of books you read _____ quite different from the kind of books you write. (be)

5 The variety of plants _____ very rich, so we should describe the structure of their DNA. (be)

Further Study

1 다음 괄호 안에서 알맞은 말을 고르시오.

1 a) Jack's brother is in (prison / the prison) for robbery.
   b) Jack went to (prison / the prison) to visit his brother.

2 a) Bill was tired, so he went to (bed / the bed) early.
   b) He helped me to make (bed / the bed).

3 a) (School / The school) is over at 3 o'clock.
   b) Mrs. White went to (school / the school) to meet her son's teacher.

4 a) Mrs. Brown goes to (church / the church) every Sunday.
   b) The workmen went to (church / the church) to repair the roof.

2 다음 중 어법상 <u>어색한</u> 것을 고르시오.

① "Do you have the time? I forgot to wear a watch."
② There are many kinds of cameras for amateurs on the shelf.
③ There are a variety of events at the resort you can enjoy every night.
④ The number of the tourists visiting the temple are increasing recently.
⑤ The vice president will take the place of the president in his or her absence.

3 다음 글을 읽고, (A)에 알맞은 말을 고르시오.

Have you ever wanted to get a spa treatment for healthier, youthful looking skin, but either couldn't find the time or didn't want to spend that much money? (A) (A variety / The variety) of anti-aging skin care products are available at a fraction of the price now. They can give you the benefits of a visit with a skin care professional in the comfort of your own home.

4 다음 주어진 단어를 이용하여 문장을 완성하시오.

1 그의 수동적인 태도를 감안할 때, 그가 성공하는 것은 불가능하다. (success, out of the question)
   Considering his passive attitude, _____.

2 그 티셔츠는 다양한 종류의 색상이 구비되어 있다. (wide, variety of)
   The T-shirts are available in _____.

3 그녀는 시대에 뒤떨어지지 않기 위하여 한 달에 두 번은 영화관에 간다. (behind)
   She goes to the cinema twice a month for fear of being _____.

4 현명한 자들은 타인의 경험으로부터 배운다. (experience)
   The wise _____ of others.

2 '아'다르고 '어'다르다!–전치사

A 다음 괄호 안에서 알맞은 말을 고르시오.

1 Arthur did not die and succeeded (in / to) the throne.

2 Water consists (in / of) two hydrogen atoms and one oxygen atom.

3 Everyone was anxious (to / for) the last of the events—fireworks.

4 Lora was anxious (about / to) leaving friends and meeting new ones.

5 (According as / According to) a Gallup poll, 67% of people say they disapprove of the law.

6 (Despite / Though) the large tax cuts, the current economic expansion is weaker.

7 (Because / Because of) the Internet, we can share information easily with others.

B 다음 〈보기〉에 주어진 단어를 이용하여 문장을 완성하시오.

Word Bank	with	about	for

1 *The Vision* mainly deals _____ fashion and trends.

2 It is said that classical music is good _____ concentration.

3 People are angry _____ the government's decision to raise the income tax.

4 Smoking is largely concerned _____ serious diseases such as lung cancer.

5 The boys are anxious _____ the upcoming match that will deliver victory to them.

6 More and more people are concerned _____ their health and want to live a long life.

C 다음 괄호 안에서 알맞은 말을 고르시오.

1 The accident (resulted from / resulted in) his carelessness.

2 Iraq's invasion of Kuwait (resulted from / resulted in) the Gulf War.

3 (In case / In case of) fire breaks out, keep a fire extinguisher in your car.

4 (In case / In case of) emergency, I keep a first-aid kit at home and in my car.

5 (Because of / Because) the increased demand, electricity went off all over town.

6 (Because of / Because) I didn't make a reservation, I had to look for a place to stay.

7 (According to / According as) the weather report, another tornado is coming soon.

Further Study

1 다음 괄호 안에서 알맞은 말을 고르시오.

1 I'm sorry (about / for) your loss.

2 I had a flat tire (in / on) the way to work, and I was late.

3 Air consists (of / in) various gases like nitrogen, oxygen, and helium.

4 (In / On) behalf of all the staff, I would like to give you a warm welcome.

5 If you want to succeed (in / to) your business, you must know how to attract customers.

2 다음 빈칸에 들어갈 말이 바르게 짝지어진 것을 고르시오.

_____ emergency, call this number for assistance from the police.
They are very _____ the destruction of natural resources.

① In spite of - good at   ② In case - anxious for
③ According to - angry about   ④ Because of - concerned with
⑤ In case of - concerned about

3 다음 글을 읽고, (A)와 (B)에 알맞은 말을 고르시오.

The sky is the region of space visible from the earth. It consists (A) (in / of) the atmosphere, which extends hundreds of miles or kilometers above the earth. Its colors result (B) (from / in) the scattering of sunlight by the gas molecules and dust particles in the atmosphere. When it is clear, the waves of blue light are scattered much more than those of any other color. As a result, it appears blue.

4 다음 주어진 단어를 이용하여 문장을 완성하시오.

1 그 보고에 따르면, 스페인이 행복지수가 가장 높다. (report)
_____, Spain has the highest level of happiness.

2 그녀가 비번일 때에는 보통 집안일을 하고 TV를 본다. (duty)
She usually does housework and watches TV when _____.

3 당신이 목표를 달성하는 것을 방해하는 도전들을 즐기려고 노력하세요. (way)
Try to enjoy challenges that stand _____ of achieving your goal.

4 여권을 잃어버리거나 도난당할 경우에 대비해서 여권을 두 장 복사해야 한다. (lost, stolen)
_____ your passport _____, you should make two copies.

The Grammar

3 Level

Concise & Core Grammar
불필요하고 잘 사용하지 않는 문법은 배제하고
핵심적인 부분만을 간결하고 정확하게 예문
중심으로 이해할 수 있도록 구성

Sentence Expansion
기초 문법을 기반으로 문장을 완성, 확장해 가는
학습 방법 적용

A Variety of Question Types
문법 포인트 확인 · 기초 문법 문제 · 응용 문제 · 문법
확장 문제 · 종합 문제

Preparation for School Tests
다양한 문제 유형을 통해 내신 대비는 물론 말하기
및 쓰기 실력 향상

Grammar Summary
배운 학습 내용을 차트 및 표로 정리하여 쉽게
암기할 수 있도록 구성

Workbook
내신 대비 및 서술형 평가 대비를 위한 충분한
분량의 문제가 수록된 워크북 제공

www.nexusEDU.kr
넥서스 초 · 중 · 고등 사이트

www.nexusbook.com
넥서스 홈페이지

Reading 시리즈

**Reading
공감
Level 1~3**

**Reading
101
Level 1~3**

**THIS IS
READING
1~4
전면 개정판**

**Smart Reading
Basic 1~2**

**Smart Reading
1~2**

**구사일생
BOOK 1~2
구문독해 204
BOOK 1~2**

**특단
어법어휘 모의고사
구문독해
독해유형**

Listening / NEW TEPS 시리즈

**Listening
공감
Level 1~3**

**After School
Listening
Level 1~3**

**The Listening
Level 1~4**

**도전! 만점
중학 영어듣기
모의고사
Level 1~3**

**만점 적중
수능 듣기
모의고사
20회 / 35회**

**NEW TEPS
실전 300+
실전 400+
실전 500+**

이것이 This is 시리즈다!

THIS IS GRAMMAR 시리즈
▶ 중 · 고등 내신에 꼭 등장하는 어법 포인트 철저 분석 및 총정리
▶ 다양하고 유용한 연습문제 및 리뷰, 리뷰 플러스 문제 수록

THIS IS READING 시리즈
▶ 실생활부터 전문적인 학술 분야까지 다양한 소재의 지문 수록
▶ 서술형 내신 대비까지 제대로 준비하는 문법 포인트 정리

THIS IS VOCABULARY 시리즈
▶ 교육부 권장 어휘를 빠짐없이 수록하여 입문 · 초급 · 중급 · 고급 · 수능 완성 · 어원편 · 뉴텝스로 어휘 학습 완성
▶ 주제별로 분류한 어휘를 연상학습을 통해 효과적으로 암기

• Reading, Vocabulary – 무료 MP3 파일 다운로드 제공
★강남구청 인터넷 수능방송 강의교재★

Concise and Core Grammar Points!

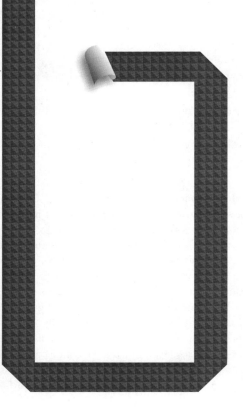

The Grammar

3 Level

Answers

NEXUS Edu

Unit 1

Exercise
P.17

A 1 quiet ⇒ quietly   2 regular ⇒ regularly
   3 surely ⇒ sure   4 happy ⇒ happily
   5 strongly ⇒ strong   6 complete ⇒ completely
   7 safe ⇒ safely   8 lately ⇒ late
   9 quick ⇒ quickly

B 1 He studied the problem briefly.
   2 Mary slept soundly in the bedroom.
   3 It was strangely quiet in the room.
   4 Some students come near the boy.
   5 He was so loved despite his faults.
   6 It's the largest eagle found in America.

C 1 Tomorrow morning we are going to go directly to the village.
   2 They are building a new school in our city next year.
   3 There are many services for free taxes in the area.
   4 The owner of the shop talks politely to the customers.
   5 Mac was frequently away from home for weeks.

A 1 목적어인 the door의 보어가 필요한 것이 아니라, 동사 opened를 수식하는 부사가 필요하다. 동사를 수식하는 것은 부사이다.
   2 부사는 동사나 형용사를 수식하는 역할을 하며, 부사가 없더라도 문장은 완벽하게 성립된다. 여기서는 동사 eat을 수식하는 부사가 필요하다.
   3 하나의 문장을 구성하기 위해 be동사 뒤에 보어인 형용사가 온다.
   4 이 문장에서 동사 play는 완전자동사로 목적어나 보어가 필요없다. 따라서 동사를 수식하는 부사가 필요하다.
   5 원급비교인 as~as...의 사이에는 문장에 맞게 형용사나 부사가 온다. be동사 뒤에는 보어가 필요하기 때문에 형용사가 와야 한다.
   6 '주어+동사'만으로 하나의 문장이 성립된 경우, 부사 completely가 와서 동사를 수식할 수 있다.
   7 부사는 동사 뒤에 위치해 동사를 수식 한다.
   8 be동사 뒤에는 보어인 형용사가 온다. lately는 부사로 '최근에'라는 뜻이다.
   9 문맥상 동사 understand를 수식하는 부사가 필요하다. 또한, 접속사 and의 앞뒤에는 같은 품사가 연결되어야 한다.

B 1 일반적으로 목적어가 있으면 부사는 목적어 뒤에 온다.
   2 목적어가 없는 자동사의 경우 일반적으로 부사는 동사 뒤에 온다.
   3 부사가 형용사를 수식하기 위해서는 우리말의 어순처럼 '부사+형용사'의 어순이 되어야 한다.
   4 동사를 수식하는 부사는 일반적으로 동사 뒤에 온다.
   5 전치사 뒤에는 명사나 명사구가 온다.
   6 분사 뒤에 다른 수식어가 올 때에는 뒤에서 앞의 명사를 수식한다.

Further Study
P.18

A (A) the only road   (B) its popularity
B 1 (A) taking   (B) to take
   2 now is the future through a digital camera.
     (=through a digital camera now is the future.)
C Chinese company's translation error
   (a translation error of Chinese company)

A

This is the only road / which completely goes across the national park. There were many tour buses in the parking lot, / which I worried would mean / the place would be too busy. The trail to the park / is sometimes a little crowded / due to its popularity.

이것은 국립공원을 완전히 가로지르는 유일한 도로이다. 주차장에 관광버스가 많은데, 이것은 그 곳이 사람들로 붐비는 것을 말해주고 있어서 걱정스럽다. 공원으로 이어지는 도로는 사람들에게 인기가 있어 때때로 약간 복잡하다.

(A) only는 내용상 '유일한' 의미의 형용사이므로 명사의 바로 앞에 위치한다.
(B) 전치사 'due to' 뒤에는 하나의 문장이 올 수 없으므로, 명사나 명사구가 와야 한다.
※ which I worried would ~에서 'I worried'는 삽입구이다.

B

This morning / I first perceived the sun's light / distracting me. The maple in front of my house / started to shed its leaves. I decided to take a few pictures / with my digital camera, / to see if I could capture some signs of seasonal change / during the day. I decided to start / by taking a picture of a falling leaf. I went outside, / saw a leaf starting to fall, / pushed the shutter button / and watched the leaf fall out of the camera's field of view. That was because I forgot the one-second delay / that happens / between the time you press the button / and the time the camera actually takes the picture. So, I missed taking a beautiful photo. I learned / that to take a digital picture / is to take a picture "one second into the future." I knew / that now is the future / through a digital camera.

오늘 아침 처음으로 내 눈길을 끄는 햇빛을 보게 되었다. 집 앞의 단풍나무 잎들이 떨어지기 시작했다. 나는 낮에 계절 변화의 흔적을 담을 수 있는지 알아보려고 디지털 카메라로 사진을 찍기로 했다. 우선 떨어지는 나뭇잎을 한 장 찍기로 했다. 밖에 나가서 떨어지기 시작하는 나뭇잎을 보고 셔터를 눌렀는데, 확인해 보니 나뭇잎은 카메라 화면에서 사라져 버리고 없었다. 그것은 셔터를 누르는 시간과 실제로 카메라가 화면을 잡는 시간 사이에 1초 정도 지연되는 것을 잊고 있었기 때문이다. 그래서 나는 예쁜 사진을 놓치고 말았다. 디지털 사진을 찍는 것은 1초 정도 지난 모습을 잡는다는 것을 알았다. 나는 디지털 카메라에서 현재의 모습은 미래의 순간임을 알았다.

(A) 전치사 뒤에는 반드시 문장이 아닌 명사의 형태가 와야 하며, 동사가 올 경우 명사 형태인 동명사로 고쳐야 한다.
(B) 주어의 위치에는 명사의 형태나 명사구(동명사, to부정사), 명사절이 올 수 있다.

C

A black family in Toronto expressed their outrage / after finding a tag on a sofa / that described the sofa's color as "nigger brown." It seems that Orangesoft, a Chinese software manufacturer, / was responsible for the tag. The Chinese software company acknowledged / its translation program was at fault / and said it was a regrettable error. The woman who purchased the sofa / met with a human rights lawyer / to consider seeking compensation. According to her, / "I had friends over from St. Lucia yesterday / and they wouldn't sit on the couch."

Toronto에 사는 한 흑인 가족은 소파 색을 nigger brown(암갈색)으로 묘사한 표시를 발견하고 모욕감을 느꼈다고 했다. 중국의 소프트웨어 제조업자인 Orangesoft가 그 표시를 한 장본인이었다. 중국의 소프트웨어 회사는 번역 프로그램이 잘못되었으며, 그것은 유감스러운 실수라는 점을 인정했다. 그 소파를 구입한 여성은 보상 청구를 고려하기 위해 인권변호사와 상담을 했다. 그녀에 따르면, 그 전날 St. Lucia에서 친구들이 왔는데, 그들이 그 의자에 앉지도 않으려고 했다는 것이다.

* 명사와 명사가 결합하는 경우 앞의 명사는 단수가 되어야 하지만, human rights lawyer는 하나의 표현으로 쓰인 것으로 예외적인 경우이다.

Unit 2

1 단순 문장-주어의 형태

Exercise

P.21

A 1 What you told me / is going to come true again.
 2 Working in this company / will be a good experience.
 3 Speaking another language / opens new doors for us.
 4 The only way to study in this country / is to join the party.
 5 A lot of people in my class / attend the class in the evening.
 6 One of the people whom I admire most / is my class teacher.
 7 Everybody in the neighborhood / participated in Christmas Festival.
 8 The test they took yesterday / consisted of long scenario questions.

B 1 Mary left her surfboard / at the beach.
 2 Thousands of languages exist / in the world.
 3 Hong Kong has seen a rapid increase / in its population.
 4 There are a lot of police cars / near my house / at night.
 5 Earthquakes also occur / in the area / near the Nansei Islands.
 6 Mike didn't show up / at Jill's party / because he had a headache.
 7 Coal and oil were formed / from plant remains / millions of years ago.

C 1 Einstein / took / a job / in a Swiss patent office.<S+V+O+부사>
 2 I / thanked / my friend / for lending me some money.<S+V+O+부사>
 3 Only a few people / are satisfied / with their jobs.<S+V+부사>
 4 I / took / a course called The Study of Islam / in Singapore.<S+V+O+부사>
 5 Hindus / call / their religious tradition / the eternal teaching.<S+V+O+C>
 6 A group of scientists / brought / help and hope / to poor farmers.<S+V+O+부사>
 7 The dream that I had last night / was / fantastic.<S+V+C>
 8 The sellers / would allow / us / to stay / through closing as their guests.<S+V+O+C+부사>

9 The helicopter tour / enabled / us / to see all the places / we couldn't drive to.<S+V+O+C>

2 단순 문장–동사의 형태

Exercise
P.23

A 1 waited for 　　　　2 angry
　　3 married 　　　　　4 discussed
　　5 familiar 　　　　　6 entered

B 2 turn 　　　　　　3 hurt
　　4 change

C 1 He kept silent and did not answer anything.
　　2 The house seemed to be large enough for the couple.
　　3 The apartments remained strong despite a few earthquakes.
　　4 I feel your product looks familiar to me.

A 1 wait는 자동사이며, 목적어가 오려면 wait for의 형태가 되어야 한다.
　　2 appear, seem, prove는 뒤에 to be가 생략되기도 하며, 보어가 필요한 동사이므로 형용사가 와야 한다.
　　3 marry는 반드시 타동사로 사용되므로 뒤에 명사 형태인 목적어가 온다.
　　4 discuss는 타동사로서 뒤에 명사형태인 목적어가 오며, talk about으로 대체할 수 있다.
　　5 remain은 '～한 상태로 남아있다'는 자동사로서, 뒤에 보어가 필요하므로 형용사가 온다.
　　6 enter는 타동사로서 뒤에 명사 형태인 목적어가 오며, go into로 대체할 수 있다.

Further Study
P.24

A 1 (A) raise (B) leave 　　2 (A) find
B 1 (A) dust (B) neat (C) turned
　　2 industrious
C 1 (A) pierces (B) makes 2 ⑤

A

Where do you place a baby little turtle / if you can't discover either of its parents? Usually young turtles are left / to live for themselves / as soon as they hatch. The answer to how you raise one / is simple: leave it alone. Turtles are protected by international agreements, / and cannot legally be taken / from the wild. If you find them / on the road, / bring them into the bush / or near watering holes.

여러분은 어린 거북이의 어미를 찾지 못한다면 어린 거북이를 어디에 두겠는가? 보통 어린 거북이들은 알에서 부화하자마자 스스로 살아가도록 내버려진다. 거북이를 기르는 방법은 단순하다. 바로 그냥 내버려두는 것이다. 국제 협약에 따라 거북이는 보호되고 있으며, 법적으로 야생 상태에서 옮길 수 없게 되었다. 길에서 거북이를 발견한다면 수풀이나 그 주변의 물이 있는 구덩이로 데려가면 된다.

(A) 목적어가 있으므로 타동사인 raise(기르다, 올리다)가 와야 한다.
(B) 목적어(it)가 있으므로 타동사인 leave가 와야 한다.
(C) 문맥상 '발견하다(find-found-found)'가 필요하다. 'found-founded-founded'는 '설립하다'의 의미이다.

B

Mom was an extraordinarily clean person. After feeding my brother and me breakfast, / she would scrub, mop, and dust everything. As we grew older, / Mom made sure / we did our part / by keeping our rooms neat. Outside, / she would tend a small flower garden, / which was the envy of the neighborhood. With Mom, / everything she touched / turned to gold. She didn't believe in doing anything halfway. She often told us / that we always had to do our best / in whatever we did.

어머니는 유별나게 청결한 분이셨다. 어머니는 나와 동생에게 아침 식사를 주고서는 모든 물건들을 문지르고, 닦고, 먼지를 털어내곤 했다. 우리가 나이를 먹자, 어머니는 우리방을 깨끗이 하는 것으로 우리의 역할을 하라고 강조하셨다. 어머니는 바깥에서 작은 정원을 손질하시곤 했는데, 이웃들은 그 정원을 부러워했다. 어머니의 손이 닿는 모든 것들은 황금으로 변했다. 어머니는 어느 것이든 대충한다는 생각을 하지 않았다. 어머니는 종종 우리에게 우리가 하는 모든 것들에 최선을 다해야 한다고 말씀하시곤 했다.

C

In the middle of the night / the sound of a wailing young child who has a fever / pierces the air. A feverish child will feel very hot or burning / but may him or herself feel cold. The first step parents need to take with a feverish child / is to get that fever down. The reality of dealing with a feverish child / can send some parents into a panic. Taking your kid's temperature / really makes one's life crazy, / especially at 3:00 in the morning. Doctors sympathize with such parents, but note that one can't ignore a fever. Sometimes, parents can't understand / that the fever itself isn't dangerous, / but it could be a sign / that there is an illness / that could cause the child some uneasiness.

한 밤중에 열이 있는 어린아이의 울부짖는 소리가 귀를 찌른다. 열이 있는 아이의 몸은 불덩이 같겠지만, 정작 아이 자신은 추위를 느낀다. 부모가 열이 있는 아이에게 해야 하는 첫 조치는 열을 내리게 하는 것이다. 사실, 열이 있는 아이를 다룰 때 어떤 부모들은 공포에 빠진다. 아이의 체온을 재면 부모들은 혼이 빠지게 되는데, 특히 새벽 3시라면 더욱 그렇다. 의사들은 그러한 부모들의 심경에 공감을 하지만, 아이의 열을 무시할 수는 없다고 알려준다. 때로는 열 자체가 해롭지 않지만 아이에게 불편함을 초래하는 어떤 질병이 있을 수 있다는 신호임을 이해하지 못하는 부모들이 있다.

(A) 주어(the sound)가 3인칭 단수 현재이므로 -s를 붙여야 한다.
(B) 주어가 동명사인 경우 단수 취급을 한다.

Unit 3

1 단순 문장-목적어의 종류

Exercise
P.27

A 1 She insists / that what Amy needs is discipline.
2 I don't know / who broke the window yesterday.
3 I gave / what I had and what I could give to the winners.
4 I used to envy / a main character in the dramas or movies.
5 I wonder / how to properly and correctly convey this emotion.
6 Most of people asked / if Christmas was Santa's or Jesus' birthday.
7 He collected / butterflies and various oddments from around the world.
8 I am enjoying / cooking and sharing delicious food with my family.

B 1 She wrote her friend a long letter.
2 He gave her some flowers on her birthday.
3 Nobody told us what to do.
4 We sent a letter to the people we met.
5 Let me cook dinner for you.

6 My father has bought a good gift for me.
7 I will try to find you those books.

C 1 you do me
2 tell me the way
3 lent me some money to
4 brought me some tapes
5 asked me for an answer

2 단순 문장-보어의 형태

Exercise
P.29

A 1 happy   2 silent
3 sweet   4 loud
5 comfortable   6 beautiful

B 1 I advised Mary to think well before starting.
2 She found the book a little too hard to read.
3 This is what happened when you took a week off.
4 When the hall lights went out, the crowd went mad.
5 I watched him take his first steps and say his first words.
6 He called him Uncle Cave Man because he lived in a cave.
7 The location has changed, but the tradition remains the same.
8 The problem is that he just doesn't understand ethnic minorities.

C 2 soft but solid   3 short
4 me to become   5 me to work hard
6 loose

A 1 look(보이다)는 뒤에 상태를 나타내는 형용사가 보어로 온다.
2 keep(~한 상태를 유지하다) 뒤에는 상태를 나타내는 형용사가 보어로 온다.
3 감각을 나타내는 동사(smell, taste, sound, look, feel)의 뒤에는 상태를 나타내는 형용사가 보어로 온다.
4 sound(들리다) 뒤에는 상태를 나타내는 형용사가 보어로 온다.
5 feel(~한 느낌이 들다) 뒤에는 어떠한 느낌인지를 나타내는 형용사가 보어로 온다.
6 동사 look(보이다)은 보어로 형용사가 필요하다.

A 1 (A) pale (B) angry
B 1 (A) you joy (B) give
C 1 what kept him alive 2 Harmony

A

Jane heard her father's loud and angry voice. Growing very pale, / she ran out into the hall. To her surprise, / her father was already halfway upstairs, / and his face turned red with rage. In the hall below / she saw her stepmother / looking troubled and getting angry.

Jane은 아버지의 화가 난 큰 목소리를 들었다. 그녀는 안색이 창백해지면서 홀(hall)로 달려 나갔다. 놀랍게도 그녀의 아버지는 이미 계단 위로 반쯤 와 계셨으며, 얼굴은 화가 난 표정이었다. 아래층 홀에는 새엄마의 난처하고 화난 표정이 보였다.

(A), (B) grow, get, turn, go, come 등의 동사 뒤에 상태를 나타내는 형용사가 오면 '~하게 되다'로 해석한다.

B

I lost touch with you for a while / and the cell phone number I had for you / no longer works. I have been thinking about you off and on, / but I haven't dared to even dream of writing a letter. I can offer you / no more than my childish best wishes / for your birthday. Nonetheless, / I hope these lines bring you joy. I wish / that I could show you / how real my feelings for you are. I wish / that I could give you this card personally / instead of mailing it to you. Would you let me give you these wishes / in the future? Happy Birthday.

내가 잠시 너와 연락을 못했고, 갖고 있던 휴대전화 번호도 연락이 되지 않더구나. 때때로 나는 네 생각을 했었지만, 난 편지 쓸 생각은 감히 꿈도 꾸지 못했어. 난 단지 네 생일을 맞아 애들처럼 안부나 물을 뿐이야. 그럼에도, 나는 이 몇 줄의 내용이 네게 기쁨을 주길 바래. 너에 대한 내 감정이 얼마나 진실한 것인지 보여줄 수 있으면 좋을 텐데. 네게 메일을 보내는 대신 이 카드를 직접 줄 수 있다면 좋을 텐데. 앞으로 내게 이런 소망을 전해줄 기회를 주겠니? 생일 축하해.

(A) 동사 bring은 '~에게 …를 가져오다'의 의미로 사용된다. 문맥상 '당신에게 즐거움을 가져온다'가 적절하다.
(B) 문맥상 '~에게 …를 주다'는 의미의 4형식 동사가 필요하다. 동사 keep은 '~에게 …를'로 사용되지 않는다.

C

It was a long car ride / to the hospital. His dad told me / how my friend, Dick, had had a mental disorder / for many years. He assured me / that whatever happened was out of our control; / we had to let Fate do its job. I walked in / as Dick yelled at the staffs / who tried to comfort him. The reaction to medication he was taking / made him think / they were poisoning his food. Sometimes he drifted in and out of consciousness. Still, he made friends at the hospital. To my surprise, / he was everybody's favorite patient. The nurses said / he was "crazy but funny." Some nurses could often rely on him / to make them laugh / when they were too stressed. They also said / he had a family / who cared for him through everything, / and that is / what kept him alive.

차를 타고 병원으로 가는 길은 멀었다. 내 친구 Dick의 아버지께서는 그가 어떻게 여러 해 동안 정신질환을 앓았는지 말해주셨다. 그는 일어나버린 일은 우리가 어찌할 수 없는 일이라며, 운명적인 일로 받아들여야 한다고 분명하게 말씀하셨다. 내가 걸어 들어갔을 때, Dick은 돌보는 간호사들에게 고함치고 있었다. 그는 약물 투여에 대한 반응으로, 간호사들이 그의 음식에 독을 넣었다고 생각했다. 때때로 그는 자기를 의식하지 못하는 경우도 있었다. 하지만, 그는 병원에서 친구들을 사귀었다. 놀랍게도, 그는 다른 사람들이 좋아하는 환자가 되어 있었다. 간호사들은 그가 미쳤지만 재미있는 사람이라고 했다. 한 간호사는 심지어 스트레스가 쌓였을 때 웃음을 만들어주는 그에게 의지할 정도라고 말했다. 그들은 또한 Dick이 그의 모든 일을 돌봐주는 가족을 두고 있으며, 그것이 그를 살아있게 해준 것이라고 했다.

Unit 4

1 복합 문장-접속사

Exercise
P.33

A 1 and 2 and 3 so
4 or 5 for 6 yet
7 for

B 1 nor 2 or 3 or
4 nor 5 for 6 but

C 2 Your father phoned this afternoon, but he didn't leave a message.
3 I didn't want to get home late, so I ran straight back.

4 Mari was not in class all day long, nor was she at home.
5 I'm not a leader now, nor do I want to be one.

2 병렬 구조-평행구조

Exercise
P.35

A 1 accurate ⇒ accurately 2 to wash ⇒ wash
3 hinder ⇒ hinders 4 to have ⇒ had
5 secure ⇒ security 6 live ⇒ alive
7 nourishing ⇒ nourishes
8 competing ⇒ competed

B 1 are 2 is 3 are
4 is 5 are

C 2 We can either fly or take the train to New York.
3 Coal is both an irreplaceable and a natural resource.
4 Not only the mosquito but also the fly spreads a disease.
5 Neither Spiderman nor Batman is going to the party.
6 Medical education can be fun(educational) as well as educational(fun).

A 1 목적어(the work) 뒤에는 보어 역할을 하는 형용사가 아니라 동사를 수식하는 부사가 와야 한다. 문맥상 부사는 생략해도 의미가 통한다.
2 either A or B(A, B 둘 중의 하나)에서 A와 B는 동일한 형태가 온다. 조동사(must) 뒤에는 동사원형이 오므로 둘 다 동사원형이 온다.
3 접속사(and)는 동일한 형태를 연결하며, 주어가 3인칭 단수 현재인 경우 동사에 -s를 붙인다.
4 not only A but also B(A뿐만 아니라 B도)에서 A, B는 같은 형태가 온다.
5 여러 개의 단어가 나열되면 마지막 단어 앞에만 접속사를 붙이며, 모두 동일한 형태가 와야 하므로 명사인 security가 온다.
6 접속사(or)의 좌우에는 같은 형태가 오며, be동사(are) 뒤에는 보어인 형용사가 온다.
7 접속사(and)는 동일한 형태를 연결하므로 주어에 연결되는 동사가 와야 한다.
8 접속사(and)의 앞과 뒤에는 주어에 연결되는 동사가 필요하다.

B 1 both A and B(A, B 둘 다)가 주어인 경우 복수동사가 따른다.
2 not only A but also B(A뿐만 아니라 B도)가 주어인 경우 B에 동사를 일치시킨다.
3 either A or B(A, B 둘 중 하나)가 주어인 경우 B에 동사를 일치시킨다.

4 neither A nor B(A, B 둘 다 아닌)가 주어인 경우 B에 동사를 일치시킨다.
5 B as well as A(A뿐만 아니라 B도)가 주어인 경우 B에 동사를 일치시킨다.

Further Study
P.36

A (A) cutting

B 1 (A) for (B) But (C) Still
2 learn to read and write, and then return

C walking and eating healthy foods will increase our energy for the rest of the day

A

In order to make their dream come true, / Mike and Amy decided not to waste money. By living temporarily with Mike's parents / and cutting their leisure expenses, / they hoped to save enough money / to buy a modest house / in two years.

그들의 꿈을 실현하기 위해 Mike와 Amy는 돈을 낭비하지 않기로 마음 먹었다. 그들은 잠시 Mike의 부모님과 함께 살고, 여가비를 적극적으로 줄여서 2년 만에 아담한 집을 살 수 있는 충분한 돈을 저축하고 싶었다.

(A) 접속사(and)로 연결되는 두 표현은 같은 형태를 가진다. 문맥상 living와 cutting은 전치사 By에 연결된다.

B

There lived a simple man / who was the person responsible / for sweeping floors and for keeping windows clean. He really did a good job, / for he was highly self-reliant / and attentive to details. He had only a little money / but he had good credit. But a new rabbi came / and insisted that everyone who lived and worked within its walls / had to be educated / enough to read and write. Still, he was illiterate / and said to the rabbi, / "I do my job well / and long to continue to do it." The rabbi frowned and said, / "I am sorry / to ask you to leave. It's my belief / that everyone in this place / should be literate. Go learn to read and write, / and then return."

마루를 청소하는 일과 유리창 청소를 담당하는 순박한 한 남자가 살았다. 그는 정말 일을 잘했는데, 왜냐하면 그는 스스로 신념이

강했고 작은 일 하나에도 세심했기 때문이다. 그는 얼마 벌지 못했지만, 신임을 얻고 있었다. 하지만 새로운 랍비가 와서, 성안에 살면서 일하는 모든 사람은 읽고 쓸 만큼 교육을 받아야 한다고 주장했다. 그러나, 그는 문맹이기 때문에, "나는 내가 할 일은 잘하고 있소. 그리고 이 일을 계속하고 싶소."라고 랍비에게 말했다. 그 랍비는 인상을 찌푸리면서, "미안하지만, 당신은 떠나야 할 것이오. 이곳에 있는 모든 사람들은 읽고 쓸 수 있어야 한다는 것이 내 신념이오. 가서 읽고 쓰는 것을 배우시오. 그리고 돌아오시오."라고 말했다.

go, come, return 등의 뒤에 to부정사가 연결되는 경우, to를 and로 교체하거나 생략하기도 한다. 이것은 '가다, 오다, 돌아오다'의 동사는 모든 동작의 기본이므로 동시에 진행되는 의미의 and로 대체될 수 있다.

C

Our bodies already knows / how to cure themselves and be healthy. Occasionally we choose not to listen to our bodies / because we don't want to hear / that we shouldn't be eating chocolate, / drinking coffee / or whatever else our body is sending signals about. It is easier / to sit on the couch in front of the TV / and eat ice cream / than to go out for a walk in nature. Both will make us feel good temporarily, / but walking and eating healthy foods / will increase our energy / for the rest of the day.

우리의 몸은 이미 자신을 어떻게 치료해야 하는지, 그리고 어떻게 건강하게 되는지 알고 있다. 때때로 우리는 쵸코릿을 먹지 말아야 한다거나 커피를 마시지 말아야 한다는 말을 들으려 하지 않고, 또 우리 몸이 무슨 신호를 보내든지 그것을 들으려 하지 않기 때문에, 우리 몸에 귀를 기울이지 않는다. 텔레비전 앞에서 의자에 앉아 아이스크림을 먹는 것이 자연 속에 산책하러 나가는 것보다 더 쉽다. 둘 다 일시적으로 우리를 기분 좋게 해주지만, 걷는 것과 건강식품을 먹는 것이 살아가는 동안 우리의 에너지를 증가시켜 줄 것이다.

Unit 5

1 주어와 동사의 일치

Exercise
P.39

A
1 are	2 was	3 is
4 have	5 were	6 is
7 have	8 has	

B
1 were ⇒ was	2 thinks ⇒ think
3 receives ⇒ receive	4 lives ⇒ live
5 stand ⇒ stands	6 decide ⇒ decides
7 have ⇒ has	8 have ⇒ has

C
1 comes	2 are	3 has
4 live	5 is	6 are
7 are	8 seems	

A 1 주어는 A number of(=many)이므로 복수형 동사가 필요하다.
   2 주어는 The number of(~의 수)이므로 단수동사가 필요하다.
   3 '분수(3분의 2)+단수명사(물질명사)'는 단수를 나타내며, '분수+복수명사'는 복수를 나타낸다.
   4 분수+복수명사가 주어이므로 복수동사가 필요하다.
   5 half+복수명사는 복수를 나타낸다.
   6 half+단수명사는 단수를 나타낸다.
   7 주어는 복수명사인 changes이므로 복수동사가 따른다.
   8 주어는 much debate이므로 단수동사가 필요하다.

B 1 주어가 a terrible earthquake이므로 단수동사인 was가 필요하다.
   2 주어인 few(불과 몇몇의)는 수를 나타내므로 복수동사가 필요하다.
   3 half(절반)이 복수명사가 결합하면 복수를 나타내며, 단수동사와 결합하면 단수를 나타낸다.
   4 people이 복수이므로 live가 와야 한다.
   5 주어가 a rock이므로 단수동사가 필요하다.
   6 Who(누구가)가 의문사로서 문장의 주어역할을 하므로 단수동사가 필요하다.
   7 A sort of drumbeat(일종의 북치는 소리)가 주어이므로 단수동사가 필요하다.
   8 문장의 주어는 The variety(다양성)이므로 단수동사가 필요하다.

2 주어+단수동사

Exercise
P.41

A
1 has	2 makes	3 has
4 is	5 dances	6 makes
7 is		

B 1 chooses 2 wears 3 means
4 has 5 is 6 appears
7 is

C 1 Ten dollars is all I have left.
2 Each child has brought some food.
3 The news was worse than I had expected.
4 Every flower has its own image.
5 Each of them has the answer.
6 Making ice cream and pies is as fun as dressing a doll.

A 1 every와 each는 무조건 단수 취급을 하므로 단수동사가 온다.
2 주어가 every bird이므로 단수동사가 필요하다.
3 학과 명칭 뒤의 -s는 복수가 아니라 단수 취급을 한다.
4 주어는 동명사(washing)이므로 단수 취급을 한다.
5 주어가 One이므로 단수동사가 필요하다.
6 주어가 동명사(Studying)인 경우 단수취급을 하므로 단수동사가 따른다.
7 주어가 시간(거리, 가격, 무게) 표현인 경우 '~라는 시간은'의 의미로서 단수 취급을 한다.

Further Study

P.42

A (A) is (B) it (C) is

B 1 (A) are (B) have (C) decide (D) have
2 taking their passports not to leave the country.

C 1 The number of Russian women who smoke has more than doubled.

A

People get passionate and heated / when talking about politics. Politics is a zero-sum game. In politics, / one party wins / and the other loses. If possible, / you should not get involved in it, / because in an environment / politics is a matter of life and death.

사람들은 정치에 관한 이야기를 할 때 열을 내고 격앙된다. 정치란 결국 남는 것 없는 제로섬(zero-sum) 게임이다. 정치에서 한 쪽이 이기면 다른 한 쪽은 진다. 어떤 환경에서는 정치란 삶과 죽음의 문제이기에, 가능하면 여러분은 정치에 관련되지 말아야 한다.

(A), (C) politics에서 -s는 학과명칭을 나타내는 표현으로서 단수로 취급한다.
(B) 문맥상 대명사도 politics를 받기 때문에 단수가 온다.

B

Every year / 20,000 Polish young people disappear, / which is large / enough to fill a medium-sized town. The 'caregivers' children meet after running away from home / are taking advantage of their difficulties / and most of them have gone unpunished. Most children who have run away from home / either commit crimes or become crime victims. An increasing number of Polish teenage girls / decide to run off abroad. Polish law doesn't provide sufficient solutions / to this. Neither the parents of the missing teenagers / nor the police who chase them / have the power to take their passports / to block them from leaving the country. This is a large loophole / in Polish legislation.

매년 2만명의 젊은 폴란드인들이 사라지는데, 이것은 중간 규모의 도시를 채울 만큼의 규모이다. 아이들이 가출을 해서 만나는 보호자들이 이들의 어려움을 이용하고 있으며, 대부분은 처벌도 받지 않았다. 가출을 하는 대부분 아이들이 범죄를 저지르거나 범죄의 희생자가 된다. 점점 많은 수의 폴란드 10대 여자아이들이 해외로 가려고 결심한다. 폴란드 법은 이에 대한 충분한 해결책을 마련해 주지 못한다. 행방불명된 아이들의 부모와 아이들을 찾는 경찰도 그들이 나라를 떠나지 못하도록 여권을 차단할 힘은 없다. 이것이 폴란드 법률의 심각한 허점이다.

(A) 주어(caregivers)가 복수이므로 복수동사가 온다.
(B) 주어는 Most children이다.
(C) 'a number of'는 복수(=many)이므로 복수동사가 온다.
(D) 'neither A nor B'가 주어인 경우, 반드시 B에 동사를 일치시킨다. the police는 복수명사로 사용되었으므로 복수동사가 온다.

C

The number of Russian women who smoke / has more than doubled / since the breakup of the Soviet Union. In 1992, just seven percent of women smoked, / compared to almost 15 percent by 2003. Over the same period, / the number of men who smoke / has risen from 56 percent to 62 percent. The Russian government needs to recognize the fact / that smoking kills one in every two smokers, / and unless it takes urgent action, / millions more Russians will die from cigarettes. The findings emphasized / that the greatest increase in smoking rates / has occurred among the least educated, / distinctly so among women. In a sign that the Russian government will take immediate action / on the tobacco epidemic, / it adopted a law / on joining the World Health Organization's Framework Convention / on Tobacco Control (FCTC).

담배를 피우는 러시아 여성의 수가 소비에트 연방의 붕괴 이래로 2배 이상 늘어났다. 2003년 여성흡연자가 거의 15% 정도인 것에 비해, 1992년에는 단지 7%의 여성이 흡연자였다. 같은 기간에 흡연을 하는 남성의 수는 56%에서 62%로 증가했다. 러시아 정부는 담배가 두 명 중 한 명꼴로 사망을 일으키고, 긴급한 조치를 취하지 않으면 수백만 명의 러시아인들이 담배로 인해 사망할 수도 있다는 사실을 알아야 한다. 흡연율의 최대 증가가 가장 교육받지 못한 사람들, 특히 여성에게 두드러지게 나타난다는 점이 눈에 띈다. 러시아 정부가 마침내 만연되고 있는 담배에 대해 즉각적인 조치를 취한다는 신호로, 세계보건기구의 FCTC(담배규제협약)에 가입하는 법안을 채택했다.

Unit 6

1 부정의 문장

Exercise
P.45

A 1 anywhere   2 any   3 never
     4 no one   5 nothing   6 ever
     7 nobody

B 2 anybody   3 anybody   4 nobody
     5 Nobody   6 nothing   7 anything

C 2 no student that knows the answer
     3 no message to anyone. I'm not a spammer
     4 nothing to happen to your twins
     5 nowhere to hide from the solar rays
     6 no food left to feed the family

A 1 이미 부정어가 있으므로 anywhere가 필요하며, not+anywhere
     는 nowhere(아무데도 ~않는)를 나타낸다.
   2 부정표현인 not과 none이 중복해서 쓸 수 없고, not ~any는
     no를 의미하므로 any가 와야 한다.
   3 대조접속사 but 뒤에 상반된 내용이 오므로 문맥상 부정표현이 필
     요하다.
   4 대조접속사 but 뒤에는 상반된 내용이 오므로 '답변하지 않는다'
     는 내용이 필요하다.
   5 내용상 부정적인 내용이 필요하며, 주어나 목적어에 부정어가 올
     수 있다.
   6 내용상 '~않다면'이 필요하지만, 이미 not이 있으므로 ever가 필
     요하다. not+ever는 never의 의미이다.
   7 문맥상 '누구도 없다'는 표현이 필요하므로 부정어가 주어로 온다.

2 도치의 문장

Exercise
P.47

A 2 d   3 e   4 b
     5 g   6 f   7 c

B 1 a   2 b   3 b
     4 a   5 a   6 b
     7 b   8 a

C 2 ever did I check the weather
     3 does the mail ever arrive before noon
     4 have I known Rosa to be dishonest
     5 did babies in the room sleep through the night

Further Study
P.48

A (A) did he

B 1 (A) nothing (B) can you
     2 does the taxi door open and close without
       your touching it

C 1 (B)

A

I was five years old / when my father introduced me / to motor sports. Dad thought it was a normal family outing / to go to a car racing event. Little did he know / that he was fueling his son with a passion / that would last for a lifetime.

내가 다섯 살이었을 때 나의 아버님이 내게 모터스포츠를 소개해 주셨다. 아버지는 자동차 경주 행사에 가는 것이 정상적인 가족 외출이라고 생각하셨다. 아버지는 한 평생 계속될 어떤 열정을 아들에게 주입하고 있다는 생각은 거의 하지 못 하셨다.

(A) 부정어나 준부정어(little, few 등)가 문두에 올 경우 뒤에는 '동사+주어'로 도치된다.

B

Fans were often used not only in Japan, / but also in Europe as well. But, only in Japan / does the taxi door open and close / without your touching it. You may think / nothing is familiar here in Japan; / everything is new experience! It's a surprise / that in Japan cell phones can be used / for banking and ticket gate passes. You find exclusive luxury cellphone stores / that require a membership before making a purchase / only in Japan. Only in Japan / can you find a mixture of many beans in food, / such as bean cakes and bean rice. These are the reasons / so many foreigners enjoy living in Japan.

부채는 종종 일본에서 뿐만 아니라 유럽에서도 사용되었다. 하지만, 일본에서는 여러분이 택시 문에 손을 대지 않고도 문이 열리고 닫힌다. 여러분들은 일본에서 모든 것이 경험한 적이 없는 낯선 것, 즉 모든 것이 새로운 경험이라는 생각을 하게 된다. 일본에서 휴대폰이 은행업무와 매표소 통과용으로 사용되는 것은 놀라운 일이다. 여러분은 오직 일본에서만 구매하기 전에 회원가입을 요구하는 호화로운 한정판 휴대폰을 보게 된다. 오직 일본에서만 콩 케이크와 콩밥 같은 음식에 콩을 섞어 먹는 것을 보게 된다. 이것들이 바로 많은 외국인들이 일본에서 즐겁게 사는 이유이다.

(A) 문맥상 모든 것이 낯설다는 내용이 필요하므로 nothing이 적절다.

(B) only+부사가 문장의 앞에 오는 것은 강조의 표현이며, 뒤에는 '동사+주어'로 도치된다.

C

Humor therapy is the art of using humor and laughter / for the relief of physical and emotional difficulties. It is said / that "a cheerful heart is a good medicine, / but a downcast spirit dries up the bones". However, not everyone will appreciate humor therapy. The only side effects of humor therapy is / that it can cause sadness, mental hurt, and alienation in persons / who are not receptive to it. Some people may consider humor for the sick or injured / as inappropriate or harmful. Therefore, it is important / to know when humor will be therapeutic / and when it will be appropriate. We should use it cautiously in cases / where the sensitivity of the person is / either uncertain or unknown.

유머치료는 사람들의 육체와 정신적인 질병의 치료를 도와주기 위해 유머와 웃음을 이용하는 기술이다. "즐거운 마음은 좋은 약이다. 하지만, 풀이 죽으면 뼈도 마른다."라는 속담이 있다. 그러나, 모든 사람이 유머치료의 진가를 인정하는 것은 아니다. 유머치료의 유일한 역효과는 그것을 받아들이지 않는 사람에게서 슬픔, 마음의 상처, 그리고 소외감을 일으킬 수 있다는 것이다. 어떤 사람들은 아프고 상처 입은 사람들에게 유머는 적절하지 못하며 해롭다고 생각한다. 그러므로, 언제 유머의 치료 효과가 있는지, 언제 유머가 적절한지 아는 것이 중요하다. 유머는 그 사람의 감수성이 불확실하거나 알 수 없는 상황에서는 조심스럽게 사용되어야 한다.

Unit 7

1 명사절

Exercise
P.51

A 1 I am proud (that) I made the best choice for my life.
2 I was convinced (that) I was right and he was wrong.
3 We proposed (that) the reports be filed within 40 days.
4 We are certain (that) all these injuries are from boat rides.
5 He insisted (that) the accident had happened on the sidewalk.
6 It is critical (that) you understand clearly what she is saying.
7 The fact (that) he is moving so well means (that) he will walk again.
8 The belief (that) arthritis pain is related to the weather is wrong.

B 1 be   2 be punished
3 should pay   4 should be
5 should, make   6 be given
7 be used

C 2 Mr. Ted will use the prize money to buy another house.
3 Peter got bonuses for doing a good job.
4 Chicago is located north or south of the equator.
5 insects have blood and ears.
6 he has letters of recommendation.

2   that S+V (=형용사/동사+전치사)

Exercise
P.53

A 2 of   3 of   4 of
5 that   6 that   7 that

B 2 I was pleased that Garry sent us the flowers.
3 I was worried that Mary was asked to resign.
4 I was delighted that they enjoyed the party.
5 I am sorry that he is in a pessimistic mood.
6 We are anxious that the uniform cost you much.
7 He is afraid that I'd get infected with disease.
8 I was frightened that Jimmy hurt the bird.

C 2 Michael was anxious that the passport was missing.
3 He was happy that they were coming to the party.
4 They were afraid that I had talked to the police.
5 They were confident of achieving a growth of four percent.

Further Study
P.54

A (A) that   (B) that

B 1 (E)

C 1 whether that is a long-term concern or not
2 of the existence of global warming

A

One day / a truck hit a pedestrian on the street. The driver argued / that the careless pedestrian was to blame / for the accident. It was difficult / to determine exactly / where the accident had taken place. Many witnesses insisted / that the accident had taken place / on the crosswalk. So, the driver was held responsible / for the accident.

어느 날 트럭이 길을 가던 보행자를 치었다. 운전수는 부주의한 보행자가 사고의 책임을 져야 한다고 주장했다. 그 사고가 어디서 발생했는지 정확히 결정하기가 어려웠다. 많은 목격자들은 그 사고가 횡단 보도에서 발생했다고 주장했다. 그래서 운전사가 그 사고의 책임을 지게 되었다.

(A) 목적절을 이끄는 접속사가 필요하다. 문맥상 '언제(when) 비난받아야 하는가'는 내용상 적절하지 않다.
(B) 문맥상 '~인지 아닌지(if)'가 아니라 단순한 목적절을 이끄는 접속사(that)가 필요하다.

B

During the season, / I usually dance around / when there is a big game. My heart rate runs high / and I usually lose about 5 pounds / from not eating / when Denver loses a game. My husband thinks / that I'm a lunatic, / but he appreciates the enthusiasm. Anyway, last May, we found out / that I was pregnant / and I was worried about the fact / that I might miss some football. After the preseason began, / I told myself / that I should be calmer and more reserved. But something was different last night. I was a little surprised / that I myself shouted and threw the clocks. As the 3rd quarter rolled into the 4th quarter / I was pumping my fists and / bouncing up and down in my

seat. Why couldn't I calm down / and just let the game go?

시즌 중 큰 시합이 있을 때 나는 보통 춤을 추며 돌아다닌다. 내 심장 박동은 빨라지고, Denver가 시합에 질 때는 먹지도 못해 대략 5파운드는 빠진다. 남편은 내가 광적이라고 생각하지만 내 열정은 인정해준다. 어쨌든, 지난 5월 내가 임신한 것을 알았고, 나는 축구시합을 놓쳐버릴 수도 있다는 사실이 걱정스러웠다. 프리시즌(preseason)이 시작 되고나서 나는 내 스스로에게 진정하고 자제해야겠다고 다짐했다. 하지만, 지난 밤은 좀 달랐다. 나는 내가 소리치고 시계를 던지는 모습에 조금 놀랐다. 3코트에서 4코트로 넘어가면서 나는 주먹을 흔들고 자리에서 몸을 들썩였다. 내가 왜 침착하지 못하고 시합을 있는 그대로 보지 못했는가?

C

There is a new proposal by the administration / to provide $500 million / to study the global warming problem. Are you concerned about climate change — global warming? I'm aware / that global warming exists. I understand / that scientific evidence supports the claim / that we've had about a one degree centigrade rise / in average temperatures over the last century. I'm also aware of the recent discoveries / that seem to have nailed down the conclusion / that much of it is man-made. I can't say / whether that is a long-term concern or not.

지구 온난화 문제를 연구하기 위해 정부가 5억 달러를 제공한다는 새로운 제안이 나왔다. 여러분은 기후 변화, 즉 지구의 온난화를 걱정하고 계십니까? 나는 지구 온난화가 일어나고 있다는 것을 인식하고 있다. 지난 한 세기에 걸쳐 지구의 온도가 약 1도 상승했다는 주장을 많은 과학적 증거들이 뒷받침하고 있는 것을 알고 있다. 나는 또한 최근 발견에서 그 상당 부분을 인간이 만든 것이라는 결론을 확정지었다는 것도 알고 있다. 나는 그것이 장기적으로 걱정거리가 되는지 여부는 말할 수 없다.

Unit 8

| 1 | 형용사절-관계대명사 I |

Exercise
P.57

A 1 which   2 whose   3 who
  4 whom   5 that   6 who
  7 whose   8 who

B 2 e 3 d 4 f
  5 b 6 g 7 c

C 2 which is located
  3 who attend(=who are attending)
  4 which was built 5 which was written

A 1 관계사절에서 선행사(tools)는 주어로 사용되므로 주격 관계대
  명사가 필요하다.
  2 선행사(animal)는 관계사절에서 소유격으로 사용되기 때문에 소
  유격 관계대명사가 필요하다.
  3 관계사절에 주어가 필요하므로 주격 관계대명사가 필요하다.
  4 선행사(someone)는 관계사절에서 목적어로 사용되므로 목적격
  관계대명사가 필요하다.
  5 관계대명사절에 주어가 필요하므로 주격 관계대명사인 that이 필
  요하다.
  6 선행사는 관계사절에서 주어역할을 하므로 주격 관계대명사가 필
  요하다.
  7 선행사는 관계사절에서 소유격으로 사용되므로 소유격 관계대명
  사인 whose가 필요하다.
  8 관계사절에 주어가 없으므로 주격 관계대명사가 필요하다.

2 형용사절–관계대명사 Ⅱ

Exercise P.59

A 1 a) which(that) b) on which c) on
  2 a) which b) from which c) from

B 1 h 2 a 3 e
  4 f 5 b 6 c
  7 g 8 d

C 2 none of whom 3 some of whom
  4 none of which 5 most of which

A 1 a. 선행사는 관계사절에서 전치사(on)의 목적어로 사용되므로,
  사물을 나타내는 목적격 관계대명사 which가 필요하다.
  b. 전치사와 목적격 관계대명사는 함께 나란히 사용될 수 있다.
  c. 전치사의 목적격 관계대명사는 생략될 수 있으며, 이 경우 전치
  사는 원래의 위치에 둔다.
  2 a. 선행사(shops)는 관계사절에서 전치사(from)의 목적어로 사
  용되므로 목적격 관계대명사가 온다.
  b. 전치사 from은 관계대명사와 나란히 사용될 수 있다.
  c. 목적격 관계대명사를 생략하는 경우 전치사는 원래의 위치에
  둔다.

A 1 (A) which (B) that
B 1 (A) which (B) which
  2 which breaks up your relationship and
  distracts you(which distracts you and
  breaks up your relationship)
C 1 most of whom respect the multi-religious
  society mutually
  2 The mutual respect (among the ethnic
  groups)

A

The Kangaroo is an animal / which lives only in
Australia. Australia is a fairly large country / that is
about the same size / as the Continental USA. But
most of its population lives only around the coastal
areas, / because two thirds of the country is desert.

캥거루는 호주에서만 서식하는 동물이다. 호주는 미국과 거의 같
은 크기를 가진 상당히 큰 나라이다. 그러나, 나라의 3분의 2가 사
막이므로 인구의 대부분은 해안 주변지역에서만 살고 있다.

(A) 관계사절에 주어가 필요하므로, 주격관계대명사(which)가 필
  요하다.
(B) 관계사절에 주어가 필요하므로, 주격관계대명사(that)가 필요
  하다.

B

Jealousy is something / which breaks up your
relationship and distracts you. You see / jealousy is a
feeling / which can cause the breakup of a relationship
/ even before you know it. I mean / jealousy is
something / which is hard to control. Jealousy can
make you do horrible things / which you normally
wouldn't even think about doing. Therefore, it is very
important / to know how to control jealousy in a
relationship.

질투는 당신의 관계를 깨버리고 주의력을 흩어버린다. 질투란 알
아차리기도 전에 관계의 단절을 일으킬 수 있는 감정이라는 것을
여러분은 알고 있다. 내 말은 질투란 억제하기 힘들다는 것이다.
질투는 여러분들이 정상적으로는 생각조차 할 수 없는 어리석은
짓을 하도록 만들어 버릴 수 있다. 그러므로, 유대관계를 맺으면서
질투를 억제하는 방법을 아는 것이 매우 중요하다.

(A) 관계사절에 주어가 없으므로 주격 관계대명사가 필요하다.
(B) 관계사절에서 동사(do)의 목적어가 필요하므로 목적격 관계대
  명사(which)가 필요하다.

C

The advertising campaign "Malaysia, Truly Asia" / is commonly heard across the world. It is sponsored by the Malaysian Government. It is designed / to attract foreign visitors to this country of 22 million people / which boasts of a diverse ethnic and religious composition. 51 percent of the population is Malay, / nearly all of whom are Muslim. Chinese make up 26 percent of the population, / most of whom are Buddhists, / while a small number are Christian. Indians constitute 7 percent of the population, / most of which are Hindu. Various ethnic groups and migrant workers, / most of whom are Indonesians, make up the remaining 16 percent of the population. In spite of the Muslim majority, / Malaysia has these various ethnic groups, / most of whom respect the multi-religious society mutually.

"Malaysia, Truly Asia"라는 광고 캠페인은 전세계에서 흔하게 듣는다. 이 캠페인은 말레이시아 정부에 의해 후원되고 있다. 이것은 매우 다양한 인종적 종교적 구성을 자랑하는 2200만의 말레이시아가 외국 관광객을 끌기 위해 기획된 것이다. 인구의 51%가 말레이 계통인데, 거의 모두가 이슬람을 믿는다. 중국계는 인구의 26%를 차지하는데, 대부분이 불교계인 반면 소수만이 기독교계이다. 인도인은 인구의 7%를 차지하며, 대부분 힌두교계이다. 다양한 인종 집단과 대부분 인도네시아 사람들인 이주근로자들이 인구의 나머지 16%를 구성하고 있다. 이슬람계가 다수임에도 불구하고 말레이시아는 3개의 다수 인종집단으로 되어 있는데, 그 대부분은 서로서로 다종교사회를 존중하고 있다.

Unit 9

1 형용사절–관계부사

Exercise
P.63

A 1 in which 2 where 3 why
4 where 5 that 6 where
7 where

B 2 where, which(that) 3 which(that), where
4 where, which(that) 5 when, which(that)

C 2 when dinosaurs dominated the earth.
3 where it was safe from robbers.
4 where she works as a waitress.
5 when we enjoy the warm weather.

A 1 선행사 the way는 관계부사 how와 함께 쓰이지 않으며, 대신 in which나 that을 사용한다.
2 선행사(the area)는 장소를 나타내며, 관계사절에서 부사로 사용되므로 where이 필요하다.
3 선행사가 관계사절에서 명사(주어,목적어,소유격)로 사용되면 관계대명사가, 부사로 사용되면 관계부사가 필요하다. 여기서는 선행사(the reason)가 부사로 사용되므로 why가 필요하다.
4 선행사(the shop)는 관계사절에서 부사로 사용되므로 관계부사가 필요하다.
5 선행사 the way는 that이나 in which와 결합한다.
6 선행사(the town)가 장소를 나타내며, 관계사절에서 부사로 사용되므로 where가 필요하다.
7 선행사(the place)는 관계사절에서 부사로 사용되므로 where이 필요하다.

2 관계사절의 다른 형태

Exercise
P.65

A 1 that 2 what 3 what
4 Whichever 5 what 6 Wherever

B 1 c 2 f 3 e
4 a 5 b 6 d
7 g

C 1 anyone what you asked me
2 what I have ordered
3 that your mom died of lung cancer
4 that I have not saved what I earned
5 that he has gained what he aimed for

A 1 선행사가 있으며, 선행사는 관계사절에서 목적어로 사용되므로 that이 필요하다.
2 anyone은 선행사가 아니며, '~에게 …를'로 사용되는 간접목적어이며, what은 목적절을 이끈다.
3 이 문장은 선행사가 없으며, discuss의 목적어로 사용되는 what절이 필요하다.
4 문맥상 '누구든지(whoever)'가 아니라 '어느 것이든지(whichever)'가 필요하다.
5 선행사가 없으며, 불완전한 문장을 이끄는 경우에는 선행사를 포함하고 있는 what(=the thing which)이 필요하다.
6 문맥상 '어느 것이든지(whichever)'가 아니라 '어디든지(wherever)'가 필요하다.

14

A (A) What   that

B 1 (A) when   (B) when   (C) why
2 advertise

C 1 produced what was in him

A

Everyone has three things in common / with everybody else in this world. The three things are: / Needs, Wants and Dreams. What most people need to discover / is that almost anything can be achieved / in their lifetimes. There are only a few details / that stand between you and the accomplishment of your dreams.

이 세상의 모든 사람들은 다른 모든 사람들과 3가지 공통점을 갖고 있다. 이 3가지는 바로 궁핍, 욕구, 그리고 꿈이다. 대부분 사람들이 알아두어야 하는 것은 이 세상을 살아가면서 어떤 일도 반드시 해낼 수 있다는 점이다. 사소한 몇 가지만이 성취되지 못해 어중간한 상태로 남을 뿐이다.

(A) 관계사절에는 목적어가 없으므로, 목적어로 사용되는 관계대명사가 필요하다. 선행사가 없으므로 선행사를 포함하는 관계사(what)가 온다.

(B) 선행사(a few details)는 관계사절에서 주어로 사용되므로 주격관계대명사(that)가 온다.

B

One of the most exciting moments in life / is when a person is finally old / enough to get a license. This is the time / when one can have independence / and go wherever one desires / whenever one wants. A person no longer has to depend on someone else / to get around all the time. However, driving a vehicle is also one of the biggest responsibilities / one will ever have / and must not be taken lightly. This is why / everyone is required to take a written test / before they are allowed to get a license. The time has come / for you to take your driver's license test! Are you fully prepared? Make sure / that you pass your road test / the first time with lots of practice. Learn / how you can be completely ready for the big test / by visiting http://www.roadtesttips.com.

인생에서 가장 짜릿한 시간 중 하나는 드디어 면허를 딸 만큼 나이가 드는 순간입니다. 이제 여러분들은 독립을 누릴 수 있으며, 준비가 되면 어디든지 갈 수 있습니다. 여러분은 더 이상 다른 사람에게 태워달라고 부탁할 필요가 없습니다. 그러나, 차를 운전하는 일은 여러분이 갖는 가장 큰 책임이며 가볍게 볼 일이 아닙니다

다. 이것 때문에 모든 사람들은 면허를 따기 전에 필기시험을 보도록 되어있는 것입니다. 여러분들이 운전면허 필기시험을 볼 시기가 왔습니다. 철저한 준비가 되었나요? 연습을 많이 해서 처음에 도로주행시험을 확실하게 통과하도록 하세요. http://www.roadtesttips.com.을 방문해서 중요한 시험에 완벽히 대비하는 방법을 배우세요.

(A) 문맥상 방법이 아니라 시간을 나타내는 관계부사(when)가 필요하다.

(B) 선행사(the time)는 관계사절에서 부사로 사용되므로, 시간의 관계부사(when)가 필요하다.

(C) 'This is why~'는 '이것 때문에'로 해석을 하며, why 앞에는 선행사 the reason이 생략되었다. 관계대명사의 경우 선행사가 생략되지 않는다.

C

Schubert spent his whole life / in poverty. But he had one noble purpose / in life. That was to write down the beautiful musical thoughts / which seemed to flow from his brain / in an endless rush of melody. As one of the most productive composers, / Schubert wrote music as freely / as one would write a friendly letter. He just produced / what was in him, / and brought us a rich treasure of music.

슈베르트는 평생 가난하게 살았다. 그러나 그는 하나의 고상한 인생목표를 갖고 있었다. 그것은 끝없이 흐르는 멜로디로 그의 머리에서 흐르는 아름다운 음악적인 생각을 작곡하는 것이었다. 가장 창작력이 풍부한 작곡자들 중 한 사람으로서 슈베르트는 사람들이 다정한 편지를 쓰는 것만큼이나 자유롭게 작곡했다. 그는 단지 그의 내부에 있는 것을 작곡했으며 우리에게 음악이라는 보배를 가져다 주었다.

Unit 10

1 의문사 의문문

Exercise

P.69

A 2 the width of the highway lane?

3 is the bridge?

4 the depth of the Atlantic ocean?

5 is an oil tanker?

6 is the moon from here?

7 is the sky from here?

B 2 d   3 g   4 b
   5 f   6 e   7 c

C 2 What brings(brought) you here?
   3 Which shoes suit me best?
   4 Why don't we go see Men In Black II?
   5 What does he look like?
   6 What made you decide to run for mayor?

2 간접의문문

Exercise   P.71

A 1 <u>Who do you think</u> would apply for this job?
   2 Could tell me <u>what the weather is like</u> today?
   3 Please tell me <u>when you received</u> the letter.
   4 Nobody knows whose side <u>the decider will</u> take.
   5 Who made it is important, but where <u>it was</u> made isn't.
   6 <u>How long do you suppose</u> the baby has been left alone at home?

B 2 has he been, he has lived
   3 did you go, you called
   4 I ride, I am

C 2 which one she wants.
   3 who left this bag here.
   4 whose painting will win the prize.
   5 what he would like for his birthday?
   6 where Bill and Teresa live?
   7 what the weather was like.
   8 why they left the country.

A 1 '의문사+do you think S+V'의 순서가 되어야 한다. who는 의문사로서 주어 역할을 하므로 Who do you think would apply~?가 되어야 한다.
   2 의문문은 종속절에서 평서문의 순서인 '의문사+S+V'의 순서가 되어야 한다.
   3 의문문(when~)이 문장에서 목적어 역할을 하므로, 간접의문문으로서 평서문의 순서가 되어야 한다.
   4 종속절인 의문문(whose side~)의 주어는 decider이므로, 평서문의 순서인 ~whose side the decider will take가 되어야 한다.
   5 의문문(where~)이 종속절에서 주어 역할을 하므로 평서문의 순서인 ~where it was made isn't (important)가 된다.(해석: 누가 그것을 만들었는가는 중요하지만, 그것이 어디서 만들어졌는가는 중요하지 않다.)
   6 생각동사(think, suppose, imagine 등)로 질문하는 의문문에서는 '의문사+do you 생각동사+S+V'의 순서가 되어야 한다. how가 형용사와 부사와 결합할 경우, '얼마나~한가'의 해석이 되며 하나의 표현으로 간주한다.

Further Study   P.72

A what the world would

B (A) what you   (B) who you are
   2 to be happy(=happiness)

C 1 wondering why your waistline is expanding

A

Just imagine / what the world would be like / if there were a universally accepted language. Our world would definitely be a better place / for all our future generations. There would be easier communication / and a less hostile and friendlier relationship among people.

세계적으로 널리 통용되는 언어가 있다면 세상은 어떻게 될까 상상해보라. 우리 미래 세대들에게 이 세상은 분명 더 좋은 곳이 될 것이다. 세상 사람들과 더 쉽게 대화를 나누고, 또 덜 적대적이고 더욱 다정한 관계가 이루어지리라.

(A) 의문문이 문장의 목적어로 사용되는 경우 '의문사+주어+동사'인 평서문의 순서로 바뀐다.

B

What are riches / and what do they have to do with you? The answer you give / shows exactly what you think of your life. Some of you will visualize riches / as an unlimited supply of money; / a large estate; a fancy yacht; a personal jet, etc. These are but objects / that reflect who you are, / and they are the tools / that you use to live your life. However, the real reason for wanting riches / is to be happy. Your riches will reflect your level of achievement; / your achievements will reflect your level of happiness. If you are not happy with your life, / then go start achieving something, / and soon you will see both happiness and riches.

부(富)란 무엇이며, 이것이 당신과 어떤 관계가 있는가? 여러분의 답변이 정확히 여러분 삶을 어떻게 생각하는가를 보여준다. 여러분 일부는 부를 무제한적으로 돈을 제공하는 것, 즉 많은 재산, 화려한 요트, 개인용 제트기 등으로 생각할 것이다. 이것은 단지 당신의 신분을 반영하는 물건일 뿐이며, 삶을 살아가는 도구에 불과하다. 하지만, 진정 부를 원하는 이유는 행복하기 위한 것이다. 당신의 부는 당신의 성취 수준을 반영할 것이며, 당신의 성취는 당신의 행복 수준을 반영할 것이다. 만약 삶에 행복을 느끼지 못한다면 다면 무엇인가를 달성하려고 해라. 그러면 곧 행복과 부를 만나게 될 것이다. 무엇인가를 달성하려고 하라. 그러면 곧 행복과 부를 만나게 될 것이다.

(A) 의문문이 문장의 목적어로 사용되었으므로 평서문의 순서가 되어야 한다.

(B) 의문문(Who are you?)이 문장의 목적어로 사용되었으므로 간접의문문인 평서문의 순서(의문사+주어+동사)가 된다.

C

Are you wondering / why your waistline is expanding? Current research suggests / that many factors work together / to influence your weight. These include genetics, eating habits, hormones / and psychological factors. However, your intimate friends can influence your weight even more / than anything else. If your close friends become obese, / it's likely you'll become obese, too. The effect has much more to do with social norms: / whom we look to / when considering appropriate social behavior. Having fat friends / makes being fat seem to be more acceptable. Consciously or unconsciously, / people look to friends / when you deciding how much to eat, / how much to exercise / and how much weight is 'too much'.

여러분은 왜 여러분의 허리선이 늘어나는지 궁금하십니까? 현재 연구결과 많은 요인들이 체중에 영향을 미친다고 한다. 여기에는 유전공학, 습관, 호르몬, 그리고 심리적인 요인들이 포함된다. 하지만, 다른 어떤 것보다 여러분의 친한 친구가 훨씬 더 체중에 영향을 미친다. 친한 친구가 비만이면 여러분 역시 비만이 되기 쉽다. 이러한 영향은 사회적 기준과 관련이 있다: 적절한 사회적 행동을 고려할 때 우리가 의지하는 사람, 뚱뚱한 친구가 있다는 것 때문에 비만을 더욱 받아들이게 만든다. 의식적이든 무의식적이든 사람들은 얼마나 먹어야 할지, 얼마나 많이 운동을 해야 하는지, 그리고 얼마나 많은 몸무게가 지나칠 정도인지를 결정할 때 친구를 기준으로 한다.

Unit 11

1 시간의 문장 I

Exercise
P.75

A 2 open
   4 will announce
   6 has changed

   3 have played
   5 are
   7 gets

B 2 d
   5 g

   3 f
   6 c

   4 b
   7 e

C 2 we were kids.
   3 his illness began.
   4 we were young.

5 I saw you in the newspaper.
6 their mother went off to work.
7 he had his accident.

A 1 시간의 부사절에서는 미래를 현재시제로 나타낸다.

   2 the moment는 시간의 접속사(when)를 대신하며, 시간의 부사절이므로 미래 대신 현재시제를 사용한다.

   3 since(~한 이래)가 사용되는 경우 주절은 '지금까지 ~해왔다'는 의미의 완료시제를 사용한다.

   4 when은 접속사가 아니라 의문사로서 간접의문문을 이끈다. 시간의 절이 명사절로 사용되면 미래를 미래시제로 나타낸다.

   5 when은 시간의 부사절을 이끄는 접속사이므로, 미래가 아닌 현재시제를 사용한다.

   6 since(~한 이래)와 함께 사용하는 주절은 완료시제를 사용한다.

   7 by the time(~할 때 즈음)은 시간의 부사절을 이끄는 접속사 역할을 하며, 시간의 부사절에서는 미래대신 현재시제를 사용한다.

2 시간의 문장 II

Exercise
P.77

A 1 when
   3 Once
   5 talking
   7 since

   2 As soon as
   4 until
   6 By the time

B 1 c
   4 a

   2 f
   5 b

   3 d
   6 e

C 2 I will take good care of your kids while you are away.

   3 He always feels excited and does his best every time he plays golf.

   4 I never thought about people holding babies until my son was born.

   5 Don't jump out. You can be safe only so long as you stay in the lifeboat.

   6 The city is pleasant for tourists so long as there is no crime.

   7 It is not very difficult, so don't be afraid as you can ask about any problems.

A 1 시간의 부사절이므로 현재시제(returns)를 사용하고 있으며, 문맥상 '~동안'이 아니라 '~할 때'가 적절하다.

   2 시간의 부사절이므로 현재시제(arrives)를 사용하고 있으며, 문맥상 '~하자마자'가 필요하다.

   3 once는 문장 앞에서 '일단 ~하기만 하면'의 의미이며, 문맥상 while(~동안)은 적절치 않다.

   4 시간의 부사절이므로 현재시제(retires)를 사용하고 있으며, 문맥

상 until이 적절하다.

5 접속사 뒤에 주어를 생략하고 분사를 사용할 수 있으며, 주어(You)의 능동적 행동이므로 현재분사가 필요하다.

6 문맥상 since(~때문에)가 아니라 by the time(~할 때 즈음)이 적절하다.

7 문맥상 '~이래로(since)'가 필요하다. (*studious 학문을 좋아하는)

Further Study

P.78

A (A) running   (B) as

B 1 (A) will remain   (B) have been falling
  2 prices will stay flat until the fourth quarter

C 1 If I have been smoking for 10 years since 15 years old and smoke continually

A

In spite of wandering deep in the forests for months, / I only encountered bears a few times. Whenever running away from me, / they beat a hasty retreat. Meeting up with both mothers and their cubs / might have been a little dangerous, though. So we made a bit of noise / as we advanced, / giving the mother bear and her cubs plenty of time / to move away.

숲 속 깊이 여러 달 돌아다녔음에도 나는 불과 몇 번 정도만 곰을 보았다. 곰은 나를 보고 도망을 갈 때마다 급하게 도망을 갔다. 하지만, 어미와 새끼 둘 다와 마주쳤다면 약간 위험했을 것이다. 그래서, 우리는 앞으로 걸어갈 때 어미 곰과 새끼들이 도망갈 시간을 충분히 갖도록 조금 시끄럽게 했다.

(A) 부사절을 이끄는 접속사 뒤에 '주어+be'를 생략하는 경우가 있다. 이것은 문장을 간략히 표현하는 분사구문을 만드는 방법이기도 하다. 이 경우 주어(a bear=it)가 능동적인 경우이므로 현재분사를 사용한다.

(B) like는 접속사로서 '~처럼'을 나타내며, as는 접속사로서 다양한 의미(~때, ~하기 때문에, ~함에 따라, ~하면서 등)를 나타낸다. 여기서는 문장을 이끄는 접속사로서 '~할 때'의 의미가 필요하다.

B

Purchasing of office paper has been on the decrease / for more than a year, / and lower demand reduced prices / in the first half of 2006. A purchasing and price recovery this year / remains very much in doubt. Economists believe / sales volume will remain the same / until the first quarter of 2007. Market prices peaked at the end of 2004 / and have been falling ever since. Most buyers believe / it might be fruitless / to try to recoup lost revenues / because there hasn't been any improvement in demand. Some buyers believe / prices will stay flat / until the fourth quarter.

신문 용지의 구매가 1년 넘게 계속 감소해왔으며, 수요 감소는 2006년 전반기의 가격을 하락시켰다. 올해 구매력과 가격의 회복은 지극히 회의적이다. 경제학자들은 판매량이 2007년 1/4분기까지는 똑같을 것이라고 믿고 있다. 2004년 말에 절정에 달했던 시장 가격은 그 이후 지금까지 계속 하락해왔다. 대부분의 구매자들은 여전히 수요가 개선되지 않았기 때문에 잃어버린 매출을 회복하려고 노력하는 것은 소용없을 것으로 믿는다. 어떤 구매자은 4/4분기까지 가격이 평행선을 그을 것으로 믿고 있다.

(A) 문맥상 '~까지 계속된다'는 내용이므로 미래시제가 온다.
(B) since(~이래로)가 있는 경우 '죽~해왔다'는 의미의 완료시제가 필요하다.

C

If I have been smoking for 10 years / since 15 years old / and smoke continually / how long will I live? Though the health risks of smoking are not uniform / across all smokers, / smokers die 10 years younger on average / than non-smokers. One in three smokers die early / from smoking-related diseases. However, quitting the habit at age 50 / can halve the smoking-related risks, / while quitting at age about 30 can practically eliminate them altogether. Smoking makes it 3 to 4 times more likely / that you will get heart disease, / and twice as likely / that you will have a stroke. Stroke victims will tell you / just how much painful such illnesses are, / if they can still talk. Half of all teenagers that smoke / will die from smoking-related diseases. On average, / they will lose 16 valuable years of life.

내가 15세부터 10년간 담배를 피워왔고, 또 계속 피운다면 나는 얼마나 오래 살까? 흡연의 건강상 위험이 모든 흡연자들에게 균일하지는 않겠지만, 흡연자들이 비흡연자들보다 평균 10년은 더 일찍 죽는다. 흡연자 3명 중 1명은 흡연관련 질병으로 일찍 죽는다. 하지만, 50세에 금연을 하면 흡연과 관련된 위험을 절반으로 줄일 수 있는 반면, 30세에 중단한다면 사실상 위험성을 모두 제거하게 된다. 흡연은 심장병에 걸릴 확률을 3~4배 정도 높이며,

18

뇌졸증에 걸릴 확률은 2배 정도 높게 한다. 뇌졸중 환자가 살아서 말을 한다면, 그러한 질병이 과연 도대체 얼마나 고통스러운지 전해줄 것이다. 담배를 피는 10대들의 절반은 흡연관련 질병으로 죽을 것이다. 평균적으로 그들은 귀중한 16년의 인생을 잃어버릴 것이다.

Unit 12

1 조건 · 가정의 문장

Exercise   P.81

A 2 c   3 b   4 e
   5 d   6 g   7 f

B 2 would hop
   3 would return
   4 would have never happened
   5 would be
   6 would be
   7 could have been considered
   8 might not have

C 1 had
   2 were(현대영어에서는 was도 가능)
   3 drive(단순가정)   4 had not bought
   5 had brought   6 had turned
   7 had started

2 소망 · 가정의 문장

Exercise   P.83

A 1 left   2 knew
   3 had known   4 have been
   5 have met   6 exist
   7 be

B 1 c   2 e   3 b
   4 d   5 g   6 f
   7 a

C 2 could have gone
   3 could have called him up
   4 could have applied
   5 could have saved
   6 could sleep

A 1 '~할 때이다'는 현재 이루어지지 않는 사실에 대한 가정이므로, 현재에 대한 가정의 시제를 따른다.
   2 주절의 시제가 현재이며, 현재에 대한 가정이므로 과거동사가 온다.
   3 과거부사(10 years ago)가 있으므로 과거에 대한 가정을 나타낸다. I wish ~는 '~라면 좋을 텐데'의미의 가정 표현이다.
   4 '~가 없었다면(If it had not been for~)'은 과거에 대한 가정이므로, 주절도 과거에 대한 가정의 시제를 필요로 한다.
   5 the world war는 과거의 일이므로 과거에 대한 가정을 나타낸다.
   6 현재 존재하는 것을 없는 것으로 가정하므로 현재에 대한 가정이다.
   7 부사절은 과거에 대한 가정이지만, 주절은 현재를 나타내는 부사(now)가 있으므로 현재에 대한 가정을 나타낸다.

Further Study   P.84

A (A) were   (B) would
B 1 (A) were   (B) turned   (C) would
   2 their jobs
C 1 would have reached Mars in 186 seconds

A

If I were prime minister, / my top priority would be the national educational and economic systems. As prime minister, / I would also grant money / for education and health issue. A good country must have competent teachers and medical staff. A prime minister should pay more attention / to the pensioners and the handicapped people.

내가 수상이라면 나의 우선적인 관심사는 국가의 교육과 경제체계가 될 것이다. 수상으로서 나는 또한 교육과 건강 문제에 자금을 제공할 것이다. 좋은 나라는 유능한 교사와 의료진을 가져야 한다. 수상은 연금 수혜자와 장애인들에게 더 많은 관심을 기울여야 한다.

현재의 내용을 가정하는 내용이므로, 'If S+V(과거동사 또는 were), S+would(could, might)+동사원형 ~'의 형태를 따라야 한다.

B

Have you heard about cars / not using gas but water? Many major car manufacturers are already building automobiles / that use this technology, / but the facts aren't well known around the world. If the technology were fully revealed to the general public now, / what would happen? We use fossil fuel, / such as petroleum and natural gas, / to generate energy for transportation. If everyone turned to water / to run their cars, / there would be much chaos in the oil industry / because of sudden demand decrease. The chaos would have a heavy impact on the economy / and many people would not make a living.

연료를 사용하지 않고 물을 이용하여 달리는 차에 대해 들어본 적이 있는가? 많은 주요 자동차 제조업자들은 이미 이런 기술을 사용하는 자동차를 만들고 있다. 하지만, 그러한 사실은 세상에 잘 알려져 있지 않다. 현재 그 기술이 일반 대중에게 완전히 알려진다면 어떻게 되겠는가? 우리는 운송 수단의 동력을 얻기 위해 천연가스와 같은 화석연료를 사용한다. 모든 사람들이 차를 움직이기 위해 물에 의지한다면 갑작스런 수요 감소로 석유 산업에 상당한 혼란이 생길 것이다. 그 혼란은 경제에 심각한 영향을 미칠 것이며, 많은 사람들은 생계를 이어가지 못할 것이다.

(A) 현재의 내용을 가정하므로 가정법 형태(If S+과거동사, were)를 취한다.

(B), (C) 가능성 없는 현재의 내용을 가정하는 내용이므로, 부사절에는 '과거동사', 주절에는 'would(could, might)+동사원형'이 온다.

C

Many people went outside / around August 27 this year / to observe the close encounter / between Earth and Mars. On August 27, / when Mars was closer to Earth / than ever in human history, / the one-way travel time of light was just 3 minutes and 6 seconds. Thus, / if you had turned a light / toward Mars that day, / it would have reached Mars / in 186 seconds. Mars was so bright / that even the lights of the city didn't get in the way. If you missed this astronomical show, / you're really out of luck. Mars will not be this close again / until the year 2287.

올해 8월 27일에는 많은 사람들이 지구와 화성이 가까워지는 현상을 관찰하기 위해 야외로 나갔다. 8월 27일, 인류 역사상 유례없이 화성이 지구와 가까워진 순간이 있었는데, 한 방향으로 빛이 쏘아졌을 때 단지 3분 6초면 다다를 수 있는 거리에 있었다. 따라서, 만약 당신이 그날 화성을 향해 빛을 쏘았다면, 그것은 186초만에 화성에 도달하였을 것이다. 화성의 빛은 너무 밝아서 도시의 빛들조차 그 빛을 막을 수 없었다. 당신이 만약 이 천문학적인 쇼를 놓쳤다면 당신은 정말 불운한 것이다. 왜냐하면, 화성은 2287년까지 다시는 이 정도로 가까워지지 않을 것이기 때문이다.

Unit 13

1	원인/이유의 문장

Exercise

P.87

A 1 Because of 2 therefore
3 because 4 so that
5 because of

B 1 due to 2 why
3 why 4 because
5 resulted from 6 resulted in

C 2 resulted from stress and spicy food.
3 to take back their areas, so we need to defend our territory.
4 would not stay closed because my suitcase had become damaged.
5 are killed and butchered. That is why we dislike and fear humans.

2	결과/목적의 문장

Exercise

P.89

A 2 so, such a 3 such a, so
4 so, such a

B 2 soft 3 well
4 pitiful 5 far away (=long)

C 2 such, nobody believed anything he said.
3 so, all the streams were frozen.
4 so, everybody took him for a college student.
5 so as not to block(in order not to).

Further Study

P.90

A (A) so (B) in
B 1 (A) because (B) why
2 mental comfort to patients
C 1 it takes around four hours to digest.
(= it takes longer to digest than mother's milk.)

A

Chinese tend to 'hide the broken arm / in the sleeve' a lot. They think / appearance matters so much / that it's better / to hide painful truth. However, last month / when some products were found corrupt and unsafe in China, / the Chinese government responded immediately to the problems / that resulted in many deaths around the globe.

중국인들은 부러진 팔을 소매 속에 감추는 경향이 있다. 그들은 외형이 상당히 중요하다고 여겨서 아픈 진실을 감추는 것이 더 좋다고 생각한다. 하지만, 지난 달 중국에서 몇몇 제품이 부패하고 안전하지 못한 것이 발견되었을 때 중국 정부는 전 세계적으로 사망 사건을 일으킨 문제 제품들에 즉각적인 반응을 보였다.

(A) 부사의 형태인 so 뒤에는 부사나 형용사가, 형용사의 형태인 such 뒤에는 명사의 형태가 반드시 필요하다. 부사(much)가 등장하므로 so가 필요하다.

(B) 어떤 일의 결과를 나타낼 때 'result in+결과의 내용'을 사용한다. 문맥상 죽음이라는 결과를 야기했으므로 result in이 필요하다.

B

Patients can have sugar pills(placebos) from doctors / and gain improvements in their health; / this is because the mental comfort doctors give patients / is often just as effective / as medication. On average, around one third of people taking placebos for complaints including pain and headache / will experience relief from symptoms. Even simply participating in a medical study / can have a positive effect on a person's health. That's why / researchers make both participants and staff unaware of / whether any particular patient receives placebos / or real medication. About 90 percent of people taking placebos in studies / see their symptoms improve.

환자들은 의사에게서 가짜 약인 설탕 덩어리를 받아 먹고 건강의 개선효과를 얻는다. 이것은 의사가 환자에게 주는 정신적 위안이 때로는 약물 치료와 마찬가지의 효과가 있기 때문이다. 평균적으로, 고통과 두통을 호소해서 가짜 약을 먹는 사람들의 3분의 1이 증상의 경감을 경험할 것이다. 심지어 단순히 의학적 연구에 참가하는 것만으로 개인의 건강에 긍정적인 효과를 미친다. 그것 때문에 연구원들은 가짜 약을 사용하면서 연구 참가자와 직원들에게는 특정 환자가 가짜 약을 받는지 실제 약물 치료를 받는지 모르게 한다. 시험에서 가짜 약을 먹은 사람들의 약 90%가 증상의 개선을 보인다.

(A) 문맥상 앞의 내용이 결과, 뒤의 문장이 원인을 나타내므로 because가 온다.

(B) 문맥상 앞의 내용이 원인, 뒤의 문장이 결과를 나타내므로 why가 온다.

C

Breast milk is more easily digested, / as it doesn't cause gas in babies. Moreover, even though dairy milk is higher in iron / it isn't easily absorbed, / resulting in the baby receiving fewer vitamins / than it should. As a result of human milk being easily digested, / a baby feeds on it more frequently; / it takes about half an hour to digest, / whereas the dairy alternative takes around four hours. This explains / why a bottle-fed child tends to sleep longer, / which is not an advantage.

모유는 아기에게 가스를 유발하지 않기 때문에 더욱 쉽게 소화된다. 더욱이나 우유가 철분은 더 높지만, 쉽게 흡수가 되지 않아서 아기는 보다 적은 양의 비타민을 흡수하는 결과가 생긴다. 모유는 쉽게 소화가 되기 때문에 아기는 더욱 자주 수유를 하게 된다. 모유의 경우 소화하는데 30분이 걸리는 반면 그 대용으로서의 우유는 약 4시간이 걸린다. 이러한 사실은 우유를 먹고 자라는 아이가 별 도움도 되지 않는 잠을 왜 그렇게 더 오래 자는지 잘 설명해 준다.

Unit 14

1　대조의 문장–양보절

Exercise

P.93

A 2 b　　　　3 a　　　　4 d
　　5 c　　　　6 f　　　　7 e

B 2 I can get a rental car.
　3 he lacks any reality.
　4 he still wasn't tired.
　5 he could not(couldn't) speak fluently.
　6 we arrived very late.
　7 There are spiders somewhere in my house.

C 2 he may work(he works), he still has to take work home with him.
　3 you complain, the UK has an excellent schooling system.
　4 you feel, there are some things you can't just take back.
　5 the night may be(the night is), somehow the sun rises once again.

Exercise
P.95

A 1 instead of   2 like
3 instead of   4 like
5 unlike   6 unlike
7 instead   8 unlike

B 2 d   3 b   4 c
5 g   6 e   7 f

C 2 lazily watched the ants
3 are just getting active
4 say half of what we know
5 preserved the seeds for planting
6 to have the deer
7 is seen as attractive

A 1 instead는 부사(그 대신에)이며, instead of(~대신에)는 전치사로서 뒤에 반드시 명사가 온다.

2 like는 전치사나 접속사로서 '~처럼'의 의미이며, unlike(~와 달리)는 전치사로서 뒤에 명사가 온다.

3 뒤에 명사 형태인 동명사가 등장하므로 전치사인 instead of(~대신에)가 필요하다.

4 뒤에 하나의 문장이 오므로 접속사 역할을 하는 like(~처럼)가 필요하다.

5 뒤에 명사(ancestors)가 오므로 전치사인 unlike가 필요하다. who~는 선행사인 ancestors를 수식한다.

6 as는 전치사인 경우 '~로서'의 의미이며, unlike(~와 달리)는 전치사로서 뒤에 명사가 온다. 문맥상 unlike가 필요하다.

7 문맥상 부사인 instead(그 대신에)가 필요하다.

8 문맥상 '다르다'는 내용이 등장하므로 unlike(~와 달리)가 적당하다.

Further Study
P.96

A (A) Unlike
B 1 (A) Nevertheless   (B) since
     2 Russian soccer team
C 1 it takes long to commute to the work(=he has to get up an hour earlier to commute)

A

Mercury is much less like the Moon / than scientists previously thought. Unlike the Moon, / Mercury has huge cliffs, / which range from hundreds of kilometers / across the planet's surface. Mercury also has a surprisingly powerful gravity.

과학자들이 전에 생각한 것보다 수성은 달과 별로 닮지 않았다. 달과는 달리, 수성은 거대한 절벽을 갖고 있는데, 그 절벽은 표면을 가로질러 수백 킬로미터 구불구불 굽어 있다. 수성은 또한 놀랍게도 강력한 중력을 갖고 있다.

(A) 문맥상 수성과 달은 닮지 않았음을 강조하므로, '~와 달리'를 나타내는 unlike가 적당하다.

B

Our soccer team gained third place / at the tournament / as we beat China 4:2. The Brazilian team celebrated a victory at the world competition / after they defeated Japan 3:2 in overtime. I think / our team could have achieved better results, / but the Russian team was not very lucky / in the semifinals match against Japan, / where they suffered defeat in overtime. Nevertheless we were excited to win the bronze / and I think it was a great achievement for us. I'm very happy / we won the bronze medal / and I don't want to think about / what would have happened / if we had played better / since the bronze medal was a good result. To my mind, / players should fight for victory in a game / and at the same time should not forget about supporters.

우리 축구 팀이 중국을 4:2로 이기고 선수권대회에서 3위를 했다. 브라질 팀이 일본 팀을 연장전에서 3:2로 이긴 후 세계선수권대회 우승을 했다. 내 생각에 우리 팀은 더 좋은 결과를 얻을 수도 있었다. 하지만, 러시아 팀은 일본 팀과 준결승전에서 운이 나빠 연장전에서 패배를 하고 말았다. 그럼에도 불구하고 우리는 동메달을 거머쥐어 흥분했으며, 내 생각에 이것은 우리에게 굉장한 업적이다. 우리는 동메달을 따서 기쁘며, 3등이면 좋은 결과이기에 좀 더 잘했으면 어떻게 되었을까라는 생각은 하고 싶지 않다. 내 생각에, 선수들은 승리를 위해 싸워야 하며, 동시에 응원하는 사람들을 잊지 말아야 할 것이다.

(A) 문맥상 otherwise(그렇지 않으면)가 아니라, nevertheless (그럼에도 불구하고)가 적당하다.

(B) 문맥상 whereas(반면에)가 아니라 since(~때문에)가 적당하다.

C

Is it fair / to want to live close to my work? My fiancée and I have a plan / to move to New York City / and the place I want to work at / is located in the center of the city. I've suggested living right in the center of the city / to walk to work, / but she would like to live out in the suburbs. Whenever we talk about it, / we get into an argument. Though her reasons are not that clear, / I think it's because of noisy neighbors, / along with a 'looking to the future' attitude / that we might need a house for kids. She doesn't work currently, / so it doesn't really matter to her / where we live, / whereas I must wake up an hour earlier every day / if we live in the suburbs.

내가 직장 가까이 살고 싶다는 것은 과연 공평한 것인가? 내 약혼녀와 나는 뉴욕으로 이사할 계획인데, 내가 근무하고 싶은 장소가 그 도시 중심에 위치해있다. 나는 직장에 걸어갈 수 있도록 도심에 살 것을 제의해 왔지만, 그녀는 교외 지역에 나가서 살고 싶어 한다. 우리는 이 이야기를 할 때마다 논쟁을 벌이게 된다. 그녀가 반대하는 이유는 분명하지 않지만, 아이가 생기면 집을 필요로 한다는 미래지향적 태도도 있고, 또한 이웃이 시끄럽기 때문이라고 생각한다. 그녀는 현재 직장을 갖고 있지 않아서, 우리가 어디에 사느냐 하는 것은 그녀에게 사실 중요하지 않다. 반면 나는 교외에 산다면 매일 한 시간 더 일찍 일어나야만 한다.

Unit 15

1   원급의 비교

Exercise
P.99

A 1 hard
    2 smoothly
    3 severe
    4 those for humans
    5 like
    6 those
    7 as
    8 than

B 2 as few as
    3 as much as
    4 as little as
    5 as few as
    6 as little as
    7 as much as
    8 as many as

C 2 as valuable as
    3 as cold as
    4 as strong as
    5 as popular as
    6 as cheap as
    7 as fluent as

A 1 be동사의 보어가 필요하므로 형용사인 hard(힘든)가 필요하다.
    2 동사 go about(돌아다니다, 진행되다)을 수식하는 표현이 필요하므로 부사가 와야 한다.
    3 동사 look은 상태를 설명하는 보어가 와야하므로 형용사가 필요하다.
    4 A와 B를 비교할 경우, A, B는 동일한 형태가 되어야 하므로 '인간의 경우 암의 위험들'을 나타내는 대명사 those가 필요하다.
    5 like는 seem, feel, look 등과 결합하여 '~처럼'의 의미로 사용된다.
    6 주어가 '인간의 청각신경'이므로 비교의 대상도 '다른 포유동물의 청각신경(auditory neurons)'이 언급되어야 하므로, neurons를 대신하는 복수형 대명사가 필요하다.

7 비교를 나타내는 than은 '비교급+than', as는 'as~ as…'의 형태로 사용된다.
8 비교급(more) 표현이 등장하므로 than이 필요하다.

2   비교 문장

Exercise
P.101

A 2 blacker – blackest
    3 more valuable – most valuable
    4 more disappointed – most disappointed
    5 prettier – prettiest
    6 more confident – most confident
    7 hotter – hottest
    8 more alike – most alike
    9 likelier – likeliest(more likely – most likely)

B 2 e   3 c   4 f
    5 b   6 g   7 d

C 2 more likely(=likelier)   3 hottest
    4 more alike   5 less dangerous
    6 most common(commonest)
    7 cheapest   8 latest

* 비교급 만드는 원칙
1 비교급에 -er, 최상급에 -est를 붙이지만, 대부분의 2음절 이상의 형용사와 -ly로 끝나는 부사에는 단어 앞에 more~, most를 붙인다. (예: careful, beautiful, seriously 등)
2 마지막 자음을 추가하는 경우 : 1음절의 형용사와 부사가 단모음+단자음으로 끝나면 비교급에서 마지막 자음을 추가한다. (예: big, fat, hot, sad, thin, wet 등)
3 a-로 시작하는 형용사 : 보어로만 사용되는 형용사로서 비교급과 최상급은 반드시 more, most를 붙여 만든다. (예: alike, afraid, ashamed 등)

Further Study
P.102

A (A) greater   (B) worse
B 1 (A) less   (B) as
    2 earn as much as
C 1 ②, ④

A

> Scientists found / that the heavier an object is the easier / it is to balance it. Once everything is set in motion / it resists change and movement. Also, once a weight has balance on a point, / the object has a stable state. The greater the weight, the more stable, / therefore the lighter the worse.
>
> 과학자들은 물체가 더 무거울수록 그 물체의 균형을 잡기가 더욱 쉽다는 것을 발견했다. 일단 모든 것은 움직이기 시작하면 변화와 움직임에 저항을 갖는다. 또한, 일단 무게가 어느 한 지점에서 거의 균형을 잡게 되면 물체는 안정을 찾는다. 무게가 무거울수록 더욱 안정된다. 그러므로 가벼우면 가벼울수록 더욱 나빠지는 것이다.

(A) '무거우면 더욱 안정된다'는 내용이므로, 'the 비교급, the 비교급'으로 표현한다.

(B) '무거우면 더욱 안정된다'는 내용이므로, 가벼울수록 나쁘다고 해야 자연스럽다.

B

> While women have made notable gains in education / since the 1980s, improvements in pay equity / haven't been achieved. As early as one year out of college, / women working full-time already earn less / than their male counterparts / even when they work in the same field. Ten years after graduation, / women fall further behind, / earning only 68 percent as much as men. Accounting for occupation, parenthood, position, and other factors / normally associated with pay, / college-educated women still earn less / than their male peers. The research indicates / that one-quarter of the pay gap remains unexplained / and is likely due to sex discrimination.
>
> 1980년 이래 여성들의 교육이 현저하게 증가한 반면, 급여의 공평성은 이루어지지 않았다. 대학 졸업 1년 후, 고용직 여성들은 같은 분야에 근무하는 남성 동료들보다 훨씬 더 적게 번다. 대학 졸업 후 10년이 되면 여성들은 훨씬 더 뒤져서 남성의 68% 정도 밖에 벌지 못한다. 직업, 부모의 신분, 지위 그리고 급여와 관련된 여러 요인들을 고려하더라도, 대졸 여성은 여전히 남성 동료보다 더 적은 급여를 받는다. 급여 차이의 4분의 1을 설명을 할 수는 없지만, 십중팔구 그것은 성적차별 때문이라는 연구결과가 있다.

(A) 내용상 여성이 남성보다 더 적게 번다는 내용이므로 less가 와야 한다.

(B) 원급비교는 'as ~ as…'의 표현을, 비교급은 '-er than, 또는 more + 형용사 or 부사 + than'의 표현을 사용한다.

C ① 판매된 사과의 무게가 최대 규모이다.
　② 판매된 오렌지의 무게가 체리의 세 배나 된다.

　③ 판매된 망고의 무게는 체리의 세 배나 된다.
　④ 배와 망고의 무게를 합하면 오렌지의 무게와 같다.
　⑤ 체리와 오렌지의 무게를 합하면 사과의 무게보다 더 많다.

Unit 16

1　동사의 단순 시제

Exercise

P.105

A 1 tells
　2 Did you take
　3 didn't get
　4 decided
　5 returned
　6 got
　7 receives

B 2 b, a　　　3 b, a　　　4 a, b

C 2 I last visited Russia when I was 14.
　3 He went to the Italian restaurant last night.
　4 The market closed at 7 on Friday.
　5 I read it last year.

A 1 시간과 조건의 부사절에서는 미래 시제 대신 현재 시제를 사용한다.
　2 과거 시제를 나타내는 부사가 있는 경우 반드시 과거 시제만 사용한다.
　3 when(~할 때, 언제)은 한순간의 시제를 나타내므로 단순 시제(과거, 현재, 미래)와 결합한다.
　4 when은 한 순간의 시제를 나타내므로 단순 시제인 과거가 와야 한다.
　5 명백한 과거를 나타내는 부사가 있으므로 과거 시제를 사용한다.
　6 과거를 나타내는 부사(ago)는 과거 시제와 결합한다.
　7 시간을 나타내는 부사절이므로 미래를 현재시제로 표현한다.

2　동사의 완료 시제

Exercise

P.107

A 1 been
　2 has served
　3 has ended
　4 gone
　5 have gone
　6 had been
　7 have been
　8 had never

B 1 b　　　2 d　　　3 f
　4 a　　　5 e　　　6 g
　7 c

C 1 a) was
　　b) had already decided
　　c) hadn't had
　　d) had already acted
　2 a) was offered
　　b) had worked

c) told 　　　　　d) asked

e) had promoted

A 1 '~에 가본 적이 있다'는 완료시제로서 'have been to + 장소'로 표현한다.

2 since(~이래로)는 계속 진행되어 온 내용이므로 완료시제와 결합한다.

3 내용상 완료시제가 와야 한다.

4 내용상 '~로 가버리고 없다'는 표현이 필요하다. 'have been to + 장소'는 '~에 가본 적이 있다'는 의미이다.

5 내용상 과거의 사실이 아니라 가격이 상승해서 지금까지 이어짐을 나타내므로 완료시제가 필요하다.

6 '~동안'을 나타내므로 완료시제가 필요하다.

7 40분 동안 기다리는 내용이 등장하므로 완료시제가 필요하다.

8 '~한 적이 있다'는 내용은 경험을 나타내며, 이 경우 완료시제를 사용한다.

Further Study
P.108

A (A) has toured　　(B) visited

B 1 (A) has lived　　(B) has been

2 she was envious of neighbor's puppies

C 1 was married

2 had been married for 25 years

A

Former U.S. President Jimmy Carter, / who promotes Habitat for Humanity, / has toured various countries / since 1994. In the summer of 2001, / he visited Asan, Korea, / to participate in a house-building project. It was part of Habitat for Humanity International's campaign / to build houses for homeless people.

미국의 전직 대통령이었던 Jimmy Carter는 인류를 위한 주거지를 장려하고 있는데, 1994년 이후로 여러 나라들을 방문하였다. 2001년 여름에, 그는 한국의 아산에, 집짓기 공사에 참여하려고 방문하였다. 이것은 집이 없는 사람들에게 집을 지어 주려는 인류를 위한 주거지 국제 운동의 일부였다.

(A) since(~이래로)가 있는 경우 주절에는 완료시제(계속 ~해왔다)가 사용된다.

(B) 명백한 과거를 나타내는 부사가 있으면 완료가 아니라 반드시 과거 시제를 사용한다.

B

Recently, in my apartment complex / there has been a birth of 8 puppies / to my neighbor's dog. The dog is a little more protective / than usual / and she seems to protect her property a little more. My female Doberman(Dobi) who has lived at the complex longer / has only known the female / who just had puppies. Now since the puppies were born and kept in the house, / my Dobi has been acting very strange and frantic. She looks somewhat slower and sadder / than usual. Does anyone have an explanation for this? She seems almost envious or jealous in a way.

최근에 우리 아파트단지 이웃집에서 강아지 10마리가 태어나는 일이 있었다. 어미는 평상시보다 더 보호막을 폈으며 주변을 더욱 경계하는 것 같았다. 아파트 단지에 더 오래 살았던 우리 집 암컷 도베르만(Dobi)은 갓 새끼를 낳았던 그 암컷 개를 알고는 있었다. 강아지들이 태어나서 집안에 갇혀 지낸 이래로, 우리 집 Dobi는 아주 이상하고 미친 듯한 행동을 보였다. 평상시보다 다소 느려졌으며, 꼭 슬픈 듯 의기소침해 보였다. 누가 이 것을 설명해줄 수 있을까? Dobi는 어떤 면에서 부러워하고 질투를 하는 것 같다.

(A) 내용상 '더 오래 살아왔다'는 내용이므로 완료시제가 필요하다.

(B) since(~이래로)가 있는 경우 주절에는 완료시제(계속 ~해왔다)가 사용된다.

C

A couple had been married for 25 years / and was going to celebrate the husband's 60th birthday. A fairy showed up / and said that because they had been such a sweet couple, / she would give them one wish each. The wife said, / "We've been so poor all these years, / and I've never gotten to see the world. / I wish we could travel all around the world." The fairy waved her wand and POOF! — / she had the travel tickets in her hands. Next, it was the husband's turn. He hesitated about / what to say / and then said, "I'd like to be married to a woman / 30 years younger than me." The fairy got upset / and waved her wand and POOF!— / he became 90 years old.

어떤 부부가 25년간 결혼생활을 해서 남편의 60세 생일을 맞았다. 한 요정이 나타나 사랑스런 부부로 보이기에 그들에게 각각 한 가지씩 소원을 들어주겠다고 말했다. 부인이 말하기를, "우린 오랫동안 가난하게 살아서 세상 구경을 하지 못했어요. 세계 일주 여행을 할 수 있으면 좋을텐데." 요정은 요술 지팡이를 흔들며 숨을 불어넣었다. 그러자 그녀의 손에 여행티켓이 쥐어졌다. 다음은 남편 차례였다. 그는 무슨 말을 해야 할지 잠시 망설였다가 말하기를, "나는 나보다 30년 젊은 여성과 결혼하고 싶어요." 그러자 요정은 화가 나서 요술지팡이를 흔들며 훅 바람을 불어넣었다. 그는 90세가 되었다.

Unit 17

1 조동사의 다양한 의미

Exercise

P.111

A 1 must   2 can't   3 had better
   4 had to   5 don't   6 needn't
   7 ought to

B 2 d   3 e   4 c
   5 f   6 a

C 2 doesn't have to   3 doesn't have to
   4 must not   5 must not
   6 don't have to   7 doesn't have to
   8 don't have to

A 1 문맥상 must(~해야 한다)가 필요하다.

   2 문맥상 can't(~할 수 없다)가 필요하다.

   3 'had better+동사원형'의 부정은 동사원형 앞에, ought to의 부정은 to부정사 앞에 not을 붙임에 주의한다.

   4 문맥상 had to(~해야 했다)가 필요하다.

   5 문맥상 don't have to(~할 필요 없다)가 필요하며, 문장 전체가 현재의 시제를 나타낸다.

   6 문맥상 needn't(~할 필요 없다)가 적절하다.

   7 문맥상 ought to(~해야 한다)가 적절하다.

2 까다로운 조동사

Exercise

P.113

A 2 can't have been   3 can't have been
   4 must have been   5 shouldn't have been
   6 should have been   7 must have been

B 1 d   2 e   3 a
   4 c   5 b   6 g
   7 i

C 2 He should have walked out of the restaurant after paying his bill.

   3 You shouldn't have wasted such a golden chance for peace.

   4 I shouldn't have worked so many part-time jobs.

   5 You should have told me Paris was such a nightmare.

Further Study

P.114

A (A) should have received

B 1 (A) must   (B) should   2 ⑤

C 1 do as the Romans do

A

The function of school is to produce knowledgeable people, / but if schools only provide knowledge, / they may destroy creativity. We often hear stories of ordinary people / who, if education had focused on creativity, / could have become great scientists. Those victims of education / should have received training / to develop creative talents / while in school. It really is a pity / that they did not.

학교의 기능은 지식이 있는 사람들을 양성하는 것이다. 그러나 만약 학교가 단지 지식만을 제공한다면 학교는 창의력을 파괴한다. 우리는 교육이 창의력에 초점을 맞추었더라면 위대한 과학자가 될 수도 있었을 평범한 사람들의 이야기를 흔히 듣는다. 그 교육의 희생자들은 학교에 다닐 때 창의적인 재능을 개발하는 훈련을 받았어야만 했다. 그들이 그러지 못했다는 것이 정말로 애석하다.

(A) 문맥상 '~학교에서 창의적 재능 개발 훈련을 받았어야 했는데'라는 내용이 필요하다. 그래서 should have received가 되어야 한다.

B

Since blood types are inherited, you have the same blood type as your parents. However, it is sometimes possible to prove that someone cannot possibly be the parent of a child. You might be unfortunate to discover that you must have been adopted; your adoptive parents should have told you about that already. You can have blonde hair and Type-O blood, and your biological parents both have brown hair and type A blood on your birth certificate. However, this doesn't necessarily mean that you were adopted. You can easily have different hair color and blood type from your biological parents, especially if you have a genetically recessive trait.

혈액형은 물려받는 것이기에, 여러분은 여러분의 부모님과 같은 혈액형을 갖고 있다. 하지만, 어떤 사람이 한 아이의 부모가 될 수 없음을 증명하는 것도 때로는 가능하다. 여러분은 불행하게도 입양되었음에 틀림없다는 사실을 발견할 지도 모른다. 결국 여러분의 부모님이 그 사실에 대해 말해주었어야 했다. 여러분이 금발에다 O형인데, 여러분 친부모님은 갈색 머리에 A형이라고 출생증명서에 나와 있다. 하지만, 그렇다고 이것이 반드시 여러분이 입양되었음을 의미하는 것은 아니다. 특히 여러분이 유전적으로 열성이

성이라면 친부모와는 다른 머리색과 혈액형을 물려받을 수 있다.

(A) 내용상 'must have+과거분사(~했음에 틀림없다)'가 적당하다.

(B) 문맥상 '양부모가 입양된 사실을 말해주었어야 했다'는 내용이므로 'should have+과거분사(=ought to have+과거분사)'가 필요하다. ought는 반드시 'ought to'로 표현된다.

C

A 38-year-old Canadian businesswoman is seeking justice / after she was thrown in jail / by Saudi Arabia's religious police / for sitting with a male colleague / in a coffee shop in Jeddah. However, if this businesswoman didn't want to be arrested, / she should not have broken the local law. If this businesswoman aimed to openly protest gender segregation / by purposely getting arrested, I acknowledge her intention. Yet, if she was trying to actually conduct a business meeting, / she should have known the local laws / and followed them. If not, she shouldn't have been there / or her husband should have been with her. When traveling abroad / one must remember / "When in Rome, do as the Romans do."

38세의 캐나다인 사업가 여성이 사우디의 Jeddah에 있는 커피점에서 남성동료와 함께 앉아있다는 이유로 사우디아라비아 종교경찰에게 걸려 감옥에 보내진 후 정식 재판을 요청하고 있다. 하지만, 이 여성사업가가 체포되지 않으려면 그곳의 법을 어기지 말았어야 했다. 그녀가 일부러 체포됨으로써 인종차별에 공개적으로 항의하기 위한 목적이었다면 그 뜻을 인정하겠다. 그러나 그녀가 실제 업무차 만난 것이라면 그녀는 법을 알고 그 법에 따랐어야 했다. 그렇지 않다면 그녀는 그곳에 있지 말았어야 했거나 남편과 함께 있었어야 했다. 해외를 여행할 때 사람들이 기억해야 할 일이 있는데, "로마에서는 로마법을 따르라"는 것이다.

Unit 18

1 사역동사

Exercise
P.117

A 1 book 2 make 3 start
  4 postponed 5 cancelled 6 to eat
  7 take

B 1 stay 2 cry 3 filled

  4 removed 5 write 6 to lend
  7 to clean 8 cleaned

C 2 grow up to be cowboys
  3 their children stop watching TV
  4 to reach the correct answer
  5 and close friends forget my birthday

A 1 'have+목적어+동사원형'은 목적어가 직접 동작을 하는 경우 사용한다.

2 사역동사 let은 'let+목적어+동사원형'으로 사용된다.

3 make가 '시키다' 의미로 사용되는 경우 'make+목적어+동사원형'으로 사용되며, 이 경우 목적어가 직접 동작을 하는 경우이다.

4 'have+목적어+과거분사'는 목적어가 '동작을 당하다' 의미의 수동적인 의미로 사용된다.

5 get 동사는 사역동사가 아니지만 '시키다' 의미로 사용되며, 'get+목적어+과거분사'는 목적어가 수동적인 의미로 사용되는 경우이다.

6 get 동사는 목적어가 능동적인 동작을 할 때 'get+목적어+to부정사'로 사용된다.

7 let은 '시키다, 허락하다'의 의미로 사용될 때 'let+목적어+동사원형'으로 나타난다.

2 지각동사

Exercise
P.119

A 1 pulled 2 using 3 standing
  4 beating 5 blooming 6 drop
  7 calling

B 2 shouting 3 happen(=happening)
  4 crawling 5 walking(=walk)
  6 called 7 whispering(=whisper)

C 2 I heard him playing the guitar.
  3 Liz felt somebody grab her arm and pull her.
  4 He was observed dancing and singing beside the road.
  5 The children were noticed lying down on the stage.

A 1 '지각동사(feel)+목적어+동사원형'은 목적어가 능동적으로 동작을 하는 경우이며, '지각동사+목적어+과거분사'는 목적어가 수동적인 의미를 나타낼 때 사용한다.

2 목적어(her)가 직접 동작을 하므로, '지각동사+목적어+동사원형(또는 -ing)'이 필요하다.

3 목적어(robbers)가 능동적인 동작을 하므로 '지각동사+목적어+동사원형(또는 -ing)'이 필요하다.

4 일반적으로 목적어가 능동적인 동작을 하는 경우, 목적보어로서 동사원형보다 -ing의 형태가 더 자주 사용된다.

5 주어인 나무가 직접 꽃을 피우는 내용이며, 접속사 and 뒤에 -ing 형태가 왔으므로 blooming이 적당하다.

6 동사가 지각동사인 경우 목적보어로 to부정사가 절대 사용되지 않는다.

7 목적어(teacher)가 직접 부르는 경우이므로 능동태인 calling이 온다.

Further Study

P.120

A (A) helped (B) know

B 1 (A) try (B) fail
  2 You have to open the door yourself

C 1 you feel fun, it to do the housework

A

When I fell ill, / I was nearly dead within days. My close friend Joanne swooped in / to support / and helped me locate doctors in San Francisco. She also let my friends know / that they were needed. Joanne helped me gain the positive outlook / I needed. She stressed the importance of surrounding myself / with encouraging people.

내가 아팠을 때 며칠간 거의 죽을 지경이었다. 절친한 내 친구 Joanne가 재빨리 도우러 와서 내가 샌프란시스코에 있는 의사를 알아보도록 도와주었다. 그녀는 또한 내 친구들에게 그들의 도움이 필요하다고 알려주기도 했다. Joanne는 내게 필요한 긍정적인 마음자세를 갖도록 도와주었다. 그녀는 내 주위에 격려하는 사람들이 있는 것이 중요하다고 강조했다.

(A) 목적어가 능동적인 동작을 하는 경우, help는 'help+목적어+동사원형 or to부정사로', get은 'get+목적어+to부정사'로 사용된다.

(B) 사역동사 let은 'let+목적어+동사원형'으로 사용된다.

B

On most subway trains, / the doors open automatically at each station. But when you are on the Metro, / the subway in Paris, / things are different. I watched a man on the Metro / try to get off the train and fail. When the train came to his station, / he got up / and stood patiently / in front of the door, / waiting for it to open. It never opened. The train simply started up again / and went on to the next station. In the Metro, / you have

to open the doors yourself / by pushing a button, / depressing a lever / or sliding them.

대부분의 지하철 전동차 문들은 각 정거장에서 자동으로 열린다. 그러나 파리의 지하철인 메트로를 타면 사정이 다르다. 나는 메트로를 탄 한 남자가 전동차에서 내리려다가 실패하는 것을 지켜보았다. 전동차가 그가 내릴 역으로 들어왔을 때 그는 자리에서 일어나 문이 열리기를 기다리며 문 앞에 끈기 있게 서 있었다. 그런 일은 일어나지 않았다(문이 열리지 않았다). 전동차는 다시 출발하여 다음 역으로 갔다. 메트로에서는 단추를 누르거나 손잡이를 내려서 누르거나, 또는 문을 옆으로 밀어서 여러분 스스로 문을 열어야 한다.

(A) 지각동사는 목적어가 능동적인가 수동적인가에 따라 '지각동사+목적어+동사원형, -ing, -ed'로 사용된다. 하지만, 목적보어 위치에 절대 to부정사가 올 수는 없다.

(B) 접속사(and)로 연결되는 내용이므로 try와 동일한 동사 형태인 동사원형이 온다.

C

When the Roboman arrived / in the mail yesterday, / I was really impressed. He had infrared vision, a color camera, and sonic sensors. Equipped with a sensor / that can read microchips in identification cards, / the robot recognized a woman / approaching from behind, / and turned to greet her by name. Now I have to get him to bounce a ball by himself. It is at this moment / that my dreams of having him clean the house / are gone. Sometimes it's very easy / to think of a robot as a human being. But it can make you feel fun, / but never expect it / to do the housework.

어제 Roboman이 우편으로 도착했을 때 나는 아주 감동했다. 적외선 눈, 컬러 카메라, 그리고 음성 감지기를 갖고 있었다. 그 로봇은 신분증의 마이크로칩을 읽을 수 있는 감지기를 장착하여 뒤에서 접근하는 여성을 인지하고는 돌아서서 이름을 부르며 인사했다. 이제 나는 그 로봇에게 혼자 공을 쳐보도록 시켜야겠다. 바로 이 순간, 그에게 집안 청소를 시켜야겠다는 내 꿈이 사라지게 된다. 때로는 로봇을 인간으로 간주하기 아주 쉽다. 하지만, 그것이 여러분을 재미있게 만들 수는 있지만, 집안일을 해줄 것으로 기대하지는 마라.

Unit 19

1 구동사

Exercise
P.123

A 1 take   2 get   3 put
    4 bring

B 1 up   2 off   3 off
    4 away

C 2 wake him up   3 Fill it in
    4 get it out   5 look it over
    6 get it back   7 switch it off
    8 tell them apart

2 다양한 구동사

Exercise
P.125

A 2 up   3 with   4 up
    5 out   6 down

B 2 give   3 put   4 (to) make
    5 find   6 pick   7 bring

C 1 e   2 h   3 f
    4 d   5 i   6 b
    7 g   8 a   9 c

Further Study
P.126

A (A) turning   (B) keep it on

B 1 (A) keep it off (B) leave it on (C) took hers off
    2 take it off and buy a cheap, bigger one.

C 1 is to write them down

A

Even if turning a computer off once a day / shortened its overall life / by only a few days, / it wouldn't pay / to keep it on all the time. Probably the best compromise is to shut your computer down / at the end of the day / and turn it back / on the next day.

비록 하루에 한번 컴퓨터를 끄는 것이 컴퓨터 수명을 며칠 정도 단축시키겠지만, 그럴더라도 계속 컴퓨터를 켜 두는 것은 별로 도움되지 않는다. 아마 가장 훌륭한 타협책은 하루 일정이 끝나고 컴퓨터를 끄는 것이며, 다음날 다시 컴퓨터를 켜는 것이다.

(A) 문맥상 '컴퓨터를 끈다'는 내용이므로 turn off가 온다.
(B) 구동사(동사+부사)의 목적어가 대명사인 경우 '동사+목적어+부사'의 형태를 취한다.

B

The ring on one's finger may get a little bit tighter / during pregnancy. I'm just curious / if I should take off my ring / when my finger begins to swell. I wonder / if I should keep it off / until after the baby is born, / and the swelling goes down. Frankly, I'd prefer to leave it on / because I personally hate the thought of not wearing my wedding ring. I've been trying to ignore my finger / which starts to swell like a sausage. However, I have contemplated buying an inexpensive, fake ring / for the time being to wear / instead of my wedding band. My friend took hers off / when she was pregnant, / and she wore a different, larger ring in its place.

손가락의 반지는 임신기간에 약간 조일 수 있다. 내 손가락이 부어오르기 시작하면 반지를 빼야하는지 알고 싶다. 나는 아이가 태어나 붓기가 가라앉을 때까지 반지를 빼어두어야 하는지 궁금하다. 솔직히 나는 반지를 계속 끼고 싶다. 왜냐하면 나는 결혼 반지를 착용하지 않는다는 생각을 개인적으로 좋아하지 않는다. 소시지처럼 붓기 시작하는 손가락을 애써 무시하려고 애썼다. 하지만, 나는 당분간 결혼반지 대신 낄 수 있는 값싼 가짜 반지 하나를 살 생각이었다. 내 친구는 임신했을 때 자신의 반지를 빼버리고, 그 자리에는 좀 더 큰 다른 반지를 끼었다.

(A), (B), (C) 구동사(동사+부사)의 경우 목적어가 대명사이면 '동사+목적어+부사'의 형태를 취한다.

C

Possibly / the most effective way to focus on your goals / is to write them down. Although this may sound like an obvious first step, / it is a step / that many people ignore. As a result, / their goals often remain unfocused, / and therefore unrealized. Go to a fairly quiet place / where you are not likely to be disturbed. Make a list of every goal you have. Include goals about finances, relationships, and your career. Be as specific / as possible.

아마도 당신이 정한 여러 목표에 집중하는 가장 효과적인 방법은 그것들을 적어두는 것이다. 이 것이 당연한 첫 단계라고 들릴지 모르지만 많은 사람들이 무시하는 단계이다. 그 결과 그들의 목표는 흔히 흐지부지 되어 결국 실현되지 못하게 된다. 당신이 방해를 받지 않을 만한 아주 조용한 곳으로 가라. 당신이 정한 모든 목표를 목록으로 만들어라. 자금, 인간관계, 그리고 직업 등에 관한 목표를 포함시켜라. 될 수 있는 한 구체적으로 작성하라.

Unit 20

1 현재분사와 과거분사

Exercise
P.129

A 1 yelling   2 sold   3 stealing
   4 boiled   5 called   6 chasing
   7 caught

B 2 a) inviting   b) invited
   3 a) providing   b) provided
   4 a) leaving   b) left
   5 a) lifting   b) lifted
   6 a) writing   b) written

C 1 eating a box while washing my car.
   2 seeing the surrounding Alps covered with snow
   3 the work finished before the start of summer
   4 the issue brought up regarding the school fees

A 1 '지각동사+목적어+동사원형 or -ing'의 형태에서 현재분사(-ing)의 사용을 선호한다.
   2 문맥상 '가장 많이 팔리는 차'가 필요하며, 주어(car)는 수동적인 동작을 하므로 수동적 의미의 과거분사가 필요하다.
   3 분사가 뒤에서 앞의 명사를 수식하며, the man이 직접 훔치는 내용이므로 능동 의미의 현재분사가 온다.
   4 주어는 eggs이므로 '끓여진다'는 의미의 과거분사가 적당하다.
   5 주어(a man)가 'Prince라고 불려지다'로 쓰이므로 수동적 의미인 과거분사가 온다.
   6 직접 뒤쫓아가는 경우이므로 능동태인 현재분사가 온다.
   7 a man이 전쟁 중 체포되는 내용이므로 수동적 의미인 과거분사가 온다.

2 분사구문

Exercise
P.131

A 1 asked   2 Keeping   3 Taking
   4 obtaining   5 Containing   6 Attacked
   7 Expecting

B 1 d   2 c   3 e
   4 b   5 a   6 f

C 2 Seen from the mountain
   3 Written in easy English
   4 Left alone
   5 Living in a remote place

A 1 If (I am) asked~에서 주어+be동사가 생략되는 경우가 많다. 즉, '접속사+분사' 형태의 문장에서 현재분사는 능동을, 과거분사는 수동을 나타낸다.
   2 분사구문의 주어(she)가 직접 곰을 기르는 내용이므로 능동적 의미인 현재분사가 온다.
   3 주어(Mrs. Cohen)가 직접 책을 가져가는 내용이므로 현재분사가 온다.
   4 주어(Saka)가 직접 visa를 획득하게 되므로 능동적 의미인 현재분사가 온다.
   5 주어(animal fat)가 직접 콜레스트롤을 포함하는 경우이므로 능동을 나타내는 현재분사가 필요하다.
   6 주어(they)가 공격을 당하는 내용이므로 수동적 의미인 과거분사가 온다.
   7 주어(Vela)가 직접 우주로 비행할 기대를 하는 내용이므로 현재분사가 온다.

Further Study
P.132

A (A) going   (B) served
B 1 (A) Coming   (B) caught
     (C) drilled   (D) allowing
   2 the remains of tiny sea animals and plants
C 1 to join a club devoted to mathematics

A

One special phenomenon happened every full moon in October. We all passed the night watching lightboats going slowly up and down the river. We enjoyed eating grilled trout and other delicious food served in abundance at the seashore as parties went on there.

매번 10월의 보름달에는 특별한 현상이 나타났다. 우리 모두는 작은 보트가 강 아래위로 천천히 지나가는 모습을 지켜보면서 밤을 보냈다. 우리는 해변에서 파티가 진행되자 불에 구운 송어와 푸짐하게 나온 다른 맛있는 음식을 즐겁게 먹었다.

(A) 지각동사의 경우 목적보어로 to부정사가 절대 올 수 없다.
(B) '명사+분사~'의 형태로서 분사는 앞의 명사를 수식해 준다. 주어인 명사가 능동적이면 현재분사(-ing)가, 수동적이면 과거분사(-ed)가 온다.

B

Crude oil is mostly found in underground areas / called reservoirs. Coming out of the ground, / oil is a thick liquid, / brown or greenish-black in color, / which is called crude oil. Oil was formed / from the remains of tiny sea plants and animals / caught between layers of rock. Over the years, / the remains were covered / by layers of mud and sediment. Heat and pressure from these layers / helped the remains turn into crude oil. Oil wells are holes / drilled down into the oil pools, / allowing the crude oil to rise to the surface.

석유는 유층(油層)이라고 불리는 땅속 지역에서 대부분 발견된다. 땅 밖으로 나올 때 석유는 걸쭉한 액체이며 색은 갈색이거나 검은 빛 나는 녹색을 하고 있는데, 그 상태를 원유라고 부른다. 석유는 암석층에 갇힌 작은 해상 식물과 동물의 잔해로 형성되었다. 많은 세월이 흘러 잔해가 여러겹의 진흙과 침전물로 덮이게 된다. 이들 층으로부터 나오는 열과 압력이 잔해가 석유로 되는 것을 도와준다. 유정(油井)은 천연가스층 밑으로 뚫은 구멍인데, 석유가 표면으로 올라오도록 해준다.

(A) 주절의 의미를 보강해주는 부사절은 분사구분으로 간략하게 줄여 사용된다. 분사(Coming)의 주어는 oil이며, come은 자동사이므로 수동적 의미인 과거분사를 사용할 수 없다. To come~ 은 '하기 위하여'가 되므로 내용상 적절하지 않다.

(C) 분사의 주어(holes)가 능동적으로 구멍을 뚫는 것은 불가능하므로, 수동적 의미를 나타내는 과거분사가 온다.

C

To be a mathematician / you don't need an expensive laboratory. The typical equipment of a mathematician / is a blackboard and chalk. It is better / to do mathematics on a blackboard / than on a piece of paper / because chalk is easier to erase, / and mathematical research is often filled with mistakes. One more thing you need to do / is to join a club / devoted to mathematics. Not many mathematicians can work alone; / they need to talk about / what they are doing. If you want to be a mathematician, / you had better expose your new ideas / to the criticism of others. It is possible / to contain hidden assumptions / that you do not see / but that are obvious to others.

수학자가 되기 위해서 비싼 실험실이 필요하지는 않다. 수학자의 전형적인 장비는 칠판과 분필이다. 분필은 보다 쉽게 지울 수 있고 수학적인 연구는 흔히 실수로 가득차있기 때문에 종이 위보다 칠판 위에서 수학을 하는 것이 더 낫다. 한 가지 더 해야 한다면 수학에 전념하는 클럽에 가입하는 것이다. 혼자서 작업하는 수학자는 많지 않다. 그들은 그들이 하고 있는 것에 대해 토론할 필요가 있다. 수학자가 되기를 원한다면 당신의 새로운 생각을 다른 사람들

른 사람들의 비판에 노출시키는 편이 낫다. 당신은 알지 못하지만, 다른 사람들에게는 분명해 보이는 어떤 숨어있는 가설을 포함하고 있을 가능성이 있다.

Unit 21

1 -ing와 -ed 형태의 형용사 I

Exercise
P.135

A 1 disappointed
2 irritating
3 exhausted
4 scared
5 tired
6 embarrassing
7 confused

B 2 a) interesting
b) interested
3 a) depressing
b) depressed
4 a) terrifying
b) terrified
5 a) disappointed
b) disappointing
6 a) embarrassing
b) embarrassed

C 2 delighted
3 boring
4 horrifying
5 frustrated
6 irritating

A 1 주어(People)가 실망을 하게되는 내용이므로 disappoint(실망시키다)는 수동적 의미인 과거분사가 된다.

2 분사의 의미상 주어(it)가 직접 동작을 하는 경우이며, 문맥상 다른 사람들을 짜증나게 하는 내용이므로 irritating이 적절하다.

3 문맥상 주어(We)가 태풍으로 인해 지치는 내용의 exhausted가 적절하다.

4 문맥상 주어(Karen)가 무섭게 되어지는 내용이므로 scare(겁을 주다)의 과거분사 형태가 온다.

5 주어(You)는 축구를 한 후에 지치게 되는 내용이 필요하므로 과거분사가 되어야 한다.

6 가주어(It)는 진주어(to send~)를 대신하며, e-mail 잘못 보내는 것은 사람을 당황케하는 것이므로 현재분사가 온다.

7 문맥상 tired와 어울리는 'confused(당황한, 헷갈리는)'가 필요하다.

Exercise

P.137

A 1 Compared   2 compared   3 boring
    4 exhausting   5 amazed   6 surprising
    7 tired

B 2 annoyed   3 discouraged
    4 depressed   5 scary
    6 excited   7 satisfying

C 2 shocked, shocking   3 bored, boring
    4 excited, exciting   5 delighted, delighting
    6 satisfying   7 discouraged
    8 satisfied
    9 entertained, entertaining
   10 wasn't amused, wasn't amusing

A 1 분사구문의 주어(the quality)는 다른 차(other teas)와 비교되는 것이므로 수동적 의미인 과거분사가 필요하다.

   2 주어(panda)는 다른 동물로 비교되어지는 경우이므로 과거분사가 온다.

   3 주인공(Jack)을 지루하게 하는 능동적 내용이므로 현재분사가 온다.

   4 분사가 명사를 수식하는 경우 그 명사가 주어이다. 주어(a day)는 사람을 지치게 하는 능동적인 의미이므로 현재분사가 온다.

   5 주어(We)는 Jane의 메달 딴 사실에 놀라게 되는 내용이므로 과거분사가 온다.

   6 가주어(It)와 진주어(that~)로 된 문장이다. 주어가 사람들을 놀라게 하는 내용이므로 현재분사가 온다.

   7 주어(you)가 지치게 되는 수동적 내용이며, 나열되는 형용사와 같은 형태가 와야 하므로 과거분사가 적절하다.

Further Study

P.138

A (A) disappointed   (B) annoying   (C) bored

B 1 (A) shocked   (B) shocking
    2 shocked, shocking

C 1 ④

A

I was very disappointed with Jackie. He was smaller and thinner / than I had expected from the advertisement / I had seen. His voice had an annoying accent, / which my son started to copy. There were not many changes in his performance / and my kid got bored very quickly with him.

나는 Jackie에게 매우 실망했다. 내가 광고를 보고 기대한 것보다 그는 더 작고 말랐다. 목소리는 듣기 거북한 액센트가 있는데, 우리 아들이 그것을 따라하기 시작했다. 연기의 변화도 많지 않았으며, 우리 아이는 Jackie에게 아주 빠르게 싫증을 느끼게 되었다.

(A) 주어가 '놀라게 되어지다'는 내용이므로 수동적 의미인 과거분사가 온다.

(B) 주어(my kid)가 지루하게 되는 내용이므로 과거분사가 온다. 'get+과거분사'는 수동태를 나타내며, '~하게 되어진다'의 의미를 타나낸다.

B

A man went into a new fruit shop / in New York. He picked some oranges / but he was shocked / when the shop assistant asked him for $1950. He gave the girl a $20 bill / and said, "Your prices are shocking." Then he left the shop. The assistant ran after him / and said, "Sir, you've forgotten your change." The man turned around / and said, "Oh, you'd better keep it. I stepped on a grape / on the way out."

뉴욕에서 한 사람이 새로 생긴 과일가게에 들어갔다. 그는 오렌지를 몇 개 골랐고 점원이 19.50달러라고 말했을 때 놀라고 말았다. 그는 그 여자 점원에게 20달러짜리 지폐를 주고, "가격이 충격적입니다"라고 말했다. 그리고 가게를 떠나자 점원이 따라와서, "잔돈을 가져 가셔야죠" 라고 했다. 그 남자는 돌아서서, "아, 가지세요. 내가 나가다가 포도를 밟았거든요."라고 했다.

(A) 주어가 놀라게 되는 내용이므로 shock(놀라게 하다)동사는 수동적 의미인 shocked가 된다.

(B) 주어(Your prices)가 사람을 놀라게 하는 내용이므로 능동적 의미인 현재분사가 온다.

C

I am delighted / to introduce you / to this exciting piece of land. From the largest dinosaur park to the most majestic mountains, / Kariba offers charming attractions for everyone. A little more exploration uncovers fascinating cultural attractions / and an exciting shopping scene. Perhaps surprisingly, / most of the city's most appealing tourist sites / offer free admission. All across Kariba, / people are preparing for delighting annual festivals and events / that expect to draw large and delighted crowds. Who says / you can't do it all in one place? Nearby you can shop, hike, golf, ski, climb, bike / or fish for trout in a tumbling stream. Kariba has fields of fluffy snow for skiing, frozen lakes for skating, / and more winter activities / than imaginable.

나는 여러분에게 이렇게 멋진 곳을 소개하게 되어 기쁩니다. Kariba는 최대규모의 공룡공원에서부터 가장 웅장한 산맥까지 모든 사람들에게 매력적인 장소를 제공합니다. 좀 더 발품을 판다면 멋진 문화유적과 쇼핑장소까지 발견할 것입니다. 놀랍게도 대부분의 시내 관광지는 입장료가 무료입니다. Kariba 전역에 걸쳐 사람들은 즐거운 축제와 행사를 준비하고 있으며 이러한 축제와 행사들이 많은 관광객을 끌어들일거라고 기대하고 있습니다. 누가 한 장소에서 그 모든 것을 할 수 없다고 말하는가? 가까이서 여러분은 쇼핑, 도보 여행, 골프, 스키, 등산, 자전거 또는 흐르는 시냇물에서 송어낚시를 할 수 있습니다. Kariba에는 스키를 탈 수 있는 푹신푹신한 눈 덮인 평지가 있고, 스케이팅을 할 수 있는 얼음 호수, 그리고 상상할 수 있는 그 이상의 많은 겨울용 활동거리가 있습니다.

Unit 22

1   be+과거분사

Exercise

A 1 been paid   2 been disconnected
   3 remain   4 disappeared
   5 permitted   6 happened
   7 operated   8 got divided

B 2 preparing, prepared
   3 inventing, invented
   4 recognized, recognized
   5 postponed, postponed
   6 exposed, exposed

C 2 d   3 b   4 c
   5 g   6 e   7 f

A 1 주어(bill)는 '지불되어지다'는 표현이 필요하므로 수동태가 필요하다.
   2 주어(telephone)가 '단절되다, 끊어지다'는 수동적 표현이므로 수동태가 와야 한다.
   3 want는 'want+목적어+to부정사'의 형태로 쓰인다. 지각동사나 사역동사를 제외하고는 목적보어로 동사원형이 올 수 없다. 동사 remain은 자동사로서 수동태로 사용될 수 없다.
   4 disappear는 자동사이며, 자동사는 스스로 발생하므로 수동태가 불가능하다.
   5 주어(smoking)는 누군가에 의해 '허락되어지다'는 내용이므로 수동태가 온다.
   6 happen은 자동사로서 능동태로만 사용된다.

   7 주어(house)는 '운영되어지다'는 표현이 적절하므로 수동태가 온다.
   8 주어(army)는 수동적 의미인 '나누어지다'는 표현이 적절하며, 수동태를 'get+과거분사'로 나타낼 수 있다.

2   주의할 수동태 표현

Exercise
P.143

A 1 a,b   2 b,a   3 b,a
   4 a,b   5 b,a

B 2 caught, were caught   3 heard, was heard
   4 found, were found

C 2 was allowed to attend Yale
   3 to be made of plastic.
   4 was told information about the program

Further Study
P.144

A (A) been stolen   (B) owned   (C) was given

B 1 (A) was placed   (B) were filled
      (C) be relieved
   2 is said to be one of the most common causes of insomnia

C 1 acquired from this process can be used as an energy source

A

A man tried to sell a painting / that had been stolen. At first the painting was owned / by Christine Jones, aged 85. She had owned it / since 1926, / when it was given to her / as a wedding present.

한 사람이 도난당한 그림을 하나 팔려고 했다. 처음에 그 그림은 85세의 Christine Jones가 소유한 것이었다. 그녀는 그 그림을 1926년부터 계속 소유했는데, 그 당시 그 그림은 결혼 선물로 그녀가 받았다.

(A) 주어(a painting)가 도난당하는 것은 steal(훔치다)을 수동태(be+stolen)로 표현하면 된다.
(B) 주어(She)가 직접 소유하는 내용이므로 능동태(had owned)가 온다.

B

Restless legs syndrome is a common sleep disorder / affecting about 1 in 10 adults. The disorder is caused / by an uncontrollable desire / to move the legs. Ten years ago, / I fractured my ankle. My leg was placed in a cast / and I was told / to keep the leg suspended / for at least a month. What I can never forget / is that my dreams were filled with unstable movements, / which would wake me up. Moreover, when trying to sleep, / my limbs become prickly / and this disorder could only be relieved / by getting up and moving around. Needless to say, / sleeping when you have this syndrome / is next to impossible. Restless legs syndrome is said to be one of the most common causes of insomnia.

하지불안 증후군은 성인 10명 중 한 명에게 나타나는 흔한 수면장애이다. 이러한 장애는 제어할 수 없을 정도로 다리를 움직이고 싶은 현상 때문에 일어난다. 10년 전에 나는 발목 골절을 당했다. 다리에 깁스를 한 상태로 적어도 2개월간 다리를 매달아 두라는 말을 들었다. 내가 잊을 수 없는 것은 온통 불안정한 동작으로 가득한 꿈을 꾸었으며, 이것이 잠을 깨우곤 한 것이다. 더욱이나 잠을 자려고 할 때 내 다리는 따끔따끔 아프고, 이런 느낌은 몸을 일으켜 움직여야 완화될 수 있었다. 말할 필요도 없이 여러분이 이런 증상이 있을 때 잠자는 것은 거의 불가능하리라. 하지불안 증후군은 불면증의 가장 흔한 원인 중 하나라고 한다.

(A) 주어(My leg)가 '놓여진다'는 내용이므로 place(~를 놓다)를 수동태(was placed)로 표현해야 한다.

(B) 주어(my dreams)가 '~로 채워진다'는 내용이므로 fill(채우다)을 수동태로 표현해야 한다.

(C) 주어(this disorder)가 '완화되어진다'는 수동적 내용이므로 relieve(완화시키다)를 수동태로 표현해야 한다.

C

How can you obtain hydrogen from water? Since water is made up of 2 hydrogen atoms and 1 oxygen atom, / water can be broken down / and separated into hydrogen and oxygen / supplying a lot of energy. To obtain hydrogen from water, / you need to build a device / that can electrolyze water. This device can be easily made / with a few tools / you can get in any hardware store. First, / you have to apply enough energy / to break its atomic bonds. A battery is connected to two electrodes, / which are submerged in water. Hydrogen bubbles from one of the electrodes, / and oxygen from the other. This is a major way / to obtain hydrogen. The hydrogen acquired from this process / can be used / as an energy source.

우리는 물에서 수소를 어떻게 얻을 수 있는가? 물은 수소 두 개와 산소 한 개의 원자로 구성되어 있으므로, 물이 분해 되어서 많은 에너지를 공급하는 수소와 산소로 분리될 수 있다. 물에서 수소를 얻기 위해서, 여러분은 물을 전기분해할 수 있는 장치를 설치해야 한다. 이러한 장치는 철물점에서 구할 수 있는 몇 개의 도구로 쉽게 만들 수 있다. 먼저, 원자의 결합을 깨기 위해 충분한 에너지를 가해야 한다. 배터리를 두 전극에 연결하고 전극은 물로 잠겨지게 된다. 전극 한 곳에서 수소의 기포가 일게 되며, 다른 쪽에서 산소 기포가 솟는다. 이것이 대량의 수소를 얻는 주된 방법이다. 수소는 이런 과정으로 얻어져서 에너지원으로 사용될 수 있다.

Unit 23

1 수동 형태의 동사구-1

Exercise
P.147

A 2 of   3 of   4 for
5 as   6 of   7 of

B 2 was robbed
3 was sent to jail
4 were destroyed by the storm
5 is spoken in many countries
6 was invented
7 is being taken to a camp by him

C 1 are said to have been robbed of
2 been convinced of
3 persuaded him of
4 was persuaded of
5 was accused of

2 수동 형태의 동사구-2

Exercise
P.149

A 1 of   2 in   3 to
4 to   5 with   6 to
7 with

B 2 a. is known   b. has known
3 a. was equipped   b. have equipped
4 a. addicted   b. were addicted
5 a. suits   b. is suited
6 a. was qualified   b. qualify

C 2 were absorbed in   3 was devoted to
4 was compared   5 is covered
6 used to   7 was associated

A 1 be composed of(~로 구성되어 있다)

2 be dressed in(~의 옷을 차려입다)

3 be addicted to(~에 중독되다)

4 be married to(~와 결혼하다 = marry)

5 be connected with(~와 관련 되어있다)

6 be accustomed to(~에 익숙해 있다)

7 be associated with(~와 관련되어 있다)

Further Study

P.150

A (A) accused of   (B) was robbed of

B 1 (A) with (B) involved

2 read aloud to children

C 1 is made up of(=is composed of) dark matter substantially.

A

A cab driver was accused of spying / with no evidence. After arrest / he was brought to the CIA, / where he was robbed of his belongings, deprived of food, / severely threatened and beaten. Finally he confessed his spying activities / out of fear of being beaten more.

어떤 택시 기사가 증거도 없이 스파이 행위로 기소되었다. 체포 후에 그는 CIA로 이송되었고, 거기서 그는 소지품을 빼앗기고 먹을 것도 받지 못하고, 심하게 협박 당하고 맞았다. 그리고 그는 더 이상 맞는 것이 두려워 스파이 행위를 털어 놓았다.

(A) 주어가 '고소되어진다'는 수동적 내용이므로 accuse(고소하다)를 수동태로 표현해야 한다.

(B) 주어(he)가 소지품을 빼앗기는 내용이므로 수동태가 필요하다. 어떤 사람이 자신의 물건을 빼앗기는 표현은 'be robbed of'를 사용한다.

B

Parental involvement in reading achievement / has been a concern / since the 1980's for both educators and parents. Reading aloud to children is a most important factor / in developing reading. Parental involvement at home is consistently associated / with higher student achievement. Reading at home protects a child / from getting addicted to television or computers. Also it actively monitors a child's time, helps with homework / and provides space to discuss school matters. Parents are able to get involved / in their child's education positively in many ways. What matters / is to do it consistently / and stick with it / because it will make an important difference / in a child's life.

부모가 독서활동에 관여하는 것이 1980년대 이래로 교육자와 부모들에게 관심사항이었다. 아이들에게 책을 큰 소리로 읽어주는 것이 독서력 개발에 매우 중요한 요인이다. 집에서 부모가 함께 하는 것이 학생의 높은 성적과 일관된 관련이 있다. 집에서 책을 읽어주면 아이들을 컴퓨터나 텔레비전의 중독으로부터 보호해 준다. 또한, 적극적으로 아이의 시간을 조정하고, 숙제를 도와주고, 그리고 학교의 일을 논의할 여유를 준다. 부모들이 아이 교육에 적극적으로 여러 면에서 관여할 수도 있다. 아이의 인생에 중요한 영향을 미치기 때문에, 일관되게 지속적으로 하는 것이 중요하다.

(A) associate(연합시키다, 관련시키다)는 'be associated with(~와 관련되다)'로 사용된다.

(B) involve(관련시키다)는 'get involved in(~에 관련되다)'으로 사용된다.

C

What is the content of the universe? Murphy, a scientist associated with NASA, explains that only a small percentage of matter of the universe is composed of what we call ordinary matter. Around 70 percent of the universe is dark energy, and about 22 percent is made up of dark matter, which makes up a substantial part of the universe's material. Although astronomers don't know what composes dark matter, they say that it is related to supersymmetry. To know what it is would answer a crucial question about the universe. Whoever solves the dark matter problem would certainly win a Nobel Prize.

우주는 무엇으로 구성되어 있는가? 미항공우주국과 관련된 과학자 Murphy는 우주의 작은 부분만 우리가 일반적으로 물질이라고 부르는 것으로 구성되어 있다고 설명한다. 우주의 약 70%는 알 수 없는 에너지이며, 22%는 알 수 없는 물질로 구성되어 있는데, 그 알 수 없는 물질이 우주의 실질적인 부분을 구성하고 있다. 천문학자들은 이 알 수 없는 물질이 무엇으로 구성되어 있는지는 모르지만 그것이 초대칭(supersymmetry)과 관련이 있다고 말한다. 그것이 무엇인지 안다면 그것은 우주 전체에 관한 중요한 질문에 대한 답이 될 것이다. 누구든 알 수 없는 물질의 의문을 푸는 사람은 분명 노벨상 수상감이다.

Unit 24

Exercise
P.153

A 2 stopping   3 to excel   4 walking
5 borrowing   6 to attend   7 helping
8 to change

B 1 d   2 g   3 a
4 c   5 f   6 h
7 b   8 e

C 2 not to eat it
3 to go with her
4 not to believe what she says
5 not to say anything
6 to return to its original shape
7 to increase his fluency in French

2 to부정사와 동명사–다른 점

Exercise
P.155

A 1 a   2 b   3 b
4 a   5 a   6 b
7 a   8 b   9 b
10 a

B 3 seeing   4 to remember
5 to think   6 answering
7 saying   8 to inform

C 2 going for a drive   3 doing it myself
4 going back home   5 eating meat
6 going there   7 mastering it

Further Study
P.156

A (A) to ask   (B) to sign   (C) to take
B 1 (A) Taking   (B) not to visit
2 to wait for him or her to calm down to take
C 1 diet-foods

A

I met Damon / in Boston at a mall a year or so ago. I was staring at the actor / being asked for an autograph. I forgot to ask for the autograph. Soon he came through / to order food / and I was amazed / at how polite and friendly he was. He stopped to sign autographs, gave me one, told me to take it easy / and walked away.

나는 약 1년 전에 Boston의 한 상가에서 Damon을 만났다. 나는 사인 요청을 받는 그를 지켜보고 있었다. 나는 그에게 사인 요청하는 것도 잊고 있었다. 이윽고 그는 음식을 주문하러 왔으며, 나는 그가 참 공손하고 다정하다는 점에 놀랐다. 그는 사인을 하기 위해 멈추었고 내게 사인을 해주고 인사를 하면서 걸어 나갔다.

(A) 내용상 사인을 받아야겠다는 생각을 잊고있는 내용이므로 'forget+to부정사'가 필요하다. 'forget+동명사'는 과거에 했던 내용을 잊어버린다는 의미이다.
(B) 문맥상 주어가 사인하기 위해 걸음을 멈춘 내용이므로 'stop+to부정사'가 필요하다. 'stop+동명사'는 '~하는 것을 중단하다'는 내용이다.
(C) tell(말해주다)은 'tell+목적어+to부정사'의 형태로 사용한다.

B

Taking a kid's temperature generates emotional extremes. The sudden increase in temperature / may scare parents. A majority of parents frequently check a feverish child's temperature / and give a child fever-reducing medication. However, excessive concern about a kid's fever / can lead parents to make some wrong moves. If a child is running around a room, / it's better / not to visit an emergency room / no matter what the temperature. If you can't hold down a child / to get a temperature, / then chances are that / he or she's not seriously sick. It's OK / to wait for him/or her to calm down / to take his/or her temperature.

아이들의 체온을 재다보면 감정이 격해질 수 있다. 갑작스런 체온 상승에 부모들은 두려워진다. 많은 부모들은 열이 있는 아이의 체온을 자주 재보고 열을 내리는 약을 주기도 한다. 하지만, 아이의 열을 지나치게 걱정해서 부모들이 잘못된 조치를 내릴 수도 있다. 아이가 방에서 돌아다닌다면 아무리 열이 있어도 응급실에는 가지 않는 것이 낫겠다. 체온을 잴 때 아이를 제지할 수 없을 정도라면 아마도 그 아이는 심각한 상태가 아니다. 그 아이의 체온을 잴 정도로 아이가 진정할 때까지 기다리는 것이 좋겠다.

(A) 문장의 주어에는 명사의 형태만이 오며, 명사의 형태로는 to부정사, 동명사, 명사구, 명사절 등이 온다.
(B) to부정사와 동명사의 부정은 반드시 그 앞에 not을 붙인다.

C

Recently some research suggest / that young animals fed diet food tend to overeat regular food. This research tells us / that children who are fed low-calorie meals / will end up eating much more / when they grow up - thus increasing their risk of obesity. Though the experiments were done on rats, / it means that the more low-calorie food one consumes, / the more one's body demands payback for the calories / it was deprived of. Thus, before feeding your children diet food / you should think it over carefully. When it comes to dieting, / most Americans are willing to resort to a shortcut / to help eat less, / such as opting for artificial sweeteners / instead of sugar. Yet, research suggests / that sugar substitutes are no key to weight loss.

최근 연구 결과 다이어트 음식을 먹인 어린 동물들은 일상적인 음식을 과식하는 경향을 보인다. 이러한 연구는 저칼로리 음식을 먹인 아이들은 성장해서 훨씬 더 많이 먹는 결과를 얻게 되고, 결국 비만의 위험성을 증가시키게 되는 것으로 나타났다. 비록 이 실험이 쥐에게 이루어진 것이지만, 이러한 실험은 저칼로리 음식을 먹으면 먹을수록 사람의 몸은 섭취하지 못한 열량에 대한 보상을 더욱 요구하는 것을 보여준다. 그러므로, 아이들에게 다이어트 음식을 먹이기 전에 조심스럽게 생각해보아야 할 것이다. 다이어트에 관한 한, 대부분의 미국 사람들은 설탕대신 인공감미료를 선택하는 등 손쉬운 방법에 의지하여 음식물 섭취를 줄이려고 한다. 그러나 그 연구는 설탕 대체품이 체중 감량에 열쇠가 될 수 없다는 것을 말하고 있다.

Unit 25

1　to+동사원형의 문장

Exercise
P.159

A 2 to choose(=one to choose)
　3 to stay
　4 to write a resume in English
　5 to blame
　6 to use instead of lemon
　7 to go in

B 2 can't afford to buy a laptop
　3 to fix(repair) the computer
　4 do exercise instead of going on a diet
　5 to win the game
　6 lose many engineers
　7 to be dead

　8 to quit climbing.

C 1 would rather walk than wait for the next bus
　2 no idea on where to go and whom to go with
　3 don't deserve to get paid more than football players
　4 may as well not say anything at all
　5 had better start listening to their voters

2　형용사+to부정사, 명사+to부정사

Exercise
P.161

A 2 d　　　　3 b　　　　4 c
　5 f　　　　6 e

B 2 willingness to care for the babies was welcomed
　3 decision to give up the right to take benefit surprised us
　4 refusal to join the league of nations disappointed us
　5 man to be scared to see the snake

C 2 very clever of Jane to work out the answer
　3 spreads too far to be operated
　4 eager to help you work it out

Further Study
P.162

A (A) are to court　(B) to court
B 1 (A) to ignore　(B) to use
　2 to have the skill to save someone's life
C 1 B　　　　2 is when to begin an action

A

Her father said, "I appreciate / that you've taken an interest in my daughter. Nevertheless, / if you are to court her, / I ask you to do so in secret." I smiled at him, / relieved that he would allow me to court his daughter. In time, if and when she accepts me, / I will make our relationship publicly known.

그녀의 아버지는 "내 딸에게 관심을 가져주어 고맙네. 그럼에도 불구하고 자네가 내 딸에게 구혼을 하고 싶다면 남몰래 해주기를 바라네."라고 말했다. 나는 그 분이 자신의 딸에게 한 구혼을 허락할 것으로 보고 안심이 되어서 그분에게 살짝 웃어보였다. 곧, 그녀가 나를 허락한다면, 그리고 허락할 때는 우리의 관계를 공개적으로 알릴 것이다. 허락한다면, 그리고 허락할 때는 우리의 관계를 공개적으로 알릴 것이다.

(A) 'If S+be to부정사~'는 '~하고 싶다면'으로 해석하며, 조건의 부사절에서는 미래를 현재로 나타내야 한다.

B

Pain is an unpleasant physical and emotional experience. Chronic pain can have negative effects / on the parts of the brain / responsible for mood and attention. More often, pain can prevent you from doing things that must be done, / if you are to survive. Not everyone has the capacity / to ignore severe pain. Under such circumstances, / pain relief is the only practical alternative, / despite any adverse effects. It is important / for you to be well informed of medications and dosage / you may need. That's why / you should know how to use / the emergency medical kit. It is vital / to have the skill / to save someone's life.

통증은 신체적으로도 감정적으로도 유쾌하지 못한 경험이다. 만성적인 통증은 기분과 주의력을 담당하는 뇌 부분에 부정적인 영향을 미칠 수 있다. 또한 통증은 여러분이 살아남으려면 해야 할 일을 못하게 막을 수도 있다. 모든 사람이 심한 통증을 무시하고 지낼 능력을 가진 것은 아니다. 이런 환경에서 통증완화제는 부작용이 있기는 하지만 유일한 실질적 선택사항이다. 여러분이 필요한 약물과 투여량을 잘 알아두는 것이 중요하다. 여러분이 구급약의 사용방법을 알아 두어야 하는 것은 이러한 이유 때문이다. 누군가의 생명을 구하기 위해 기술을 습득하는 것은 매우 중요하다.

(A) capacity을 수식하는 형용사의 형태가 필요하다. 형용사처럼 뒤에서 명사나 대명사를 수식하는 것은 분사(-ing. -ed)와 to부정사이다.

(B) '의문사+to부정사'는 명사구로서 문장의 목적어로 사용될 수 있다.

C

You may / think intuition is the capability / to see the future and is an inner awareness / that goes beyond logical thought. Yet, in fact intuition is the ability / to alert you / if you are in trouble. Then what's stopping you from listening to that? Many times we hear from our intuition / what we should be doing, / but we don't trust it. Your friends or family give contradictory advice, / or you are too afraid to follow it. I've learned through experience / that my life flows more smoothly / if I follow my intuitive voice. Using the logical side of your brain is useful / for solving lots of problems, / but if you don't use your intuition / you are not going to make the best decisions. The core problem is / when to begin an action.

여러분은 직관이란 미래를 보는 능력이며, 논리적인 사고를 뛰어넘는 내적 인식이라고 생각한다. 그러나, 실제 직관이란 여러분이 어려움에 처해 있다면 여러분에게 경고를 주는 능력이다. 그런데 무엇이 여러분으로 하여금 귀를 기울이지 못하게 하는가? 많은 경우 우리는 직관적으로 무엇을 해야 한다는 것을 듣게 되지만 그것을 신뢰하지는 않는다. 여러분의 친구나 가족이 반대의견을 주거나, 여러분이 거기에 따르기에는 두려움이 앞서는 것이다. 나는 경험상 내가 나의 직관적 목소리를 따르면 삶의 흐름이 매끄럽게 진행되는 것을 배웠다. 뇌의 논리적인 면을 사용하면 많은 문제를 해결하는 데에 유용하지만, 직관을 이용하지 않을 경우 최선의 결정을 내리지 못하게 될 것이다. 핵심적인 문제는 언제 행동을 시작하느냐이다.

Unit 26

1 다양한 명사표현

Exercise

P.165

A 2 a reading lamp
   3 the twins' mother
   4 The garage door
   5 the children's position
   6 the computer keyboard
   7 the kitchen table
   8 my sister's husband

B 1 are, They   2 a pair of, They
   3 are, them   4 are, them
   5 were, a pot of

C 1 cow   2 nephew   3 cock
   4 widow   5 bachelor   6 heroine
   7 bride

2 명사를 만드는 접미사

Exercise
P.167

A 1 ②　　　　2 ③　　　　3 ④
　　4 ④　　　　5 ②　　　　6 ⑤
　　7 ⑤　　　　8 ①

B 1 ⑤　　　　2 ⑤　　　　3 ④
　　4 ②

C 1 descendant　　　2 assistant
　　3 protestant　　　　4 servant
　　5 consultant　　　　6 attendant
　　7 applicant

Further Study
P.168

A (A) breadth　(B) length　(C) depth
B 1 (A) hostility　(B) patient
　　2 how to do as adults do around them
C 1 father-in-law

A

How is the breadth of a huge area like an ocean measured? I wonder / how the length of a country, the height of a mountain / or the depth of a sea is measured. Of course, the answer is / that we have satellite data / on which we can accurately measure the relative distances / between faraway points.

바다처럼 거대한 지역의 넓이를 어떻게 측정하는가? 나는 한 나라의 길이, 산의 높이, 또는 바다의 깊이를 어떻게 재는지 궁금하다. 물론, 답은 우리가 실제 멀리 있는 두 지점의 상대적인 거리를 정확히 잴 수 있는 위성자료를 갖고 있다는 것이다.

(A) 문맥상 바다와 같은 넓은 지역을 나타내므로 넓이(breadth)가 필요하다.
(B) 문맥상 한 나라의 길이(length)가 필요하다.
(C) 문맥상 바다의 깊이(depth)가 필요하다.

B

If a child lives with criticism, / he learns to blame. If a child lives with hostility, / he learns to fight. If a child lives with ridicule, / he learns to be shy. But do not despair. If a child lives with tolerance, / he learns to be patient. If a child lives with encouragement, / he learns confidence. If a child lives with applause, he learns to appreciate. If a child lives with fairness, / he learns justice. If a child lives with acceptance and friendship, / he learns to find love in the world. <Children Learn What They Live—Dorothy Law Nolie>

아이가 비난 속에서 산다면 그는 비난하는 것을 배운다. 아이가 적대감 속에서 산다면 그는 싸우는 것을 배운다. 아이가 비웃음을 받으며 산다면, 소심하게 된다. 하지만, 절망하지는 마라. 아이가 인내력을 갖고 산다면 그는 참는 것을 배운다. 아이가 격려를 받고 산다면 그는 자신감을 배운다. 아이가 칭찬을 받고 산다면 그는 감사해 하는 것을 배운다. 아이가 공정함 속에서 산다면 그는 정의롭게 산다. 아이가 인정을 받고 우정을 간직하고 산다면 그는 세상에서 사랑을 찾는 방법을 배운다.

(A) hospitality(환대), hostility(적대감)
(B) impatient(성급한), patient(인내력 있는)

C

When Richard died, / I kept in contact / with his dad, his brothers, his wife and their children. I'm not close to his mother. His parents have been divorced for years / and my relationship with mother-in-law is a long, / complicated story. Although I still call Richard's dad my 'father-in-law' / and I'm still "Aunt" Rosa to / those nieces and nephews, I know / that legally I'm not related to them anymore. My kids, however, will always be related to them. Emotionally I will always feel / that connection to them. For me, that won't go away; / at least, it hasn't yet.

Richard가 죽었을 때 나는 그의 아버지, 그의 형제, 그의 부인, 그리고 그의 아이들과 계속 연락을 취했다. 나는 그의 어머니와 가깝지는 않았다. 그의 부모님은 여러 해 전에 이혼했으며, 나와 시어머니와의 관계는 길고 복잡한 이야기가 있었다. 비록 내가 여전히 Richard의 아버지를 시아버지라고 부르고 조카와 조카딸들에게 여전히 내가 Rosa 숙모라고 불리지만, 법적으로 나는 그들과 더 이상 관련이 없다는 것을 안다. 하지만, 내 아이들은 항상 그들과 관련되어 있을 것이다. 정서적으로 나는 항상 그들과 연결 관계를 느끼고 있다. 나로서는 그것이 사라지지 않는다. 적어도 아직은 사라지지 않았다.

Unit 27

1 It/There 관련 문장

Exercise
P.171

A 1 There 2 it 3 It
   4 it 5 It 6 there
   7 there

B 2 c 3 b 4 f
   5 d 6 e 7 h
   8 g

C 1 certain that appearance is very important.
   2 possible to get rich by playing the game.
   3 Napoleon that invented canned food(=canned food that Napoleon invented)?
   4 to go outside with nothing to do.
   5 to be a disagreement over the best answer.

2 대명사 one, another, the other, others

Exercise
P.173

A 1 one 2 it 3 It
   4 one 5 It 6 ones
   7 one

B 1 another 2 Others
   3 the other 4 another, the other
   5 another 6 the others

C 2 like rock music
   3 others like to have curly hair
   4 energetic and active
   5 night people(=night owls)
   6 spend their holidays in a beach
   7 war, fire, or flood

Further Study
P.174

A (A) one   (B) the other
B 1 (A) others   (B) it
   2 is your mind that controls your life
C 1 D

A

People frequently talk about having an angel / on one shoulder / and the devil on the other. The devil is the thoughts / telling you to do something wrong / in order to gain short term personal satisfaction. The angel is your conscience / telling you not to listen to the devil.

사람들은 한쪽 어깨에는 천사가 있고, 다른 한쪽에는 악마가 있다는 이야기를 자주 한다. 악마는 단기간의 개인적 만족감을 얻기 위해 여러분에게 그릇된 일을 하도록 말해주는 생각이다. 천사는 여러분에게 악마 말을 듣지 말라고 말해주는 양심이다.

(A), (B) 2개의 대상을 대명사로 나타낼 경우에, '하나(one)는~, 나머지 하나(the other)는~'으로 표현한다.

B

Why is it / that some people are fortunate / enough to succeed / with seemingly no effort, / while others struggle all their lives to make ends meet? The main cause can't be a physical one; / otherwise only good looking people would be successful / and other people would be subjected to slave labor. Yet there are countless examples / that plain-looking people are insanely successful. We know it is a mental ability / that determines your success. Success blossoms from your mind: / your mental outlook impacts the way you live. In other words it is your mind / that controls your life.

아무 노력 없이 운 좋게 성공을 하는 사람들이 있는 반면, 어떤 사람들은 빚지지 않고 살기 위해 한 평생 노력을 하는 것은 왜 그런가? 그 이유는 신체적인 것이 아니다. 만약 그렇지 않다면 오직 외모가 수려한 사람만이 성공을 하고 세상의 나머지는 노예처럼 일을 할 운명이란 말인가. 그러나, 평범하게 생긴 사람들이 비상식적으로 성공을 한 예는 무수히 많다. 성공을 결정하는 것은 정신적 능력임을 우리는 알고 있다. 성공은 마음에서 꽃이 피워 오르며, 마음속 사고방식이 여러분의 살아가는 방식에 영향을 미친다. 달리 말해, 당신의 삶을 통제하는 것은 바로 당신의 마음이다.

(A) some~, others~의 표현으로 some은 정확한 수가 아닌 '몇몇'이며, others는 '(막연한) 다른 것들'을 나타낸다.

(B) 앞에 언급된 성공의 자격을 언급하므로, 정해진 대상을 나타내는 it이 필요하다.

C

Tips-for-Travel has completely renewed its website! It's got not only small changes / but an entirely new concept. We think / that it looks more professional / than the previous one. It will give us the chance / to expand our programs to several more countries, / and it'll be easier / to find out and use our new site. However, we also fear / that the changes in our colors and logo make the frequent visitors not recognize us. So we are sending this newsletter / to all our contacts to assure you / that we are the same company and the same people. Please take a look at our new site!

Tips-for-Travel이 웹사이트를 새롭게 단장했습니다. 그리고 작은 변화뿐만 아니라 전적으로 새로운 개념을 실었습니다. 새로

사이트가 이전의 것보다 더욱 전문적으로 보인다고 생각합니다. 이것은 우리의 프로그램이 더 많은 다른 나라로 넓혀나갈 기회를 우리에게 제공할 것이며, 우리의 새로운 사이트를 찾고 이용하기가 더욱 쉬울 것입니다. 하지만, 우리의 색상과 로고가 변화함에 따라 단골 방문객들이 우리를 알아보지 못하게 될까 걱정스럽습니다. 그래서 우리는 전과 같이 동일한 단체이며 동일한 사람들임을 확인시키기 위해 이러한 편지를 우리 접속자인 여러분들에게 보내는 것입니다. 우리의 새로운 사이트에 접속해 보세요.

Unit 28

1 수량표현의 대명사

Exercise
P.177

A 2 most(all) 3 both 4 both
5 All 6 neither

B 1 every 2 each 3 every
4 each 5 every 6 every
7 each

C 2 d 3 c 4 e
5 b 6 h 7 f

2 재귀대명사

Exercise
P.179

A 1 yourself 2 himself 3 myself
4 oneself 5 yourself 6 itself

---

7 yourself 8 yourself 9 herself

B 2 yourself 3 myself 4 himself
5 yourself 6 ourselves 7 yourself

C 2 take care of himself 3 defend yourself
4 blame himself 5 looked at herself
6 made himself 7 devoted herself

A 1 명령문이므로 주어는 2인칭(you)이며, make oneself comfortable은 '편히 쉬다'를 의미한다.
2 apply oneself to는 '~에 열중하다'는 의미이다.
3 주어(I)가 목적어와 동일 인물이기 때문에 재귀대명사가 온다.
4 주어가 목적어로 오면 재귀대명사가 오며, 주어의 형태를 따르므로 oneself가 된다.
5 명령문의 형태에서 주어는 you이므로 yourself가 온다.
6 of itself는 '저절로'라는 뜻이다.
7 명령문에서는 주어가 you이며, '마음대로 해라'는 의미는 'suit yourself'로 표현한다.
8 주어가 목적어와 동일인이므로 재귀대명사를 사용한다.
9 '혼잣말하다'는 주어가 스스로에게 말하는 경우이므로 'tell oneself'로 나타낸다. 주어에 맞게 herself가 필요하다.

Further Study
P.180

A (A) yourself (B) It

B 1 (A) him (B) himself (C) him
2 described himself as a shy, humble, and innocent man

C 1 of your house is the most favored position for every plant

A

When you attempt to do something and fail, you have to ask yourself / why you have failed to do / what you intended. Answering this question in a new, unexpected way / is the essential creative act. It will improve your chances of succeeding / next time.

여러분이 어떤 일을 시도해 보고 실패하면, 여러분은 왜 의도했던 일에 실패했을까 하고 자문해 보아야 한다. 이 질문에 대해 새롭고도 예상하지 못했던 방법으로 답변하는 것이 꼭 필요한 창조적 활동이다. 그렇게 하면, 다음 번에는 여러분이 성공할 가능성이 높아진다.

(A) 내용상 '자신에게 물어보다'는 내용으로서, 주어와 목적어가 같기 때문에 재귀대명사를 써야 한다.
(B) 앞에 나온 'the essential creative act'를 가리키므로, 단수 대명사를 써야 한다.

B

Moreno's twinkling eyes and thin beard / gave him a natural pride and arrogance / but he always described himself / as a shy, humble, and innocent man. Moreno was one of only nine entertainers / to win all four major entertainment awards: / the Tony, the Oscar, the Emmy and the Grammy. Moreno also won all four awards / in the shortest amount of time: / within a 16 year period. Although he described himself / as 'an ordinary character actor', / British people have described him / as 'the greatest gift.'

Moreno의 반짝이는 눈과 가느다란 턱수염은 그에게 자연스럽게 자부심과 거만함을 갖게 해주지만, 그는 항상 자신을 수줍고 겸손하고 순수한 사람이라고 말한다. Moreno는 지금까지 4대 주요 연예상인 오스카, 토니, 그래미, 그리고 에미상을 휩쓴 단지 9명 중 한 사람이었다. 그는 또한 16년이라는 가장 짧은 시간에 4개의 상을 수상했다. 그가 자신을 평범한 성격배우로 묘사했지만, 영국 사람들은 그를 가장 재능있는 사람으로 묘사했다.

(A) 주어와 목적어가 동일하지 않으므로 him이 온다.

(B) 주어와 목적어가 동일하므로 재귀대명사를 써야 한다.

(C) 주어(British people)와 목적어(Moreno)가 다르므로 대명사 him을 써야 한다.

C

Most plants must hold their leaves / above those of competitors in the environment. Without access to sunlight, / they can't gather energy. Most of the plants in nature need many hours of sunshine daily / in order to grow satisfactorily. Leaves must create a broad enough area of photosynthetic tissue / to capture as much sunlight as possible. A large surface area means / greater chances of gaining light. A good general rule to remember / is that less sun just means slower growth, / or may ultimately result in a smaller and less vigorous plant. Usually mornings provide the most intense sunlight / for maximum plant growth. Thus the east side of your house / is the most favored position for every plant.

대부분의 식물은 그들의 잎을 주변 환경의 경쟁자보다 높이 올려야 한다. 햇빛을 가까이 하지 않으면 그들은 에너지를 모을 수 없다. 대부분의 자연환경에 있는 식물은 제대로 자라기 위해서는 매일 많은 시간의 햇빛을 받아야 한다. 나뭇잎은 가능하면 많은 햇빛을 얻기 위해 넓은 면을 가진 광합성 조직을 만들어내야 한다. 넓은 표면이 있어야 햇빛을 얻을 가능성이 더욱 높다. 기억해야 할 일반적인 원칙은 햇빛이 적으면 성장이 더 느리고, 결국 식물은 더 작고 생기가 줄어든다는 것이다. 보통 식물을 가장 잘 자라게 해주는 가장 강렬한 햇빛은 아침에 제공된다. 그러므로, 여러분 집의 동쪽은 모든 식물들이 가장 좋아하는 위치이다.

Unit 29

1   까다로운 형용사

Exercise
P.183

A 2 a wooden horse   3 silken thread
  4 the stony wall   5 a woolen sweater
  6 a man-like steely machine

B 2 officers responsible   3 people involved
  4 involved process   5 people present
  6 present law   7 concerned doctor
  8 people concerned

C 2 see people falling asleep after lunch
  3 a few people involved in the union movements
  4 take time to make something special for your father
  5 math well enough to teach it to her sister

2   파생어

Exercise
P.185

A 1 b   2 g   3 d
  4 c   5 a   6 e
  7 f

B 1 childish   2 industrious   3 sensitive
  4 successive   5 considerate   6 confident
  7 sensible

C 1 ①   2 ②

Further Study
P.186

A (A) successive   (B) temporary

B 1 (A) like   (B) brilliantly   (C) alive
  2 supremely delighted

C 1 (A) substances present   (B) valuable   (C) sensitive
  2 skin

A

Generally, a citizen who has resided for five successive years / will obtain the right of permanent residence. In order to obtain the right of temporary residence, / a citizen must contact the local government authorities. The applicant can be granted the right / to reside five years.

일반적으로 5년 연속으로 거주한 시민은 영주권을 얻을 것이다. 임시 거주권을 얻으려는 시민은 그 지역 행정 담당자를 만나야 한다. 신청자는 5년간의 거주 권리를 받을 수 있다.

(A) successive: 연속적인   successful: 성공적인
(B) temporary: 순간의, 일시의   contemporary: 동시대의

B

Falling in love is like being wrapped / in a magical cloud. The air feels fresher, / the flowers smell sweeter, / food tastes more delicious, / and the stars shine more brilliantly / in the night sky. You feel light and happy / as though you are sailing through life. Your problems and challenges suddenly seem insignificant. Your body feels alive, / and you jump out of bed each morning / with a smile on your face. You are in a state of supreme delight.

사랑에 빠지는 것은 신비한 구름에 싸여 있는 것과 같다. 공기의 느낌이 더 신선해지고, 꽃 냄새가 더 향긋해지고, 음식 맛이 더 좋아지며, 밤하늘의 별이 더 찬란하게 반짝이게 된다. 당신은 마치 인생을 순항하듯이 경쾌하고 행복한 느낌을 갖게 된다. 당신의 고민과 난제들이 갑자기 대수롭지 않은 것으로 보이게 된다. 몸에 활력을 느끼면서 당신은 아침마다 얼굴에 미소를 띤 채 잠자리에서 힘차게 나오게 된다. 당신의 즐거움은 최고의 상태가 된다.

(A) alike는 서술적 용법으로 사용되는 형용사로서 목적어를 둔 문장에서 사용할 수 없다. like는 'A is like B', 'A look like B'의 형태로 사용된다.
(B) 동사(shine)를 수식하는 부사가 필요하다.
(C) 문맥상 보어로 사용되는 alive(살아있는)가 필요하다. lived는 live의 과거형이며, 'long-lived man(오래 사는 사람)'처럼 부사와 결합해 형용사로 사용되기도 한다.

C

Aloe vera has been used externally / to heal various skin conditions, / such as burns and eczema. The lower leaves of the Aloe vera plants are used / for medicinal purposes, / protecting the immune system and improving digestive function. Its multiple beneficial properties may come from the substances / present in the gel of the plant's leaves. The light gel cream is valuable / in soothing the eye area, / reducing swellings and removing little wrinkles. Aloe gel is also useful / for dry skin conditions, / especially sensitive facial skin. One should always use the inner gel of the plant / and not the aloe latex / which is the yellow substance / that comes from the inner side of the skin of the plant.

알로에는 화상이나 습진과 같은 다양한 피부 상태를 치료하기 위해 몸에 바르는 용도로 사용되어 왔다. 알로에 잎의 아랫부분은 면역 체계를 보호하고 소화기능을 개선하는 의학적 용도로 사용된다. 알로에의 여러 가지 유익한 성분은 잎의 젤에 존재하는 물질에서 나온다. 가벼운 젤 크림은 눈 부위를 진정시키고 부어오른 부분을 완화시켜주고 잔주름을 없애는데 아주 좋다. 알로에는 또한 건조한 피부, 특히 민감한 얼굴 피부에 유용하다. 사람들은 항상 알로에의 안쪽 젤 부분을 사용해야 하며, 껍질 안쪽에서 나오는 노란 물질부분인 알로에 라텍스를 사용해서는 안 된다.

Unit 30

1 다양한 부사

Exercise
P.189

A 2 eagerly   3 bravely   4 carefully
  5 late   6 early   7 quickly
B 1 still   2 still   3 yet
  4 already   5 already   6 yet
  7 yet
C 2 Frankly   3 Fortunately   4 Obviously
  5 Personally

2 혼동하기 쉬운 형용사와 부사

Exercise
P.191

A 1 lively   2 costly   3 lately
  4 near   5 highly   6 hardly
  7 elderly   8 hard
B 2 d   3 e   4 b
  5 c   6 g   7 f
C 1 pretty   2 longed (=has longed)
  3 well (=better)   4 long
  5 slowled   6 fast

A

1 감각을 나타내는 동사(feel, look, sound, smell, taste) 뒤에는 상태를 나타내는 보어가 오므로 형용사가 필요하다.

2 문맥상 '값비싼'이란 뜻의 형용사가 와야 하며, 일반적으로 명사 뒤의 -ly는 형용사를 만든다.

3 late(늦은, 늦게)와 lately(최근에)를 구분하여 사용해야 하며, 문맥상 여기서는 lately가 적당하다.

4 near(가까운, 가까이)와 nearly(거의)를 구분하여 사용해야 한다.

5 think highly of(~를 중시하다)에서 highly는 정도를 나타내는 부사(높이, 매우)이다.

6 문맥상 '거의 ~않는'이란 의미의 부사가 필요하며, hard는 형용사(힘든, 열심히 하는)와 부사(열심히)로 쓰인다.

7 elder(더 나이 먹은)와 elderly(연로한, 나이 먹은)를 구분하여 사용해야 한다. 단순한 노인을 나타내는 내용이므로 elderly가 온다.

8 문맥상 '힘든'이란 의미의 형용사가 온다. hardly는 부정 부사로서 '거의~않는'의 의미이다.

Further Study

P.192

A (A) pretty (B) well

B 1 (A) always feel (B) hardly
  2 creates and maintains good relationships.

C 1 a diabetic patient frequently tests his or her blood sugar levels on a regular basis.

A

For the first 2 weeks of my ownership of the N95, / I was pretty unhappy. I was a very heavy mobile phone user, / but the battery lasted only 7 hours per day. Now, though, I get well over 2 days / from the battery. So everything is well now.

내가 N95을 소유한 지 처음 2주 동안은 아주 불쾌했다. 내가 휴대폰을 많이 사용하는 사람이긴 하지만, 배터리는 하루에 겨우 7시간 지속됐다. 그러나 이제는 배터리가 2일 정도는 족히 간다. 이제 모든 것이 만족스럽다.

(A) 문맥상 pretty(매우)가 필요하며, prettily는 형용사 pretty(예쁜)의 부사 형태이다.

(B) 문맥상 보어인 형용사가 필요하며, well(만족스런, 좋은)은 형용사로 사용되었다.

B

Dick would show up in Florida a lot / and always feel so zealous and happy. He'd travel with his little backpack / that was still smaller / than my purse. Lately I have been thinking about / how he hardly ever had any baggage. I think / that his free spirit and his curiosity enabled him / to travel lightly with little baggage. He didn't hesitate to touch hundreds of lives / and was willing to stay in contact with everyone. He not only created relationships with people all over the world, / but he maintained them. My friend once said / that in a relationship / there is the gardener / and there is the flower. Dick was a gardener.

Dick은 플로리다에 자주 모습을 보였는데, 항상 열정적이고 행복해 했다. 그는 작은 배낭을 메고 여행을 가곤 하는데, 그 가방이 나의 서류가방보다도 더 작았다. 최근에 나는 그가 어떻게 짐도 없이 여행하는지 생각해보았다. 그의 자유로운 기질과 호기심 때문에 짐도 별로 없이 가볍게 여행을 할 수 있었다고 생각한다. 그는 주저하지 않고 수백 명의 사람들과 기꺼이 접촉을 하고, 또 계속 만남을 유지해 갔다. 그는 전 세계 사람들과 관계를 만들어 낼 뿐만 아니라 유지하기도 했다. 내 친구가 말하길 인간관계에서는 정원사가 있고 꽃이 있다고 했는데 Dick은 바로 정원사였다.

(A) 빈도부사는 be동사나 조동사의 뒤에, 일반 동사의 앞에 온다.

(B) 부정부사(hardly, seldom, rarely 등)는 빈도부사의 위치인 조동사와 be동사의 뒤, 일반 동사의 앞에 온다. hard는 형용사(힘든, 열심히 하는)와 부사(열심히)로 사용된다. 문장의 문맥상 hardly가 필요하다.

C

When you think about diabetes / you usually think / it has something to do with sugar. But sadly, that's not all to it. A patient is diagnosed as having prediabetes / when glucose called blood sugar is higher than normal / but not high enough to be diagnosed as diabetes. Our body needs glucose to function properly, / but occasionally it becomes incapable of processing the sugar / that it gets from foods. Once the body can't process sugar efficiently, / it is diagnosed as diabetes. Knowing that the symptoms are in the early stages / can aid in getting the proper treatment. This is why / a diabetic patient frequently test his or her blood sugar levels / on a regular basis.

여러분들이 당뇨병을 생각할 때 일반적으로는 당분과 관계있다고 생각을 한다. 하지만, 아쉽게도 모두가 꼭 그런 것은 아니다. 혈당이라고 불리는 포도당이 정상보다 높게 나오지만 당뇨라는 진단을 받을 만큼은 아닌 경우, 환자는 당뇨병 전증(前症)이라고 진단을 받는다. 몸이 제대로 기능을 발휘하기 위해서는 포도당을 필요로로 하지만, 가끔씩 몸은 우리가 먹는 음식에서 나오는 당분을 처리할 수 없는 경우가 있다. 일단 우리 몸이 당분을 효율적으로 처리할 수 없게 되면 당뇨병의 진단이 나온다. 증세가 초기 단계라는 것을 알게 되면 적절한 치료에 도움이 된다. 이것 때문에 당뇨환자가 혈당치를 정기적으로 자주 검사해야 하는 것이다.

Unit 31

1 '아' 다르고 '어' 다르다—관사

Exercise

A 1 the 2 × 3 ×
4 the 5 × 6 the
7 ×

B 2 is 3 are 4 is
5 are 6 is

C 2 a tree, and the driver of the car
3 ate at a restaurant near the hotel
4 a variety of events throughout the year
5 out of the question in apartment buildings

B 1 주어가 A number of(= many)이므로 복수동사가 온다.
2 주어가 The number of(~의 수)이므로 단수동사가 온다.
3 주어가 a range of services이므로 are가 와야 한다.
4 주어가 The kind of flowers이므로 단수동사가 온다.
5 주어가 A variety of cultures(다양한 문화들)이므로 복수동사가 온다.
6 The variety of(~의 다양성)가 주어이므로 단수동사가 온다.

2 '아' 다르고 '어' 다르다—전치사

Exercise
P.197

A 2 succeeded to 3 succeed in
4 resulted from 5 attended to
6 resulted in

B 1 Because of 2 Because 3 to
4 as 5 Despite 6 Though
7 In case of 8 In case
**전치가 뒤에는 명사(구)가 오며, 접속사 뒤에는 하나의 문장이 온다. 그러므로 전치사인지 접속사인지 구분을 해야 한다.

C 1 with 2 about 3 about
4 with 5 for 6 about

Further Study
P.198

A (A) because of (B) despite
B 1 (A) as (B) according to
C 1 Wessex

A

When Ben's family moved / into a white neighborhood, the kids would tease Ben / because of his terrible Spanish accent. The move was good for him / despite the culture shock, / because now Ben could only speak English. Little by little, / Ben learned to speak and write the English language.

Ben의 가족이 백인들 마을로 이사 갔을 때, 아이들은 Ben의 형편 없는 스페인어 억양 때문에 그를 놀려댔다. 문화적 충격은 있었으나 현재 Ben이 영어를 말할 수 있다는 것 때문에도 이사를 간 것은 Ben에게 좋은 일이었다. 조금씩 Ben은 영어 말하기와 쓰기를 배워갔다.

(A) because(접속사)는 문장과, because of(전치사)는 명사와 결합한다. 뒤에 명사 형태(my terrible Spanish accent)가 오므로 because of가 필요하다.
(B) 문맥상 '~에도 불구하고(despite, in spite of)'가 필요하다.

B

Many people keep big cats / as pets across U.S., / in spite of risk. How would you feel / if you discovered / that a tiger is living next door in your suburban neighborhood? Like puppies, / big cats are quite appealing / when they're young and playful. In fact, / the country may have more pet tigers / than there are estimated / to be remaining in their wild habitats in Asia, / according to research / done for the National Geographic Ultimate Explorer television documentary. Acquiring large cats is legal / and surprisingly easy in many states / and counties in the United States. But most owners end up with trouble and damage.

미국 전역에 걸쳐 많은 사람들이 위험을 무릅쓰고 애완동물로 큰 고양이과 동물을 기른다. 교외 지역에 거주하는 여러분 이웃에 호랑이가 산다는 것을 안다면 여러분은 어떤 느낌이겠는가? 강아지처럼, 큰 고양이과는 어리고 재롱부릴 때는 아주 매력적이다. 사실, National Geographic의 텔레비전 기록영상인 Ultimate Explorer에서 이루어진 연구에 따르면, 미국에는 아시아 야생 서식지에 남아있다고 추산되는 것 이상으로 많은 애완용 호랑이들이 있다고 한다. 덩치 큰 고양이과 동물을 구하는 것이 미국의 많은 주에서는 합법적이고 놀랍게도 쉬운 일이다. 하지만, 결국 대부분의 주인에게는 시끄러운 일과 손해를 배상하는 것으로 끝난다.

(A) 문맥상 '~로서'가 필요하므로 as가 필요하다. 'like+명사'는 '~처럼'의 의미이다.

(B) according to(전치사)는 뒤에 명사가, according as(접속사)는 뒤에 문장이 온다. 뒤에는 문장이 아니라 done 이하가 research를 수식하는 형태가 오므로 according to가 필요하다.

C

Wessex is one of the kingdoms / of Anglo-Saxon Britain. According to the documents pertaining to its origin, / Ethelwulf succeeded to the throne of Wessex / at his father's death in 839, / while the eastern provinces went to his son or brother. A similar division took place / on Ethelwulf's death / between his two sons Ethelbald and Ethelberht. Later, the former was succeeded in 865 by Ethelred / and the latter by Alfred in 871. This was the period of the great Danish invasion. Shortly afterwards Ethelred accepted Alfred's overlordship. By 886 Alfred's authority was recognized / in all the provinces of England / which were not under Danish rule. From this time onwards / the history of Wessex is the history of England.

Wessex는 Anglo–Saxon Britain 왕국들 중 하나이다. 왕국의 기원에 관한 기록 서류에 따르면, Ethelwulf가 839년 그의 아버지가 죽자 Wessex의 왕위를 물려받았다. 반면, 동부 지역은 그의 아들과 형제에게 넘어갔다. 비슷한 분할이 Ethelwulf의 사후에 그의 두 아들 Ethelbald와 Ehtelberht 사이에 발생했다. 훗날, 전자인 Ethelbald의 경우 865년 Ethelred에 의해, 후자인 Ethelberht는 871년 Alfred에 의해 계승되었다. 이 때는 덴마크 제국의 침입 시기였다. 그 직후 Ethelred가 Alfred의 대군주 지위를 인정했다. 886년까지 Alfred의 권력은 덴마크의 지배 하에 있지 않은 영국의 모든 지방 세력에게 인정을 받았다. 이때부터 계속해서 Wessex의 역사는 영국의 역사가 되었다.

Workbook Answers

Unit 1

A

1 in spite of
2 despite
3 watching
4 egg-laying
5 frightening
6 somebody strange
7 something special

B

1 happy → happily
2 cheap something → something cheap
3 fluent → fluently
4 neat → neatly
5 dined → dining
6 friend → friendly

C

1 Are you for or against
2 has been unusually cold this year
3 was something strange about
4 Quitting smoking is heavily influenced
5 big black furry

Further Study

1

1 surrounding
2 missing
3 participating
4 injured
5 driving

2 ③

3 badly, clear

4

1 joining two villages
2 made in this factory
3 left their telephone out of order
4 will be nothing

Unit 2

A

1 silent   2 makes
3 is   4 Taking
5 depends   6 To stay, to destroy

B

1 Either Sally or John
2 No one in the earth
3 The importance of luck in achieving one's goals
4 One of the most important steps you must take
5 To forget about the most embarrassing moment in your life
6 the world
7 Excluding those from voting who are already socially isolated
8 Introducing a new management style and overcoming its huge losses

C

1 What you know and what you do
2 One third of the apples
3 The most serious disease connected with smoking
4 Sewage containing human waste
5 The company where I work

Further Study

1

1 Different ways of speaking are found between men and women.
  - ways of speaking = S
  - are found = V

2 Overall, getting up early and going to bed early is good for health.
  - getting up early and going to bed early = S
  - is = V
  - good = C

3 Following these simple guidelines will have a good effect on the environment.
  - Following these simple guidelines = S
  - will have = V
  - a good effect = O

4 Maintaining friendship with anybody requires a lot of patience and understanding.
  - Maintaining friendship with anybody = S
  - requires = V
  - a lot of patience and understanding = O

5 Taking pictures and collecting old paintings as a
student made your pocket empty.
          s   v   o   oc

6 Doing things together such as camping and
traveling is an important part of friendship.

2 ①

3 was, like

4
1 will do you good
2 proportion of older people, increasing
3 economy, accounts for
4 strange feeling crept over

2 단순 문장–동사의 형태   P.8~9

A
1 popular   2 quiet
3 lies   4 laid
5 married

B
1 Ø, about   2 at/in, Ø
3 Ø, to   4 at, Ø
5 to, Ø   6 with, Ø

C
1 envied
2 me
3 worries about
4 agree with
5 resembled
6 answer

Further Study

1
1 on 삭제
2 like 삭제
3 happily → happy
4 with 삭제
5 about 삭제
6 about 삭제

2 ③

3 lay, sat

4
1 ordered them to leave
2 were poorly informed
3 have multiple meanings
4 to apply for the job

Unit 3

1 단순 문장–목적어의 종류   P. 10~11

A
1 him, his well-shaped figure
2 many market observers
3 that animal intelligence can be measured
4 hearing all about your adventures
5 me, what I really needed
6 how to send videos from this camera to an e-mail
address

B
1 for   2 for
3 to   4 of

C
1 Scott gave her a pretty doll at Christmas.
2 They ordered some pizza for us.
3 She gave me what I really wanted.
4 I don't know what to do after graduation.
5 The brand-new car cost me an arm and a leg.
6 My teacher asked a question of me.

Further Study

1
1 coming → to come
2 for → of/about
3 to → for
4 have → having
5 buy → buying

2
1 ①   2 ⑤

3 tell, to wait

4
1 prepared well for
2 is enjoying every moment
3 deals with the life and death
4 who will be their teacher

2 단순 문장–보어의 형태 　　　　 P. 12~13

A

1 to make
2 to bond
3 surprised
4 to shout
5 good
6 called
7 making

B

1 be → to be
2 truly → true
3 doing → to do
4 beautifully → beautiful
5 silently → silent
6 doing → to do

C

1 young
2 the book a little difficult for me
3 him to be dismissed
4 relieved to learn that the danger was gone
5 them turn down his job application
6 him very unpopular with the staff

Further Study

1

1 true
2 run
3 hard
4 happily
5 shyly

2

1 ①
2 ③

3 bad, to flow

4

1 such as maple leaves, turn red
2 grow old, the truth of
3 get better in a few days
4 difficult to keep warm

Unit 4

1 복합 문장–접속사 　　　　 P. 14~15

A

1 and
2 and
3 nor
4 or
5 and
6 for
7 but

B

1 ③
2 ②
3 ③
4 ①
5 ③
6 ①

C

1 are both interesting and
2 was not only a doctor but also
3 go to school by bus or
4 he neither smokes nor
5 so I went to bed
6 for her mother was sick

Further Study

1

1 but
2 and
3 so
4 for
5 or
6 but also

2 ④

3 and, but

4

1 was neither television nor radio
2 or you will get toothache
3 so I couldn't see what was happening
4 not only love me, trust me

2 병렬 구조 　　　　 P. 16~17

A

1 am
2 is
3 is
4 had
5 sincerity
6 watching
7 or

B

1 gets up
2 are
3 collecting
4 like
5 are
6 got

C

1 Both fish and milk are good for our health.
2 I saw Susie's sister/her sister as well as Susie at the shopping mall.
3 Thomson has not only an electric guitar but also a classical guitar.
4 They play either basketball or computer games after school.
5 He likes neither fishing nor swimming.
6 His speech is both boring and difficult.

Further Study

1
1 skillful → skillfully
2 calling → called
3 to speak → speaking
4 receives → received
5 building → build
6 honest → honesty

2 ①

3 watching, break

4
1 we learn culture as well as language
2 waste food but also damages your health
3 are often required by, and
4 either mow the lawn or wash the car

Unit 5

1 주어와 동사의 일치   P. 18~19

A

1 was	2 has
3 have	4 are
5 are	6 is
7 was	

B

1 remains → remain
2 was → were
3 was → were
4 were → was
5 keep → keeps
6 was → were
7 are → is
8 has → have
9 have → has
10 seem → seems

C

1 is	2 is
3 remains	4 were
5 is	6 does
7 seems	8 was

Further Study

1
1 is	2 is
3 were	4 have
5 is	6 makes

2 ①

3 were

4
1 ability to apply his knowledge
2 A number of passengers were injured
3 are still a few minutes left
4 has been damaged

2 주어+단수동사 P. 20~21

A
1 has   2 has
3 is   4 is
5 is   6 makes
7 is

B
1 prevent → prevents
2 are → is
3 are → is
4 are → is
5 were → was
6 are → is
7 have become → has become

C
1 Nodding your head up and down means "yes" in this country.
2 Learning a foreign language is a process that takes a lifetime.
3 To earn the respect of your children is a real success in life.
4 To laugh often and much brings you a healthier life.

Further Study

1
1 have → has
2 require → requires
3 are → is
4 were → was
5 are → is
6 perform → performs
7 are → is

2
1 ②   2 ①
3 is, is

4
1 state is facing
2 is a long time to spend
3 diabetes is still regarded
4 a number of young boys took up arms

Unit 6

1 부정의 문장 P. 22~23

A
1 Neither   2 any
3 Nobody   4 anything
5 any   6 anywhere

B
1 Both   2 any
3 either   4 Neither
5 Not, all

C
1 none of the girls sitting there
2 neither of these books
3 never experienced this problem before
4 nowhere to get some drinking water

Further Study

1
1 Nobody   2 anything
3 anybody   4 None
5 Neither   6 No

2 ⑤

3 no, any

4
1 everyone of his family
2 ready to grab chances
3 there is none
4 money doesn't always bring happiness

2 도치의 문장 P. 24~25

A
1 will I   2 comes the bus
3 could barely 4 did I know
5 can we   6 does
7 is

B
1 was   2 did
3 has he   4 could he
5 never did

C

1 have we received complaints about her
2 did she know that her boyfriend had a twin sister
3 can I believe what he said about the incident
4 will I leave the office before it gets dark
5 has the city developed since we moved three years ago
6 does the weather change in some parts of the world

Further Study

1
1 do they go for a walk
2 have I seen such a splendid sight
3 could she understand what the book was about
4 did Mr. Jones spend money buying clothes and shoes

2 ②

3 all, do

4
1 comes our teacher
2 have I had a chance
3 does he have trouble
4 did I dream

Unit 7

| **1** | 명사절 | P. 26~27 |

A

1	That	2	whether
3	Whether	4	that
5	should	6	be allowed

B

1	b	2	b
3	a	4	b
5	b	6	a
7	b	8	a

C

1 he bought
2 many Japanese people celebrate
3 I locked
4 Jennifer will get married
5 Canada has

Further Study

1
1 be   2 give
3 be   4 save
5 be

2 ⑤

3 that, if

4
1 critical that you (should) follow
2 her son had failed the entrance exam
3 can deny the fact
4 know if/whether, feed the chickens first

| **2** | that S+V | P. 28~29 |

A

1	to	2	on
3	of	4	that
5	that	6	that

B

1 taking → take
2 to → of
3 to → of
4 of → to
5 get → getting

C

1 she has an expensive necklace
2 he was a spy
3 I (should) go out in the rain
4 you are healthy
5 she returned home safe
6 the room was too cold
7 I heard of your father's death

Further Study

1
1 to   2 to
3 that   4 of

2 ③

3 of, that

4
1 complained, he was treated
2 he could not make himself understood
3 are not aware of
4 are pleased that

52

Unit 8

1 형용사절-관계대명사 I
P. 30~31

A
1 that
2 whose
3 living
4 appointed
5 whom
6 who

B
1 ×
2 ○
3 ×
4 ○
5 ×
6 ×
7 ○

C
1 who(m)/that is now in New York
2 (which/that is) located in the suburbs
3 whom/who performed with many other artists
4 which/that was first used in Africa
5 which/that many tourists are looking at

Further Study

1
1 whose
2 which
3 whose
4 who
5 whom
6 which

2 ③

3 which

4
1 (who(m)/that) my brother fell in love with
2 (who/that is) sitting next to the door
3 who/that sang many famous songs
4 (which is) spoken in the province

2 형용사절-관계대명사 II
P. 32~33

A
1 two of which
2 about which
3 which
4 which
5 much
6 of which

B
1 which → for which 또는 looking → looking for
2 on that I slept → that I slept on 또는 that → which
3 which → on which 또는 sitting → sitting on
4 much → many
5 which → of which 또는 fond → fond of
6 that → which
7 was → were

C
1 none of whom
2 some of which
3 none of which
4 most of which
5 most of whom
6 some of whom

Further Study

1
1 which
2 which
3 to
4 whom
5 which joins

2 ③

3 which, were

4
1 who likes to wear white clothes
2 who/that is talking to Jessica
3 most of which are brand-new
4 (which is) located in

Unit 9

A

1 where
2 the way
3 when
4 when
5 why

B

1 why she dislikes me
2 where roads meet
3 when the new school year begins
4 why Mr. Kim is absent from work for a few days
5 where I was the guest of honor

C

1 where the Olympic Games took place in 2008
2 where they had many devoted fans
3 how the young boy made a million dollars
4 when the World Cup soccer tournament took place in Korea
5 why I cannot agree with you

Further Study

1

1 where
2 why
3 when
4 how
5 which

2 ②

3 where, indicate

4

1 the village where I used to paint
2 The reason why/that I applied for this company
3 where goods from foreign countries
4 the way he wanted

A

1 what
2 whoever
3 However
4 Whenever
5 Whoever
6 what

B

1 Whenever
2 wherever
3 whatever
4 Whatever
5 whomever
6 However

C

1 b
2 a
3 b
4 a
5 c
6 c
7 c

Further Study

1

1 Whatever
2 whomever
3 what
4 whoever
5 what

2 ③

3 What, who

4

1 No matter where you may go/Wherever you may go
2 whomever you recommend
3 What I want to say
4 whenever she has

Unit 10

A

1 Why
2 took
3 Where
4 did you see
5 From whom
6 For what reason

B

1 Whose
2 What
3 Whom
4 Why
5 Who

C

1 How many students are there in the auditorium?
2 Who showed her the way to the station?
3 Which book did they choose?
4 How much did you pay for your hat?
5 Where has your father gone?
6 Which do you like better, spring or autumn?

1
1 How → What
2 Where → What
3 What reason → For what reason 또는 fined → fined for
4 How → Which
5 From what → From whom

2
1 ①   2 ④
3 what, Who

4
1 How about going for a swim
2 Whom did you sit next to
3 Who immigrated
4 What national holiday do Korean people

| **2** | **간접의문문** | P. 40~41 |

A
1 which is
2 who will
3 you went
4 Where do you think
5 what
6 it will

B
1 Who do you think will help me cut the wheat field today?
2 I wonder how your father makes a living.
3 I asked her what the population of Seoul is/was.
4 Whom do you suppose he is looking for?

C
1 Who broke the window?
2 When will their train arrive?
3 Where does your brother live?
4 How far is it from Seoul to Busan?

1
1 is the mayor of the town → the mayor of the town is
2 Do you suppose which way → Which way do you suppose
3 What do you know → Do you know what
4 does she like → she likes
5 Why do you know → Do you know why
6 is the best title of this passage → the best title of this passage is

2 ②

3 where they had, that

4
1 What do you think the second largest country
2 tell me how long you have been working/have worked
3 when the bank closes
4 why you applied for the job

Unit 11

| **1** | **시간의 문장 I** | P. 42~43 |

A
1 will pay	2 have been
3 have been	4 finishes
5 comes	6 arrive

B
1 went	2 will, be
3 walks	4 was, cooked
5 was, waiting	6 had, kept
7 had	8 Have, met

C
1 before	2 before
3 while	4 since
5 By the time	

1

1 While   2 after
3 since   4 before

2 ②

3 when, ever since

4

1 since I came here
2 I was reading a newspaper
3 when I go to the supermarket
4 will have already started

A

1 as soon as   2 while
3 did I know   4 as long as
5 Once   6 While

B

1 while having dinner
2 when hearing a child crying softly
3 before going out to ride a bike
4 After spending all his money

C

1 midnight did she return home,
   midnight that she returned home
2 they lose it do people know the blessing of health
   they lose it that people know the blessing of health
3 last week did Scott realize he was wrong,
   last week that Scott realized he was wrong

1

1 whenever   2 as long as
3 As soon as   4 Once

2 ③

3 as long as, that

4

1 until she was in her 70's
2 As soon as he heard of the accident
3 When opening the door/When we opened the door
4 As they grew older

Unit 12

A

1 tell   2 had
3 were   4 would be
5 Otherwise   6 had taken

B

1 I knew how to drive a car, I could take you home
2 I hadn't followed your advice, I would have been deceived
3 it had not rained hard last night, the road would not be very muddy
4 my mother's tender care, I would not be strong and healthy
5 had not been ill, I would have attended the meeting

C

1 I didn't have the book, I could not lend it to you
2 he didn't have open-heart surgery, he is not alive
3 he is not a man of sense, he does such a thing
4 I don't get up early, I cannot eat breakfast with my family

1

1 Had   2 does
3 were not   4 have bought
5 had not been

2 ③

3 If, As

4

1 If I were in your position
2 If you had driven carefully
3 had listened to, wouldn't be in trouble
4 Otherwise I would have missed

2 소망 · 가정의 문장 P. 48~49

A

1 could
2 went
3 had told
4 unless
5 were not
6 could not have passed

B

1 I wish I could have gone with him.
2 I wish I had a car.
3 I wish he could visit us more often.
4 I wish I had been there yesterday.

C

1 we left here now
2 as if he were a baby
3 he had been born in better times
4 he had been a true Christian
5 your kind help, it had not been for your kind help

Further Study

1

1 were
2 went
3 unless
4 had taken
5 Without

2 ①

3 stopped, realized, should appreciate

4

1 as if he had lived in the U.S.A.
2 It's time that the government did
3 Without your timely advice
4 unless you are willing to change

Unit 13

1 원인 · 이유의 문장 P. 50~51

A

1 for
2 Because
3 because
4 Because of
5 why
6 resulted in
7 resulted form

B

1 Due to → As/Because/Since
2 so → because/since/as
3 Because → Because of/Due to/Owing to
4 because → why
5 from → in

C

1 for the gasoline was out
2 due to her weak sight
3 is causing me a lot of problems
4 because of heavy rain
5 resulted from the end of the 2nd World War
6 because they believe meat is not good for their health

Further Study

1

1 to
2 because of
3 for
4 from
5 why

2 ②

3 when, why

4

1 I do not despise him
2 because/as/since it has a lot of fat and sugar
3 Due to this year's cold weather
4 resulted in the death of three passengers

P. 52~53

A

1 so as not to
2 lest
3 so
4 such
5 so as not to
6 such
7 in order to

B

1 so as not
2 able
3 in order
4 so that
5 so wise

C

1 so, hot
2 such, great
3 such, that
4 so, that

Further Study

1

1 lest
2 so
3 such
4 so that
5 in order

2 ③

3 so, so

4

1 in order that, could cross the road
2 such a tiny kitchen that
3 As a result, she missed an important test
4 lest we should forget

Unit 14

1 대조의 문장-양보절 P. 54~55

A

1 In spite of
2 Despite
3 Even though
4 However
5 Frightened
6 However

B

1 an old man → old a man
2 roughly → rough
3 yet 삭제 또는 Though 삭제
4 so → as
5 As → Even though/Though/Although
6 in spite → in spite of

7 of 삭제

C

1 Even, though
2 In, spite
3 Though, tired
4 However
5 In, spite
6 No, matter, how

Further Study

1

1 However, painful
2 Even, though
3 as, she, is
4 In, spite, of

2 ⑤

3 Despite, even though

4

1 However/No matter how difficult a thing is
2 Even if you don't like the decision
3 Even though/Though/Although their offer was obviously unfair
4 In spite of/Despite our effort

2 대조의 문장-연결사 P. 56~57

A

1 whereas
2 instead
3 on the contrary
4 Like
5 Nevertheless
6 on the other hand

B

1 instead of
2 yet
3 like
4 instead
5 nevertheless

C

1 ②
2 ③
3 ⑤
4 ②
5 ③
6 ⑤

1
1 yet
2 unlike
3 Still
4 In spite of
5 However

2 ③

3 yet, as

4
1 Unlike her mother
2 yet she missed
3 but it is still a matter of concern
4 look at/on the bright side

Unit 15

| **1** | 원급의 비교 | P. 58~59 |

A
1 I
2 than
3 as
4 as
5 large
6 that

B
1 than → as
2 like → as
3 much → more
4 Japan → Japan's
5 the original book → that of the original book
6 as larger than → as large as 또는 as larger than → larger than
7 sharper → sharp

C
1 seven times as old
2 as delicious as
3 four times as tall
4 not as/so fast as
5 not as/so quick as
6 as fresh as

1
1 cheap
2 as
3 as
4 that of snakes
5 I

2 ④

3 than, many

4
1 advised me to eat as little as possible
2 twice as many bedrooms as my uncle's
3 earned twice as much as
4 not as/so expensive as

| **2** | 비교의 문장 | P. 60~61 |

A
1 latter
2 hotter
3 later
4 by far
5 the most
6 much
7 the less

B
1 the least → the less
2 as → than
3 happyest → happiest
4 many → much
5 farther → further
6 elder → older

C
1 the most delicious apple that I've ever eaten
2 the most beautiful scenery that I've ever seen
3 the biggest animal in the world
4 the longest river in the U.S.A.
5 Rome best

1
1 high
2 cities
3 brightest
4 later
5 further
6 much

2 ④

3 even, latest

4
1 the second biggest continent is
2 The hotter, the more crowded

3 much/even/far cheaper than new cars
4 I eat less than she/my sister

Unit 16

1 동사의 단순시제 P. 62~63

A

1 will drop
2 come
3 did you finish
4 rains
5 has gone
6 will come
7 was

B

1 has, lost
2 rises
3 watched
4 agrees
5 suffered
6 has, suffered
7 broke
8 will, experiment
9 will, be

C

1 will come → comes
2 visits → will visit
3 will start → start
4 have been → was
5 was → is
6 will rain → rains
7 is working → has worked/has been working

Further Study

1

1 finish
2 has taught/has been teaching
3 attended
4 took
5 stay

2 ⑤

3 before, jumps

4

1 brushes his teeth
2 Before you leave
3 lay down on the bed
4 I met an American captain

2 동사의 완료시제 P. 64~65

A

1 for
2 have been
3 have been
4 has already left
5 have happened
6 had bought

B

1 has, gone
2 have, forgotten
3 have, been, married
4 has, been

C

1 no doubt that he was a spy
2 that he was ignorant of the fact
3 that he did such a thing
4 had forgotten my instructions

Further Study

1

1 have known
2 had already gone
3 since
4 has gone

2

1 has done
2 have been
3 has belonged
4 have visited

3 had been, had

4

1 has walked two miles a day
2 he was transferred to Busan
3 has changed in recent years
4 she has sold life insurance

Unit 17

1 조동사의 다양한 의미　P. 66~67

A

1 cook	2 must
3 had better not	4 May
5 don't have to	6 ought not to

B

1 doesn't have to	2 must not
3 may	4 must
5 may not	

C

1 shall, we, make, it
2 used, to, wash, clothes
3 Would, you, like, to
4 can't, be, had, better, not

Further Study

1

1 must	2 used, to
3 had better	4 can't be

2 ⑤

3 must, has to

4

1 must not/should not/ought not to drink alcoholic beverages
2 had better take a break
3 You need not have/You don't need to have
4 used to go to the cinema

2 까다로운 조동사　P. 68~69

A

1 could
2 would
3 must be
4 should have watched
5 must have been

B

1 may have	2 need not have
3 must have	4 shouldn't have
5 should have	6 cannot have

C

1 should, have, told
2 need/should, not, have, brought
3 cannot, have, written
4 must, have, forgotten
5 should, not, have, used

Further Study

1

1 cannot have rained → must have rained
2 can → could
3 need have left → may have left
4 cannot have joined → should have joined

2 ④

3 should have been, have to

4

1 you need not leave in such a hurry
2 He may have written to her
3 You should have followed
4 should not have built my house

Unit 18

1 사역동사　P. 70~71

A

1 finish	2 to bring
3 use	4 repaired
5 to tell	6 play

B

1 leave	2 (to) pack
3 clean up	4 picked
5 to practice	6 checked up

C

1 had my room painted
2 got the waiter to clean up
3 let anyone control
4 was made to shed
5 had the repairman fix
6 was made to move into

Further Study

1

1 tested   2 to paint
3 broken   4 pulled
5 to kneel   6 come

2 ①

3 feel, prevent

4

1 had their windows broken
2 make her patients relax
3 Let me point out
4 (to) spread out the payment

---

2 지각동사   P. 72~73

A

1 crawling   2 painting
3 running   4 knocked
5 waiting   6 displayed
7 approaching

B

1 flying/fly   2 running/run
3 falling down   4 caught
5 stand

C

1 writing   2 crossing
3 playing   4 stand
5 entering   6 holding

Further Study

1

1 sung   2 beating
3 striking/strike   4 walk/walking
5 call/calling

2 ③

3 sleeping, approaching

4

1 was noticed running out of
2 saw a poor man injured
3 this opera sung in Italian
4 heard the rain patter/pattering

Unit 19

1 구동사   P. 74~75

A

1 on   2 put it on
3 turn off   4 cope with
5 broke out   6 call me up
7 put off

B

1 resembles   2 serve
3 explain   4 discuss
5 mentioned   6 remove
7 postpone   8 canceled

C

1 wake me up
2 carry them out
3 give away a car/give a car away
4 put it off

Further Study

1

1 turned out   2 work out
3 ran out   4 broke up
5 get through

2 ①

3 Turn it down, switched off

4

1 The flood was brought about
2 The electricity was cut off
3 was carried on for four hours
4 The boy was brought up

---

2 다양한 구동사   P. 76~77

A

1 put out   2 turned down
3 give off   4 broke out
5 ran away   6 made up for

B

1 died   2 selected
3 overcome   4 causes
5 spent   6 requires
7 investigate   8 endure

C

1	stands for	2	go with
3	stood by	4	came into
5	figure out	6	ran after
7	put on		

Further Study

1

1	③	2	②
3	④	4	④

2 ②

3 to, of

4
1 didn't come up to our expectation
2 forget to look it up
3 worked out the difficulty
4 came across some old pictures

Unit 20

1 현재분사와 과거분사   P. 78~79

A

1	coming	2	lying
3	playing	4	sleeping
5	locked	6	long-lasting

B

1	waiting	2	held
3	covered	4	educating
5	flying		

C
1 singing, merrily
2 surrounded
3 expressed
4 living
5 written
6 staring
7 tied

Further Study

1

1	fixed	2	well-dressed
3	carried	4	built
5	drowning	6	wondering

2 ④

3 unified, existing

4
1 The girl injured at the accident
2 The language spoken
3 was terrified
4 he remained standing

2 분사구문   P. 80~81

A

1	eating	2	Taking
3	crossed	4	Written
5	Seeing	6	Not knowing

B
1 Not knowing what to say
2 There being no bus service
3 (being) followed by their wives
4 (being) carefully read
5 (Being) Written in easy English

C

1	e	2	f
3	a	4	g
5	h	6	c
7	b	8	d

Further Study

1

1	Compared	2	Robbed
3	Seen	4	taken
5	covered		

2 ②

3 Situated, forming

4
1 Not being able to swim well
2 (Being) Deceived often
3 spent
4 Walking a dog on the street or in the park

Unit 21

1 -ing와 -ed 형태의 형용사 I   P. 82~83

A

1 touched	2 boring
3 disappointed	4 fascinating
5 pleasing	6 scared

B

1 exciting	2 excited
3 tiring	4 tired
5 boring	6 bored
7 surprising	8 surprised

C

1 pleasing, pleased
2 annoyed, annoying
3 satisfied, satisfying
4 irritating, irritated
5 confused, confusing

Further Study

1

1 pleased	2 encouraging
3 exciting	4 satisfied
5 embarrassed	

2 ①

3 amazing, embarrassing

4
1 very surprising news
2 was enormously exciting
3 was frightened
4 (you're) confused

2 -ing와 -ed 형태의 형용사 II   P. 84~85

A

1 tiring	2 interesting
3 exciting	4 bored
5 interesting	6 satisfied
7 disappointed	8 fascinating

B

1 disillusioning → disillusioned
2 intrigued → intriguing
3 troubling → troubled

4 interested → interesting
5 bored → boring
6 touched → touching
7 amazing → amazed, amazed → amazing
8 exhausting → exhausted

C

1 confusing
2 shocked
3 encouraged
4 exciting
5 impressed
6 embarrassing
7 frightening
8 bewildering

Further Study

1

1 amusing	2 disappointing
3 depressing	4 assured

2 ③

3 irritated, excited

4
1 find, boring
2 were astonished
3 was ashamed
4 feel insulted

Unit 22

1 be+과거분사   P. 86~87

A

1 disappears	2 was taken
3 arise	4 be paid
5 to be canceled	6 was laughed at

B

1 been seen	2 is spoken
3 be found	4 be looked after
5 being built	6 be followed
7 painted	8 was signed

C

1 mend, is being mended
2 observed, is observed

3 change, be changed
4 was scolded, scold
5 ascribes, be ascribed

Further Study

1
1 be answered   2 be endured
3 be scolded   4 consists
5 are mistaken   6 occurred
7 disappeared

2 ①

3 is located, is hidden

4
1 are spoken to
2 is based on his experience
3 has not been used
4 His ambition was supported by

2 주의할 수동태 표현   P. 88~89

A
1 stop   2 was found
3 to have   4 to be made
5 to   6 to be frustrated

B
1 was heard to
2 was elected captain
3 was seen entering
4 was made to wait

C
1 consider, be considered
2 discuss, be discussed
3 be judged, judge
4 told, was told
5 caught, was caught

Further Study

1
1 is forbidden   2 to smile
3 be recognized   4 was advised
5 been done

2 ④

3 been heard, believe

4

1 is invariably followed by
2 He was put on trial
3 have to be made
4 Have you been taught

Unit 23

1 수동 형태의 동사구 Ⅰ   P. 90~91

A
1 was stolen   2 as
3 for   4 is said
5 was robbed of   6 was situated

B
1 was persuaded of her innocence
2 was informed of some changes
3 is said that, is said to have
4 was stolen
5 was accused of giving

C
1 known by
2 is thought to be
3 was convinced of
4 is believed that

Further Study

1
1 was accused of lying (by him)
2 was deprived of sight by the accident
3 was informed of the risks of the surgery (by the doctor)
4 is said that the council has decided to demolish the old community center

2 ③

3 robbed of, stolen

4
1 was reminded of the appointment
2 are persuaded
3 be notified
4 is said that he will be

2 수동태형 동사구 II

A

1 to
2 am not acquainted with
3 is qualified for
4 was absorbed in
5 was addicted to
6 is made up of
7 crowded with

B

1 of
2 in
3 with
4 to
5 on
6 for

C

1 was dismayed, dismayed
2 is situated, situated
3 is covered, covered
4 is filled, filled
5 are equipped, equipped

Further Study

1
1 of
2 in
3 to
4 to
5 with
6 of
7 to

2 ③

3 is regarded, referred

4
1 His daughters were provided with
2 be associated with
3 skipping breakfast is related to
4 was faced with, challenges

Unit 24

1 to부정사와 동명사의 닮은 점
P. 94~95

A

1 helping
2 not being
3 of
4 to seek
5 for
6 our son to be
7 not to have
8 your

B

1 I → my
2 his → him
3 to not talk → not to talk
4 realizing → to realize
5 of → for
6 to watching → to watch/watching
7 to meet → meeting

C

1 my reading
2 his having won
3 this room's/room being
4 the concert's/concert being
5 leaving

Further Study

1
1 sit on
2 being taught
3 not to
4 for him
5 for not
6 my

2 ③

3 putting, to remember

4
1 not remembering
2 for him to sympathize
3 doesn't mind my eating food
4 interrupting me

2 to부정사와 동명사의 다른 점
P. 96~97

A

1 driving
2 be
3 make
4 seeing
5 meeting
6 giving

B

1 posting
2 to post
3 not bringing
4 are used to make purchases

C

1 I was opposed to staying behind.
2 What do you say to going out for dinner tonight?
3 I cannot help following her directions.
4 I look forward to hearing your positive response.
5 He devoted his whole life to studying the Bible.
6 I regretted not saying good-bye to my friends at work.

Further Study

1

1 see → seeing
2 to run → running
3 making → to make
4 to quit → quitting
5 taking → take

2 ③

3 teaching, to do

4

1 They will not object to passing
2 remember seeing her
3 regretted having drunk
4 stop walking to catch

Unit 25

1	to+동사원형의 문장	P. 98~99

A

1 go	2 to buy
3 watch	4 to stay
5 whether	6 know

B

1 which one to	2 when to
3 where to	4 what to
5 whom to	6 how to

C

1 couldn't afford to pay the school fees
2 happened to meet an old friend
3 failed to attract people's attention
4 prove to be the greatest player
5 tend to learn from their parents

Further Study

1

1 mean	2 deserves
3 proved	4 failed
5 tend	

2 ③

3 to help, to buy

4

1 not to see
2 where to stay
3 may well be disappointed
4 how to dive

2	형용사+to , 명사+to	P. 100~101

A

1 to tell	2 free
3 to travel	4 can't
5 willingness	6 start
7 reach	

B

1 willing	2 available
3 reluctant	4 sure
5 adequate	6 free

C

1 His attempt to fulfill
2 Her refusal to sell
3 his failure to win the competition
4 the government's permission to import rice

Further Study

1

1 are to get there on time
2 is to arrive
3 are to stay

2 ③

3 be sent, to use

4

1 too wide to swim across
2 the last man to deceive
3 to increase
4 unwillingness to forgive

Unit 26

A

1 toilet paper
2 sleeping pills
3 drinking water
4 children's books
5 my brother's room
6 the glasses frame

B

1 cube   2 jar
3 bar   4 bottle
5 flock   6 sheet

C

1 mare   2 cock
3 bull   4 heroine
5 widower   6 mock
7 spinster   8 nephew

Further Study

1

1 herd   2 flock
3 compasses   4 arms
5 boys'

2 ①

3 a bachelor, a spinster, relatives

4

1 a pair of shorts and a T-shirt
2 a herd of cows
3 heroes and heroines
4 graduated from Robertson Girls' High School

A

1 bondage   2 burial
3 likelihood   4 attendant
5 appraisal   6 moisture

B

1 failure   2 departure
3 width   4 depth
5 breath   6 truth
7 growth   8 shortage
9 length   10 engineer
11 descendant   12 consultant
13 bondage   14 leakage
15 applicant   16 assistant
17 participant   18 approval
19 salvage   20 revival

C

1 ③   2 ②
3 ⑤   4 ③

Further Study

1

1 breath   2 heritage
3 length   4 approval
5 pressure   6 livelihood

2 ②

3 approval, applications

4

1 The joy of parenthood
2 the warmth of the welcome
3 Too much exposure
4 was disappointed at the poor attendance

Unit 27

1 It/There 관련문장   P. 106~107

A

1	it	2	it
3	that	4	that
5	There are	6	found it

B

1 that Tom went there yesterday
2 that I first met her in Rome
3 that game was scheduled to be held
4 that complained about the price of the food in the restaurant
5 the meeting was half over that he came

C

1 illegal to serve alcohol on campus
2 quite natural for you to refuse his offer
3 hard to untie the package
4 my duty to protect my family and my country

Further Study

1

1	it	2	It
3	There	4	There
5	were	6	was
7	it		

2 ③

3 its

4
1 It, to learn
2 is always heavy traffic
3 was a fishing rod that
4 made it clear that

2 대명사   P. 108~109

A

1	one	2	ones
3	the other	4	the others
5	others		

B

1	others	2	it
3	none	4	another
5	no	6	the other
7	one	8	the others
9	the one		

C

1	others	2	another
3	none	4	another

Further Study

1

1	one	2	ones
3	the other	4	None
5	others	6	none

2 ①

3 Some, Others

4
1 One should respect
2 the others think differently
3 None, passed the examination
4 one is red, another is blue, the others

Unit 28

1 수량표현의 대명사   P. 110~111

A

1	almost	2	Most
3	Few	4	Most
5	Little	6	Either
7	is		

B

1	neither	2	Every
3	none	4	Everybody

C

1	every	2	None
3	Both	4	each
5	either	6	Neither

Further Study

1

1	neither	2	few
3	man	4	Neither
5	a few	6	is

2 ⑤

3 most, it

4

1 Either you or I/Either of us should speak about
2 Neither of us cares about
3 spent most of his salary
4 a few people came

2 재귀대명사 P. 112~113

A

1	yourself	2	Help yourself
3	myself	4	himself
5	themselves	6	herself

B

1	herself	2	myself
3	himself	4	myself
5	itself	6	ourselves

C

1	herself	2	yourself
3	myself	4	himself
5	themselves	6	themselves

Further Study

1

1	himself	2	yourself
3	me	4	itself

2 ①

3 themselves, them

4

1 they introduced themselves one by one
2 entertained themselves
3 Tom often occupies himself
4 devoted herself

Unit 29

1 까다로운 형용사 P. 114~115

A

1 asleep
2 alive
3 only
4 good enough
5 people present
6 enough information

B

1 certain, certain
2 late, late
3 present, present

C

1 There are enough chairs to seat
2 the person responsible for customer service
3 interesting enough to draw people's attention
4 He lay awake all night long
5 All the students involved in the fight

Further Study

1

1	④	2	③
3	①	4	②
5	④		

2 ③

3 old enough, a child alone

4

1 stupid enough to repeat
2 fall asleep
3 many people concerned about
4 his dreams and inspirations are still alive

2 파생어 P. 116~117

A

1	sensitive	2	respective
3	momentous	4	memorable
5	confidential	6	industrial
7	considerable	8	childlike

B

1	respective	2	considerate

3 confidential   4 imaginative
5 sensitive   6 industrial

C

1 considerate   2 confident
3 favorable   4 practical
5 sensory   6 successive

Further Study

1
1 sensitive   2 respectable
3 imaginable   4 successful
5 memorial
2 ④
3 generous, minimum, maximum
4
1 healthy food
2 five successive victories
3 completely confidential
4 five sensory organs

Unit 30

A

1 still   2 yet
3 already   4 after
5 frequently talk   6 Unfortunately

B

1 regularly   2 badly
3 patiently   4 suddenly
5 selfishly   6 perfectly

C

1 closely
2 continuously
3 Briefly/Simply
4 slightly
5 barely/rarely/hardly

Further Study

1
1 yet   2 before
3 clearly   4 yet
5 heavily   6 still
2 ①
3 terribly, barely helps
4
1 haven't received any response, yet
2 almost run over
3 In addition, can get a discount
4 can hardly stand

A

1 nearly   2 costly
3 hard   4 timely
5 Highly

B

1 fast   2 soon
3 enough   4 easily

C

1 well, well
2 pretty, pretty
3 last, last
4 ill, ill
5 long, long

Further Study

1
1 lately   2 high
3 rarely   4 hardly, harshly
5 Most   6 near, badly
2 ①
3 pretty, unlike
4
1 be served shortly after
2 didn't live long
3 nearly one million people gathered
4 well organized

Unit 31

1   '아' 다르고 '어' 다르다—관사   P. 122~123

A

1 behind time
2 The number
3 The
4 A number
5 A variety
6 out of the question

B

1 an, the   2 a, the
3 the, an   4 a, the
5 a, the   6 a, the

C

1 is   2 are
3 are   4 is
5 is

Further Study

1

1 prison, the prison
2 bed, the bed
3 School, the school
4 church, the church

2 ④

3 A variety

4

1 his success is out of the question
2 a wide variety of colors
3 behind the times
4 from the experience

2   '아' 다르고 '어' 다르다—전치사   P. 124~125

A

1 to   2 of
3 for   4 about
5 According to   6 Despite
7 Because of

B

1 with   2 for
3 about   4 with
5 for   6 about

C

1 resulted from
2 resulted in
3 In case
4 In case of
5 Because of
6 Because
7 According to

Further Study

1

1 for   2 on
3 of   4 On
5 in

2 ⑤

3 of, from

4

1 According to the report
2 she is off duty
3 in the way
4 In case, is lost or stolen